AF559931

Water and Sustainable Tourism

Water and Sustainable Tourism

Ramakanth Rajput

Water and Sustainable Tourism

ISBN 978-93-5111-880-0

Published in 2016 in India by

RANDOM PUBLICATIONS

4376-A/4B, Gali Murari Lal, Ansari Road
New Delhi-110 002
Phone : +9111-43580356, 011-23289044, 011-43142548
e-mail: sales@randompublications.com,
info@randompublications.com, randomexports@gmail.com

Type Setting by : Friends Media, Delhi-110089

Digitally Printed at : Replika Press Pvt. Ltd.

Preface

Water is one of the world's most precious natural resources. In tourism, it is both a critical resource and asset for most destinations. Clean, accessible water is an integral resource, running most of the tourism sector's businesses, from hotels and restaurants, to leisure facilities and transportation. Wetland tourism is a growing segment, with many of the world's coastlines and lakes being some of the most popular tourist destinations today. Many of those natural attractions where water is an essential element are key to the tourism sector and thus a source of tourism-related employment and income in countries worldwide.

Yet freshwater reserves are being threatened by a growing world population, excessive water consumption, weak water management, poor sanitation and global climate change. Increased water demand by tourists and local communities has an impact not only on human needs but also on flora and fauna.

Without good planning and adaptation, development opportunities are missed and millions of lives are put at risk. At the global level, tourism does not consume excessive quantities of water - the challenge is rather to be found at destination level regarding the competition for water. Overall, tourism consumes 1% of water, as compared to agriculture's 70%. Consumption can be additionally cut by up to 23% through investments in water efficiency in the tourism sector, boosting its contribution to economic growth and jobs.

Tourism's contribution to water preservation is key on two accounts: the sustainable development of tourism in water destinations and the effective management of water resources in tourism activities and operations.

– ***Author***

Contents

1

Water Population Growth and Environmental Quality

There is a long history of study and debate about the interactions between population growth and the environment. According to the British thinker Malthus, for example, a growing population exerts pressure on agricultural land, causing environmental degradation, and forcing the cultivation of land of poorer and poorer quality. This environmental degradation ultimately reduces agricultural yields and food availability, causes famines and diseases and death, thereby reducing the rate of population growth. Population growth, because it can place increased pressure on the assimilative capacity of the environment, is also seen as a major cause of air, water, and solid-waste pollution. The result, Malthus theorized, is an equilibrium population that enjoys low levels of both income and environmental quality. Malthus suggested positive and preventative forced control of human population, along with abolition of poor laws.

Malthus theory, published between 1798 and 1826, has been analyzed and criticized ever since. The American thinker Henry George, for example, observed with his characteristic piquancy in dismissing Malthus: "Both the jayhawk and the man eat chickens; but the more jayhawks, the fewer chickens, while the more men, the more chickens." Similarly, the American economist Julian Lincoln Simoncriticised Malthus's theory. He noted that the facts of human history have proven the predictions of Malthus and of the Neo-Malthusians to be flawed. Massive geometric population growth in the 20th century did not result in a Malthusian catastrophe.

The possible reasons include: increase in human knowledge, rapid increases in productivity, innovation and application of knowledge, general improvements in farming methods (industrial agriculture), mechanization of work (tractors), the introduction of high-yield varieties of wheat and other plants (Green Revolution), the use of pesticides to control crop pests. More recent scholarly articles concede that while there is no question that population growth may contribute to environmental degradation, its effects can be modified by economic growth and modern technology. Research in environmental economics has uncovered a relationship between environmental quality, measured by ambient concentrations of air pollutants and per capita income. This so-called environmental Kuznets curve shows environmental quality worsening up until about $5,000 of per capita income on purchasing parity basis, and improving thereafter. The key requirement, for this to be true, is continued adoption of technology and scientific management of resources, continued increases in productivity in every economic sector, entrepreneurial innovation and economic expansion.

Other data suggests that population density has little correlation to environmental quality and human quality of life. India's population density, in 2011, was about 368 human beings per square kilometer. Many countries with population density similar or higher than India enjoy environmental quality as well as human quality of life far superior than India.

For example: Singapore (7148 /km^2), Hong Kong-China (6349 /km^2), South Korea (487 /km^2), Netherlands (403 /km^2), Belgium (355 / km^2), Japan (337/ km^2), England (395 /km^2), the state of Florida (353 / km^2), the state of New York (412 / km^2), the state of Massachusetts (840 / km^2), the state of North Rhine-Westphalia (523 / km^2), the region of Île-de-France (974 / km^2), and the region of Lombardy (417 / km^2).

CAUSE OF WATER POLLUTION

A 2007 study finds that discharge of untreated sewage is single most important cause for pollution of surface and ground water in India. There is a large gap between generation and treatment of domestic wastewater in India. The problem is not only that India lacks sufficient treatment capacity but also that the sewage treatment plants that exist do not operate and are not maintained. Majority of the government-owned sewage treatment plants remain closed most of the time due to improper design or poor maintenance or lack of reliable electricity supply to operate the plants, together with absentee employees and poor management. The wastewater generated in these areas normally percolates in the soil or evaporates. The uncollected wastes accumulate in the urban areas cause unhygienic conditions and release pollutants that leaches to surface and groundwater.

A 1992 World Health Organization study is claimed to have reported that out of India's 3,119 towns and cities, just 209 have partial sewage treatment facilities, and only 8 have full wastewater treatment facilities. Downstream, the untreated water is used for drinking, bathing, and washing. A 1995 report claimed 114 Indian cities were dumping untreatedsewage and partially cremated bodies directly into the Ganges River. Open defecation is widespread even in urban areas of India. This situation is typical of India as well as other developing countries. According to another 2005 report, sewage discharged from cities and towns is the predominant cause of water pollution in India. Investment is needed to bridge the gap between 29000 million litre per day of sewage India generates, and a treatment capacity of mere 6000 million litre per day. A large number of Indian rivers are severely polluted as a result of discharge of domestic sewage.

The Central Pollution Control Board, a Ministry of Environment & Forests Government of India entity, has established a National Water Quality Monitoring Network comprising 1429 monitoring stations in 27 states and 6 in Union Territories on various rivers and water bodies across the country. This effort monitors water quality year round. The monitoring network covers 293 rivers, 94 lakes, 9 tanks, 41 ponds, 8 creeks, 23 canals, 18 drains and 411 wells distributed across India. Water samples are routinely analyzed for 28 parameters including dissolved oxygen, bacteriological and other internationally established parameters for water quality. Additionally 9 trace metals parameters and 28 pesticide residues are analyzed. Biomonitoring is also carried out on specific locations.

The scientific analysis of water samples from 1995 to 2008 indicates that the organic and bacterial contamination are severe in water bodies of India. This is mainly due to discharge of domestic wastewater in untreated form, mostly from the urban centres of India.

In 2008, the water quality monitoring found almost all rivers with high levels of BOD. The worst pollution, in decreasing order, were found in river Markanda (590 mg O/l), followed by river Kali (364), river Amlakhadi (353), Yamuna canal (247), river Yamuna at Delhi (70) and river Betwa (58). For context, a water sample with a 5 day BOD between 1 and 2 mg O/L indicates a very clean water, 3 to 8 mg O/L indicates a moderately clean water, 8 to 20 indicates borderline water, and greater than 20 mg O/L indicates ecologically-unsafe polluted water.

The Mithi River, which flows through the city of Mumbai, is heavily polluted. The levels of BOD are severe near the cities and major towns. In rural parts of India, the river BOD levels were sufficient to support aquatic life.

Total coliform and fecal coliform densities in the rivers of India range between 500 to 100,000 MPN/100 ml. The presence of coliform suggests that the water is being contaminated with the fecal material of humans, livestocks, pets and other animals. Rivers Yamuna,Ganga, Gomti, Ghaggar, Chambal, Mahi, Vardha are amongst the other most coliform polluted water bodies in India. For context, coliform must be below 104 MPN/100 ml, preferably absent from water for it to be considered safe for general human use, and for irrigation where coliform may cause disease outbreak from contaminated-water in agriculture.

In 2006, 47 percent of water quality monitoring stations in India reported a total average annual coliform levels above 500 MPN/100 ml. During 2008, 33 percent of all water quality monitoring stations reported a total coliform levels exceeding those levels, suggesting recent effort to add pollution control infrastructure and upgrade treatment plants in India, may be reversing the water pollution trend. Treatment of domestic sewage and subsequent utilization of treated sewage for irrigation can prevent pollution of water bodies, reduce the demand for fresh water in irrigation sector and become a resource for irrigation. Since 2005, Indian wastewater treatment plant market has been growing annually at the rate of 10 to 12 percent. The United States is the largest supplier of treatment equipment and supplies to India, with 40 percent market share of new installation. At this rate of expansion, and assuming the government of India continues on its path of reform, major investments in sewage treatment plants and electricity infrastructure development, India will nearly triple its water treatment capacity by 2015, and treatment capacity supply will match India's daily sewage water treatment requirements by about 2020.

Water resources have not been linked to either domestic or international violent conflict as was previously anticipated by some observers. Possible exceptions, notes a 2004 report, include some communal violence related to distribution of water from the Kaveri River and political tensions surrounding actual and potential population displacements by dam projects, particularly on the Narmada River.

A 1997 article claimed Punjab is another hotbed of pollution, for example, Buddha Nullah, a rivulet which run through Malwaregion of Punjab, India, and after passing through highly populated Ludhiana district, before draining into Sutlej River, a tributary of the Indus river, is today an important case point in the recent studies, which suggest this as another Bhopal in making.

A joint study by PGIMER and Punjab Pollution Control Board in 2008, revealed that in villages along the Nullah, calcium, magnesium, fluoride, mercury, beta-endosulphan and heptachlor pesticide were more than permissible limit (MPL) in ground and tap waters. Plus the water had high concentration of COD and BOD (chemical and biochemical oxygen demand), ammonia, phosphate, chloride, chromium, arsenic and chlorpyrifos pesticide. The ground water also contains nickel and selenium, while the tap water has high concentration of lead, nickel and cadmium. The Hindon River, which flows through the city of Ghaziabad, highly polluted and groundwater of this city has coloured and poisoned by industrial effluents, Hindon Vahini is strongly opposing of water pollution activities. Flooding during monsoons worsens India's water pollution problem, as it washes and moves all sorts of solid garbage and contaminated soils into its rivers and wetlands.

The annual average precipitation in India is about 4000 billion cubic metres. From this, with the state of Indian infrastructure in 2005, the available water resource through the rivers is about 1869 billion cubic meters. Accounting to uneven distribution of rain over the country each year, water resources available for utilization, including ground water, is claimed to be about 1122 billion cubic meters. Much of this water is unsafe, because pollution degrades water quality.

Water pollution severely limits the amount of water available to Indian consumer, its industry and its agriculture.

THE GANGES

To know why 1,000 Indian children die of diarrhoeal sickness every day, take a wary stroll along the Ganges in Varanasi. As it enters the city, Hinduism's sacred river contains 60,000 faecal coliform bacteria per 100 millilitres, 120 times more than is considered safe for bathing. Four miles downstream, with inputs from 24 gushing sewers and 60,000 pilgrim-bathers, the concentration is 3,000 times over the safety limit. In places, the Ganges becomes black and septic. Corpses, of semi-cremated adults or enshrouded babies, drift slowly by. — *The Economist on December 11, 2008*

More than 400 million people live along the Ganges River. An estimated 2,000,000 persons ritually bathe daily in the river, which is considered holy by Hindus. Ganges river pollution from sewage and semi-cremated remains is thus a major health risk.

THE YAMUNA

NewsWeek describes Delhi's sacred Yamuna River as "a putrid ribbon of black sludge" where fecal bacteria is 10,000 over safety limits despite a 15-year programme to address the problem. Cholera epidemics are not unknown. NewsWeek observes India's messy democracy is particularly ill equipped to handle the conflicting pressures of rapid growth and poverty. Even though India revised its national water policy in 2002 to encourage community participation and decentralize water management, the country's Byzantine bureaucracy ensures that it remains a "mere statement of intent." Responsibility for managing water issues is fragmented among a dozen different ministries and departments without any coordination. The government bureaucracy and state-run project department has failed to solve the problem, despite having spent many years and $500 million on this project.

METHODS OF WATER POLLUTION

Methods of controlling water pollution fall into three general categories: physical, chemical, and biological. For example, one form of water pollution consists of suspended solids such as fine dirt and dead organisms. These materials can be removed from water by simply allowing the water to sit quietly for a period of time, thereby allowing the pollutants to settle out, or by passing the water through a filter. (The solid pollutants are then trapped in the filter.) Chemical reactions can be used to remove pollutants from water. For example, the addition of alum (potassium aluminum sulfate) and lime (calcium hydroxide) to water results in the formation of a thick, sticky precipitate. When the precipitate begins to settle out, it traps and carries with it solid particles, dead bacteria, and other components of polluted water. Biological agents can also be used to remove pollutants from water. Aerobic bacteria (those that need oxygen to survive) and anaerobic bacteria (those that do not require oxygen) attack certain chemicals in polluted water and convert them to a harmless form.

SOLID POLLUTANTS

Solid pollutants consist of garbage, sewage sludge, paper, plastics, and many other forms of waste materials. One method of dealing with solid pollutants is simply to bury them in dumps or landfills. Another approach is to compost them, a process in which microorganisms turn certain types of pollutants into useful fertilizers. Finally, solid pollutants can also be incinerated (burned).

TRADE AND ENVIRONMENT

The main goal is to make the complex relationship between the environment and international trade more understandable from the developing countries' perspective. It also aims to dispel the idea that the relationship between trade and environment can easily be described as either negative or positive. It is extremely complex and varies from country to country. There are both threats and opportunities in this relationship for developing countries pursuing economic development and environmental protection. The conclusions that can be drawn from this that from the developing countries' perspective is to exploit the opportunities and reduce the threats, and in so doing, to maximize the net positive contribution that trade can make sustainable development. A broader and clearer understanding of the linkages between trade, environment, and development is a prerequisite for seizing those opportunities and reducing those threats.

On the other hand, environmental requirements however, may be used for protectionist purposes and may operate as a non-tariff barrier. In future, there is a likelihood of more trade embargos in the name of environment, especially in cases where countries fail to comply with certain environmental standard requirements. Thus, the outcome of the various case studies has the potential for strengthening the hand of protectionist lobbies, in the name of conservation and protection of the environment.

Finally, the threat of embargo can also be used to make countries adhere to certain environmental policies and regulations, which they would otherwise not adopt due to various socio-economic compulsions. Moreover, these environmental friendly policies demand the attention and cooperation of international institutions such as the World Bank as well as NGOs and other grassroots environmental groups. Protecting the environment is a luxury good, often only afforded to the wealthy countries.

Therefore, these policies should be coupled with ones that encourage the transfer and exchange of environmentally friendly technologies and the build up of industries oriented to sustainable development.

WATER QUALITY CONSERVATION

India is endowed with diverse geological formations from oldest achaeans to recent alluviums and characterized by varying climatic conditions in different parts of the country. The natural chemical content of groundwater is influenced by depth of the soils and sub-surface geological formations through which groundwater remains in contact.

In general, greater part of the country, groundwater is of good quality and suitable for drinking, agricultural or industrial purposes. Groundwater in shallow aquifers is generally suitable for use for different purposes and is mainly of Calcium Bicarbonate and mixed type. However, other types of water are also available including Sodium-Chloride water. The quality in deeper aquifers also varies from place to place and is generally found suitable for common uses. There is salinity problem in the coastal tracts and high incidence of fluoride, arsenic, iron & heavy metals etc. in isolated pockets have also been reported. The main groundwater quality problems in India are as follows.

SALINITY

Salinity in groundwater can be of broadly categorized into two types, *i.e.* inland salinity and coastal salinity.

INLAND SALINITY

Inland salinity in groundwater is prevalent mainly in the arid and semi-arid regions of Rajasthan, Haryana, Punjab and Gujarat, Uttar Pradesh, Delhi, Andhra Pradesh, Maharashtra, Karnataka and Tamil Nadu.

There are several places in Rajasthan and southern Haryana where EC values of groundwater is quite high making water non-potable. In some areas of Rajasthan and Gujarat, groundwater salinity is so high that the well water is directly used for salt manufacturing by solar evaporation. Inland salinity is also caused due to practice of surface water irrigation without consideration of groundwater status. The gradual rise of groundwater levels with time has resulted in water logging and heavy evaporation in semi-arid regions lead to salinity problem in command areas.

COASTAL SALINITY

The Indian subcontinent has a dynamic coast line of about 7500 km length. It stretches from Rann of Kutch in Gujarat to Konkan and Malabar coast to Kanyakumari in the south to northwards along the Coromandal coast to Sunderbans in West Bengal.

The western coast is characterized by wide continental shelf and is marked by backwaters and mud flats while the eastern coast has a narrow continental shelf and is characterized by deltaic and estuarine land forms. Groundwater in coastal areas occurs under unconfined to confined conditions in a wide range of unconsolidated and consolidated formations. Normally, saline water bodies owe their origin to entrapped sea water (connate water), sea water ingress, leachates from navigation canals constructed along the coast, leachates from salt pans etc. In India, salinity problems have been observed in a number of places in most of the coastal states of the country. Problem of salinity ingress has been conspicuously noticed in Minjur area of Tamil Nadu and Mangrol – Chorwad-Porbander belt along the Saurashtra coast. Under Hydrology Project (PhaseII), National Institute of Hydrology, Roorkee has taken-up a purpose driven study related to seawater intrusion in Minsar river basin in Porbandar district of Gujarat.

FLUORIDE

85% of rural population of the country uses groundwater for drinking and domestic purposes. High concentration of fluoride in groundwater beyond the permissible limit of 1.5 mg/l poses the health problem. The occurrences of fluoride beyond permissible limit (> 1.5 mg/l) has been observed based on the chemical analysis of water samples collected from the groundwater observation wells.

ARSENIC

The occurrence of arsenic in groundwater was first reported in 1980 in West Bengal. In West Bengal, 79 blocks in 8 districts have arsenic beyond the permissible limit of 0.05 mg/l. The most affected districts are on the eastern side of Bhagirathi river in the districts of Malda, Murshidabad, Nadia, North 24 Parganas and South 24 Parganas and western side of the districts of Howrah, Hugli and Bardhman. The occurrence of arsenic in groundwater is mainly in the intermediate aquifers upto the depth of 100 m. The deeper aquifers are free from arsenic contamination. Apart from West Bengal, arsenic contamination in groundwater has been found in the states of Bihar, Chhattisgarh, Uttar Pradesh and Assam. Arsenic in groundwater has been reported in 15 districts In Bihar, 9 districts in U.P. and one district each in Chhatisgarh and Assam states. The occurrence of arsenic in the states of Bihar, West Bengal and Uttar Pradesh is in alluvium formation but in the state of Chhattisgarh, it is in the volcanic rocks exclusively confined to N-S trending Dongargarh-Kotri ancient rift zone. It has also been reported in Dhemaji district of Assam.

IRON

High concentration of iron (>1.0 mg/l) in groundwater has been observed in more than 1.1 lakh habitations in the country. Groundwater contaminated by iron has been reported from the states of Andhra Pradesh, Assam, Bihar, Chhattisgarh, Goa, Gujarat, Haryana, J&K, Jharkhand, Karnataka, Kerala, Madhya Pradesh, Maharashtra, Manipur, Meghalaya, Orissa, Punjab, Rajasthan,

Tamil Nadu, Tripura, Uttar Pradesh, West Bengal and UT of Andaman & Nicobar.

NITRATE

Nitrate is a very common constituent in the groundwater, especially in shallow aquifers. The source is mainly from anthropogenic activities. High concentration of nitrate in water beyond the permissible limit of 45 mg/l causes health problems. High nitrate concentration in groundwater in India has been found in almost all hydrogeological formations.

Implementation of water pollution prevention strategies and restoration of ecological systems are integral components of all development plans. To preserve our water and environment, we need to make systematic changes in the way we grow our food, manufacture the goods, and dispose off the waste. In India, agriculture is the biggest user and polluter of water. If pollution by agriculture is reduced, it would improve water quality and would also eliminate cost incurred for treatment of diseases. Like all other inputs, there is an optimal quantity of fertilizer for given conditions and excess application does not improve the crop yield. Pricing of fertilizers and pesticides as well as appropriate legislation to regulate their use will also go a long way in stopping indiscriminate use. Industries need to carefully treat their waste discharges. Manufacturers may reduce water pollution by reusing materials and chemicals and switching over to less toxic alternatives. Industrial symbiosis, in which the unusable wastes from one product/firm become the input for another, is an attractive solution. Also, there is a need to encourage reductions or replacement of toxic chemicals, possibly through fiscal measures.

URBAN WATER SUPPLY AND SANITATION

The urban water supply and sanitation sector in the country is suffering from inadequate levels of service, an increasing demand-supply gap, poor sanitary conditions and deteriorating financial and technical performance. Supply of water is highly erratic and unreliable. Transmission and distribution networks are old and poorly maintained, and generally of a poor quality. Consequently physical losses are typically high, ranging from 25 to over 50 per cent. Low pressures and intermittent supplies allow back siphoning, which results in contamination of water in the distribution network. Water is typically available for only 2-8 hours a day in most Indian cities. The situation is even worse in summer when water is available only for a few minutes, sometimes not at all.

Sanitation and water management should be looked at simultaneously. Too often attention is focused on drinking water supply, leaving sanitation and wastewater treatment for later. However, for every 100 litres of water going into a house about 90 litres will have to leave the plot again. Water supply is an institutional process and an institutional framework for effective water supply and sanitation has to comply with the functions of policy, regulation and sector organization, management of quality, infrastructure and on-site sanitation.

It is desirable to think of water supply, sanitation and wastewater in an integrated way. Urban centres in India are facing an ironical situation today. On one hand, there is the acute water scarcity and on the other, the streets are often flooded during the monsoons. This has led to serious problems with quality and quantity of groundwater. This is despite the fact that all these cities receive good rainfall. However, this rainfall occurs during short spells of high intensity. Because of such short duration of heavy rain, most of the rain falling on the surface tends to flow away rapidly leaving very little for recharge of groundwater. As water shortage increases, alternative sources of water supply are gaining importance. These include sewage recycle, rainwater harvesting, etc. It should be made mandatory for each industry to install water management solutions to recycle its waste water for reuse. Major step in this front is through the development of industrial effluent recycle solution which integrates physio-chemical, biological and membrane separation processes for optimum water recovery. They achieve water management through water recycle and source reduction, and waste management through product recovery and waste minimization.

PEOPLE PARTICIPATION AND CAPACITY BUILDING

For making the people of various sections of the society aware about the different issues of water resources management, a participatory approach may be adopted. Mass communication programmes may be launched using the modern communication means for educating the people about water conservation and efficient utilization of water. Capacity building should be perceived as the process whereby a community equips itself to become an active and well-informed partner in decision making. The process of capacity building must be aimed at both increasing access to water resources and changing the power relationships between the stakeholders. Capacity building is not only limited to officials and technicians but must also include the general awareness of the local population regarding their responsibilities in sustainable management of the water resources. Policy decisions in any water resources project should be directed to improve knowledge, attitude and practices about the linkages between health and hygiene, provide higher water supply service levels and to improve environment through safe disposal of human waste.

Sustainable management of water requires decentralized decisions by giving authority, responsibility and financial support to communities to manage their natural resources and thereby protect the environment.

GROUNDWATER POLLUTION

Interactions between groundwater and surface water are complex. Consequently, groundwater pollution, sometimes referred to as groundwater contamination, is not as easily classified as surface water pollution. By its very nature, groundwater aquifers are susceptible to contamination from sources that may not directly affect surface water bodies, and the distinction of point vs. nonpoint source may be irrelevant.

A spill of a chemical contaminant on soil, located away from a surface water body, may not necessarily create point source or non-point source pollution, but nonetheless may contaminate the aquifer below. Analysis of groundwater contamination may focus on soil characteristics and hydrology, as well as the nature of the contaminant itself.

CAUSES OF WATER POLLUTION

When you consider the many different causes of water pollution, it's not difficult to understand why drinking water contamination is such a widespread problem. Water pollution occurs both when harmful substances directly enter the water supply, as well as through changes that occur in the environment as a result of pollution causing activities. When you realize how many different types of water pollution there are, it's easy to see why water filtration systems are a necessity for every home.

COMMON CAUSES OF WATER POLLUTION

OIL

Petroleum often pollutes water in the form of oil. Oil spills from ships and super- tankers, and from off-shore oil drilling operations cause pollution. Oil and petrol that leaks from cars and trucks also washes off roads and into waterways through storm water drains. Oil forms a thin layer on top of water and act like a lid on the surface and the water. Animals and plants living in the water can't breathe, the oil coats the feathers of water birds, and the fur of animals that swim in the water, causing them to become sick and, if there is a great amount of oil on their bodies, to die. Even the insects that live on the surface of the water are badly affected.

FERTILIZERS

Fertilizers contain nutrients such as nitrates and phosphates that help plants to grow. That's why farmers use them. When fertilizers are washed into rivers and streams the nitrates and phosphates cause excessive growth of water plants. The plants clogs the waterways, use up oxygen in the water, and block light to deeper waters. This is harmful to the fish and other invertebrates that live in water because it make it hard for the animals to breathe.

SOIL

Pollution of waterways is also caused when silt and soil washes off ploughed fields, construction and logging sites, and from river banks when it rains.

SEWAGE AND OTHER ORGANIC POLLUTANTS

When material such as leaves and grass clippings, and waste from farm animals enters the water, it rots and breaks down and uses up the oxygen in the water. Many types of fish and other aquatic animals cannot survive. Organisms such as bacteria and viruses enter waterways through untreated sewage in storm-water drains, run-off from septic tanks, and from boats whose owners dump sewage into the water. These microscopic pollutants cause sickness in people and in animals that drink or live in the water.

CHEMICALS

Chemical pollution entering rivers and streams causes great destruction. The chemicals can come from factories, construction sites, mining operations, and from homes when people pour chemicals down the sink or down the toilet.

PLASTICS

Floating plastic is ugly, and harmful to the environment. Plastic rubbish is not biodegradable (it doesn't rot away after we have used it) It can choke animals that try to eat it, and drown those that get tangled in it.

LITTER

When people drop litter such as plastic and cans, food wrappers and cigarette butts, they can be washed by the rain into rivers and other waterways through storm water drains in the streets. At the beach, it is important that people take home their litter or put it into garbage bins at the beach so that it doesn't get into the sea.

Other Causes of Water Pollution Include:

- Air Pollution
- Carbon Dioxide
- Fuel Additives
- Increased Water Temperature
- Industrial Development
- Landfills
- Mining Activities
- Gasoline
- Household Cleaning Products
- Personal Care Products
- Sediment.

THE EFFECTS OF WATER POLLUTION

The effects of water pollution are far-reaching. And it's not only humans who are affected. All plants and animals must endure poisonous drinking water, river and lake ecosystems that have become unbalanced and can no longer support biodiversity.

Deforestation from acid rain can occur as well. On the whole, water pollution has long-term effects on our health and economic productivity. Fight water pollution to keep our planet safe. The effects of water pollution differ from region to region, depending on the pollutants in the water and environmental factors. Common effects of water pollution include unhealthy or poisonous water, sick animals that pass their sickness on to humans, ecosystems that are unable to support a normal diverse animal and plant habitat and more.

POLLUTION AFFECTS THE FOOD CHAIN

Pollution in the form of organic material enters waterways in many different forms as sewage, as leaves and grass clippings, or as runoff from livestock feedlots and pastures. When natural bacteria and protozoan in the water break down this organic material, they destroyed the whole things.

POLLUTION AFFECT AQUATIC ECOSYSTEMS

In nature nothing exists alone. Living things relate to each other as well as to their non-living, but supporting, environments.These complex relationships are called ecosystems. Each body of water is a delicately balanced ecosystem in continuous interaction with the surrounding air and land. Whatever occurs on the land and in the air also affects the water. If a substance enters a river or lake, the water can purify itself biologically — but only to a degree. Whether it is in the smallest stream or lake — or even in the mighty oceans — the water can absorb only so much. It reaches a point where the natural cleaning processes can no longer cope. For example, various species of fish now suffer from tumors and lesions, and their reproductive capacities are decreasing

POLLUTION AFFECT MARINE LIFE

Lakes many are persistent toxic chemicals such as DDT. Populations of fish consuming birds and mammals also seem to be on the decline. Of the ten most highly valued species of fish in Lake Ontario, seven have now almost totally vanished. People dump hazardous materials into the ocean to get rid of them. Sewage and waste from factories and cities can reach the ocean. This pollution is very harmful. It can kill the plants and animals living in the ocean. Dangerous chemicals like mercury kill the aquatic environment very quickly.

WATER POLLUTION'S CHAIN REACTION

One of the many causes of water pollution is sewage and fertilizers that contain nutrients such as nitrates and phosphates. When these enter our water system in excess levels, the growth of aquatic plants and algae is overstimulated. As a result of the excessive growth of these aquatic plants, our waterways are clogged. They use up dissolved oxygen as they decompose, and block light to deeper waters. Subsequently, the respiration ability or fish and other invertebrates that reside in water are also damaged.

HEALTH IMPACTS OF WATER POLLUTION

It is a well-known fact that clean water is absolutely essential for healthy living. Adequate supply of fresh and clean drinking water is a basic need for all human beings on the earth, yet it has been observed that millions of people worldwide are deprived of this. Freshwater resources all over the world are threatened not only by over exploitation and poor management but also by ecological degradation.

The main source of freshwater pollution can be attributed to discharge of untreated waste, dumping of industrial effluent, and run-off from agricultural fields. Industrial growth, urbanization and the increasing use of synthetic organic substances have serious and adverse impacts on freshwater bodies. It is a generally accepted fact that the developed countries suffer from problems of chemical discharge into the water sources mainly groundwater, while developing countries face problems of agricultural run-off in water sources. Polluted water like chemicals in drinking water causes problem to health and leads to water-borne diseases which can be prevented by taking measures can be taken even at the household level.

GROUNDWATER AND ITS CONTAMINATION

Many areas of groundwater and surface water are now contaminated with heavy metals, POPs (persistent organic pollutants), and nutrients that have an adverse affect on health. Water-borne diseases and water-caused health problems are mostly due to inadequate and incompetent management of water resources. Safe water for all can only be assured when access, sustainability, and equity can be guaranteed. Access can be defined as the number of people who are guaranteed safe drinking water and sufficient quantities of it. There has to be an effort to sustain it, and there has to be a fair and equal distribution of water to all segments of the society. Urban areas generally have a higher coverage of safe water than the rural areas. Even within an area there is variation: areas that can pay for the services have access to safe water whereas areas that cannot pay for the services have to make do with water from hand pumps and other sources.

In the urban areas water gets contaminated in many different ways, some of the most common reasons being leaky water pipe joints in areas where the water pipe and sewage line pass close together. Sometimes the water gets polluted at source due to various reasons and mainly due to inflow of sewage into the source.

Pesticides. Run-off from farms, backyards, and golf courses contain pesticides such as DDT that in turn contaminate the water. Leechate from landfill sites is another major contaminating source. Its effects on the ecosystems and health are endocrine and reproductive damage in wildlife. Groundwater is susceptible to contamination, as pesticides are mobile in the soil. It is a matter of concern as these chemicals are persistent in the soil and water.

Sewage. Untreated or inadequately treated municipal sewage is a major source of groundwater and surface water pollution in the developing countries. The organic material that is discharged with municipal waste into the watercourses uses substantial oxygen for biological degradation thereby upsetting the ecological balance of rivers and lakes. Sewage also carries microbial pathogens that are the cause of the spread of disease.

Nutrients. Domestic waste water, agricultural run-off, and industrial effluents contain phosphorus and nitrogen, fertilizer run-off, manure from livestock operations, which increase the level of nutrients in water bodies and can cause eutrophication in the lakes and rivers and continue on to the coastal areas. The nitrates come mainly from the fertilizer that is added to the fields. Excessive use of fertilizers cause nitrate contamination of groundwater, with the result that nitrate levels in drinking water is far above the safety levels recommended. Good agricultural practices can help in reducing the amount of nitrates in the soil and thereby lower its content in the water.

Synthetic organics. Many of the 100 000 synthetic compounds in use today are found in the aquatic environment and accumulate in the food chain. POPs or Persistent organic pollutants, represent the most harmful element for the ecosystem and for human health, for example, industrial chemicals and agricultural pesticides. These chemicals can accumulate in fish and cause serious damage to human health. Where pesticides are used on a large-scale, groundwater gets contaminated and this leads to the chemical contamination of drinking water.

Acidification. Acidification of surface water, mainly lakes and reservoirs, is one of the major environmental impacts of transport over long distance of air pollutants such as sulphur dioxide from power plants, other heavy industry such as steel plants, and motor vehicles. This problem is more severe in the US and in parts of Europe.

CHEMICALS IN DRINKING WATER

Chemicals in water can be both naturally occurring or introduced by human interference and can have serious health effects.

Fluoride. Fluoride in the water is essential for protection against dental caries and weakening of the bones, but higher levels can have an adverse effect on health. In India, high fluoride content is found naturally in the waters in

Rajasthan.*Arsenic*. Arsenic occurs naturally or is possibly aggrevated by over powering aquifers and by phosphorus from fertilizers. High concentrations of arsenic in water can have an adverse effect on health.A few years back, high concentrations of this element was found in drinking water in six districts in West Bengal. A majority of people in the area was found suffering from arsenic skin lesions. It was felt that arsenic contamination in the groundwater was due to natural causes. The government is trying to provide an alternative drinking water source and a method through which the arsenic content from water can be removed.

Lead. Pipes, fittings, solder, and the service connections of some household plumbing systems contain lead that contaminates the drinking water source.

Recreational use of water. Untreated sewage, industrial effluents, and agricultural waste are often discharged into the water bodies such as the lakes, coastal areas and rivers endangering their use for recreational purposes such as swimming and canoeing.

Petrochemicals. Petrochemicals contaminate the groundwater from underground petroleum storage tanks.

Other heavy metals. These contaminants come from mining waste and tailings, landfills, or hazardous waste dumps.

Chlorinated solvents. Metal and plastic effluents, fabric cleaning, electronic and aircraft manufacturing are often discharged and contaminate groundwater.

DISEASES

Water-borne diseases are infectious diseases spread primarily through contaminated water. Though these diseases are spread either directly or through flies or filth, water is the chief medium for spread of these diseases and hence they are termed as water-borne diseases.

Most intestinal (enteric) diseases are infectious and are transmitted through faecal waste. Pathogens – which include virus, bacteria, protozoa, and parasitic worms – are disease-producing agents found in the faeces of infected persons. These diseases are more prevalent in areas with poor sanitary conditions. These pathogens travel through water sources and interfuses directly through persons handling food and water. Since these diseases are highly infectious, extreme care and hygiene should be maintained by people looking after an infected patient. Hepatitis, cholera, dysentery, and typhoid are the more common water-borne diseases that affect large populations in the tropical regions.

A large number of chemicals that either exist naturally in the land or are added due to human activity dissolve in the water, thereby contaminating it and leading to various diseases.

Pesticides. The organophosphates and the carbonates present in pesticides affect and damage the nervous system and can cause cancer. Some of the pesticides contain carcinogens that exceed recommended levels. They contain chlorides that cause reproductive and endocrinal damage. *Lead.* Lead is hazardous to health as it accumulates in the body and affects the central nervous system. Children and pregnant women are most at risk.

Fluoride. Excess fluorides can cause yellowing of the teeth and damage to the spinal cord and other crippling diseases.

Nitrates. Drinking water that gets contaminated with nitrates can prove fatal especially to infants that drink formula milk as it restricts the amount of oxygen that reaches the brain causing the 'blue baby' syndrome. It is also linked to digestive tract cancers. It causes algae to bloom resulting in eutrophication in surface water.

Petrochemicals. Benzene and other petrochemicals can cause cancer even at low exposure levels.*Chlorinated solvents.* These are linked to reproduction disorders and to some cancers.

Arsenic. Arsenic poisoning through water can cause liver and nervous system damage, vascular diseases and also skin cancer.

Other heavy metals. –Heavy metals cause damage to the nervous system and the kidney, and other metabolic disruptions.

Salts. It makes the fresh water unusable for drinking and irrigation purposes.

Exposure to polluted water can cause diarrhoea, skin irritation, respiratory problems, and other diseases, depending on the pollutant that is in the water body. Stagnant water and other untreated water provide a habitat for the mosquito and a host of other parasites and insects that cause a large number of diseases especially in the tropical regions. Among these, malaria is undoubtedly the most widely distributed and causes most damage to human health.

PREVENTIVE MEASURES

Water-borne epidemics and health hazards in the aquatic environment are mainly due to improper management of water resources. Proper management of water resources has become the need of the hour as this would ultimately lead to a cleaner and healthier environment.

In order to prevent the spread of water-borne infectious diseases, people should take adequate precautions. The city water supply should be properly checked and necessary steps taken to disinfect it. Water pipes should be regularly checked for leaks and cracks. At home, the water should be boiled, filtered, or other methods and necessary steps taken to ensure that it is free from infection.

MINAMATA: ENVIRONMENTAL CONTAMINATION WITH METHYL MERCURY

In Minamata, Japan, inorganic mercury was used in the industrial production of acetaldehyde. It was discharged into the nearby bay as waste water and was ingested by organisms in the bottom sediments. Fish and other creatures in the sea were soon contaminated and eventually residents of this area who consumed the fish suffered from MeHg (methyl mercury) intoxication, later known as the Minamata disease. The disease was first detected in 1956 but the mercury emissions continued until 1968. But even after the emission of mercury stopped, the bottom sediment of the polluted water contained high levels of this mercury.

Various measures were taken to deal with this disease. Environmental pollution control, which included cessation of the mercury process; industrial effluent control, environmental restoration of the bay; and restrictions on the intake of fish from the bay. This apart research and investigative activities were promoted assiduously, and compensation and help was offered by the Japanese Government to all those affected by the disease.

The Minamata disease proved a turning point, towards progress in environment protection measures. This experience clearly showed that health and environment considerations must be integrated into the process of economic and industrial development from an early stage.

POLLUTION OF DRINKING WATER

Water is an important factor in the life of organisms. It supports life system and its shortage has been to main concerns of human beings.

Environmentalists and social scientists are warning about the availability of fresh water to human consumption after 2020 AD. Almost all the developing countries are going to face shortage of fresh water for human consumption by 2020 AD. Industrialization, development of civilization and population growth have increased dependence on natural resources, which are fast depleting. Availability of fresh water is a must for human consumption.

The fresh water resources are fast depleting or either getting polluted due to careless handling of water resources by the developing countries. The present paper mainly deals with the fresh water pollution in irrigation canals of Godavari delta System from its source of generation (Dowalaiswaram Barrage) upto the field input.

Generally the canal water in Godavari delta system will be utilized for water requirements of irrigable crops as well as for drinking purpose in the region. As regards pollution of fresh water in irrigation canals of Godavari Delta System, two important aspects are to be considered. One is pollution of canal water from source of generation (Dowalaiswaram barrage) to field input, while the fresh water is being carried through irrigation canals. Another is due to pollution caused to canal water by disorderly development of prawn/fish culture in the region. Apart from the above, there are industrial pollutants (due to large scale industrialization) etc. while they are being allowed to flow into irrigation canals and drains causes pollution.

POLLUTION OF CANAL WATER

Generally the canal water, from reservoirs or barrages are drawn through main canal, and distributed through branch canals, distributaries, field channels to the field. As far as Godavari delta is concerned, the irrigation canals and branch canals are passing through many of the towns, villages, hamlets, hutments etc. The main source of drinking water in the villages is through village drinking water tanks, fed by irrigation water.

Civilization and Industrialization has made mans pursuit for development more difficult. From the time immemorial, the drinking water tanks are source of fresh water for drinking purpose in the villages, in preference to urban areas. Now the position has changed. They are no more fresh water ponds, but containing polluted canal water only. The water pollution even in the villages is predominantly high; some times they also have to depend on ground water or private water resources for drinking purposes. This is due to large scale water pollution in canals from its source of generation to field input.

All the irrigation canals are passing by the towns, villages, hamlets hutments, carrying fresh water. There is considerable waste land *i.e.* government or poramboke (canal poramboke or drain poramboke) available on either side of delta canals or drains, allowing for possible widening of canals/ drains at a later stage. Thanks to the tbresightedness of "Apara Bhagiratha" Sir Arthur Cotton, the Eminent British Engineer, who constructed Godavari Anicut (old) and canal system in the year 1854.

At present all the canal banks and berms are encroached and occupied by local people for construction of dwelling houses, pucca lavatories etc. thus allowing all human waste/effluents into fresh water canal. The canal banks and berths are the open lavatories on the village nearby. For many of the villages and towns, the main outlets of drainage and sewage water are irrigation canals only.

The irrigation canals which are passing nearby the villages and towns are the dumping yards for the human and animal wastes sewage etc. In some places, the medical and surgical wastes and industrial wastes are dumped into fresh water canals. By the time the water reaches the tail end, it is contaminated with the full of the said effluents.

The million dollar questions asked now are: 1) Who is responsible for the above situation? 2. What are the existing Acts/laws to control the situation? 3. What are the remedial measures? The people at large and encroachers and hutment dwellers who have encroached into govt. land/poramboke in particular are responsible for the above situation.

The water (Prevention and control of pollution) Act, 1974 authorized central government to constitute The central pollution control Board" to exercise the powers conferred on and to perform the functions assigned to the board under the Act, authorized the State government, to constitute State Boards. If the canal water are to be made, free from pollution, the encroachments on the either side of the canals and canal berms (public lavatories) are to be evicted. All the sewage water freely flowing into the canal is to be stopped. Public awareness is to be created among the people not to throw objectionable matter such as garbage, sewage waste, human and animal wastes etc. into the irrigation canals. It is a socio-economic problem; the State government must take } effective measures.

Supreme Court in M.C. Mehta Vs. Union of India in Olium Gas Leakage case (AIR 1987, SC 1086) have evolved 'the Rule of absolute Liability" developed from the rule of strict liability and awarded damages to the victims. The wrong doers are to be punished under 'absolute liability' for which no defence is available. The same principle must be applied in case of offenders of water pollution, who ever may be.

POLLUTION OF FRESH WATER

Seafood has created a sensation in the world trade because of its health attitudes. It is the fastest moving commodity with persistent demand and high unit value. Seafood sector is growing into a multi billion dollar industry, with immense potential for the future. Prawns are the largest contribution to Indian fishing exports, accounting for an export share of 22 in volume, 48 in value. Prawns exports have been growing steadily from India in the recent years, mainly due to increase in production from capture as well as from culture. The export of marine products from India amounted to 3500 crores in the year 1995-96 and it stood at 6400 crores in the year 2000-01. Sea food exports alone constitute about 3.14 of the gross export earnings of our country, which is a vital to the Indian economy.

In view of the good return on prawn/fish culture, many of the irrigation lands under paddy cultivation are being converted into prawn/fish tanks, in Godavari Delta, including that of "Coastal Regulation Zone". This indiscriminate conversion of paddy fields is causing water pollution, including imbalance in eco-system.

The question of prohibiting or regulating aquaculture, prawn culture and shrimp culture came up for consideration for the Apex Court in S. Jagannath Vs. Union of India (AIR 1997 SC 811).

The court gave the following directions in this case:

1. We declare that the notification issued in G.O.Ms.No.120, dated 4.10.1999 is valid.
2. The respondents shall forthwith take adequate steps for stoppage and regulation of effluents discharged from the industries and municipalities into Kolleru Lake and strictly adhere to the standards laid down by the Ministry of Environment, Government of India for the purpose of preservation and maintenance of the lake and ecology

in accordance with law and state shall make all endeavours to bring back Kolleru Lake to its pristine glory.

3. No Pisci culture/aquaculture/shrimp culture should be permitted to be undertaken with the Kolleru lake sanctuary and only traditional methods of fishing as directed in G.o.ms.No.120, dated 4.10.1999 should be permitted. Any person intending to take recourse to aqua culture or Pisci culture or shrimp culture must file requisite applications before the appropriate aqua culture authority provided their lands fell outside the notification-dated 4.10.1999 and the area of sanctuary.
4. State shall ensure for removal of all encroachments of Kolleru Lake bed area in accordance with G.O.ms.No.l20, dt.4.10.1999. However, the enforcement authorities failed to remove encroachments in Kolleru Lake, further the authorities tailed to check conversion of agriculture lands into aqua culture, though such activities are going on without obtaining permissions from the proper authorities.

The method of irrigation adopted in Godavari Delta is by 'flooding method' mainly of 'strip border method". In this the irrigable land is levelled and divided into suitable size along plots by 0.30 mt. high field lands into a number of long and narrow strips. Water is allowed at the head or upper end of each strip and it flows along the strip in the form of a thin 5 to 7.5 cm stretch of water to the lower end of the strip. The irrigation system is mainly from field to field initially. The drainage water from one plot is collected and discharged into field drainage. The drainage system is not pucca as that of canal system. With the result the drainage water from upper field will flood over the adjacent field to join to nearest drainage course. Under this process of field to field irrigation, the drainage water of upper field will be input for lower field. This process of water utilization will not cause any effect so far as all the field block is under cultivation. If some land is under prawn/fish culture, the drainage water of prawn/fish tanks will be input for irrigation land. The problem has been aggravated due to smaller plots of land holding by the ryots, in Godavari delta.

Due to successive use of same water for different tanks, apart from change of physical and chemical properties. The water will acquire 'dielectric characteristics'. Ultimately the water gets polluted and will not be suitable for drinking purpose.

How the questions that arise are:

1. How far it is admissible to allow prawn/fish culture to interfere with the irrigation system developed exclusively for crop water requirements?
2. Can government centre and state, ban prawn/fish culture which are hazardously polluting water for human consumption in view of the tremendous foreign exchange earning capacity?

It is a socio-economic problem. No Government can ill afford to loose the tremendous foreign exchange earnings out of sea food exports. More over small and marginal farmers are dependent on culture. The only solution seems to be segregation of total irrigable land under delta system into two zones, one for raising irrigable crops and another for cultivating prawn/fish tanks.

The lands or areas surrounded by fisherman villages must be classified as zones for culture etc. The remodelling of the Irrigation system can be taken up by "Marine products Export Development Authority out of the funds available with them, by way of Export Cess.

The irrigation canal water is polluted, before it reaches the consumers in the villages for drinking purposes. Art. 21 of the constitution which guarantees Right to life. The Constitutional Review Committee while suggesting certain additions to Art. 21 (*i.e.* 21A to 21C) ignored to include "right to have a clean environment" under Art 21 therefore this may be incorporated as Art. 21 D. Thus making it as a fundamental Right.

Both central and state government and people in particular are responsible for the large scale pollution of canal water. It is a violation of fundamental rights, guaranteed to the citizen. Then the judiciary must act upon, when the executive is inactive. It is obvious that "the Water (Prevention and Control of Pollution Act 1974" even though enacted as far back as 1974 could not yield concrete results, so far obviously.

The supreme court has banned raising of culture in 'Coastal Regulation Zone". If the constitutional rights of getting free water and air to be enforced to the citizens, still more stringent laws to be enacted. A statue which will give an immediate action will only serve the purpose.

The Water Act, 1974 and Environment (Protection) Act, 1986 may be amended which empower the pollution control Boards to take appropriate action instead of filing the cases in courts. Further it should also enable a magistrate atleast First Class Magistrate to initiate action 'suo moto' without waiting for Board to initiate action.

RECENT EFFORTS TO ADDRESS WATER ISSUES

The government of India envisions a US$154 billion project to interlink all major river networks in India. This initiative would connect water-deficient areas to water-abundant ones by interlinking 37 Indian rivers. One of the largest projects anywhere in the world, it would transfer water through 30 links across 9,600 kilometres. It would connect 32 dams and use 56 million tons of cement and 2 million tons of steel. The project aims a transformation of India's water treatment, management, transmission and distribution. The Indian government has proposed reforms to attract investment and privatization of its water networks. Water companies from all over the world have established a presence in India to pursue an estimated 70 projects worth several billion dollars in 20

Indian cities. India is debating the social and environmental impact of this project. One of the first projects under consideration is the linking of Ken and Betwa rivers in northern India.

AIR POLLUTION

FUEL WOOD AND BIOMASS BURNING

Fuelwood and biomass burning is the primary reason for near-permanent haze and smokeobserved above rural and urban India, and in satellite pictures of the country. Fuelwood and biomass cakes are used for cooking and general heating needs. These are burnt in cook stoves known as *chullah* or *chulha* in some parts of India. These cook stoves are present in over 100 million Indian households, and are used two to three times a day, daily. As of 2009, majority of Indians still use traditional fuels such as dried cow dung, agricultural wastes, and firewood as cooking fuel. This form of fuel is inefficient source of energy, its burning releases high levels of smoke, PM10 particulate matter, NOX, SOX, PAHs, polyaromatics, formaldehyde, carbon monoxide and other air pollutants. Some reports, including one by the World Health Organization, claim 300,000 to 400,000 people die of indoor air pollution and carbon monoxide poisoning in India because of biomass burning and use of chullahs. Burning of biomass and firewood will not stop, unless electricity or clean burning fuel and combustion technologies become reliably available and widely adopted in rural and urban India.

India is the world's largest consumer of fuelwood, agricultural waste and biomass for energy purposes. From the most recent available nationwide study, India used 148.7 million tonnes coal replacement worth of fuelwood and biomass annually for domestic energy use. India's national average annual per capita consumption of fuel wood, agri wate and biomass cakes was 206 kilogram coal equivalent. In 2010 terms, with India's population increased to about 1.2 billion, the country burns over 200 million tonnes of coal replacement worth of fuel wood and biomass every year to meet its energy need for cooking and other domestic use. The study found that the households consumed around 95 million tonnes of fuelwood, one-third of which was logs and the rest was twigs. Twigs were mostly consumed in the villages, and logs were more popular in cities of India. The overall contribution of fuelwood, including sawdust and wood waste, was about 46% of the total, the rest being agri waste and biomass dung cakes. Traditional fuel (fuelwood, crop residue and dung cake) dominates domestic energy use in rural India and accounts for about 90% of the total. In urban areas, this traditional fuel constitutes about 24% of the total.

Fuel wood, agri waste and biomass cake burning releases over 165 million tonnes of combustion products into India's indoor and outdoor air every year. To place this volume of emission in context, the Environmental Protection Agency (EPA) of the United States estimates that fire wood smoke contributes over 420,000 tonnes of fine particles throughout the United States – mostly during the winter months. United States consumes about one-tenth of fuelwood consumed by India, and mostly for fireplace and home heating purposes. EPA estimates that residential wood combustion in the USA accounts for 44 percent of total organic matter emissions and 62 percent of the PAH, which are probable human carcinogens and are of great concern to EPA. The fuelwood sourced residential wood smoke makes up over 50 percent of the wintertime particle pollution problem in California. In 2010, the state of California had about the same number of vehicles as all of India.

India burns tenfold more fuelwood every year than the United States, the fuelwood quality in India is different than the dry firewood of the United States, and the Indian stoves in use are less efficient thereby producing more smoke and air pollutants per kilogram equivalent. India has less land area and less emission air space than the United States. In summary, the impact on indoor and outdoor air pollution by fuelwood and biomass cake burning is far worse in India.

A United Nations study finds firewood and biomass stoves can be made more efficient in India. Animal dung, now used in inefficient stoves, could be used to produce biogas, a cleaner fuel with higher utilization efficiency. In addition, an excellent fertilizer can be produced from the slurry from biogas plants. Switching to gaseous fuels would bring the greatest gains in terms of both thermal efficiency and reduction in air pollution, but would require more investment. A combination of technologies may be the best way forward.

Between 2001 and 2010, India has made progress in adding electrical power generation capacity, bringing electricity to rural areas, and reforming market to improve availability and distribution of liquified cleaner burning fuels in urban and rural area. Over the same period, scientific data collection and analysis show improvement in India's air quality, with some regions witnessing 30 to 65% reduction in NOx, SOx and suspended particulate matter. Even at these lower levels, the emissions are higher than those recommended by the World Health Organization. Continued progress is necessary.

Scientific studies conclude biomass combustion in India is the country's dominant source of carbonaceous aerosols, emitting 0.25 teragram per year of black carbon into air, 0.94 teragram per year of organic matter, and 2.04 teragram per year of small particulates with diameter less than 2.5 microns. Biomass burning, as domestic fuel in India, accounts for about 3 times as much black carbon air pollution as all other sources combined, including vehicles and industrial sources.

Other sources of pollution in Indian cities are vehicles and emissions from industry. Until 1992, India protected its automobile industry using license raj. Many two wheel, three wheel and four wheel vehicles lacked catalytic converters. Per vehicle emissions were amongst the highest in the world. The refining of oil and supply of fuel was owned, regulated and run by the government; the fuel quality was lax. In 2005, India adopted emission standard of Bharat Stage IV for vehicles, which is equivalent to Euro IV European standards for vehicle emissions. Nevertheless, the old pre-2005 vehicles, and even pre-1992 vehicles are still on Indian streets.

FUEL ADULTERATION

Some Indian taxis and auto-rickshaws run on adulterated fuel blends. Adulteration of gasoline and diesel with lower-priced fuels is common in South Asia, including India. Some adulterants increase emissions of harmful pollutants from vehicles, worsening urban air pollution. Financial incentives arising from differential taxes are generally the primary cause of fuel adulteration. In India and other developing countries, gasoline carries a much higher tax than diesel, which in turn is taxed more than kerosene meant as a cooking fuel, while some solvents and lubricants carry little or no tax. As fuel prices rise, the public transport driver cuts costs by blending the cheaper hydrocarbon into highly taxed hydrocarbon. The blending may be as much as 20-30 percent. For a low wage driver, the adulteration can yield short term savings that are significant over the month. The consequences to long term air pollution, quality of life and effect on health are simply ignored. Also ignored are the reduced life of vehicle engine and higher maintenance costs, particularly if the taxi, auto-rickshaw or truck is being rented for a daily fee.

Adulterated fuel increases tailpipe emissions of hydrocarbons (HC), carbon monoxide (CO), oxides of nitrogen (NOx) and particulate matter (PM). Air toxin emissions — which fall into the category of unregulated emissions— of primary concern are benzene and polyaromatic hydrocarbons (PAHs), both well known carcinogens. Kerosene is more difficult to burn than gasoline; its addition results in higher levels of HC, CO and PM emissions even from catalyst-equipped cars. The higher sulfur level of kerosene is another issue. The permissible level of fuel sulfur in India, in 2002, was 0.25 percent by weight as against 0.10 percent for gasoline. The higher levels of sulfur can deactivate the catalyst. Once the catalyst becomes deactivated, the amount of pollution from the vehicle dramatically increases. Fuel adulteration is essentially an unintended consequence of tax policies and the attempt to control fuel prices, in the name of fairness. Air pollution is the ultimate result. This problem is not unique to India, but prevalent in many developing countries including those outside of south Asia. This problem is largely absent in economies that do not regulate the ability of fuel producers to innovate or price based on market demand.

TRAFFIC CONGESTION

Traffic congestion is severe in India's cities and towns. Traffic congestion is caused for several reasons, some of which are: increase in number of vehicles per kilometer of available road, a lack of intra-city divided-lane highways and intra-city expressways networks, lack of inter-city expressways, traffic accidents and chaos from poor enforcement of traffic laws.

Traffic congestion reduces average traffic speed. At low speeds, scientific studies reveal, vehicles burn fuel inefficiently and pollute more per trip. For example, a study in the United States found that for the same trip, cars consumed more fuel and polluted more if the traffic was congested, than when traffic flowed freely. At average trip speeds between 20 to 40 kilometres per hour, the cars pollutant emission was twice as much as when the average speed was 55 to 75 kilometres per hour. At average trip speeds between 5 to 20 kilometres per hour, the cars pollutant emissions were 4 to 8 times as much as when the average speed was 55 to 70 kilometres per hour. Fuel efficiencies similarly were much worse with traffic congestion.

Traffic gridlock in Delhi and other India cities is extreme. The average trip speed on many Indian city roads is less than 20 kilometres per hour; a 10 kilometer trip can take 30 minutes, or more. At such speeds, vehicles in India emit air pollutants 4 to 8 times more than they would with less traffic congestion; Indian vehicles also consume a lot more carbon footprint fuel per trip, than they would if the traffic congestion was less.

In cities like Bangalore, around 50% of children suffer from asthma.

RECENT TRENDS IN INDIA'S AIR QUALITY

With the last 15 years of economic development and regulatory reforms, India has made progress in improving its air quality. The table presents the average emissions sampled at many locations, over time, and data analyzed by scientific methods, by multiple agencies, including The World Bank. For context and comparison, the table also includes average values for Sweden in 2008, observed and analyzed by same methods. Over 1995-2008, average nationwide levels of major air pollutants have dropped by between 25-45 percent in India.

India's Central Pollution Control Board now routinely monitors four air pollutants namely sulphur dioxide (SO_2), oxides of nitrogen (NOx), suspended particulate matter (SPM) and respirable particulate matter (PM10). These are target air pollutants for regular monitoring at 308 operating stations in 115 cities/towns in 25 states and 4 Union Territories of India. The monitoring of meteorological parameters such as wind speed and direction, relative humidity and temperature has also been integrated with the monitoring of air quality. The monitoring of these pollutants is carried out for 24 hours (4-hourly sampling for gaseous pollutants and 8-hourly sampling for particulate matter) with a frequency of twice a week, to yield 104 observations in a year.

For 2010, the key findings of India's central pollution control board are:

- Most Indian cities continue to violate India's and world air quality PM10 targets. Respirable particulate matter pollution remains a key challenge for India. Despite the general non-attainment, some cities showed far more improvement than others. A decreasing trend has been observed in PM10 levels in cities like Solapur and Ahmedabad over the last few years. This improvement may be due to local measures taken to reduce sulphur in diesel and stringent enforcement by Gujarat government.

- A decreasing trend has been observed in sulphur dioxide levels in residential areas of many cities such as Delhi, Mumbai, Lucknow, Bhopal during last few years. The decreasing trend in sulphur dioxide levels may be due to recently introduced clean fuel standards, and the increasing use of LPG as domestic fuel instead of coal or fuelwood, and the use of LPG instead of diesel in certain vehicles.
- A decreasing trend has been observed in nitrogen dioxide levels in residential areas of some cities such as Bhopal and Solapur during last few years. The decreasing trend in sulphur dioxide levels may be due to recently introduced vehicle emission standards, and the increasing use of LPG as domestic fuel instead of coal or fuelwood.
- Most Indian cities greatly exceed acceptable levels of suspended particulate matter. This may be because of refuse and biomass burning, vehicles, power plant emissions, industrial sources.
- The Indian air quality monitoring stations reported lower levels of PM10 and suspended particulate matter during monsoon months possibly due to wet deposition and air scrubbing by rainfall. Higher levels of particulates were observed during winter months possibly due to lower mixing heights and more calm conditions. In other words, India's air quality worsens in winter months, and improves with the onset of monsoon season.

For its 2008 annual report, Central Pollution Control Board used 346 operating Air Quality Monitoring Stations, covering 130 cities / towns in 26 States and 4 Union Territories. With the weekly data collected and then averaged over the year, Central Pollution Control Board reported the following annual trends from 1998 to 2008:

- The average annual SOx and NOx emissions level and periodic violations in industrial areas of India were significantly and surprisingly lower than the emission and violations in residential areas of India.
- The 24-hour average PM10 and suspended particulate matter emissions and violations in almost all areas of India violated India's and WHO targets. The PM10 and suspended particulate matter concentrations, in industrial areas of India were, however, lower than those in residential areas of India. Residential areas of India were the source of over 90% of the most serious and repeated violations in particulate air pollution.

- Of the four major Indian cities, air pollution was consistently worst in Delhi, every year over 5 year period (2004–2008). Kolkata was a close second, followed by Mumbai. Chennai air pollution was least of the four.
- The states of Kerala and Meghalaya, relative to other Indian states, experienced on average some of lowest air pollution levels. The cities of Thiruvananthapuram, Kottayam and Shillong, relative to other Indian cities and towns, experienced some of lowest air pollution levels.
- Air Quality data collected from the monitoring station at Taj Mahal, Agra since year 1991 to 2008, suggests that both particulate and acid rain pollutants at Taj Mahal have been declining over the years. The 2008 average annual air pollutant concentrations were between 38 to 67% lower than those in 1991.

SOLID WASTE POLLUTION

Trash and garbage is a common sight in urban and rural areas of India. It is a major source of pollution. Indian cities alone generate more than 100 million tons of solid waste a year. Street corners are piled with trash. Public places and sidewalks are despoiled with filth and litter, rivers and canals act as garbage dumps. In part, India's garbage crisis is from rising consumption. India's waste problem also points to a stunning failure of governance. In 2000, India's Supreme Court directed all Indian cities to implement a comprehensive waste-management programme that would include household collection of segregated waste, recycling and composting. These directions have simply been ignored. No major city runs a comprehensive programme of the kind envisioned by the Supreme Court. Indeed, forget waste segregation and recycling directive of the India's Supreme Court, the Organization for Economic Cooperation and Development estimates that up to 40 percent of municipal waste in India remains simply uncollected. Even medical waste, theoretically controlled by stringent rules that require hospitals to operate incinerators, is routinely dumped with regular municipal garbage. A recent study found that about half of India's medical waste is improperly disposed of.

Municipalities in Indian cities and towns have waste collection employees. However, these are unionized government workers and their work performance is neither measured nor monitored.

Some of the few solid waste landfills India has, near its major cities, are overflowing and poorly managed. They have become significant sources of greenhouse emissions and breeding sites for disease vectors such as flies, mosquitoes, cockroaches, rats, and other pests.

In 2011, several Indian cities embarked on waste-to-energy projects of the type in use in Germany, Switzerland and Japan. For example, New Delhi is implementing two incinerator projects aimed at turning the city's trash problem into electricity resource. These plants are being welcomed for addressing the city's chronic problems of excess untreated waste and a shortage of electric power. They are also being welcomed by those who seek to prevent water pollution, hygiene problems, and eliminate rotting trash that produces potent greenhouse gas methane. The projects are being opposed by waste collection workers and local unions who fear changing technology may deprive them of their livelihood and way of life.

Along with waste-to-energy projects, some cities and towns such as Pune, Maharashtra are introducing competition and the privatization of solid waste collection, street cleaning operations and bio-mining to dispose the waste. A scientific study suggests public private partnership is, in Indian context, more useful in solid waste management. According to this study, government and municipal corporations must encourage PPP-based local management through collection, transport and segregation and disposal of solid waste.

NOISE POLLUTION

The Supreme Court of India gave a significant verdict on noise pollution in 2005. Unnecessary honking of vehicles makes for a highdecibel level of noise in cities. The use of loudspeakers for political purposes and by temples and mosques make for noise pollution inresidential areas because using more speakers in an programmes the noise is increase. In January 2010, Government of India published norms of permissible noise levels in urban and rural areas.

LAND POLLUTION

In March 2009, the issue of Uranium poisoning in Punjab came into light, caused by fly ash ponds of thermal power stations, which reportedly lead to severe birth defects in children in the Faridkot and Bhatinda districts of Punjab.

GREENHOUSE GAS EMISSIONS

India was the third largest emitter of carbon dioxide in 2009 at 1.65 Gt per year, after China (6.9 Gt per year) and the United States (5.2 Gt per year). With 17 percent of world population, India contributed some 5 percent of human-sourced carbon dioxide emission; compared to China's 24 percent share. On per capita basis, India emitted about 1.4 tons of carbon dioxide per person, in comparison to the United States' 17 tons per person, and a world average of 5.3 tons per person.

About 65 percent of India's carbon dioxide emissions in 2009 was from heating, domestic uses and power sector. About 9 percent of India's emissions were from transportation (cars, trains, two wheelers, airplanes, others). India's coal-fired, oil-fired and natural gas-fired thermal power plants are inefficient and offer significant potential for CO_2 emission reduction through better technology. Compared to the average emissions from coal-fired, oil-fired and natural gas-fired thermal power plants in European Union (EU-27) countries, India's thermal power plants emit 50 to 120 percent more CO2 per kWh produced. This is in significant part to inefficient thermal power plants installed in India prior to its economic liberalization in the 1990s.

Between 1990 and 2009, India's carbon dioxide emissions per GDP purchasing power parity basis have decreased by over 10 percent, a trend similar to China. Meanwhile, between 1990 and 2009, Russia's carbon dioxide emissions per GDP purchasing power parity basis have increased by 40 percent. India has one of the better records in the world, of an economy that is growing efficiently on CO2 emissions basis. In other words, over the last 20 years, India has reduced CO2 emissions with each unit of GDP increase. Per Copenhagen Accord, India aims to further reduce emissions intensity of its growing GDP by 20 to 25 percent before 2020, with technology transfer and international cooperation. Nevertheless, it is expected, that like China, India's absolute carbon dioxide emissions will rise in years ahead, even as International Energy Agency's Annex I countries expect their absolute CO2 emissions to drop.

A significant source of greenhouse gas emissions from India is from black carbon, NOx, methane and other air pollutants. These pollutants are emitted in large quantities in India every day from incomplete and inefficient combustion of biomass (fuel wood, crop waste and cattle dung). A majority of Indian population lacks access to clean burning fuels, and uses biomass combustion as cooking fuel. India's poorly managed solid wastes, inadequate sewage treatment plants, water pollution and agriculture are other sources of greenhouse gas emissions.

NASA's Lau has proposed that as the aerosol particles rise on the warm, convecting air, they produce more rain over northern India and the Himalayan foothill, which further warms the atmosphere and fuels a "heat pump" that draws yet more warm air to the region. This phenomenon, Lau believes, changes the timing and intensity of the monsoon, effectively transferring heat from the low-lying lands over the subcontinent to the atmosphere over the Tibetan Plateau, which in turn warms the high-altitude land surface and hastens glacial retreat. His modeling shows that aerosols—particularly black carbon and dust—likely cause as much of the glacial retreat in the region as greenhouse gases via this "heat pump" effect.

IRRIGATION WATER MANAGEMENT

An adequate water supply is important for plant growth. When rainfall is not sufficient, the plants must receive additional water from irrigation. Various methods can be used to supply irrigation water to the plants. Each method has its advantages and disadvantages. These should be taken into account when choosing the method which is best suited to the local circumstances.

IRRIGATION AND ARTIFICIAL APPLICATION OF WATER

Irrigation may be defined as the science of artificial application of water to the land or soil. It is used to assist in the growing of agricultural crops, maintenance of landscapes, and revegetation of disturbed soils in dry areas and during periods of inadequate rainfall.

Additionally, irrigation also has a few other uses in crop production, which include protecting plants against frost, suppressing weed growing in grain fields and helping in preventing soil consolidation. In contrast, agriculture that relies only on direct rainfall is referred to as rain-fed or dryland farming. Irrigation systems are also used for dust suppression, disposal of sewage, and in mining. Irrigation is often studied together with drainage, which is the natural or artificial removal of surface and sub-surface water from a given area. Irrigation is also a term used in medical/dental fields to refer to flushing and washing out anything with water or another liquid.

VARIOUS TYPES OF IRRIGATION

Various types of irrigation techniques differ in how the water obtained from the source is distributed within the field. In general, the goal is to supply the entire field uniformly with water, so that each plant has the amount of water it needs, neither too much nor too little.The modern methods are efficient enough to achieve this goal.

SURFACE IRRIGATION SYSTEMS

In surface irrigation systems, water moves over and across the land by simple gravity flow in order to wet it and to infiltrate into the soil. Surface irrigation can be subdivided into furrow, *borderstrip or basin irrigation*. It is often called flood irrigation when the irrigation results in flooding or near flooding of the cultivated land.

Historically, this has been the most common method of irrigating agricultural land. Where water levels from the irrigation source permit, the levels are controlled by dikes, usually plugged by soil.

This is often seen in terraced rice fields (rice paddies), where the method is used to flood or control the level of water in each distinct field. In some cases, the water is pumped, or lifted by human or animal power to the level of the land.

Localized

Localized irrigation is a system where water is distributed under low pressure through a piped network, in a pre-determined pattern, and applied as a small discharge to each plant or adjacent to it. Drip irrigation, spray or micro-sprinkler irrigation and bubbler irrigation belong to this category of irrigation methods.

Drip

Drip irrigation, also known as trickle irrigation, functions as its name suggests.In this system water falls drop by drop just at the position of roots. Water is delivered at or near the root zone of plants, drop by drop. This method can be the most water-efficient method of irrigation, if managed properly, since evaporation and run-off are minimized. In modern agriculture, drip irrigation is often combined with plastic mulch, further reducing evaporation, and is also the means of delivery of fertilizer. The process is known as *fertigation*. Deep percolation, where water moves below the root zone, can occur if a drip system is operated for too long or if the delivery rate is too high. Drip irrigation methods range from very high-tech and computerized to low-tech and labour-intensive. Lower water pressures are usually needed than for most other types of systems, with the exception of low energy centre pivot systems and surface irrigation systems, and the system can be designed for uniformity throughout a field or for precise water delivery to individual plants in a landscape containing a mix of plant species.

Although it is difficult to regulate pressure on steep slopes, pressure compensating emitters are available, so the field does not have to be level. High-tech solutions involve precisely calibrated emitters located along lines of tubing that extend from a computerized set of valves.

Sprinkler

In sprinkler or overhead irrigation, water is piped to one or more central locations within the field and distributed by overhead high-pressure sprinklers or guns. A system utilizing sprinklers, sprays, or guns mounted overhead on permanently installed risers is often referred to as a *solid-set* irrigation system.

Higher pressure sprinklers that rotate are called *rotors* and are driven by a ball drive, gear drive, or impact mechanism. Rotors can be designed to rotate in a full or partial circle.

Guns are similar to rotors, except that they generally operate at very high pressures of 40 to 130 lbf/in^2 (275 to 900 kPa) and flows of 50 to 1200 US gal/min (3 to 76 L/s), usually with nozzle diameters in the range of 0.5 to 1.9 inches (10 to 50 mm). Guns are used not only for irrigation, but also for industrial applications such as dust suppression and logging.

Sprinklers can also be mounted on moving platforms connected to the water source by a hose. Automatically moving wheeled systems known as *traveling sprinklers* may irrigate areas such as small farms, sports fields, parks, pastures, and cemeteries unattended. Most of these utilize a length of polyethylene tubing wound on a steel drum.

As the tubing is wound on the drum powered by the irrigation water or a small gas engine, the sprinkler is pulled across the field. When the sprinkler arrives back at the reel the system shuts off. This type of system is known to most people as a "waterreel" traveling irrigation sprinkler and they are used extensively for dust suppression, irrigation, and land application of waste water. Other travellers use a flat rubber hose that is dragged along behind while the sprinkler platform is pulled by a cable. These cable-type travellers are definitely old technology and their use is limited in today's modern irrigation projects.

Centre Pivot

Centre pivot irrigation is a form of sprinkler irrigation consisting of several segments of pipe (usually galvanized steel or aluminum) joined together and supported by trusses, mounted on wheeled towers with sprinklers positioned along its length. The system moves in a circular pattern and is fed with water from the pivot point at the centre of the arc. These systems are found and used in all parts of the world and allow irrigation of all types of terrain. Newer systems have drop sprinkler heads as shown in the image that follows.

Most centre pivot systems now have drops hanging from a u-shaped pipe attached at the top of the pipe with sprinkler heads that are positioned a few feet (at most) above the crop, thus limiting evaporative losses. Drops can also be used with drag hoses or bubblers that deposit the water directly on the ground between crops.

Crops are often planted in a circle to conform to the centre pivot. This type of system is known as LEPA (Low Energy Precision Application). Originally, most centre pivots were water powered. These were replaced by hydraulic systems (*T-L Irrigation*) and electric motor driven systems (Reinke, Valley, Zimmatic). Many modern pivots feature GPS devices.

Lateral Move (Side Roll, Wheel Line)

A series of pipes, each with a wheel of about 1.5 m diameter permanently affixed to its midpoint and sprinklers along its length, are coupled together at one edge of a field. Water is supplied at one end using a large hose. After sufficient water has been applied, the hose is removed and the remaining assembly rotated either by hand or with a purpose-built mechanism, so that the sprinklers move 10 m across the field. The hose is reconnected.

The process is repeated until the opposite edge of the field is reached. This system is less expensive to install than a centre pivot, but much more labour intensive to operate, and it is limited in the amount of water it can carry.

Most systems utilize 4 or 5-inch (130 mm) diameter aluminum pipe. One feature of a lateral move system is that it consists of sections that can be easily disconnected. They are most often used for small or oddly shaped fields, such as those found in hilly or mountainous regions, or in regions where labour is inexpensive. Subirrigation also sometimes called *seepage irrigation* has been used for many years in field crops in areas with high water tables. It is a method of artificially raising the water table to allow the soil to be moistened from below the plants' root zone. Often those systems are located on permanent grasslands in lowlands or river valleys and combined with drainage infrastructure. A system of pumping stations, canals, weirs and gates allows it to increase or decrease the water level in a network of ditches and thereby control the water table.

Sub-irrigation is also used in commercial greenhouse production, usually for potted plants. Water is delivered from below, absorbed upwards, and the excess collected for recycling.

Typically, a solution of water and nutrients floods a container or flows through a trough for a short period of time, 10–20 minutes, and is then pumped back into a holding tank for reuse. Sub-irrigation in greenhouses requires fairly sophisticated, expensive equipment and management. Advantages are water and nutrient conservation, and labour-saving through lowered system maintenance and automation. It is similar in principle and action to subsurface drip irrigation.

Manual using Buckets or Watering Cans

These systems have low requirements for infrastructure and technical equipment but need high labour inputs. Irrigation using watering cans is to be found for example in peri-urban agriculture around large cities in some African countries.

Automatic, Non-electric using Buckets and Ropes

Besides the common manual watering by bucket, an automated, natural version of this also exist. Using plain polyester ropes combined with a prepared ground mixture can be used to water plants from a vessel filled with water.

The ground mixture would need to be made depending on the plant itself, yet would mostly consist of black potting soil, vermiculite and perlite. This system would (with certain crops) allow to save expenses as it does not consume any electricity and only little water (unlike sprinklers, water timers,...). However, it may only be used with certain crops (probably mostly larger crops that do not need a humid environment; perhaps *e.g.* paprikas).

Using Water Condensed from Humid Air

In countries where at night, humid air sweeps the countryside, water can be obtained from the humid air by condensation onto cold surfaces. This is for example practiced in the vineyards at Lanzarote using stones to condense water or with various fog collectors based on canvas or foil sheets.

IRRIGATION WATER QUALITY CRITERIA

Salt-affected soils develop from a wide range of factors including: soil type, field slope and drainage, irrigation system type and management, fertilizer and manuring practices, and other soil and water management practices. In Colorado, perhaps the most critical factor in predicting, managing, and reducing salt-affected soils is the quality of irrigation water being used. Besides affecting crop yield and soil physical conditions, irrigation water quality can affect fertility needs, irrigation system performance and longevity, and how the water can be applied. Therefore, knowledge of irrigation water quality is critical to understanding what management changes are necessary for long-term productivity.

IRRIGATION WATER QUALITY CRITERIA

Soil scientists use the following categories to describe irrigation water effects on crop production and soil quality:

- Salinity hazard - total soluble salt content
- Sodium hazard - relative proportion of sodium to calcium and magnesium ions
- pH - acid or basic
- Alkalinity - carbonate and bicarbonate
- *Specific ions*: chloride, sulfate, boron, and nitrate.

Another potential irrigation water quality impairment that may affect suitability for cropping systems is microbial pathogens.

Table. General Guidelines for Salinity Hazard of Irrigation Water based Upon Conductivity.

Limitations for use	*Electrical Conductivity*
	(dS/m)*
None	£0.75
Some	0.76 – 1.5
Moderate	1.51 – 3.00
Severe	£3.00

Note: *dS/m at 25ºC = mmhos/cmLeaching required at higher range.Good drainage needed and sensitive plants may have difficulty at germination.

SALINITY HAZARD

The most influential water quality guideline on crop productivity is the water salinity hazard as measured by electrical conductivity (EC_w). The primary effect of high EC_w water on crop productivity is the inability of the plant to compete with ions in the soil solution for water (physiological drought). The higher the EC, the less water is available to plants, even though the soil may appear wet.

Because plants can only transpire "pure" water, usable plant water in the soil solution decreases dramatically as EC increases. Actual yield reductions from irrigating with high EC water varies substantially. Factors influencing yield reductions include soil type, drainage, salt type, irrigation system and management.

Table. Potential Yield Reduction from Saline Water for Selected Irrigated Crops.

	% Yield Reduction			
Crop	*0%*	*10%*	*25%*	*50%*
	EC_w			
Barley	5.3	6.7	8.7	12
Wheat	4.0	4.9	6.4	8.7
Sugarbeet	4.7	5.8	7.5	10
Alfalfa	1.3	2.2	3.6	5.9
Potato	1.1	1.7	2.5	3.9
Corn (grain)	1.1	1.7	2.5	3.9
Corn (silage)	1.2	2.1	3.5	5.7
Onion	0.8	1.2	1.8	2.9
Dry Beans	0.7	1.0	1.5	2.4

Note:

EC_w = electrical conductivity of the irrigation water in dS/m at 25oC. Sensitive during germination. EC_w should not exceed 3 dS/m for garden beets and sugarbeets.

The amount of water transpired through a crop is directly related to yield; therefore, irrigation water with high EC_w reduces yield potential (Table). Beyond effects on the immediate crop is the long term impact of salt loading through the irrigation water. Water with an EC_w of only 1.15 dS/m contains approximately 2,000 pounds of salt for every acre foot of water. You can use conversion factors in Table to make this calculation for other water EC levels.

Table. Conversion Factors for Irrigation Water Quality Laboratory Reports.

Component	To Convert	Multiply By	To Obtain
Water nutrient or TDS	mg/L	1.0	ppm
Water salinity hazard	1 dS/m	1.0	1 mmho/cm
Water salinity hazard	1 mmho/cm	1,000	1 μmho/cm
Water salinity hazard	EC_w (dS/m) for EC <5 dS/m	640	TDS (mg/L)
Water salinity hazard	EC_w (dS/m) for EC >5 dS/m	800	TDS (mg/L)
Water NO_3N, SO_4-S,B applied	ppm	0.23	lb per acre inch of water
Irrigation water	acre inch	27,150	gallons of water

Other terms that laboratories and literature sources use to report salinity hazard are: salts, salinity, electrical conductivity (EC_w), or total dissolved solids (TDS). These terms are all comparable and all quantify the amount of dissolved "salts" (or ions, charged particles) in a water sample. However, TDS is a direct measurement of dissolved ions and EC is an indirect measurement of ions by an electrode. Although people frequently confuse the term "salinity" with common table salt or sodium chloride (NaCl), EC measures salinity from all the ions dissolved in a sample. This includes negatively charged ions (*e.g.*, Cl, NO_3) and positively charged ions (*e.g.*, Ca, Na). Another common source of confusion is the variety of unit systems used with EC_w. The preferred unit is deciSiemens per meter (dS/m), however millimhos per centimeter (mmho/cm) and micromhos per centimeter (μmho/cm) are still frequently used.

DEFINITIONS

Abbrev.	*Meaning*
mg/L	Milligrams per litre
meq/L	Milliequivalents per litre
ppm	Parts per million
dS/m	DeciSiemens per meter
μS/cm	MicroSiemens per centimeter
mmho/cm	Millimhos per centimeter
TDS	Total dissolved solids

SODIUM HAZARD

Infiltration/Permeability Problems

Although plant growth is primarily limited by the salinity (EC_w) level of the irrigation water, the application of water with a sodium imbalance can further reduce yield under certain soil texture conditions. Reductions in water infiltration can occur when irrigation water contains high sodium relative to the calcium and magnesium contents. This condition, termed "sodicity," results from excessive soil accumulation of sodium. Sodic water is not the same as saline water. Sodicity causes swelling and dispersion of soil clays, surface crusting and pore plugging. This degraded soil structure condition in turn obstructs infiltration and may increase run-off. Sodicity causes a decrease in the downward movement of water into and through the soil, and actively growing plants roots may not get adequate water, despite pooling of water on the soil surface after irrigation.

The most common measure to assess sodicity in water and soil is called the Sodium Adsorption Ratio (SAR). The SAR defines sodicity in terms of the relative concentration of sodium (Na) compared to the sum of calcium (Ca) and magnesium (Mg) ions in a sample. The SAR assesses the potential for infiltration problems due to a sodium imbalance in irrigation water. The SAR is mathematically written below, where Na, Ca and Mg are the concentrations of these ions in milliequivalents per litre (meq/L). Concentrations of these ions in water samples are typically provided in milligrams per litre (mg/L). To convert Na, Ca, and Mg from mg/L to meq/L, you should divide the concentration by 22.9, 20, and 12.15 respectively. For most irrigation waters encountered in Colorado the standard SAR formula provided above is suitable to express the potential sodium hazard. However, for irrigation water with high bicarbonate (HCO_3) content, an "adjusted" SAR (SAR_{ADJ}) can be calculated. In this case, the amount of calcium is adjusted for the water's alkalinity, is recommended in place of the standard SAR. Your laboratory may calculate an adjusted SAR in situations where the HCO_3 is greater than 200 mg/L or pH is greater than 8.5.

$$SAR = \frac{Na^{+} meq / L}{\sqrt{\frac{\left(Ca^{++}{}_{meq/L}\right) + \left(Mg^{++}{}_{meq/L}\right)}{2}}}$$

meq/L = mg/L divided by atomic weight of ion divided by ionic charge (Na = 23.0 mg/meq, Ca = 20.0 mg/meq, Mg = 12.15 mg/meq) The potential soil infiltration and permeability problems created from applications of irrigation water with high "sodicity" cannot be adequately assessed on the basis of the SAR alone.

This is because the swelling potential of low salinity (EC_w) water is greater than high EC_w waters at the same sodium content. Therefore, a more accurate evaluation of the infiltration/permeability hazard requires using the electrical conductivity (EC_w) together with the SAR.

Table. Guidelines for Assessment of Sodium Hazard of Irrigation Water Based on SAR and EC_w.

	Potential for Water Infiltration Problem	
Irrigation water SAR	*Unlikely*	*Likely*
	------ EC_w (dS/m) ------	
0-3	>0.7	<0.2
3-6	>1.2	<0.4
6-12	>1.9	<0.5.
12-20	>2.9	<1.0
20-40	>5.0	<3.0

Many factors including soil texture, organic matter, cropping system, irrigation system and management affect how sodium in irrigation water affects soils. Soils most likely to show reduced infiltration and crusting from water with elevated SAR (greater than 6) are those containing more than 30% expansive (smectite) clay. Soils containing more than 30% clay include most soils in the clay loam, silty clay loam textural classes and finer and some sandy clay loams. In Colorado, smectite clays are common in areas with agricultural production.

Table. Susceptibility Ranges for Crops to Foliar Injury from Saline Sprinkler Water.

	Na or Cl Concentration (mg/L) Causing			
	Foliar Injury			
Na concentration	<46	46-230	231-460	>460
Cl concentration	<175	175-350	351-700	>700
	Apricot	Pepper	Alfalfa	Sugarbeet
	Plum	Potato	Barley	Sunflower
	Tomato	Corn	Sorghum	

pH and Alkalinity

The acidity or basicity of irrigation water is expressed as pH (< 7.0 acidic; > 7.0 basic). The normal pH range for irrigation water is from 6.5 to 8.4. Abnormally low pH's are not common in Colorado, but may cause accelerated irrigation system corrosion where they occur. High pH's above 8.5 are often caused by high bicarbonate (HCO_3) and carbonate (CO_3) concentrations, known as alkalinity.

High carbonates cause calcium and magnesium ions to form insoluble minerals leaving sodium as the dominant ion in solution. As described in the sodium hazard section, this alkaline water could intensify the impact of high SAR water on sodic soil conditions. Excessive bicarbonate concentrates can also be problematic for drip or micro-spray irrigation systems when calcite or scale build up causes reduced flow rates through orifices or emitters. In these situations, correction by injecting sulfuric or other acidic materials into the system may be required.

Chloride

Chloride is a common ion in Colorado irrigation waters. Although chloride is essential to plants in very low amounts, it can cause toxicity to sensitive crops at high concentrations.

Like sodium, high chloride concentrations cause more problems when applied with sprinkler irrigation. Leaf burn under sprinkler from both sodium and chloride can be reduced by night time irrigation or application on cool, cloudy days.

Drop nozzles and drag hoses are also recommended when applying any saline irrigation water through a sprinkler system to avoid direct contact with leaf surfaces.

Table. Chloride Classification of Irrigation Water.

Chloride (ppm)	*Effect on Crops*
Below 70	Generally safe for all plants.
70-140	Sensitive plants show injury.
141-350	Moderately tolerant plants show injury.
Above 350	Can cause severe problems.

Boron

Boron is another element that is essential in low amounts, but toxic at higher concentrations. In fact, toxicity can occur on sensitive crops at concentrations less than 1.0 ppm.

Colorado soils and irrigation waters contain enough B that additional B fertilizer is not required in most situations. Because B toxicity can occur at such low concentrations, an irrigation water analysis is advised for ground water before applying additional B to crops.

Table. Boron Sensitivity of Selected Colorado Plants (B Concentration, mg/ L*)

Sensitive	Moderately Sensitive	Moderately Tolerant	Tolerant
0.76-1.0	1.1-2.0	2.1-4.0	4.1-6.0
Wheat	Carrot	Lettuce	Alfalfa
Barley	Potato	Cabbage	Sugar beet
Sunflower	Cucumber	Corn	Tomato
Dry Bean		Oats	

Sulfate

The sulfate ion is a major contributor to salinity in many of Colorado irrigation waters. As with boron, sulfate in irrigation water has fertility benefits, and irrigation water in Colorado often has enough sulfate for maximum production for most crops. Exceptions are sandy fields with <1 per cent organic matter and <10 ppm SO-S in irrigation water.

Nitrogen

Nitrogen in irrigation water (N) is largely a fertility issue, and nitrate-nitrogen (NO_3-N) can be a significant N source in the South Platte, San Luis Valley, and parts of the Arkansas River basins. The nitrate ion often occurs at higher concentrations than ammonium in irrigation water. Waters high in N can cause quality problems in crops such as barley and sugar beets and excessive vegetative growth in some vegetables. However, these problems can usually be overcome by good fertilizer and irrigation management. Regardless of the crop, nitrate should be credited towards the fertilizer rate especially when the concentration exceeds 10 ppm NO_3-N (45 ppm NO_3^-).

IMPORTANCE OF IRRIGATION SYSTEM

John Skutsch and Darren Evans have made a valuable contribution to the debate on irrigation maintenance. They suggest that widespread evidence points to a considerable shortfall between recommended maintenance expenditure for public-sector irrigation schemes and the amounts actually spent. In a variety of projects researched during the 1990s in India, Indonesia, Pakistan and Sri Lanka, the ratio per hectare of actual spend to recommended spend was only 24-47 per cent.

In the first years of a new scheme, maintenance neglect may have no dramatic effect. Irrigation staff can freeride on the freeboard produced by the vertical distance by which the channel flow's usual height exceeds the required operating level. Cropping systems, too, may show some resilience. But sooner or later maintenance underfunding begins to bite. Schemes in arid and semi-arid areas, where crops are entirely dependent on irrigation under managed rotations, are more sensitive to neglect than projects in the humid tropics that have paddy rice under continuous irrigation supplementary to monsoon rains.

The biggest losses come through crop output decline as the volume of irrigation water delivered eventually begins to decline. This may show itself as a fall in tonnage efficiency or in a diminution of the irrigated area. Moreover, as Carruthers and Morrison indicate, farmers shift to lower value crops so as to be able to reduce risk by limiting the use of inputs. Impeded drainage can lead to waterlogging and salinity and to an increase in the incidence of water-related diseases associated with blocked channels and stagnant water. Skutsch and Evans, commenting on the serious social and financial implications for farmers, write:

Those in the more favoured parts of the system may continue to receive an adequate water supply, while those at the tail-end can face ruin. Poor maintenance thus directly aggravates existing inequities within the farming community. It initiates a vicious circle of decline: reduced water supply; lost output; farmers' anger, despair and reduced investment; reduced water fee collections; vandalism and conflict. Smallholder farmers operate on a narrow margin between relative success and failure. Land is often mortgaged against the following harvest to pay for the cost of agricultural inputs. A single disastrous cropping season can mean the loss of a farmer's land and enforced migration to the cities to seek work.

This process brings with it the premature obsolescence of irrigation projects. The search for new capital funding begins in order to renovate the assets far earlier than would have been necessary under a satisfactory maintenance regime. A cycle of build-neglect-rebuild is in place. Partly as a result of this, most development bank finance for irrigation is now for the rehabilitation of existing schemes. Skutsch estimates that about two-thirds of recent international lending has been for systems that have suffered early technical failure. Already in 1995 Jones's overview of World Bank lending for irrigation projects could conclude: 'O&M problems can be seen in the Bank's financing of so many rehabilitation projects. Almost all of them, when scrutinized, turn out to be deferred maintenance projects.

Why, then, is maintenance neglected? As so often is the case in the social sciences, the question is simple but the answer is fiendishly complex. In part, farmers themselves are responsible. As is commonly the case with public-sector irrigation schemes, they see maintenance as the proper task of government.

If farmers are required to allocate greater resources to maintenance, either in terms of increased payments or of increased responsibility...they must see a clear incentive in better cash returns, reduced costs or improved control over water. Particularly on rice-growing schemes in monsoon climates, farmers may see little urgency in paying today to avoid increasing problems tomorrow, particularly if the government has traditionally stepped in to rehabilitate defective systems. In part, government and irrigation department staff are responsible for the neglect of maintenance.

Too often, national, regional and local élites regard the public sector as a milch cow whose teats are there to be squeezed for easy profits. No simpler way exists of doing this than by pushing superfluous staff into administrative posts as a favour to family, professional or political allies. As a consequence the 'establishment' of the department becomes excessively large, draining resources from OM&M. Moreover, operations activities in any case enjoy precedence over maintenance.

Technical and engineering staff, trained in design and construction, are likely to be unmotivated by the bread-and-butter tasks of OM&M, which offer poor rewards and prospects. For senior staff, administrators and engineers, new projects are likely to be the most highly sought after given their prestige and the rent-skimming opportunities they offer. A rule of thumb of some international consultants in parts of the developing world is that capital rather than current spending is favoured by country élites in government because 40 per cent of capital costs go in pay-offs.

At a level more mundane but of real importance, irrigation departments commonly remit the charges they collect from farmers to the finance ministry. That ministry may give other sectors more support than agriculture when it provides revenue financing. As the sum allocated to OM&M is decoupled from the fees collected from farmers, irrigation agencies have no incentive to maximize their revenue collection. There is a parallel here with the breaking of the line in prudential responsibility, itself a 'decoupling' of loan provider and loan user. In part, the development banks themselves are responsible for maintenance neglect. If they lend money on schemes that 15 years later are choked with weeds, silted up, waterlogged, saline, exhibiting high distribution losses and with defective equipment, then their original cost-benefit analyses must have been *seriously* erroneous. The McNamara effect and a weak record in post-project evaluation are partially to blame here. The development banks need not fear that their loans will never be repaid, because the dollar flow of principal and interest comes from national government treasuries, not from the deficient project.

Several authors have proposed policy changes aimed at ending the buildneglect-rebuild syndrome. Such proposals include the following:

- An information system should be put in place that is capable of defining in detail the volume of water used.
- A dependable delivery system should be achieved.
- An agency willing and able to collect fees should be built, with a transparent management system.
- Farmers should be required to contribute an agreed number of maintenance days each year.

- Fees paid by farmers should increase but only after
  - The managing agency details all costs, levels of service and benefits,
  - Users are surveyed on their willingness and ability to pay,
  - The charging mechanism is agreed,
  - Users participate in setting the levels of service
  - Fees are linked to the level of service.
- Recognized sanctions for non-payment should be enforced.
- Feeding back the charges paid by farmers directly to OM&M.
- Maintenance should be carried out by private or autonomous self-accounting agencies.
- Engineers and planners should design irrigation projects for low maintenance, less costly management and greater effective lives.
- Improvement and modernization projects would be considered only for those schemes where a regular review of their individual maintenance standard shows them to be satisfactory or better.
- Lending agencies should provide financial support for a transitional period following construction.
- Tradeable abstraction rights should be introduced.
- Irrigation management should be transferred to farmers themselves.

MANAGING COMMON PROPERTY RESOURCES

The above list of thirteen proposals for ending the build-neglect-rebuild cycle ends with irrigation management transfer from the public sector to farmers themselves. In the 1990s of such a possibility was able to draw upon and contribute to, a vigorous literature exploring the subject of common property resource management. The published papers and books demonstrate a welcome (if rare) willingness of economists and sociologists to work together in common cause. Below, synthesis of the relevant literature, particularly as it applies to the management of irrigation systems.

In every society common property resources exist, each of which is the common location of work by human agents or actors-the two terms are deployed here interchangeably. Agents may be individual persons, families or institutions. Such common property resources may be constituted by specific natural environments, such as a commons used for grazing livestock, or by some complex resource integrating features of the natural environment with the means of production created by human society, such as an irrigation scheme. The 'common property' characteristic of the resource is that a number of separate actors enjoy rights of access and use of the resource-rights that are recognized in law or are customary practice.

In the day-to-day work located on the common resource, each agent may be motivated only by the *private* interest of that person, family or institution.

This is of special importance in three ways. *First,* each actor may seek to appropriate as much of the resource for itself, without regard for other agents' interests. *Second,* each actor may choose to maintain the productivity of the resource only to the degree that the private costs borne by the actor in such efforts are outweighed by the private advantages, without regard for other agents' interests. *Third,* insofar as the use of the common resource creates negative side-effects, the actor may seek to reduce these side-effects only to the extent that their cost outweighs their production advantage, without regard for other agents' interests. So, for any single actor, private interest may prevail over the common interest in respect of resource appropriation, resource maintenance and resource degradation.

Production of outputs from a common resource-the milk yield of ruminants or the tonnage of grain-may grow vigorously over time. Work motivated by the private interests of the agent can stimulate long hours in the field, a sharp tactical appreciation of gains and losses from adaptive action and an eager search for innovative practices. In respect of the productivity of the common resource, these are powerful advantages.

However, with the passage of time the common property resource itself and the patterns of productive activity on it may show signs of enfeeblement and impending long-term collapse. Now, the disadvantages imposed by each single agent's actions on other persons, families and institutions have become disproportionately large. The struggle by actors over the appropriation of the resource can weaken friendship, create mistrust and result in disabling and destructive legal and physical conflicts as well as the exhaustion of the resource itself. Maintenance and protection of the common resource may decline below what is required for its long-term sustainability. Each agent's indifference to the negative effects of its actions on others may bring with it both bitter social disputes as well as the poisoning of the common resource.

Such a trajectory may lead to demands for a reconstitution of the social relationships between actors in the management of the common property resource. Where government cannot or will not lead this collective activity, a non-governmental local entity for collective action (LECA) may be created. The core objectives of the LECA are likely to be fourfold. *First,* the shared use of the resource should be recognized by the participant agents as being equitable. *Second,* the maintenance of the resource should be adequate to ensure its long-term viability. *Third,* the production of negative externalities should be sufficiently well regulated that their collective cost to the new institution's actors is acceptable and does not threaten systemic sustainability. *Fourth,* the transaction costs of meeting the first three objectives are acceptable to actors in the light of the benefits they bring.

There is a problem. A successful LECA brings all-round advantages to its actor-members. But every agent knows that if *he and he alone* continues to pursue his private interest, he reaps the benefits of unrestrained action as well as the benefits deriving from the collective agreement. This is known as the freerider problem. As freerider numbers grow, the advantages of collective action diminish and the LECA collapses.

So each LECA needs to engage in forms of moral persuasion in order that its actors honour the collective agreement made. It will also monitor members' activities to ensure that they do not breach the rules and that, when this occurs, sanctions are exercised against such infractions. The collective also faces costs of bargaining, contract formulation and information search in pursuit of a collective economic strategy. Together, all these costs of motivation, control and co-ordination are termed transaction costs. Even in a study as exhaustive as Anna Blomqvist's in South India it was never possible to assign these costs a monetary value. The greater the LECA's legitimacy, *i.e.* the greater the internalization of its values and ideas within and outside the institution, the less costly is monitoring and enforcement. Blomqvist concluded from her experience that LECAs are most likely to succeed when the members are culturally homogeneous, small in number, highly dependent on the common resource and benefit equally from collective action.

ABSTRACTION CHARGES AND SUSTAINABLE CATCHMENT MANAGEMENT

The subject of abstraction charging is related to the debate on sustainability, beginning with the approach of Richard Dubourg whose contributions to the study of hydroeconomics are within the neoclassical framework. Dubourg suggests that aggregate sustainability is a situation where natural capital as well as non-natural capital are non-declining and specifically where 'critical capital' such as water, within the natural capital category, is non-declining.

From these definitions he deduces impeccably that aggregate sustainability is consistent with catchment management policies in which abstraction of surface water and groundwater is equal to effective rainfall. It has to be said that the adoption of such a definition of sustainable abstraction would be extraordinarily dangerous.

Abstraction at a rate equal to effective rainfall may be capable of leaving surface and groundwater stocks unchanged over the course of a year so that the critical capital stock is maintained. But a rate of abstraction at this maximum rate would have the effect of capturing the entire river flow at some point or points in the catchment. In effect, Dubourg's definition ignores completely what in the USA is termed the environmental need for water in river systems-all on the basis of three mathematical constraints. In *Introduction to the Economics of Water Resources* I have suggested an alternative, multi-dimensional approach. After defining the concept of a 'sustainable society', it is suggested that water resource planning in such a society has six principal fields of action:

- The protection of water's hydrocyclical capacity to renew its ground and surface-water flows and stocks;
- The conservation of society's species and natural habitats in all their fresh and saltwater environments;
- The husbandry of water in its supply and use;
- The supply of freshwater sufficient to meet the biological, cultural and economic needs of society's human populations;
- The purification of water from domestic, agricultural and industrial effluents;
- The drainage of water and the protection of rural and urban communities against flood.

Abstraction charges can contribute positively to the first three of these fields and, below, it is shown how this can be done, using what I shall call *full cost incentive charging*.

The preparation of a tariff scheme should take as its starting point the regulatory controls put in place by the catchment authority in carrying out its responsibilities. In the development of these controls, there is an important role for social cost-effectiveness analysis and social cost-benefit analysis. These techniques have a place, alongside environmental impact assessment, in comparing alternative regulatory options. The design of environmental regulation should be an economic process as well as an ecological one.

The tariff regime introduced to any specific catchment (or region) will be contingent on its physical geography, its habitats and species, its human settlement patterns, its economy and the power relationships which hold between various social and economic groups. So what we require are criteria for tariff design which can be applied in the appropriate way to any single area with all its unique characteristics. I propose three such criteria for full cost incentive charging.

- *First,* the annual income from abstraction charges should be hypothecated to the environmental regulator such that, when added to the income received from discharge fees, fishing licences, navigation permits, etc., abstraction fee income is sufficient to cover all the state's capital and current account expenditures on environmental regulation, research and database development, compensation payments, etc. In providing the regulator with hypothecated income, it is likely to increase their relative power as an agency of government. As Kraemer writes of Germany since 1988: 'On the whole, the water resource taxes contributed to capacity building within the water management administration in the German Länder and thus partly overcame the implementation deficit in water resource management'. It will also provide a budget to finance the legal costs of modifying or terminating abstraction licences that threaten the hydrocycle or undermine nature conservation. Higher abstraction charges will also give a price signal to water companies to reduce their storage and distribution leakage between the points of abstraction and the user's gate.

- *Second,* where the full cost abstraction tariff still leaves an excess of demand for abstracted water over its licensed supply, the charge should be raised so that market clearing takes place.
- *Third,* specification of the components of the abstraction charge should provide incentives for abstraction behaviour that is economically efficient and that avoids environmental degradation. Price per unit volume should be invariant with total volume abstracted, unless there are countervailing economic or environmental arguments. Price should be discounted where abstractors recycle their off-take to surface or groundwater sources. (Discharge fees should be used to handle the water quality aspects of recycled water.) Charges should be higher for abstracted water of higher quality. Seasonal variations in effective rainfall and economic demand should be dealt with through the licensed volume provisions laid down by the regulator and by the market-clearing criterion. Charges should be higher for upstream sources and for abstraction in locations where species and habitats are more threatened by abstraction.

The institutional framework that would be most appropriate for full cost incentive charging deserves discussion and my ideas here have been strongly influenced by Karin Kemper's *The Cost of Free Water*. The basic approach is a negotiation model in which there exists a public-sector catchment agency that, through a negotiating forum, develops its policies with the advice of water companies, direct abstractors, environmental organizations and water user associations representing the domestic sector, irrigated agriculture, mining and manufacturing, etc. The original prototype for such negotiation models is the French water parliaments. Central government retains the statutory right to determine which public and private institutions may enjoy the right to abstract water, on what scale, in what locations, at what time of year, at what price-but it delegates such rights to the catchment agency.

The agency, with the assistance of its partners in the negotiating forum and with a full understanding of existing customary rights, then assigns formal abstraction rights on a time-limited basis to specific abstractors or groups of abstractors. The time limit would be 10 years, rolled over each year except where the agency allows the licence to expire. Where these 10-year rights need to be modified or rescinded for hydrological, environmental or economic reasons, compensation would be payable to the abstractor so affected. Rules would also exist to address third party impacts. Abstraction rights assigned to abstractors could be freely traded provided the agency had approved such transfers in the light of their social, economic and environmental impacts. Full cost incentive charging would be the basis of the price paid by abstractors for their water.

It has the objectives of:

- Underpinning environmental regulation with a hypothecated income source;
- Requiring abstractors (and therefore final users) to cover the full costs of regulation;
- Bringing the quantity of water demanded by abstractors into line with regulatory limits; and
- Giving price signals that promote both allocative efficiency as well as abstraction practices that avoid damage to riverine eco-systems.

No charge would be made for abstractions below a minimum scale-the transaction costs of such charges would be high compared with the volumes abstracted.

Arrangements would be made to monitor abstraction with respect to its location, time and quantity, as well as to invoice abstractors, to collect the charges owed and to enforce all agreements. Such transaction costs would be included in the full costing tariff of abstraction charges. The creation of this institutional framework imposes social, economic and political costs on the parties concerned, structural costs of change both real and financial in their nature. Therefore the negotiating forum may agree that it is sensible for full cost incentive charging to be phased in gradually.

Irrigation Management Transfer on Mexico

Local associations of water users serve the same functions as irrigation agencies, but on a very localized level. In some countries such as Nepal and the Philippines, the major portion of the irrigated area is managed locally, through village-based water user associations. Typically such associations manage very small irrigation canals that were constructed by the users, perhaps centuries ago and the associations have grown up around the need for operating and maintaining these canals. In many developing countries such traditional canal systems have been the target of modernisation efforts by government agencies, often funded through international development assistance. The relatively crude physical infrastructure of many of these canal systems was rebuilt and absorbed into the domain of the government agency, which replaced the management functions of the indigenous water user associations.

Today, local water user associations are recognised as resources of 'social capital' which will have an increasingly important role to play in the coming decades. Instead of absorbing such associations into the state organisation, the capacity of associations is developed so that they can improve the performance of their own irrigation and drainage systems. This participatory approach was re-invented in the Philippines in the 1970s and has since evolved into a global trend that combines participation with various degrees of privatisation. In many developing countries a major focus of this process is the institutional challenge of establishing new water user associations which can serve the management functions previously handled by government.

A particularly fruitful source for a case study of this trend is Mexico. With 5 million irrigated hectares it was the seventh largest irrigator in the world in 1995. It began the irrigation management transfer process as early as 1989 and the experience has been extensively researched. Finally, Mexico has for a number of years been considered as a paradigm for this form of institutional transformation. The case study draws heavily on the work of Kloezen, Garcés-Restrepo and Johnson.

The broad political and economic context within which Mexico introduced irrigation management transfer was central government's neoliberal response to the economic crisis of the 1980s and the unsatisfactory performance of the irrigation districts under the management of the National Water Commission. Transfer has been a top-down process motivated by the international development banks, the main objective being to reduce public expenditure on irrigation OM&M whilst promoting greater user participation in irrigation management. It has been accompanied by a new National Water Act, revision of the Constitution to give legal foundation for the privatization of the *ejidos* (land reform communities) in all irrigation districts and termination of guaranteed crop prices and subsidized credit. 'Dismantling the public sector, including the public irrigation sector, would not have been possible without the commitment at the highest political levels to reduce staff working in the public sector'.

The institutional transformation has been rapid and radical. In its first phase the National Water Commission retained management of the headworks and the main canals. Water user associations took over financial and managerial responsibility for OM&M below the main canal. In the second phase the Commission is left with management of the reservoirs and surface-water-pumping stations; a District Federation of the user associations takes on the OM&M of the main canals. These associations are non-governmental local entities for collective action.

The high speed of the process and the low resistance of farmers have surprised many observers. It seems that transfer was preceded by other neoliberal reforms in agriculture. Farmers knew the Commission's traditional OM&M was to be terminated and OM&M had in any case declined in quality. Reform came first in the larger districts in the north, where many large private producers were known to support change. Lastly, the programme built on a strong organizational base-the *ejidos* themselves and the private farmers' co-operatives and unions.

Government informed farmers of the impending change-there seems to have been no serious consultation-and instructed them to select their delegates to the new user associations. Thereafter, delegates to each association elected from among themselves a president, a treasurer and a secretary. The Commission worked with the new user groups for 6 months or more from the time of transfer and provided their leaders and technical staff with extensive training in OM&M and financial management. The Commission also granted concessions to the associations to use its machinery and equipment so that there would be no capital expenditure required in advance.

Prior to transfer the National Water Commission was wholly responsible at the district level for the planning of annual and seasonal water allocations. Similarly the Commission employed the heads of the irrigation units into which each district was divided. These units were more or less independent hydraulic blocks with sizes ranging from 3,000 to 20,000 ha. Unit heads and their channel-keepers were responsible for daily OM&M at all system levels down to the farm inlets. Farmers paid their fees at the unit office and were given water by the channel-keeper.

After transfer, hydraulic committees were introduced at district level for allocation planning; these committees were composed of representatives from the Commission, the state government and each user association in that district. At the same time the district 'units' were replaced by 'modules'-two or more per unit-and it is at this level that the new water user associations manage.

They collect irrigation water fees directly from farmers and employ their own module managers, channel-keepers, maintenance personnel and administrative staff. Based on the volume of water a module takes from the Commission and on the proportional amount of main infrastructure serving a module, each association must pay a percentage of the total fees it collects to the Commission.

The specific subject of this case study is the Alto Río Lerma Irrigation District. Located in the State of Guanajuato, it has an area of 113,000 ha. There are some 24,000 farmers of whom 55 per cent are from the *ejidos* and 45 per cent are private growers. The average landholding is 5 ha. Private holdings average twice the size of *ejido* holdings. The district's climate is sub-humid with annual precipitation of 750mm and potential evapotranspiration of 1900mm. Eighty millimetres of rain falls in the winter season from November to April and 670 mm falls from May to November. Average temperature is 19 °C and relative humidity is 60 per cent.

The Alto Río Lerma Irrigation District enjoys access to both surface water and groundwater. The river has four storage dams with a combined capacity of 2,140 mcm, as well as five diversion dams. The distribution network has 475 km of main canals and 1,660 km of secondary and tertiary canals, as well as 1,030 km of drainage canals. There are 1,710 deep wells exploiting three different aquifers with a total annual recharge of 500 mcm. Seventy per cent of the irrigated hectarage uses surface water and 30 per cent uses groundwater. Wheat and barley are the main crops in the dry winter months. Sorghum, maize and beans predominate in the wet summer season. All farmers grow vegetables and the private growers do so for the export market.

At the start of each agricultural year in November the hydraulic committee decides on the total area that can be safely irrigated in the district and by each of the eleven modules. This total area is derived from the combined volume of water in the four storage dams. The committee next sets the number of times that irrigation services can be delivered to each farmer in each season, typically 3-5 times in the winter and once in the summer. Each module receives its allocated share of surface water over the year and, given the module's ability to restrict the area irrigated by users, farmers can request water at any time within the constraints of the seasonal maximum. Farmers pay a fee to their water user association prior to each individual irrigation and get a receipt that has to be shown to the channel-keeper before water is allocated to their fields.

Kloezen and his colleagues show a keen awareness of the political and macroeconomic context of irrigation management transfer as well as a familiarity, for example, with Fox's sociological work on building social capital from below. However, the language of common property resources, freeriding and transaction costs is absent from their reports. What we do learn is that the number of staff engaged in governance, OM&M, administration, monitoring and evaluation *rose* by 13 per cent between the 'before' and 'after' transfer periods of 1992 and 1996. The proportion of persons employed by the National Water Commission dropped from 100 per cent to 38 per cent. The associations feel that the Commission staff numbers are excessive and that:

...an unspecified percentage of these...staff are residual personnel that for political and labour-union-related reasons remain within the agency with no specific task. This has been one of the major reasons why the modules wanted to create the [District Federation of the user associations] which will take over management of the main system. They feel that this will be much more cost-effective than the current arrangement.

As already indicated, the water user associations hire all their own staff. In doing so they have shown reluctance to employ ex-Commission personnel. The associations argue that Commission channel-keepers and other staff were often out of control, poor workers, unaccountable, given to rent-seeking behaviour and were likely to involve the trade unions in module management in a divisive manner.

To what degree do farmers accept that the shared use of the resource is now equitable? The importance of the new, district-wide, hydraulic committees should be noted, but the allocation planning method has not changed at this level. However, there is evidence that correspondence between the volume of water assigned to modules and the actual volumes received by them is better than before transfer. This is probably because every association was represented on the hydraulic committee, with each module insisting on receiving the volume it had been assigned and had paid for.

With respect to individual farmers, a detailed, post-transfer study shows that in the sample area 'there is no clear bias towards head- or tail-end farmers and that all farmers receive sufficient water to meet crop requirements'. In a sample of farmers, 34 per cent said water distribution amongst them was poor before transfer and good after it, compared with only 15 per cent who held the reverse opinion.

Probably the most important contribution to equitable distribution of the resource has come from the associations' control over channel-keepers. Bribes exacted by Commission employees under the previous regime were impossible for farmers to eradicate. The downward shift in power to water users now gives them the control over rent-seeking behaviour that they lacked.

To what degree has infrastructural operation and maintenance been improved? With respect to operation, the post-transfer study indicated an improvement in water adequacy at field level, in the timeliness of water delivery and in access to the channel-keepers. In the sample of farmers, 40 per cent said the service provided by the channel-keepers was poor before transfer and good after it, compared with only 14 per cent who held the reverse opinion. Eighty-three per cent of farmers believe that the water user associations should now retain responsibility for operation of the main and secondary systems.

The transfer process included free concessionary use of Commission machinery such as draglines and hydraulic excavators. This was a flying start for users. Significantly, some of this equipment was in serious disrepair so the modules bought twenty-nine pieces of new heavy machinery from their user fee income and also received equipment from a World Bank programme.

Maintenance expenditure in constant peso prices almost doubled in the before- and after-transfer comparison. There was an approximately threefold increase in the desilting of secondary canals and drains. Farmers' perceptions of the condition of the irrigation and drainage network were that the network had improved considerably.

To what degree have negative externalities arising from individual farmers' actions declined since the user associations were set up? Kloezen and his colleagues address this question only with respect to overabstraction of groundwater. By customary practice, modules exclude from the surface-water supply those areas that have access to wells. But groundwater users are permitted to use the canal network to distribute their pumped supplies.

Unfortunately the aquifers in the district are definitely being overexploited by about 20 per cent of annual recharge. By 1996 the water table was falling by 2-5 m annually. Groundwater mining does not appear to have become worse since transfer, but transfer has been unable to diminish it. To conclude this case study, the new arrangements for the financing of capital and current costs are examined. We have already seen that the association pays fees to the Commission for its services, that the association charges the farmer for each irrigation, that there has been a decline in bribes paid to channel-keepers and that charges to farmers have been used not only for prime costs but also for equipment purchase.

Forty per cent of farmers surveyed report that payment procedures are now less cumbersome compared with only 2 per cent holding the reverse opinion. Sixty-nine per cent stated that bribery of channel-keepers had been reduced. But many farmers still come to the module office to complain of keepers demanding private payments and this has often led to workers being dismissed. Keepers are also rotated between module sections to prevent the growth of patron-client relations. Nevertheless as many as 30 per cent of farmers surveyed were willing to admit that they bribe keepers to irrigate more than the farmer's entitled area or to get water at different times from those programmed.

So the indirect charges are higher than the official ones-as are the wages of keepers. Under the Commission, charges were way below prime costs, let alone the full cost of the service. To prepare the way for a more self-reliant organization, the Commission increased the charge by some 400 per cent 2 years prior to transfer. It then remained unchanged in nominal pesos through and after transfer. But inflation halved the real value of the charge in the first 2 years of the associations' existence.

What is undoubtedly impressive is that in terms of the ratio of fees actually collected to actual OM&M expenditure, both given in pesos at current prices, the rate jumped from an average of 50 per cent in 1989-91 to 123 per cent in 1993-6. These facts remind us that in irrigation economics the estimation of the cost of water to farming families and agribusinesses should be based on the payments *actually* made, not on those that are *supposed* to be made. Kloezen and his colleagues never attempt to measure what proportion of the full cost of irrigation services is met by farmers' actual payments, but it seems likely to be considerably less than 100 per cent. This raises the question: 'What organisation in future will be responsible for infrastructural investment and rehabilitation, how will it raise the required finance and how will these costs be repaid?'

For the 1996-7 winter season the associations used the hydraulic committee to raise the irrigation fee by more than one-third. They also pushed the Commission to transfer OM&M responsibility for the main canal to a newly created District Federation of the user associations. In 1997 the average percentage of farmers' irrigation fees paid to the Commission was correspondingly slashed from 25 per cent to 9.5 per cent.

Tradable Abstraction Rights in Australia

Up to this point, consideration of abstraction has covered the right to abstract and the charges that a catchment agency might levy on farmers for the enjoyment of that right. *Tradeable* abstraction rights (TARs) have been discussed only briefly-although long enough to recommend that, with appropriate safeguards, such rights should be widely introduced. This case study reviews the introduction since the early 1980s of TARs within irrigated agriculture by the State of Victoria in Australia. The case study updates by 4 years one that I published in 1997.

In every catchment, some users of water will value their abstraction rights more than other users, for example because they employ water more productively. In that situation, trading in such rights can be financially attractive to both the existing owner of such rights and the party that wishes to see them transferred. To understand trading in abstraction rights we need to come to grips with the relevant law, with differential valuations of water and with the legal, hydrological and engineering means for implementing transfers. In this field, valuable work has been carried out by Robert Hearne and William Easter, in Chile, although when they were writing their report less than 1 per cent of all abstractions operated through such water markets there.

In Australia, the practice is now extensively developed and there the main objective of TARs has been the more efficient use of scarce irrigation water. The Australian water economy is said to be in its mature phase, where the long-term average total cost function is rising sharply, where there is intense competition for existing supplies and where the hydrosocial infrastructure requires costly rehabilitation.

Victoria is one of the constituent states of federal Australia and lies in its south-east corner. The dominant physiographic feature is the Great Dividing Range, running east-west in the eastern two-thirds of the state. This creates a rainshadow in northern Victoria, where average annual rainfall is 450 mm in the Goulburn-Murray Irrigation District (GMID). This is the largest irrigation area in Australia, covering some 820,000 ha and it represents the bulk of water trading in the state. Irrigation is sourced from reservoirs on regulated surfacewater flows. Meat and dairy products are the principal agricultural output; higher-valued crops such as horticultural products are constrained by the red-brown soil type. Surface-water resources have been extensively developed in the past and any further supply growth would require inter-basin transfers. The GMID is principally designed to provide security of supply during a prolonged series of drought years. The main water dams are operated on a carry-over basis, where water is accumulated in years of high river flows for use in drier years.

Australia's modern history of property rights in water begins in the 1880s, when Victoria introduced new water laws based on the recommendations of a

Royal Commission chaired by Alfred Deakin. He proposed that water allocations should be tied to the land, that rights to water should be vested in the British Crown and that allocations to landholders should be the responsibility of the state governments. Riparian owners retained limited common-law rights for domestic use, stock watering, gardens and a maximum of 2 ha of irrigated land for fodder crops. Over the next 15 years, similar legislation was introduced in the other federal states. Using the new legislation, the states ventured into large irrigation projects, providing water to farmers far below average total cost. Areas were established in which government constructed massive irrigation and drainage infrastructures, such as the Goulburn-Murray Irrigation District itself, the Murrumbidgee Irrigation Area in New South Wales and Riverland in South Australia.

The subsidy of water led to overuse and this was consolidated by the historical overallocation of water to irrigated farms. As argued in the work of Pigram and co-workers: This has its roots in the social objectives of past governments for the development and use of water resources. The overriding objectives were an equitable distribution of water among farms and the promotion of regional development and closer settlement of inland areas. All farmers were considered to have an equal right to the available water, irrespective of how much was needed to irrigate the proposed crops to be grown on the farms, or of any consideration of how efficiently the water would be used. As water rights became capitalized into land values, individuals had the economic incentive to retain their entire water rights through demonstrating a history of use. In many cases, this actually translated into a history of over-use.

By 1990, the arrangements in the GMID were that irrigators paid for a water right based on both the amount of land they held that was suitable for gravity-fed irrigation and the irrigation district in which they were located. An annual charge applied to the water right, invariant with the volume of use. Subject to availability, 'sales water' was also available, at a volumetric charge based on the water right charge. These water rights in their specific form were assigned by a licensing system for a fixed period of 15 years, with an expectation of reissue. The authorities could vary the volume licensed, usually in times of shortage. However, before 1987-8, no arrangements existed for *transferring* farmers' abstraction rights.

An Australian interest in TARs (also known as tradeable water rights or transferable water entitlements) began to surface in the mid-1970s. For some, the introduction of TARs seemed to offer a new flexibility to existing arrangements, with clear economic and environmental advantages. *First,* we have already seen that the maturing of the Australian water economy in recent decades is associated with high average total cost for the long-term supply curve. So, TARs offered a new direction that, by reallocating water supply, would reduce the pressure for aggregate supply expansion. This reallocative effect would not be merely within the farming sector. There was also the prospect of reducing agricultural overuse to open up supplies for a range of urban and industrial uses.

Second, supply reallocation within agriculture was a major objective. There was a widespread belief by the mid-1980s that TARs would switch water from lower to higher water-productivity uses in the farming sector. In Australia, at that time, the agricultural sector accounted for 80 per cent of total water use. In Victoria, each year, up to one-third of irrigators were using less than their full water right allotment. Specific switches into river red gum watering, salinity dilution and dairy farming were forecast. *Third,* environmental benefits were expected from transferability. The new policy promised to reduce the scale of infrastructure construction for inter-basin transfers, with all their negative externalities. Development proposals were meeting increased resistance from environmental groups. Moreover, reductions in agricultural overuse promised to have a positive environmental effect through a reduction in waterlogging, salinization and biocide dispersion.

The redistribution of abstraction rights could have been sought by the administrative processes of the licensing system. But this would have been met by political resistance from the farms on which volumes were to be reduced and land values consequentially cut. Tradeable abstraction rights offered these farms a pay-off. For landholders wishing to move out of irrigation, but to remain in dryland agriculture, transferability allows water entitlements to be sold separately from the land. Previously, the options for such irrigators were either to cancel their water rights licence (or not renew it) and get nothing for the right, or sell the entire irrigation holding and buy a dryland property elsewhere. Transferability can permit a more flexible retirement plan for an irrigator, or facilitate a long-term change in enterprise or financial structure of the farm business.

The fundamental requirement of a workable and efficient market in abstraction rights is a clear specification of property rights in water such that:

- Rights in land and rights in water must be separable;
- The volume of water that an individual or institution has available for transfer must be clearly stated, as well as any special conditions on its use-such volumes are likely to be conditional on rainfall, or surface flows or groundwater stocks;
- The right to transfer such water at a privately negotiated price must exist;
- The period over which such a transfer is deemed to be effective, temporary or permanent, must be known;
- The power of government to restrict or terminate abstraction rights at a future date must be known.

In Victoria, TARs were cautiously introduced in 1987-8 with a *temporary* scheme, before permanent transfers were considered. In the GMID the transfer period was to be for 1 year, only between irrigators and only within the same supply system. There was no volumetric limitation but stock and domestic allocations had to be retained. A state agency assessed possible third-party effects and could refuse the transfer if these were significant. The arrangements were not to affect significantly delivery and drainage channel capacity or salinity. Finally, the price was determined between buyer and seller but the agency's fixed fee was A$70.

A new Water Act in 1989 permitted *permanent* transfers of abstraction rights between farmers, with effect from 1991-2. Transfers out of agriculture were still proscribed. However, despite these references to 'permanence' in trading, the state assignation of water rights through the licensing system, meant that a purchaser of abstraction rights could not be assured in law that such water rights would continue indefinitely. The state government retained long-term flexibility in its management powers.

TARs impose certain transaction costs. In the GMID case they seem to be modest because of the legitimacy of the institutions, the support from farmers for the general approach to the new rights and the competence and honesty of Victoria's state administration. Incremental supply costs also exist if distribution and drainage structures cannot handle the increased water volumes. However, in Australia, water agencies have taken the easy administrative option of simply refusing transfers where existing capacities would be exceeded.

The outcomes of Victorian TARs in the early years after they were first introduced are considered next. The scale of change can be measured by the volume of abstraction transfers as a percentage of all abstractions. With respect to benefits, we are looking for: the avoidance of new infrastructure expenditure as a result of the redistribution of abstractions within and between user categories; an increase in agricultural productivity as a result of abstraction redistribution within farming; and a fall in waterlogging, salinity and pollution from run-off because of the reduction in agricultural overuse.

In the 2 years 1987-8 and 1988-9 the trading of abstraction rights in Victoria (most of it in the GMID) averaged 25 mcm, less than 2 per cent of total abstractions. Price per megalitre ranged from A$8 to A$20. Gross margins increased. But at this point the judgement was that 'Despite widespread endorsement of the concept in Victoria, transfer activity has been sporadic in that state'.

In Victoria by 1990-1 trade was still 'insignificant compared to the total volume'. In a mail survey of all 299 permanent water transfers within the GMID up to 1994, with a 63 per cent response rate from buyers, purchases made up between 0 per cent and 2.3 per cent of total allocations when the responses were grouped by district. What the survey showed was that sellers were releasing sleeper water (*i.e.* unused allocations) and that farmers in financial distress were also selling. In a smaller number of cases, farmers either wished to cut their irrigation agriculture, or to farm without irrigation, or to retire. In respect of purchasers, the single most important reason for buying water, applicable to 65 per cent of respondents, was that they 'wanted to secure existing crops against future drought'.

Stringer suggested that in Victoria as a whole in 1991-4, the average percentage of allocated water traded in each of those years was 0.33 per cent. In the Murray region as a whole in 1993-4, the volume of transfers was 17 mcm for temporary transfers and 8 mcm for permanent transfers. For 1994-5, these figures changed dramatically.

Temporary transfers soared to 265 mcm whereas permanent transfers fell to 2 mcm. At this point it could be argued that by the mid-1990s TARs in Victoria had created a space for single-season switching of abstraction, most active in years of low rainfall. By the year 2000 Australian statistical reporting of TARs had become much fuller and more informative as a result of work by the Australian National Commission for Irrigation and Drainage. Its *Benchmarking Report* contains data for nine Goulburn-Murray systems known as Murray Valley, Shepparton, Central Goulburn, Rochester, Pyramid-Boort, Torrumbarry, Nyah, Tresco and Woorinen. In all of these except the last the percentage of surface-water irrigation supply points that are metered lies in the range 87-98 per cent.

A broking service exists in all nine systems to facilitate the trading process between users. In 1998-9 temporary trading took place in all nine systems, averaging 11 per cent of total abstraction entitlements for that year. Six of the nine systems reported permanent trading that averaged 2 per cent of entitlements in those six areas.

From the perspective of this book, the material on why one set of irrigators sell their TARs and others purchase them is of particular interest. A substantial paper by Björnlund and McKay throws some light here.

The authors state that the main use of irrigation water is in the cultivation of pastures for dairy cattle. Some activity is found too in horticulture and viticulture. Mixed grazing and cropping is said to have low-value water use. Purchasers of tradeable abstraction rights were shown to be seeking to ease their reliance on annual sales water and temporary water market purchases. TAR sellers are smaller than buyers in terms of irrigated area; water trading can be seen to be integrated with a long-term consolidation and amalgamation of farm properties.

Sellers were asked how they used the cash proceeds of their permanent sales-note that a permanent sale does not imply the sale of a farm's entire water entitlement:10 per cent was invested in laser grading, 5 per cent in improved drainage and another 5 per cent in other irrigation equipment. Fifty per cent of the sample said the money was used for general consumption purposes, related or not to the farm as an enterprise; 21 per cent went to debt reduction; 6 per cent to non-irrigation equipment; and 3 per cent for the purchase of another farm.

Clearly the subject is ideally suited to an irrigation economics case study, for both the permanent and temporary markets, into the differential motivation of buyer-seller *pairs*.

A BLOCKED CHANNEL

One aspect of this blocked channel concerns payments for abstraction rights. I have given a very full account of the criteria that can be used by a state authority in constructing an abstraction tariff for farmers and the relevance of such a tariff to effective catchment management. But there is no accompanying case study to test these ideas-merely brief, illustrative examples. In contrast there is an extended discussion of the recent history of tradeable abstraction rights in Victoria, but the theoretical material is adhoc and fragmented.

Despite this the research reports of Wim Kloezen, Carlos Garcés Restrepo and Sam Johnson seem to me to be wholly successful in coming to grips with the dynamic institutional changes of this catchment. Perhaps it is because they were a team with varied disciplinary backgrounds, which is so important in water resource planning. Perhaps it is that irrigation management transfer is quintessentially a compound of private economic interests and political power set within a given hydrological context-and that Kloezen and his colleagues have a good grasp of hydropolitics. In contrast, the language of many economists is so distant from the complex drives of individuals, families and organizations and so wedded to a vision of the determining interplay of measurable quantities, that they fail to understand the nature and exercise of power.

ABSTRACTION CHARGES IN RIVERS AND LAKES

Rivers, lakes and aquifers are common property resources, except where access to them is privatized. This is why common property resource analysis, including the appraisal of transaction costs, is of such great relevance to a full understanding of the management of water resources. In particular, rivers, lakes and aquifers are resources from which water is abstracted for use in agriculture, industry and households. They are also resources used as sinks for the disposal of waste water and drainage water.

Abstraction usually takes place where the abstracting actor enjoys formal legal rights to do so, or where abstraction is an accepted customary practice. In such cases the abstractor may be required to pay a charge either to a public agency or to a private owner of rights in water. Abstraction rights may also be traded. One objective of these two sections is to provide a general economic analysis of the subject capable of international application to specific case studies. The second objective is to recommend the most appropriate basis for government abstraction tariffs. The scope of abstraction charging includes water consumers abstracting directly for their own use, such as farmers, mining companies and manufacturers. One also includes water service companies that abstract not for their own use but in order to provide a public water supply to irrigators and to urban areas.

A useful analytic starting point is to establish that abstraction charges are a form of economic rent. The modern theory of rent was first developed in the early nineteenth century. Its application was to British agriculture and the common situation where capitalist farmers used land owned by the aristocracy and the gentry and paid rent for that right. At that time, agriculture contributed about one-third of Britain's total output. The classical school of economists argued that the appropriation of land has the consequent effect of the creation of rent. Thus, Ricardo writes: 'Rent is that portion of the produce of the earth, which is paid to the landlord for the use of the original and indestructible powers of the soil'.

It is true that we may now doubt that any power of the soil is indestructible. Nevertheless, since Ricardo's time, economists have used rent theory whenever they are dealing with a natural resource of economic value that can be privately appropriated and that is in restricted supply. Clearly, this makes rent theory applicable to natural supplies of freshwater. These flows are of economic value, rights in their abstraction can be privately appropriated and groundwater as well as surface water are in restricted supply in any given year.

However, the supposed inelasticity of the water supply deserves closer scrutiny. Within a catchment, short-term elasticity is perversely high where substantial stocks are held in a catchment's reservoirs or where aquifer stocks are high and groundwater pumping capacity is not fully utilized. But it is the elasticity of the planning supply function of water over the medium and long term that is at issue here. It is certainly true that total rainfall in the catchment less evaporation sets a hydrological constraint on long-term catchment abstraction, as Dubourg suggests. But the recycling and reuse of water weakens this natural barrier whilst the desalination of sea water and abstracted water imports from another catchment, can smash it. The problem is that the wider one casts the net for additional supply, the greater are its unit costs. It is the exponential character of this planning function which maintains the truth of the statement that, in the majority of the world's catchments with substantial populations, abstracted water is indeed in restricted supply.

Returning to the classical theory of differential rent, this assumed that competition existed between farmers for access to land and between landowners in supplying land. In such a situation, it is theorized that land rent on the least fertile tract of land worth cultivating would be zero and here the farmer would earn the going rate of profit on capital for the private sectors of the economy as a whole.

Land which was more fertile (or better located) would bring the owner a higher flow of rental receipts such that the farmer, after paying this higher rent, would still receive only the going rate of profit. Rent could therefore be seen as the transformation of the surplus profits of capital, driven by the competition for land of differential fertility.

Ricardo had only a limited interest in non-competitive markets in the supply of land for rent. As a consequence, his theory is essentially demand-driven. This neglect of the supply-side determinants of land rent restricts the scope of differential rent theory in its application to abstraction charges levied by government. Such charges typically exist where an agency of the state licenses abstraction to specified individuals and institutions and where no property right exists to abstract ground and surface water without such a licence. Here, property rights on the supply side are assigned by a state monopoly. So analysis needs a means to interpret the legislative practice of charge-setting by state institutions in different catchments, regions or countries.

Having argued that abstraction charges are a form of economic rent, but that differential rent theory does not provide a basis to explain charge-setting by the state, the best way to proceed is to develop a taxonomy of charge-setting principles. Such principles can then provide the basis for interpretive empirical work in specific catchments, as well as a starting point for policy review of existing legislative practice. Various charge-setting principles are set out below and each is glossed in turn. Note that these charging principles are in respect of the right to appropriate the scarce resource for outstream purposes. They do not include the cost of supply-side infrastructure.

Nor are the public-sector costs of flood management, navigation, etc. included here:

- *No charge:* This is the lower limiting case. In the majority of the world's countries, government abstraction charges simply do not exist. In some cases the argument is that, since surface water and groundwater are a gift of Nature or of God, the state has no business in taxing it. This may explain the situation in Scotland, for example. In other cases, what is lacking is the administrative capacity to levy the tax.
- *A revenue-maximizing charge:* This is the upper limiting case. In principle government could raise all its revenue requirements from this single tax. In practice, of course, such a principle is never applied.
- *A market-clearing charge:* In countries and regions that are arid or semi-arid, or where levels of water consumption are high compared with effective rainfall, users may wish to gain access to more water

than is available, at least in the absence of inter-catchment transfers. In this case, government may put in place a demand-management policy in which a general abstraction charge is applied that, although it is not revenue-maximizing, does broadly match the demand by abstractors to the annual flows available. No pure examples exist of this, the closest being the public auction of tickets for fixed time and flow in the centuries-old water market of Alicante in Spain. Schiffler and his colleagues at the German Development Institute recorded for the case of Jordan that supply-fix policies in the early 1990s were under considerable pressure and that a demand-management philosophy was taking shape. Politically, it was impossible to tax water abstracted for use by farmers, but an abstraction tax on industry had been introduced there.

- *An environmental regulation charge:* In this case one is considering a country which has a well-developed national policy for water resource management. The necessity for a regulator of the freshwater environment is accepted and abstraction charges are levied and hypothecated to finance the costs of regulation. ('Hypothecation' is a term widely used in economics to refer to cases where government income from a defined tax is reserved for a specific expenditure category.) This charge may take the form of an average total cost levy equal to the total financial costs of regulation (including compensation payments for rescinded abstraction rights and any other miscellaneous items) divided by the total volume of water abstracted during the year.
- *A Pigovian charge:* Here, the principle is that government should set a charge which is differentiated according to the external costs imposed on society by each class of abstractor. K. William Kapp later formulated the parallel concept of 'social cost', covering 'all direct and indirect losses sustained by third persons or the general public as a result of unrestrained economic activities'. An example of the kinds of damage done by overabstraction is that of the Hueco Bolsón aquifer on the Mexican-USA border. Over a period of 70 years the water table fell by 25 metres (m), resulting in increased pumping costs, subsidence and contamination by increased flows of saline and polluted waters into the freshwater source. As a general rule, whilst abstraction charges may include a component in recognition of overabstraction, the *differentiation* of the charge on the basis of the monetary evaluation of the external costs never takes place because of the extreme difficulty of measuring them. Indeed, many institutional economists even deny that such measurement has any meaning. Kraemer refers to the overwhelming problems of applying a Pigovian

tax in his introduction to the development of German abstraction charging after 1988.

- *An incentives charge:* Incentive charging in a catchment or region can be defined as the use of a water tariff-a table of fixed charges-to give price signals to abstractors that reinforce water resource management based on environmental standards and regulatory controls. The best-developed system of incentive charging is probably that of the Federal Republic of Germany. An incentive tariff can include the following components:
  - A licence fee to have a new water abstraction installation approved by the regulatory authority. For example, Foster in their comprehensive introduction to the hydrogeological, legal and administrative aspects of groundwater licensing in Latin America indicate that installation fees are common and are hypothecated.
  - A charge per unit volume. This may be invariable with total volume consumed. Alternatively, it may rise with the volume drawn off. The total charge payable may be based either on the licensed volume or the actual volume abstracted. As Schiffler point out, a significant drawback of a rising block tariff is that it hits hardest those abstractors requiring large volumes simply because of the size of the farm or factory. It should also be observed that abstraction charging is never imposed where the installation's capacity falls below a minimum level set by government. This is the case at Keveral Farm.
  - A charge reduction for the quantity of water directly recycled to surface waters after use. To take the example of Didcot power station in the UK, in the mid-1990s this had a licence to abstract 142 million litres of water per day. The licence required 50-66 per cent of the water abstracted to be returned to the river, depending on flow conditions. Unit price was lower because of this non-consumptive use. In contrast, spray irrigation provided virtually no return flow to river or aquifer and so was undiscounted.
  - A charge that is greater for higher quality water. This is found in Germany for water drawn from deep aquifers.
  - A charge which varies with the seasons. The volumetric rate is higher in those months when demand is greater and higher too when precipitation is less.
  - A charge which is greater for certain locations. These include
    (*a*) Upstream sources, because the length of the river exposed to abstraction impacts is greater,

(*b*) Rivers, lakes and aquifers most threatened by past or present overdraft;

(*c*) Regions with lower effective rainfall.

INTENSIVE IRRIGATION AND WATER LOGGING

Most anti-dam movements in india have emerged from move ments of people facing displacement due to the submergence of large areas upstream of dam sites. These struggles are expressions of a conflict of interests between those who bear the social and ecological costs of dams and those who benefit from them.

However, large dams have diverse and complex ecological impacts. and they often generate environmental costs for those very groups who are supposed to be the beneficiaries. Waterlogging and salini sation are twin problems caused by the wasteful use of water.

Waterlogging is caused by the interaction of a large number of factors such as irrigation intensity, soil characteristics, drainage. seepage from reservoirs, distributaries and field channels. Since large-scale irrigation systems are linked to the uniformity of water distribution, which enforces the uniformity of cropping patterns. and uniformity in the landscape, waterlogging becomes inevitable in areas with undulating topography and water retentive soils. In such cases, farmers who are supposed to be the 'beneficiaries' become victims of irrigation projects and irrigation authorities. In areas where irrigation has led to the transformation of productive lands into waterlogged wastelands, conflicts arise between farmers and the state. The 'Mitt) Bachao Andolan' in the Tawacomman area is an example of such conflicts." In the Krishna basin, conflic generated by irrigation projects were highlighted by the farmer agitations in the command area of the Malaprabha project.

The Malaprabha project was completed in 1972-73. With the introduction of canal irrigation, nearly 2,364 hectares of land i the project area has become waterlogged and saline' Before the introduction of perennial irrigation, the undulating semi-arid land in the project area was used for growing water prudent crops like jowar and pulses. Due to a sudden change from rainfed agriculture to intensive canal irrigation, the low lying areas have become waterlogged. The cultivation of water demanding crops like hybrid cotton has aggravated the problem. In addition, seepage from canals has also raised the water level. The Malaprabha project includes a storage dam of 1,068 million cum capacity near Saundatti in Belgaum district which feeds the 138 km Malaprabha right bank, 168 km left bank canal, and the Kolachi right bank canal. The soils in the command area are black cotton soils, which have high water retention capacity and are prone to waterloggin, Intensive irrigation of black cotton soils has been known to be prescription for creating wastelands. While irrigation has bet viewed as a means to improve land productivity, in cases like if Malaprabha command area, it has led to the destruction of productivity. Further, the shift from rainfed food crops to an irrigated cash crop like cotton was expected to improve the prosperity of farmer However, it led to indebtedness as well as loss of fertile fan. through waterlogging.

To utilise the irrigation waters, farmers began to cultivate 'Varalaxmi' cotton which was initially sold at Rs. 1,000 per quintal. Farmers took loans from banks to develop land, purchase seeds, chemical fertilisers and pesticides. The total loan taken by the farmers increased from Rs. 50 lakhs in 1974 to over Rs. 5.5 crores by 1980. The prices of chemical fertilisers increased from Rs. 75 to Rs. 103 per bag. The cost of the Varalaxmi seed increased from Rs. 60 to Rs. 170 per kg. In the meantime the price of cotton crashed from Rs. 1,000 per quintal in 1974 to Rs. 350 per quintal in 1980.

While farmers were caught in the trap of unfulfilled commercial promise, banks demanded repayments of loans, and the irrigation authorities demanded a development tax known as betterment levy of Rs. 500 to Rs. 1,600 per acre. The water tax was raised from Rs. 18 to Rs. 30 per acre for jowar, Rs. 18 to Rs. 50 per acre for Varalaxmi. A tax of Rs. 10 per acre was fixed even if water was not utilised. For the farmers, this amounted to gross injustice, since they had not benefited from the irrigation project. In addition, the compensation for acquiring land for the dam and canals had not been paid to 75 per cent of the farmers even after seven to eight years.

The farmers therefore organised themselves as the Malaprabha Niravari Pradesh Ryota Samvya Samithi' (Co-ordination Committee of Farmers of Malaprabha Ittihsyrf Area) in March 1980. When the local authorities did not pay heed to the farmers' demands, they launched a non-cooperation movement for nonpayment of taxes. The authorities responded by refusing to issue the certificates required by the farmers' children in order to in schools and colleges. On 19 June, the farmers went on a hunger strike in front of the Tebsildar's office in Naragund town. On 30 June, 10,()00 farmers collected to support those on hunger strike. On 7 July, a massive rally was organised in Navalgund, and the farmers went on a hunger strike. Seeing that no response was forthcoming from the authorities, the farmers organised a 'bunch' on 21 July. When 5,000 to 6,000 farmers had gathered in Navalgund, their tractors were damaged and the rally was stoned. The protest then took a violent turn. The angry farmers seized the irrigation office department, burnt down one truck and fifteen jeeps. The police in turn opened fire and a young boy, Basappa Shivappa of Algavadi, was killed on the spot.

In Naragund town, the police opened fire at a procession of 10,000 people, shooting one youth. The protesting farmers responded by beating a police officer and a constable to death. The protests rapidly spread to Ghataprabha, Tungabhadra, and other parts of Karnataka. During the protests thousands of farmers were arrested and forty were killed. Finally, the government had to put a moratorium on the collection of water taxes.and the betterment levy. According to a rough estimate, the concessions granted to farmers to end the Malaprabha agitation amounted to Rs. 85 crores.

However, the high costs of irrigation in the Malaprabha project have been forgotten. No lessons have been drawn for planning water projects, and bureaucrats, technocrats and politicians continue-to get carried away by the euphoria for large dams and intensive irrigation projects. The creation of waterlogged wasteland through intensive irrigation is not specific to the Malaprabha command area. Compared to other projects in the Krishna basin, waterlogging, salinity and alkalinity are most serious in the Tungabhadra project. Nearly 1,500 hectares of land is likely to become waterlogged under the left bank canal.

In the right bank canal 6,000 hectares have been affected by waterlogging. Under the right bank high level canal 12,000 hectares have been affected by waterlogging. In all, 19,500 hectares have been destroyed by waterlogging in the Tungabhadra project within an irrigation period of thirty-five years.

In the Bhadra project, of 1,24,392 hectares irrigated, 7,900 hectares have been devastated by waterlogging. In the Malaprabha project, of the total potential of 2,12,086 hectares, only 12,186 hectares have been actually irrigated. Of this irrigated area, 50 per cent has been waterlogged. In the Ghataprabha project, where a higher average has been irrigated than what was actually planned, out of 3,58,542 hectares irrigated, 19,948 hectares have been devastated by waterlogging.

In Andhra Pradesh, under the Nagarjunasagar project (NSP) the groundwater level has risen alarmingly within ten years, thereby indicating a trend towards waterlogging. In Maharashtra, the Maharashtra Irrigation Commission claims that 28,000 hectares of land have been affected by waterlogging in the Deccan Canals, *i.e.*, Nira and Mutha Canals. The irrigation commission of 1976 had estimated the total waterlogged area in the basin at 7,828 hectares (6,583 hectares in Karnataka and 1,245 hectares in Maharashtra) and 15,502 hectares affected by salinity. At present 4,45,985 hectares have been affected by salinity. Waterlogging is ecologically linked to large dams because large darns involve the transport of huge quantities of water for intensive irrigation. In fact, the primary rationale given in defence of large dams is to induce a shift from protective irrigation, which is ensured by indigenous irrigation systems, to intensive irrigation for commercial crops. The inevitable ecological impact of overuse of water for irrigation is a build up of water beyond the drainage capacity of the ecosystem. The need for artificial drainage systems arises because the natural drainage processes of the local ecosystem are violated. Waterlogging is thus a symptom of the conflict between water use in the commerciaVmarket economy, and water use for the maintenance of the water cycle including a balance between water entering an ecosystem and water leaving it. By violating the ecological laws of water flow, large dams lead to ecological destruction on the one hand and political conflict on the other.

RIVER DIVERSIONS AND REGIONAL CONFLICTS OVER WATER

Large dams are constructed for allowing major diversions of water from the natural drainage flow of the river. These diversions result in a major change in the distribution patterns of water in a basin, especially when they involve inter-basin transfers. They therefore generate new conflicts over the distribution of water between different regions. Regional conflicts become inter-state conflicts, and are rapidly enmeshed in inter-state and centre-state politics. The Telugu Ganga Canal, which takes off from the Srisailam Dam, is probably the most conflict-ridden river diversion project in contemporary India.

Krishna is the second largest river of peninsular India. Its catchment lies in the Western Ghats and it flows east through the states of Maharashtra, Karnataka and Andhra Pradesh. Krishna is an inter-state river, and conflicts have arisen between the co-riparian states over the allocation of its waters to their respective territories for purposes of development.

The Krishna basin like other regions of India had indigenous irrigation works such as tanks, wells and anicuts. There were nearly 27,000 small tanks and diversions on the Krishna river system, mostly in Andhra Pradesh and Karnataka. To these were added new canals during the colonial period for commercial agriculture. These were:

1. The Krishna Delta Canals built in 1855.
2. The Nira Canals in Maharashtra constructed in I885 irrigating about 150,000 acres.
3. The Kurnool Cuddapah Canal in Andhra Pradesh built in 1886, irrigating 100,000 acres.

The majority of the area irrigated by the Krishna Delta Canals and Kurnool Cuddapah Canal (1.11 million acres) lies outside the basin of the Krishna. In 1951, the status of the diversion of Krishna waters was as follows: 411.4 TMCF of water was diverted annually for the irrigation of 2,302,377 acres. Of this 290.1 TMCF was used by Andhra Pradesh, 430 TMCF by Maharashtra, and 78.3 TMCF by Karnataka.

After independence, the large-scale diversion of river waters increased. In July 1951 the Planning Commission convened an inter-state conference to discuss the utilisation of Krishna waters. The dependable annual flow in the Krishna basin based on the recorded gaugings at Vijayawada was agreed at 1,715 TMCF so the balance of flow for new projects remained 970.5 TMCF which was rounded off to 1,000 TMCF and allocations were made between the different states as follows:

For the balance flow in excess of 1,000 TMCF, if any, the allocation for the above states was in the ratio 30:30:1:39. The state of Bombay was allowed to divert the waters to the west across the Western Ghats for the hydro-electric project at Koyna up to a limit of 67.5 TMCF. The agreement provided for a review of the allocations after twenty years. In 1953, states were; reorganised on a linguistic basis, Madras was divided into Andhra and Madras. In 1956 the state of Andhra Pradesh was created by the merger of parts of Hyderabad and Andhra. As a result of territorial changes, the riparian states sharing the Krishna waters are Maharashtra, Karnataka and Andhra Pradesh. An inter-state conference was convened in New Delhi under the auspices of the Union Minister of Irrigation and Power on September 1960, to recast the allocations of Krishna waters made in 1981. However, efforts to reach an agreement among the states proved unsuccessful and widely divergent views were expressed by the different states. ~ three man commission headed by N.D. Gulhati was set up. The commission undertook the first ever attempt 'at a basin-wide survey of the technical implementation relevant to water resources development.'

As observed by Tripathi, the Commission in examining the river flow of both these rivers was greatly hampered by the lack of regular reliable and continuous observations of water discharge at various points in river... The Commission stated that the flow records prior to 1936 were based on formulae different from those followed after 1936. Therefore the Commission stated that it [was] not possible to determine the flow for 86 per cent dependability or for 75 per cent dependability or for any other criterion of dependability. Because of the lack of adequate data of river flow, the Commission could not give positive answers to the terms of reference as regards the availability of water supplies on the river systems. State-wise allocation of Krishna waters was, therefore, not possible owing to the lack of scientifically observed data. The Irrigation Minister decided that adequate river data should be collected over a number of years and analysed continuously. However, tentative allocation was made for ongoing projects.

In spite of interim re-allocations, conflicts over Krishna waters continued with each state accusing the other of higher withdrawals from the river than its legitimate share. Maharashtra and Karnataka wanted a tribunal set up under Section 3 of the Interstate Water Disputes Act, 1956.

The Bachawat Tribunal was appointed in 1969 to resolve the Krishna water state conflicts. In 1973 the Bachawat Committee gave its award. The availability of water was assessed at 2,060 TMCF and on the basis of 75 per cent dependability, Andhra Pradesh was allocated 800 TMCF. The award fixed a formula for sharing both during surplus and lean years and was binding on the states until AD 2000.

Mrs. Gandhi the then Prime Minister consulted the co-riparian states to provide drinking water to Madras which had been facing severe shortages. The three states readily agreed to part with S TMCF each. The Chief Minister of Andhra Pradesh later hailed the Krishna water supply scheme to Madras as the Telugu Ganga. The agreement was reached on 14 April 1976. On 17 October 1977, it was agreed that a 330 km long open canal would carry 15 TMCF to Madras.

While the decision to supply drinking water to Madras was agreed by all the states, conflicts arose when Andhra Pradesh decided to use the Telugu Ganga project for irrigation. The Rs. 850 crore project now envisages extension of irrigation to 5.75 lakh acres in three districts of Rayalseema-Kurnool, Cuddapah and Chittoor and one district in the Andhra region-Nellore, in addition to the supply of 15 TMCF of drinking water to Madras. Nearly 42.4 per cent of Kurnool district lies in the Krishna basin. Cuddapah and Chittoor as well as the rest of Kurnool lie in the Pennar basin. Karnataka had questioned the diversion of water outside the basin to the KWDT arguing that only in-basin needs should be considered in determining a state's equitable share, a state should be permitted to divert its share of water outside the basin. Andhra Pradesh maintained that out of basin needs are a relevant factor and that diversions outside the basin for irrigation needs only should be permitted. Using precedence from the American Law, the Bachawat Tribunal held that the diversion of Krishna water outside the basin was legal. The river basin as an integral unit was thus substituted by the state as an administrative unit. The conflicting demands and distributive patterns emerging from the integrity of the basin versus the integrity of the state ifs a major reason for inter-state conflicts between riparian states not getting fully resolved.

Another fundamental reason for the intractable nature of river conflicts arises from the rights established through the priority of Project use in time and the rights based on the priority of need in the long term. Andhra Pradesh contends that the diversion of an additional 275 TMCF of Krishna waters to feed the districts of Kurnool and Cuddapah in Rayalseema for irrigation of 2.75 lakh acres, is within the scope of the Bachawat award as the Tribunal permitted Andhra Pradesh to take advantage of the surplus flows down the river at Vijayawada. As the Bachawat Tribunal stated, 'the state of An&a Pradesh will be at liberty to use in any year the remaining water that may be flowing in the Krishna river'.

Karnataka has objected to the Telugu Ganga irrigation scheme on the grounds that its own projects to harness Krishna waters are still incomplete and what appears to be excess, currently, will be used in the future. Karnataka has made it clear that surplus Krishna waters would not be available for the Telugu Ganga project. Maharashtra has also opposed the Telugu Ganga project on the ground that it violates the inter-state agreement reached in October 1977. The government of Maharashtra has observed that the state has vast chronic drought affected areas. Almost 75 per cent of the Krishna basin area in Maharashtra is drought prone and the state has plans to use the Krishna water allocated to it by the Krishna Tribunal. It has, therefore, to make sure that at the time of review of the award, its legitimate claim to the surplus available water in the Krishna river is not in any way jeopardised by pre-emptive efforts to commit this surplus water to projects like the Telugu Ganga. Karnataka-and Maharashtra governments are resisting the project on the grounds that Andhra Pradesh has already used its allocation and the Telugu Ganga project would enable Andhra Pradesh to establish its right on larger volumes of water through prior utilisation.

Andhra Pradesh has already invested Rs. 200 crores and has 5,000 labourers working on the construction of the canal. Of the 406 km length of the canal, 190 km pass through the reserved forests of the Nellamali Range, for which central environmental clearance has not been obtained so far. At present the work is confined to reservoirs and canals in the non-forest areas. Water for the project is to be drawn from the Srisailam Dam through the head regulator at Pothireddypadu, which has a total carrying capacity of 11,000 cusecs.

The first 16 km of the canal is shared with the Srisailam right branch canal. The common canals run up to Bankacherla cross regulator where the Srisailam right branch canal and the Telugu Ganga Canal branch off to the right and left, respectively. The Telugu Ganga Canal is in fact the old Srisailam left branch canal extending into the Segileru Valley. Water to be drawn for the Telugu Ganga project is to be stored in four reservoirs at Yellgodu, Brahamasagar, Somashila and Kandaleru. At Mithakanda? near the Bankacherla regulator, a 100 feet high ridge divides the Krishna and the Pennar basins, where the water would be transferred outside the Krishna basin. The canal would pass through Kurnool and Cuddapah districts from where the water would flow into the Pennar river at Chenumukapalli. The flow down the river would be picked up at the Somashila Dam and passed on to the Kandaleru reservoir before it reaches Madras. The construction work continues even though the controversy over the Telugu Ganga project remains unresolved.

Andhra Pradesh derives its legitimacy from two arguments. First, it claims it is using only surplus waters for the project, and the right to surplus waters had been granted to it by the Tribunal. Second, it claims that if there is scarcity, then the arid drought prone regions of Rayalseema should not be asked to sacrifice irrigation waters. Instead, Maharashtra should be asked to stop diverting large volumes of water out of the Krishna basin into the Arabian Ocean for power generation for industrial centres. The river Krishna emerges in the Western Ghats and flows eastward down the gentle slopes. The western face of the Western Ghats falls steeply down altitudes of 1,000 to 2,000 feet, providing excellent sites for power generation. However, the water used for hydro-electricity has to be diverted out of the basin, and dropped into the sea. Currently, the power projects in Maharashtra which divert water westwards are the Tata and Koyna Hydel Projects. The former diverts 42.6 TMC and the latter diverts 67.5 TMC.

In this conflict between the demands for power generation and the demands for irrigation in drought prone areas, the Krishna Tribunal protected existing diversions while giving priority to irrigation for future use. As it stated:

In the Krishna Basin, water is a scarce commodity. Westward diversion of water for power generation seriously restricts the use of water for downstream irrigation.... Power for Bombay and Maharashtra industry is generated at the cost of depriving the low rainfall areas on the eastern side of the water solely needed for irrigation.

The Tribunal, however, allowed the expansion of hydel projects on the condition that over a period of twenty years they would return to the existing capacity. When the next Krishna Tribunal meets in the year 2020 to review the sharing and utilisation of Krishna waters, the concepts of justice and rights as related to water will have undergone dramatic changes, as will the basin itself.

SOURCES OF IRRIGATION WATER AND GROUNDWATER

Sources of irrigation water can be groundwater extracted from springs or by using wells, surface water withdrawn from rivers, lakes or reservoirs or non-conventional sources like treated wastewater, desalinated water or drainage water. A special form of irrigation using surface water is spate irrigation, also called floodwater harvesting.

In case of a flood (spate) water is diverted to normally dry river beds (wadis) using a network of dams, gates and channels and spread over large areas. The moisture stored in the soil will be used thereafter to grow crops. Spate irrigation areas are in particular located in semi-arid or arid, mountainous regions. While floodwater harvesting belongs to the accepted irrigation methods, rainwater harvesting is usually not considered as a form of irrigation. Rainwater harvesting is the collection of run-off water from roofs or unused land and the concentration of this. Some of Ancient India's water systems were pulled by oxen.

Around 90% of wastewater produced globally remains untreated, causing widespread water pollution, especially in low-income countries. Increasingly, agriculture is using untreated wastewater as a source of irrigation water. Cities provide lucrative markets for fresh produce, so are attractive to farmers.

However, because agriculture has to compete for increasingly scarce water resources with industry and municipal users, there is often no alternative for farmers but to use water polluted with urban waste, including sewage, directly to water their crops. There can be significant health hazards related to using water loaded with pathogens in this way, especially if people eat raw vegetables that have been irrigated with the polluted water. The International Water Management Institute has worked in India, Pakistan, Vietnam, Ghana, Ethiopia, Mexico and other countries on various projects aimed at assessing and reducing risks of wastewater irrigation. They advocate a 'multiple-barrier' approach to wastewater use, where farmers are encouraged to adopt various risk-reducing behaviours. These include ceasing irrigation a few days before harvesting to allow pathogens to die off in the sunlight, applying water carefully so it does not contaminate leaves likely to be eaten raw, cleaning vegetables with disinfectant or allowing fecal sludge used in farming to dry before being used as a human manure. The World Health Organization has developed guidelines for safe water use.

WATER SCARCITY

Fifty years ago, the common perception was that water was an infinite resource. At that time, there were fewer than half the current number of people on the planet. People were not as wealthy as today, consumed fewer calories and ate less meat, so less water was needed to produce their food. They required a third of the volume of water we presently take from rivers. Today, the competition for water resources is much more intense. This is because there are now more than seven billion people on the planet, their consumption of water-thirsty meat and vegetables is rising, and there is increasing competition for water from industry, urbanisation and biofuel crops. To avoid a global water crisis, farmers will have to strive to increase productivity to meet growing demands for food, while industry and cities find ways to use water more efficiently.

Successful agriculture is dependent upon farmers having sufficient access to water. However, water scarcity is already a critical constraint to farming in many parts of the world. With regards to agriculture, the World Bank targets food production and water management as an increasingly global issue that is fostering a growing debate. Physical water scarcity is where there is not enough water to meet all demands, including that needed for ecosystems to function effectively. Arid regions frequently suffer from physical water scarcity. It also occurs where water seems abundant but where resources are over-committed.

This can happen where there is overdevelopment of hydraulic infrastructure, usually for irrigation. Symptoms of physical water scarcity include environmental degradation and declining groundwater. Economic scarcity, meanwhile, is caused by a lack of investment in water or insufficient human capacity to satisfy the demand for water. Symptoms of economic water scarcity include a lack of infrastructure, with people often having to fetch water from rivers for domestic and agricultural uses. Some 2.8 billion people currently live in water-scarce areas.

How an in-ground Irrigation System Works

Most commercial and residential irrigation systems are "in ground" systems, which means that everything is buried in the ground. With the pipes, sprinklers, emitters (drippers), and irrigation valves being hidden, it makes for a cleaner, more presentable landscape without garden hoses or other items having to be moved around manually. This does, however, create some drawbacks in the maintenance of a completely buried system.

Controllers, Zones, and Valves

Most irrigation systems are divided into zones. A zone is a single irrigation valve and one or a group of drippers or sprinklers that are connected by pipes or tubes. Irrigation systems are divided into zones because there is usually not enough pressure and available flow to run sprinklers for an entire yard or sports field at once.

Each zone has a solenoid valve on it that is controlled via wire by an irrigation controller. The irrigation controller is either a mechanical (now the "dinosaur" type) or electrical device that signals a zone to turn on at a specific time and keeps it on for a specified amount of time. "Smart Controller" is a recent term used to describe a controller that is capable of adjusting the watering time by itself in response to current environmental conditions. The smart controller determines current conditions by means of historic weather data for the local area, a soil moisture sensors (water potential or water content), rain sensor, or in more sophisticated systems satellite feed weather station, or a combination of these.

Emitters and Sprinklers

When a zone comes on, the water flows through the lateral lines and ultimately ends up at the irrigation emitter (drip) or sprinkler heads. Many sprinklers have pipe thread inlets on the bottom of them which allows a fitting and the pipe to be attached to them. The sprinklers are usually installed with the top of the head flush with the ground surface. When the water is pressurized, the head will pop up out of the ground and water the desired area until the valve closes and shuts off that zone. Once there is no more water pressure in the lateral line, the sprinkler head will retract back into the ground. Emitters are generally laid on the soil surface or buried a few inches to reduce evaporation losses.

Problems in Irrigation

Irrigation can lead to a number of problems:

- Competition for surface water rights.
- Depletion of underground aquifers.
- Ground subsidence (*e.g.* New Orleans, Louisiana)
- Underirrigation or irrigation giving only just enough water for the plant (*e.g.* in drip line irrigation) gives poor soil salinity control which leads to increased soil salinity with consequent build up of toxic salts on soil surface in areas with high evaporation. This requires either

leaching to remove these salts and a method of drainage to carry the salts away. When using drip lines, the leaching is best done regularly at certain intervals (with only a slight excess of water), so that the salt is flushed back under the plant's roots.

- Overirrigation because of poor distribution uniformity or management wastes water, chemicals, and may lead to water pollution.
- Deep drainage (from over-irrigation) may result in rising water tables which in some instances will lead to problems of irrigation salinity requiring watertable control by some form of subsurface land drainage.
- Irrigation with saline or high-sodium water may damage soil structure owing to the formation of alkaline soil

CONSISTS OF IRRIGATION SYSTEM

The irrigation system consists of a (main) intake structure or (main) pumping station, a conveyance system, a distribution system, a field application system and a drainage system.

The (main) intake structure, or (main) pumping station, directs water from the source of supply, such as a reservoir or a river, into the irrigation system. The conveyance system assures the transport of water from the main intake structure or main pumping station up to the field ditches. The distribution system assures the transport of water through field ditches to the irrigated fields. The field application system assures the transport of water within the fields. The drainage system removes the excess water (caused by rainfall and/ or irrigation) from the fields.

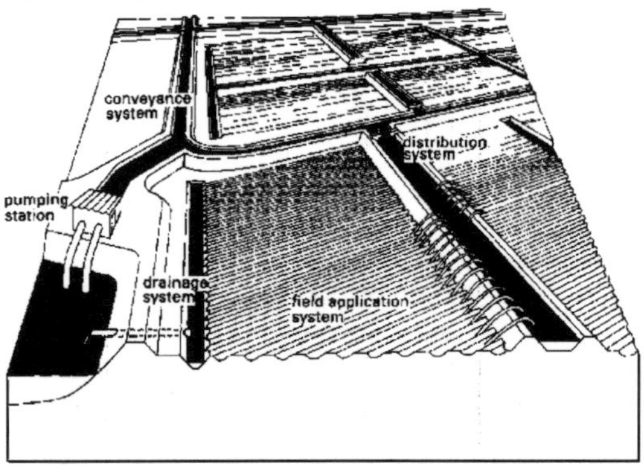

Fig. An Irrigation System

MAIN INTAKE STRUCTURE AND PUMPING STATION

Main Intake Structure

The intake structure is built at the entry to the irrigation system. Its purpose is to direct water from the original source of supply (lake, river, reservoir etc.) into the irrigation system.

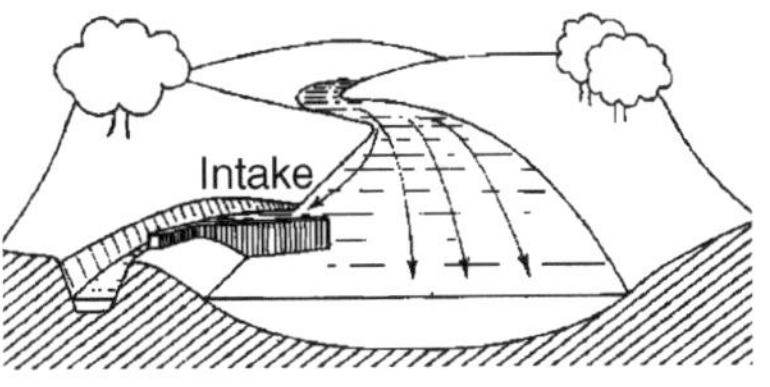

Fig. An Intake Structure

Pumping Station

In some cases, the irrigation water source lies below the level of the irrigated fields. Then a pump must be used to supply water to the irrigation system.

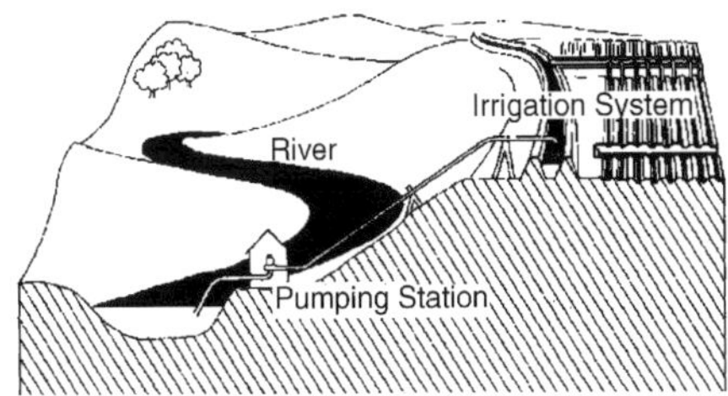

Fig. A Pumping Station

There are several types of pumps, but the most commonly used in irrigation is the centrifugal pump.

The centrifugal pump consists of a case in which an element, called an impeller, rotates driven by a motor. Water enters the case at the centre, through the suction pipe. The water is immediately caught by the rapidly rotating impeller and expelled through the discharge pipe. The centrifugal pump will only operate when the case is completely filled with water.

CONVEYANCE AND DISTRIBUTION SYSTEM

The conveyance and distribution systems consist of canals transporting the water through the whole irrigation system. Canal structures are required for the control and measurement of the water flow.

OPEN CANALS

An open canal, channel, or ditch, is an open waterway whose purpose is to carry water from one place to another. Channels and canals refer to main waterways supplying water to one or more farms. Field ditches have smaller dimensions and convey water from the farm entrance to the irrigated fields.

CANAL CHARACTERISTICS

According to the shape of their cross-section, canals are called rectangular (a), triangular (b), trapezoidal (c), circular (d), parabolic (e) and irregular or natural (f). The most commonly used canal cross-section in irrigation and drainage, is the trapezoidal cross-section. For the purposes of this publication, only this type of canal will be considered. The typical cross-section of a trapezoidal canal.

The freeboard of the canal is the height of the bank above the highest water level anticipated. It is required to guard against overtopping by waves or unexpected rises in the water level. The side slope of the canal is expressed as ratio, namely the vertical distance or height to the horizontal distance or width. For example, if the side slope of the canal has a ratio of 1:2 (one to two), this means that the horizontal distance (w) is two times the vertical distance (h).

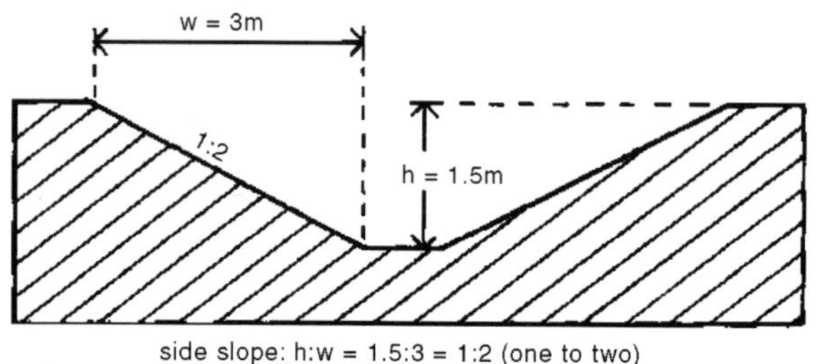

Fig. A Side Slope of 1:2 (One to Two)

The bottom slope of the canal does not appear on the drawing of the cross-section but on the longitudinal section. It is commonly expressed in per cent or per mil.

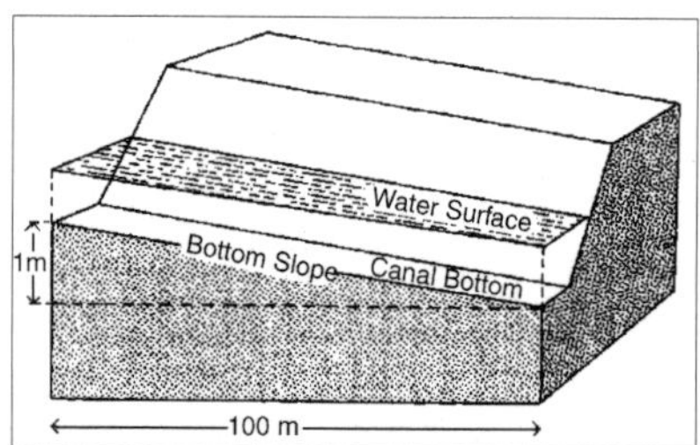

Fig. A Bottom Slope of a Canal

An example of the calculation of the bottom slope of a canal is given below:

The bottom slope (%) =

$$\frac{\text{Height difference (metres)}}{\text{Horizontal distance (metres)}} \times 100$$

$$\frac{1\,\text{m}}{100\,\text{m}} \times 100 = 1\%$$

or,

$$\text{The bottom slope (\%)} = \frac{\text{Height difference (metres)}}{\text{Horizontal distance (metres)}} \times 1000$$

$$= \frac{1\,\text{m}}{100\,\text{m}} \times 1000 = 10‰$$

EARTHEN CANALS

Earthen canals are simply dug in the ground and the bank is made up from the removed earth. The disadvantages of earthen canals are the risk of the side slopes collapsing and the water loss due to seepage. They also require continuous maintenance in order to control weed growth and to repair damage done by livestock and rodent.

LINED CANALS

Earthen canals can be lined with impermeable materials to prevent excessive seepage and growth of weeds. Lining canals is also an effective way to control canal bottom and bank erosion. The materials mostly used for canal lining are concrete (in precast slabs or cast in place), brick or rock masonry and asphaltic concrete (a mixture of sand, gravel and asphalt). The construction cost is much higher than for earthen canals. Maintenance is reduced for lined canals, but skilled labour is required.

CANAL STRUCTURES

The flow of irrigation water in the canals must always be under control. For this purpose, canal structures are required. They help regulate the flow and deliver the correct amount of water to the different branches of the system and onward to the irrigated fields. There are four main types of structures: erosion control structures, distribution control structures, crossing structures and water measurement structures.

Erosion Control Structures

Canal Erosion

Canal bottom slope and water velocity are closely related, as the following example will show. A cardboard sheet is lifted on one side 2 cm from the ground. A small ball is placed at the edge of the lifted side of the sheet. It starts rolling downward, following the slope direction. The sheet edge is now lifted 5 cm from the ground creating a steeper slope. The same ball placed on the top edge of the sheet rolls downward, but this time much faster. The steeper the slope, the higher the velocity of the ball.

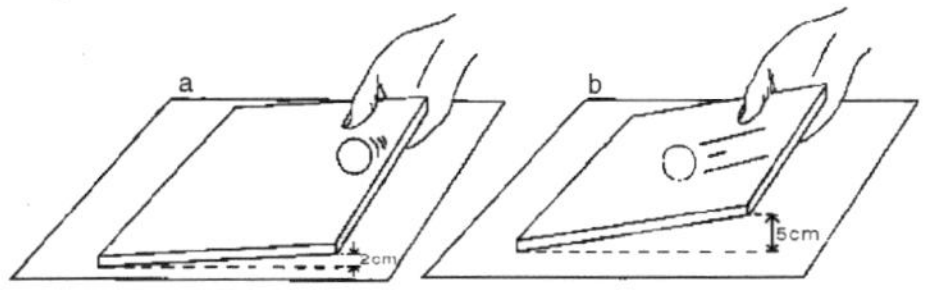

Fig. The Relationship between Slope and Velocity

Water poured on the top edge of the sheet reacts exactly the same as the ball. It flows downward and the steeper the slope, the higher the velocity of the flow. Water flowing in steep canals can reach very high velocities. Soil particles along the bottom and banks of an earthen canal are then lifted, carried away by the water flow and deposited downstream where they may block the canal and silt up structures. The canal is said to be under erosion; the banks might eventually collapse.

Drop Structures and Chutes

Drop structures or chutes are required to reduce the bottom slope of canals lying on steeply sloping land in order to avoid high velocity of the flow and risk of erosion.

These structures permit the canal to be constructed as a series of relatively flat sections, each at a different elevation.

Drop structures take the water abruptly from a higher section of the canal to a lower one. In a chute, the water does not drop freely but is carried through a steep, lined canal section. Chutes are used where there are big differences in the elevation of the canal.

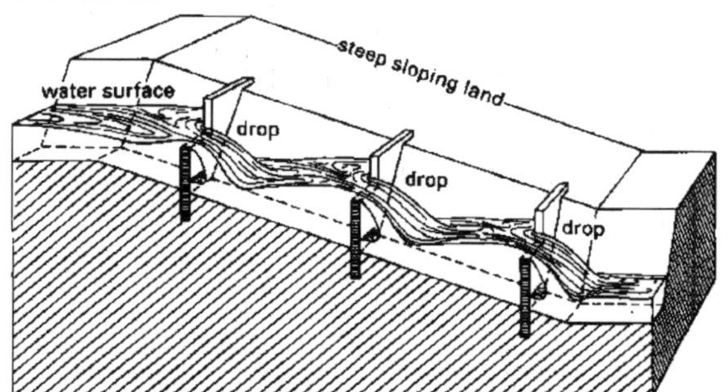

Fig. Longitudinal Section of a Series of Drop Structures

Distribution Control Structures

Distribution control structures are required for easy and accurate water distribution within the irrigation system and on the farm. Division boxes are used to divide or direct the flow of water between two or more canals or ditches. Water enters the box through an opening on one side and flows out through openings on the other sides. These openings are equipped with gates.

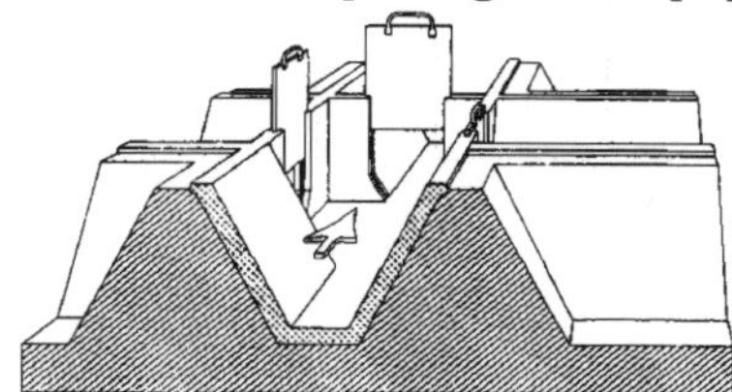

Fig. A Division Box with Three Gates

Turnouts

Turnouts are constructed in the bank of a canal. They divert part of the water from the canal to a smaller one.

Turnouts can be concrete structures, or pipe structures.

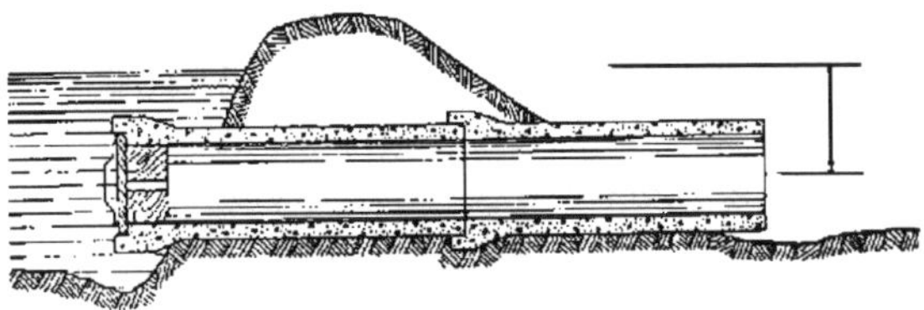

Fig. A Pipe Turnout

Checks

To divert water from the field ditch to the field, it is often necessary to raise the water level in the ditch. Checks are structures placed across the ditch to block it temporarily and to raise the upstream water level. Checks can be permanent structures or portable.

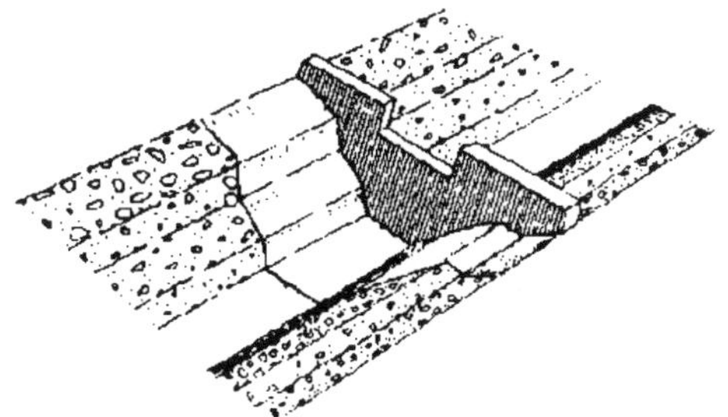

Fig. A Permanent Concrete Check

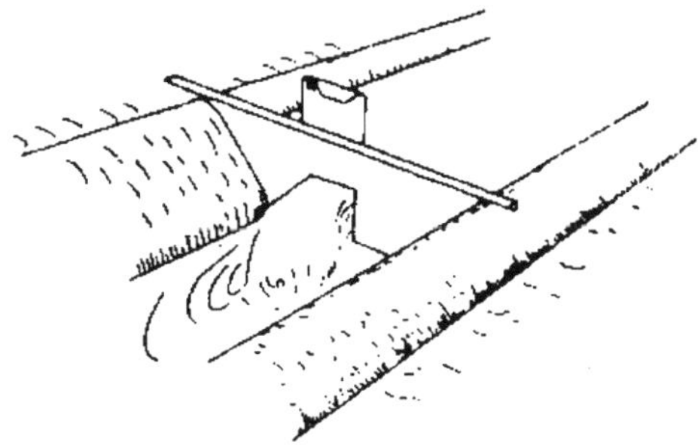

Fig. A Portable Metal Check

CROSSING STRUCTURES

It is often necessary to carry irrigation water across roads, hillsides and natural depressions. Crossing structures, such as flumes, culverts and inverted siphons, are then required.

Flumes

Flumes are used to carry irrigation water across gullies, ravines or other natural depressions. They are open canals made of wood (bamboo), metal or concrete which often need to be supported by pillars.

Culverts

Culverts are used to carry the water across roads. The structure consists of masonry or concrete headwalls at the inlet and outlet connected by a buried pipeline.

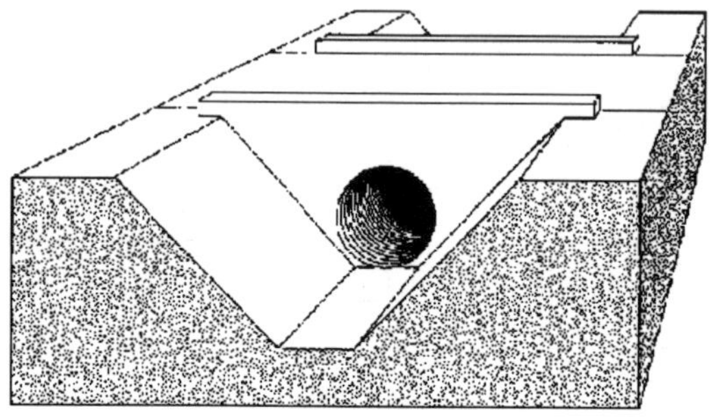

Fig. A Culvert

Inverted Siphons

When water has to be carried across a road which is at the same level as or below the canal bottom, an inverted siphon is used instead of a culvert. The structure consists of an inlet and outlet connected by a pipeline. Inverted siphons are also used to carry water across wide depressions.

Fig. An Inverted Siphon

Water Measurement Structures

The principal objective of measuring irrigation water is to permit efficient distribution and application. By measuring the flow of water, a farmer knows how much water is applied during each irrigation. In irrigation schemes where water costs are charged to the farmer, water measurement provides a basis for estimating water charges. The most commonly used water measuring structures are weirs and flumes. In these structures, the water depth is read on a scale which is part of the structure. Using this reading, the flow-rate is then computed from standard formulas or obtained from standard tables prepared specially for the structure.

Weirs

In its simplest form, a weir consists of a wall of timber, metal or concrete with an opening with fixed dimensions cut in its edge. The opening, called a notch, may be rectangular, trapezoidal or triangular.

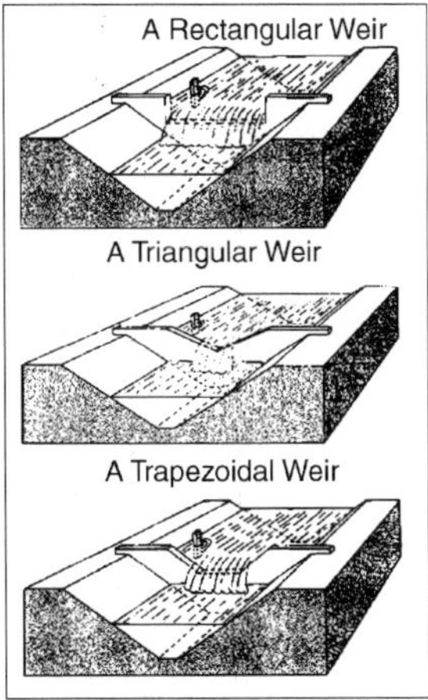

Fig. Some Examples of Weirs

Parshall Flumes

The Parshall flume consists of a metal or concrete channel structure with three main sections:

- A converging section at the upstream end, leading to;
- A constricted or throat section,
- A diverging section at the downstream end.

Depending on the flow condition (free flow or submerged flow), the water depth readings are taken on one scale only (the upstream one) or on both scales simultaneously.

Cut-throat Flume

The cut-throat flume is similar to the Parshall flume, but has no throat section, only converging and diverging sections. Unlike the Parshall flume, the cut-throat flume has a flat bottom. Because it is easier to construct and install, the cut-throat flume is often preferred to the Parshall flume.

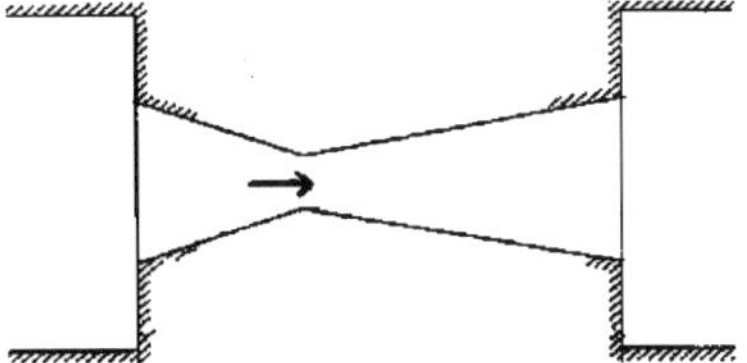

Fig. A Cut-throat Flume

FIELD APPLICATION SYSTEMS

There are many methods of applying water to the field. The simplest one consists of bringing water from the source of supply, such as a well, to each plant with a bucket or a water-can.

This is a very time-consuming method and it involves quite heavy work. However, it can be used successfully to irrigate small plots of land, such as vegetable gardens, that are in the neighbourhood of a water source. More sophisticated methods of water application are used in larger irrigation systems. There are three basic methods: surface irrigation, sprinkler irrigation and drip irrigation.

Surface Irrigation

Surface irrigation is the application of water to the fields at ground level. Either the entire field is flooded or the water is directed into furrows or borders.

Furrow Irrigation

Furrows are narrow ditches dug on the field between the rows of crops. The water runs along them as it moves down the slope of the field. The water flows from the field ditch into the furrows by opening up the bank or dyke of the ditch or by means of syphons or spiles. Siphons are small curved pipes that deliver water over the ditch bank. Spiles are small pipes buried in the ditch bank.

Border Irrigation

In border irrigation, the field to be irrigated is divided into strips (also called borders or borderstrips) by parallel dykes or border ridges. The water is released from the field ditch onto the border through gate structures called outlets. The water can also be released by means of siphons or spiles. The sheet of flowing water moves down the slope of the border, guided by the border ridges.

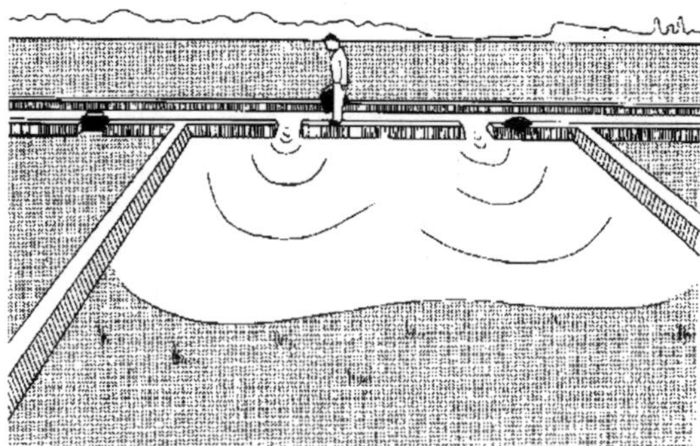

Fig. Border Irrigation

Basin Irrigation

Basins are horizontal, flat plots of land, surrounded by small dykes or bunds. The banks prevent the water from flowing to the surrounding fields. Basin irrigation is commonly used for rice grown on flat lands or in terraces on hillsides. Trees can also be grown in basins, where one tree usually is located in the centre of a small basin.

Sprinkler Irrigation

With sprinkler irrigation, artificial rainfall is created. The water is led to the field through a pipe system in which the water is under pressure. The spraying is accomplished by using several rotating sprinkler heads or spray nozzles or a single gun type sprinkler.

Drip Irrigation

In drip irrigation, also called trickle irrigation, the water is led to the field through a pipe system. On the field, next to the row of plants or trees, a tube is installed. At regular intervals, near the plants or trees, a hole is made in the tube and equipped with an emitter. The water is supplied slowly, drop by drop, to the plants through these emitters.

Drainage System

A drainage system is necessary to remove excess water from the irrigated land. This excess water may be *e.g.* waste water from irrigation or surface run-off from rainfall. It may also include leakage or seepage water from the distribution system.

NEED FOR DRAINAGE

During rain or irrigation, the fields become wet. The water infiltrates into the soil and is stored in its pores.

When all the pores are filled with water, the soil is said to be saturated and no more water can be absorbed; when rain or irrigation continues, pools may form on the soil surface. Part of the water present in thc saturated upper soil layers flows downward into deeper layers and is replaced by water infiltrating from the surface pools.

When there is no more water left on the soil surface, the downward flow continues for a while and air re-enters in the pores of the soil. This soil is not saturated anymore.

However, saturation may have lasted too long for the plants' health. Plant roots require air as well as water and most plants cannot withstand saturated soil for long periods (rice is an exception).

Besides damage to the crop, a very wet soil makes the use of machinery difficult, if not impossible.

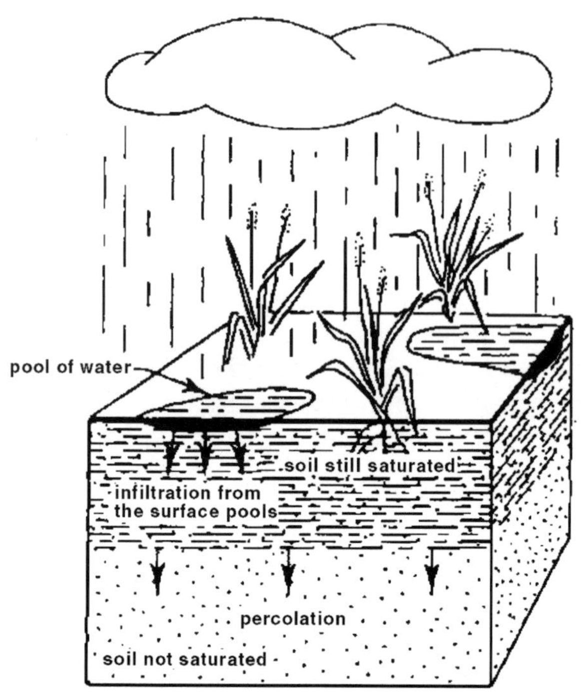

Fig. Water Percolates to Deeper Layers and Infiltrates from the Pools

The water flowing from the saturated soil downward to deeper layers, feeds the groundwater reservoir. As a result, the groundwater level (often called groundwater table or simply water table) rises. Following heavy rainfall or continuous over-irrigation, the groundwater table may even reach and saturate part of the rootzone. Again, if this situation lasts too long, the plants may suffer. Measures to control the rise of the water table are thus necessary. The removal of excess water either from the ground surface or from the rootzone, is called drainage. Excess water may be caused by rainfall or by using too much irrigation water, but may also have other origins such as canal seepage or floods.

In very dry areas there is often accumulation of salts in the soil. Most crops do not grow well on salty soil. Salts can be washed out by percolating irrigation water through the rootzone of the crops. To achieve sufficient percolation, farmers will apply more water to the field than the crops need. But the salty percolation water will cause the water table to rise. Drainage to control the water table, therefore, also serves to control the salinity of the soil.

DIFFERENT TYPES OF DRAINAGE

Drainage can be either natural or artificial. Many areas have some natural drainage; this means that excess water flows from the farmers' fields to swamps or to lakes and rivers. Natural drainage, however, is often inadequate and artificial or man-made drainage is required. There are two types of artificial drainage: Surface drainage and subsurface drainage.

Surface Drainage

Surface drainage is the removal of excess water from the surface of the land. This is normally accomplished by shallow ditches, also called open drains. The shallow ditches discharge into larger and deeper collector drains. In order to facilitate the flow of excess water towards the drains, the field is given an artificial slope by means of land grading.

Subsurface Drainage

Subsurface drainage is the removal of water from the rootzone. It is accomplished by deep open drains or buried pipe drains.

Pipe Drains

Pipe drains are buried pipes with openings through which the soil water can enter. The pipes convey the water to a collector drain.

Drain pipes are made of clay, concrete or plastic. They are usually placed in trenches by machines. In clay and concrete pipes (usually 30 cm long and 5 - 10 cm in diameter) drainage water enters the pipes through the joints. Flexible plastic drains are much longer (up to 200 m) and the water enters through perforations distributed over the entire length of the pipe.

Open drains use land that otherwise could be used for crops. They restrict the use of machines. They also require a large number of bridges and culverts for road crossings and access to the fields. Open drains require frequent maintenance (weed control, repairs, etc.).

In contrast to open drains, buried pipes cause no loss of cultivable land and maintenance requirements are very limited. The installation costs, however, of pipe drains may be higher due to the materials, the equipment and the skilled manpower involved.

Deep Open Drains

The excess water from the rootzone flows into the open drains. The disadvantage of this type of subsurface drainage is that it makes the use of machinery difficult.

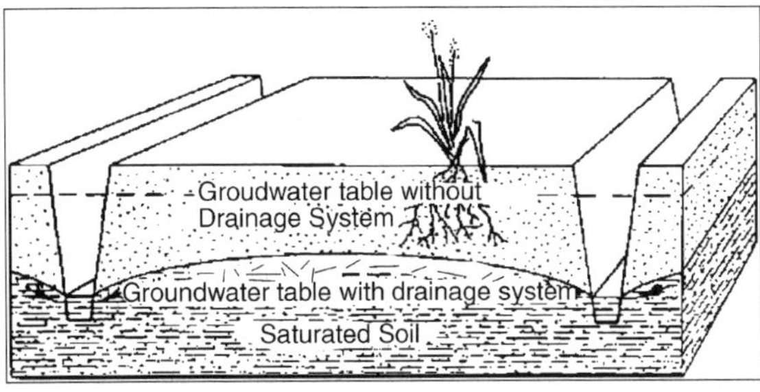

Fig. Control of the Groundwater Table by Means of Deep Open Drains

SOILS SALINIZATION

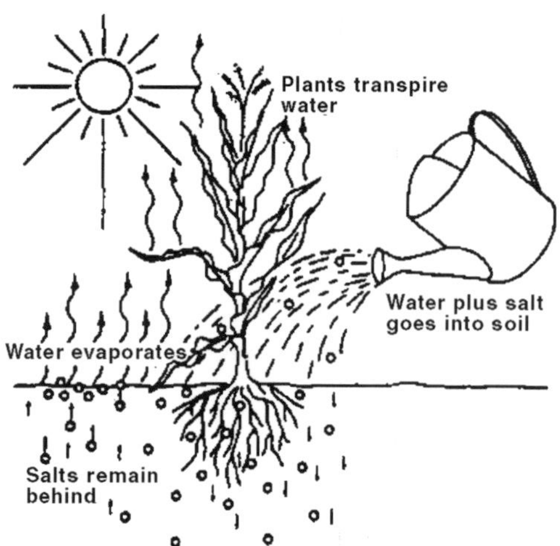

Fig. Salinization, Caused by Salty Irrigation Water

A soil may be rich in salts because the parent rock from which it was formed contains salts. Sea water is another source of salts in low-lying areas along the coast. A very common source of salts in irrigated soils is the irrigation water itself. Most irrigation waters contain some salts. After irrigation, the water added to the soil is used by the crop or evaporates directly from the moist soil. The salt, however, is left behind in the soil. If not removed, it accumulates in the soil; this process is called salinization.

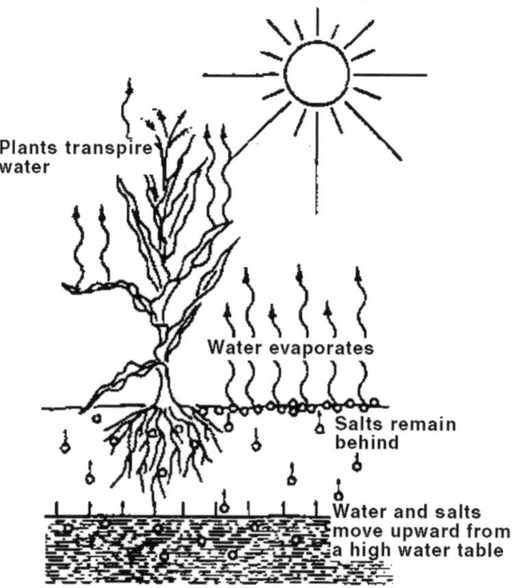

Fig. Salinization, Caused by a High

Very salty soils are sometimes recognizable by a white layer of dry salt on the soil surface. Salty groundwater may also contribute to salinization. When the water table rises (*e.g.* following irrigation in the absence of proper drainage), the salty groundwater may reach the upper soil layers and, thus, supply salts to the rootzone.Soils that contain a harmful amount of salt are often referred to as salty or saline soils. Soil, or water, that has a high content of salt is said to have a high salinity.

WATER SALINITY

Water salinity is the amount of salt contained in the water. It is also called the "salt concentration" and may be expressed in grams of salt per litre of water (grams/litre or g/l) or in milligrams per litre (which is the same as parts per million, p.p.m). However, the salinity of both water and soil is easily measured by means of an electrical device. It is then expressed in terms of electrical conductivity: millimhos/cm or micromhos/cm. A salt concentration of 1 gram per litre is about 1.5 millimhos/cm. Thus a concentration of 3 grams per litre will be about the same as 4.5 millimhos/cm.

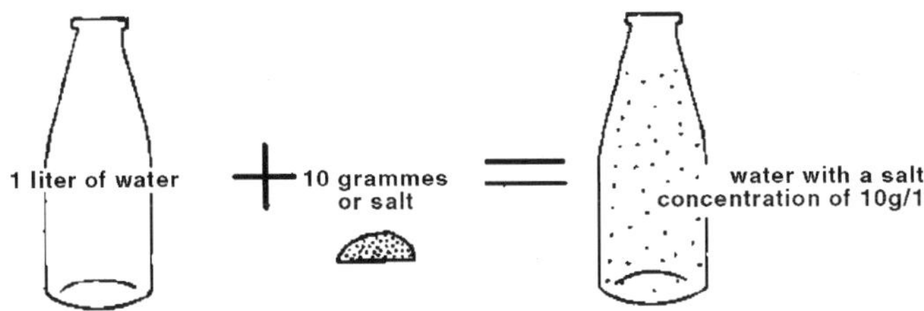

Fig. A Salt Concentration of 10 g/l

Soil Salinity

The salt concentration in the water extracted from a saturated soil (called saturation extract) defines the salinity of this soil. If this water contains less than 3 grams of salt per litre, the soil is said to be non saline. If the salt concentration of the saturation extract contains more than 12 g/l, the soil is said to be highly saline.

Table. Salt Concentration of the Soil Water (Saturation Extract)

In g/l	*In Millimhos/cm*	*Salinity*
0 - 3	0 - 4.5	non saline
3 - 6	4.5 - 9	slightly saline
6 - 12	9 - 18	medium saline
more than 12	more than 18	highly saline

CROPS AND SALINE SOILS

Most crops do not grow well on soils that contain salts. One reason is that salt causes a reduction in the rate and amount of water that the plant roots can take up from the soil. Also, some salts are toxic to plants when present in high concentration. Some plants are more tolerant to a high salt concentration than others. Some examples are given in the following table:

Highly Tolerant	*Moderately Tolerant*	*Sensitive*
Date palm	Wheat	Red clover
Barley	Tomato	Peas
Sugarbeet	Oats	Beans
Cotton	Alfalfa	Sugarcane
Asparagus	Rice	Pear
Spinach	Maize	Apple
	Flax	Orange
	Potatoes	Prune
	Carrot	Plum
	Onion	Almond
	Cucumber	Apricot
	Pomegranate	Peach
	Fig	
	Olive	
	Grape	

The highly tolerant crops can withstand a salt concentration of the saturation extract up to 10 g/l. The moderately tolerant crops can withstand salt concentration up to 5 g/l. The limit of the sensitive group is about 2.5 g/l.

Sodicity

Salty soils usually contain several types of salt. One of these is sodium salt. Where the concentration of sodium salts is high relative to other types of salt, a sodic soil may develop.

Sodic soils are characterized by a poor soil structure: they have a low infiltration rate, they are poorly aerated and difficult to cultivate. Thus, sodic soils adversely affect the plants' growth.

IMPROVEMENT OF SALINE AND SODIC SOILS

Numerous areas in the world are naturally saline or sodic or have become saline due to improper irrigation practices. Crop growth on many of these is poor. However, their productivity can be improved by a number of measures.

Improvement of Saline Soils

Improvement of a saline soil implies the reduction of the salt concentration of the soil to a level that is not harmful to the crops. To that end, more water is applied to the field than is required for crop growth. This additional water infiltrates into the soil and percolates through the rootzone. During percolation, it takes up part of the salts in the soil and takes these along to deeper soil layers.

In fact, the water washes the salts out of the rootzone. This washing process is called leaching.

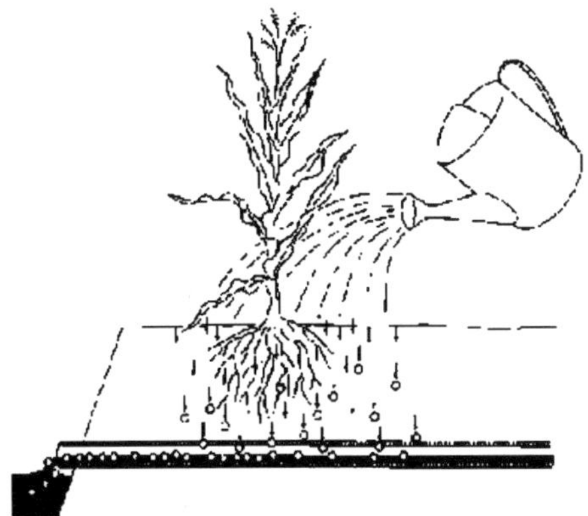

Fig. Leaching of Salts

The additional water required for leaching must be removed from the rootzone by means of a subsurface drainage system. If not removed, it could cause a rise of the groundwater table which would bring the salts back into the rootzone.

Thus, improvement of saline soils includes, essentially, leaching and subsurface drainage.

PREVENTION OF SALINIZATION

Soils will become salty if salts are allowed to accumulate. Proper irrigation management and adequate drainage are not only important measures for the improvement of salty soils, they are also essential for the prevention of salinization.

Irrigation Water Quality

The suitability of water for irrigation depends on the amount and the type of salt the irrigation water contains. The higher the salt concentration of the irrigation water, the greater the risk of salinization. The following Table gives an idea of the risk of salinization:

Salt Concentration of the Irrigation water in g/l	*Soil Salinization risk*	*Restriction on use*
Less than 0.5 g/l	No risk	No restriction on its use
0.5 - 2 g/l	Slight to moderate risk	should be used with approp riate water management practices
More than 2 g/l	High Risk	Not generally advised for use unless consulted with specialists

The type of salt in the irrigation water will influence the risk of developing sodicity: the higher the concentration of sodium present in the irrigation water (particularly compared to other soils), the higher the risk.

Irrigation Management and Drainage

Irrigation systems are never fully efficient. Some water is always lost in canals and on the farmers' fields. Part of this seeps into the soil. While this will help leach salt out of the rootzone, it will also contribute to a rise of the water table; a high water table is risky because it may cause the salts to return to the rootzone. Therefore, both the water losses and the water table must be strictly controlled. This requires careful management of the irrigation system and a good subsurface drainage system.

AGRICULTURAL WATER CRISIS

The agriculture development in China relies more and more heavily on water sources. Based on the analysis of the existing problems and the improvement of society, science and technology, rational development and high efficient use of agricultural water resources is unique strategy accounting for water crisis involving in grain supply to 1.6 billion Chinese in the mid-21st century. Water crisis is affected by many factors. The following countermeasures should be taken:

ENERGETICALLY INCREASING INPUT TO THE CONSTRUCTION

While the development of water saving in agriculture, the input to the construction of water conservancy infrastructure should be increased so as to develop various water source for irrigation. Some important water projects for the development of national economy should be constructed to change the status of water shortage in the north part of China and the coastal regions, to improve the production condition of the important production bases of grain and cotton, and to promote the agriculture development.

Developing rain irrigation is very important not only to the agriculture development on rain-fed land, but also to the high efficient use of irrigation water and the relaxation of contradiction between the demand and the supply. The utilization degree of rain and flood during flood season should be raised by structure and non-structure measures in order to combine flood control with generating benefit, *i.e.* utilizing resources while controlling disaster. It will play an outstanding role in relaxation of water crisis and flood disaster. The treatment and reuse of wastewater and low quality water will not only relax the water crisis in irrigation, but also improve and protect the ecological environment.

Vigorously Developing High Efficient Use of Agricultural Water Use

At present, the production efficiency of irrigation water is still less than 40%, accordingly which decrease the utilization efficiency of rain and irrigation water and worsen the water crisis. The water production efficiency can be improved by taking synthesis agricultural measures to decrease crop's invalid water consumption. These agricultural measures include: planting the crops and breed with the characteristics of low water consumption and high production; improving utilization ratio of soil water and protecting soil moisture; high efficient allocation and control of water and fertilizer; covering planting; improving crop's drought resistance and water utilization efficiency by chemical measures.

The development of high efficient use of agricultural water use relies not only on technology, but also on the following sufficient studies: studying and establishing the strategy and target of the development of agricultural water saving; study on the basic gist putting forward the general target and task of agricultural water saving; for different stage and region, study on the requirement on agricultural water saving by national economy development, the national economic base supporting the development of agricultural water saving, farmer's income, investment ability and interesting, as well as the development strategy and technologic principle; for different stage, study on the mechanism prompting agricultural water saving and its change and control measures; study on the stage of industrialization of agricultural water saving.

The development of high efficient use of agricultural water use must be sustainable and accord with the following three criterions: firstly, sustainablity–can effectively protect, rationally and high efficiently utilize water resources and make the utilization sustainable; Secondly, efficiency-can markedly raise economic efficiency, including water saving, production increase, land saving, energy saving, ecological environmental benefit, profit of non-agricultural capital input, and so on; Finally, high scientific and technological characteristic-should be scientific and technologic and can fully meet the requirement on high efficient use of agricultural water use at different development stage.

High Efficient use of agricultural water use is the foundation supporting the sustainable development of agricultural and the sustainable utilization of water resources.

Energetically Improving and Protecting

The simple improvement with protection target should be transferred to the improvement with exploitation target in order to combine tightly ecological benefit with economic benefit. The exploitation should be combined with and promotes the improvement. Strengthening the construction of water conservancy infrastructure on farmland in order to raise the farmland's ability of resisting water-logging and saline disasters, and rationally utilize the water resources. The pollution of the agricultural water resources should be effectively prevented and improved by the rational and effective use of fertilizer and bad water source.

Intensifying the Management For High Efficient

It is recognized in the World that 50% of potential of irrigation water saving is from the improvement of management. There is a very big gap in management plane of water resources between China and the developed countries. Firstly, the policies and codes prompting high efficient use of water resources are not perfect. There is short of mechanism and management measures encouraging high efficient use of agricultural water use. Secondly, the technical system supporting high efficient use of water resources has not been established. The potential of water resources far has not been fully developed. Thirdly, there is short of engineering measure which can support the improvement of management, because of the low project standards of many agricultural water projects.

Therefore, to resolve the water crisis, the water management must be changed from an extensive pattern to an intensive pattern, including:

- Establishing the management system supporting rational and high efficient use of water resources to make the unified management of water resources available.
- Establishing the price system prompting rational use of water resources to form a sound market mechanism for the management of water use.
- Establishing the guarantee system prompting high efficient use of agricultural water use, including investment mechanism.

Strengthening Scientific Study and Research

With the contradiction between the demand and the supply is day and day outstanding and the national economy is developing, many technical problems related to the high efficient water use are waiting for resolving and new technical problems appear in succession. All the problems need to be profoundly studied. The technical integration and innovate system supporting the high efficient use of agricultural water use should be established. The science and education should benefit the development of water resources. The development of series products of high efficient water use should be strengthened. The efficiency of water use should be raised.

Reforming the Mechanism of Water Management

The technical reform and management system reform of irrigation districts must be pressed on to reach the target of high efficient use of water resources and solidify the agricultural production on irrigated area on which the crop's production account for third-fourth of the entire country. The technical reform of irrigation districts is basis of high efficient water use, and the management system reform of irrigation districts is its assurance. The management system reform of irrigation districts will benefit not only for the exertion and increase of value of state's capital, but also for the sustainable development of irrigation agriculture and high efficient water use, even for food security. So it is one of the important measures accounting for the water crisis, and is also a key component of the prosecution and management system reform in agriculture and rural. This reform should be in line with the development of market agriculture and integration of prosecution to be one part of the socialism market economy.

Because of the limit of natural condition, immense requirement of the society and economy development, weak economic base, and so on, the sustainable development of agriculture is facing severe water crisis. With the population increase, people's living standard raise and cultivated land decrease, the press on cultivated land, specially on irrigated cultivated land, will be more and more heavy. Water will dominate the fortune of China's agriculture and the survival and development of 1.6 billion Chinese in the 21st century. Based on the analysis of water crisis, social practice and the advancement of science and technology, the essential measure accounting for the water crisis faced by the sustainable development of agriculture is high efficient use of agricultural water use. The raise of water use efficiency and water production efficiency is key strategic measure related to the survival and development of 1.6 billion Chinese in the 21st century.

The development of agriculture and water is a huge system engineering. The water crisis must be roundly resolved from system viewpoint. It should be realised the water's complexity. Don't keep eyes only on water. The problem of water resources should be roundly resolved from system viewpoint and by means of carrying out the comprehensive prevention and cure strategy, to reach effect which is more than the addition of single strategy's effect.The utilization efficiency and production efficiency of water resources must be raised by means of system engineering and carrying out the comprehensive measures including water projects, agricultural biologic measure, modern management technology, information engineering technology and meteorology, to basically resolve the contradiction between water supply and demand, and to support the rapid development of society and economy in China in the 21st century.

WATER CRISIS LIMITS THE AGRICULTURE

Since the founding of the People's Republic of China, a large amount of water conservancy infrastructure have been constructed and strongly encouraged the development of the industry and agriculture and urban construction, resisted flood, protected environment, and obviously raised the people's living standards. With the increase in population and rapid development of the society and economy, the water supply obviously cannot meet the water demand and resulted in water shortage.

According to statistics, drought disaster bring with more serious affection than flood disaster. Therefore, a critical problem facing by the development of China's society and economy is how to satisfy the water demand of society and economy.

Water shortage resulted in:

- The production from rain-fed land which area is more than 50% of total cultivated area in China has to rely on climate, and is low and unstable. Consequently, the agricultural development has badly been limited.
- The water shortage resulted from water pollution is also remarkable.
- In the northern part of China, a series of the ecological and environmental problems occurred and day and day worsened, including drying up of rivers, bad overdraft of groundwater, decline of groundwater table in broad area, and so on.
- Large amounts of wastewater and sewage without treatment have been directly and indirectly used for irrigation, specially in the northern part of China, and gradually become an important component part of agricultural water use. The use of wastewater and sewage without treatment resulted in the pollution of soil water in farmland and groundwater and the excess content of pollutants in agricultural products which are harmful to the people's health. This kind of harm is very severe.

Except for the water shortage and the water environmental problem, China's water crisis still includes the frequent flood disaster and the low capability of resisting natural disasters. Flood disaster is still a serious danger to the sustainable development of China's agriculture.

WATER CRISIS IN THE 21ST CENTURY IN CHINA

The water demand and supply in the 21st century in China will face:

- Due to too fast increase in water demand and limited increase in water supply, the lag between demand and supply will further be widened;
- Because of the existing water source drying up, water projects aging and inadequate maintenance, and so on, the water supply sharp decline;
- In the northern part of China, the available water supply obviously decrease with deep development of water resources and the water consumption increase in river basin;
- The warmer and warmer climate may aggravate water crisis;
- With industrial and domestic water use increase, water pollution will more and more seriously threaten water supply and safety of water use;
- People don't fully understand the seriousness of water crisis, thereby water projects aren't enough and management is backward. Water supply lag water demand with extravagant water use. The low water use efficiency and water production efficiency further worsen the water crisis.

The 21st century will be an era of the great development of economy, and an era which China's population will reach the peak of 1.6 billion. Water is an important constraining factor for the economy development. If the problem of water shortage cannot be resolved, the sustainable development of society and economy must be seriously imperiled.

Moreover, the water crisis mainly affect the agriculture development by:

- Competition for water among regions, between industry and agriculture, between urban and rural, will continue for a long time and be more serious.
- Competition for water between agriculture and environment will stand out, specially in the northern part of China.
- With the development of economy and the raise of people's living standards, the water demand by other agriculture, including forestry, animal husbandry, fishery and subsidiary, must extremely increase. Accordingly, competition for water within agriculture sector will be more outstanding.

THE DEVELOPMENT OF IRRIGATION AREA AND AGRICULTURAL WATER USE

Rural economy rapidly developed and grain production steady increased, but the increment of agricultural water use was limited. Though the actual irrigation water use is affected by many factors including yearly hydrologic and meteorologic conditions, the general trend of water use in the whole country still can be concluded.

The decrease of irrigation water use was mainly due to effective agricultural water saving and shortage of water supply for agriculture in water scarcity regions.

With the development and popularization of agricultural water saving, the efficiency of agricultural water use is being raised. The actual irrigation area increased by about 8,200 thousand hm^2 from 1980 to 1999, but the change of irrigation water use was tiny. In general, the average water use per hm^2 decreased from 8,750 m^3 in 1980 to 7,270 m^3 in 1999. The water use of per unit area decreased by 17%. These agricultural statistics are shown in Table. The water use by forest, herd and fishery fast increased while irrigation water use decreasing. Sequentially, the water demand by ecological environment had better been met.

Table. Irrigation Area and Water Use

Year	*Irrigation Water Use (B m^3)*	*Actual Irrigation Area (10^3 hm^2)*	*Unit water use (m^3/hm^2)*
1980	358.1	40 920	8 750
1999	356.4	49 090	7 260
Increment	–1.7	8 170	–1 490

WATER DEMAND

Based on the analysis of the relationship between water resources and the sustainable development of national economy, the characteristic of water resources, factors of water resources rational allocation supporting the sustainable development, status of water use and supply, as well as the existing problems, the water demand before the mid-21st century have been predicted.

The prediction on water demand by industry, agriculture and domesticity in different target years are shown in Table.

Table. Prediction on Water Demand (B m^3)

Year	*Urban*	*Rural*	*Industry*	*Irrigation*	*Other Agriculture*	*Total*
2010	40.5	30.2	149.8	387.9	34.0	642.4
2030	64.1	30.9	191.1	387.2	38.5	711.8
2050	81.5	30.6	199.8	377.5	42.5	731.9

Table indicates the basic increasing trend of water use: faster increasing of industrial and domestic water use, little increasing of agricultural water use, steady growth of proportion of industrial and domestic water use in total water use, decrease of proportion of agricultural water use. However, because of natural condition, the agricultural development in China has to rely on irrigation.

So the proportion of irrigation water use in total national economy water use always is highest among the sectors. According to the status and the development trend, three main problems, such as flood disaster, water shortage and water environment worsen, especially the water shortage will more and more heavily limit the development of agriculture, society and economy.

How to resolve the contradiction between the sustainable development of agriculture and water supply is one of the focus related to the sustainable development of society and economy.

CURVE NUMBERS, RECENT DEVELOPMENTS

The Curve Number procedure of the U.S. Dept. of Agriculture, Natural Resources Conservation Service (NRCS) (formerly Soil Conservation Service, SCS) has elicited questions and concern since its conception. This arises, for the most part, because users read into the procedure what they wish was covered. The actual intent of the procedure is often disregarded. Too, the basic reference for Curve Numbers, the National Engineering Handbook of the SCS, has been revised several times, not always by individuals or committees that understood the significance of their statements. The Natural Resources Conservation Service and the Agricultural Research Service, both agencies of the U.S. Department of Agriculture, formed a joint work group to assess the state of the Curve Number procedure and to chart its future development.

The joint work group recognized three distinctly different modes of application for Curve Numbers:

1. Determination of run-off volume of a given return period, given total event rainfall for that return period;
2. Determine direct run-off for individual events, explaining the variability from event to event, as used in continuous simulation models;
3. Determine infiltration rates for short time intervals as used with unit hydrograph development of flood hydrographs.

The first mode of application represents the historical basis of the procedure, so receives the most attention. Use as a surrogate for an infiltration is very common and follows from the historical basis, so must be considered. The application in continuous simulation models is an extension beyond the scope of the committee.

Discussions within the committee made it apparent that a portion of the difficulty surrounding the procedure was attributable to the presentation of the procedure in the National Engineering Handbook.

The first task then was to rewrite those portions of the Handbook pertaining to the procedure. Problems identified ranged from incorrect and misleading statements to incomplete documentation. For example, it was incorrectly stated that S includes Ia, whereas it can be shown mathematically that S does not include Ia.

Fortunately, this is only significant for continuous simulation. Another example was a table that related antecedent rainfall to antecedent moisture condition (AMC). This was not intended to have nationwide application, though it was treated as such. Folklore concerning Curve Numbers could also be attributed to problems with documentation. A folklore example is that the Curve Number Run-off Equation is an infiltration equation.

In rewriting the Curve Number portions of the Handbook, the work group agreed that:

- Committee must Abelieve in≅ concepts expressed;
- References will be included if possible; and
- Results must be technically defensible.

The results of the rewrite include such items as:

- Reference to Antecedent Moisture Condition (AMC) was removed. Variability is incorporated by considering the curve number as a random variable and the AMC–I and AMC–III conditions as bounds on the distribution.
- Reiteration of desirability of locally determined curve numbers. This was part of the original documentation but tended to be neglected.
- Explicit expression of Curve Number run-off equation as a transformation of rainfall frequency distribution to run-off frequency distribution. This was demonstrated in the original documentation but again was often neglected.

- Expression of AMC-I and AMC–III as measures of dispersion about the central tendency (AMC II). This is a corollary of treating the CN as a random variable.
- Mathematical proof showing that S does not include Ia. This is only significant because of the previous missunderstanding.

As the work group progressed on the rewriting, they reached a level of agreement on principles allowing work to begin on two other areas of need. These were to reconsider the hydrologic soils classifications recognizing the vastly expanded data base available today and the capabilities of modern computers, and to reconsider the tables of curve numbers in terms of the expanded rainfall-run-off database available.

CONCEPT OF HYDROLOGIC SOIL GROUPS

There has been a vast increase in basic soils property data since Musgrave first proposed the concept of hydrologic soil groups in Handbook of Agriculture. The data are now available in an electronic database. Modern tools of data mining were explored for analysis of this mass of data. Both neural networks and fuzzy sets were tried with fuzzy sets being adopted.

Originally, Soil Hydrologic Groups were assigned to soil series and phase of series by soil scientists based upon their interpretation of the published criteria. The soil scientist=s interpretation of the published criteria has varied across time and between states or regions. Thus, the hydrologic group criteria are not applied consistently across the United States. This is most evident in the comparison of soils with similar soil hydrologic and physical properties and dissimilar hydrologic group placement.

The Hydrologic Soil Groups are A, B, C, D and dual groups A/D, B/D and C/D. Soils in hydrologic group A have low run-off potential. Soils that have a moderate rate of infiltration when thoroughly wet are in hydrologic group B. Hydrologic group C soils that have a slow rate of infiltration rate when thoroughly wet. Soils in hydrologic group D have a high run-off potential. Dual Hydrologic Soil Groups (A/D, B/D, and C/D) are given for certain wet soils that could be adequately drained. The first letter applies to the drained and the second to the undrained condition. Soils are assigned to dual groups if the shallow depth to a permanent water table is the sole criteria for assigning a soil to hydrologic group D.

A model or rule based automated system that provides for objective placement of soils into Hydrologic Soil Groups was developed. The fuzzy system model for assigning soils to hydrologic soil groups is based on the published hydrologic group assumptions and criteria.

The soil surface is taken to be bare and the soil is not permanently frozen. The soil physical and hydrologic characteristic which make up the hydrologic grouping criteria are the depth to permanent water, depth to a restrictive layer, minimum saturated hydraulic conductivity in the soil=s upper 100 cm, and the soil=s texture.

There are three components to the fuzzy systems model: the Property, the Evaluation, and the Rule. The Property is an SQL (Standard Query Language) statement that retrieves the needed soil data from the soil survey database. An example of a Property is the depth to a restrictive layer.

The Evaluation=s function is to apply the data received from the SQL statement to a statement of the property=s relevance to the soil=s hydrologic grouping. In the case of the depth to a restrictive layer, the Evaluation determines the fit or truthfulness of the statement, AThe run-off characteristics of the soil increases as a soil=s depth a restrictive layer becomes shallower.

At some depth, the restrictive layer in the soil has a maximum contribution to run-off and the Evaluation is true. The result of an Evaluation is some number between 0 and 1. This number represents the truthfulness of the statement being evaluated.

The closer the number is to 1 the closer the soil=s property fits the grouping criterion. Conversely, the closer the number is to 0 the less the soil property=s contribution to the hydrologic grouping of soils. In the restrictive layer example, an Evaluation output of 1 would mean that the soil=s restrictive layer is shallower than 50cm. Any output less than 1 would mean that the depth to any soil restrictive layer is greater than 50cm. This numeric output from the evaluation is passed to the Rule. The Rule is the third component of the fuzzy system model. The Rule serves two functions that result in a soil=s Hydrologic Soil Group placement.

The first function is to provide tools for the construction and implementation of the grouping system=s model and to bring the various hydrologic grouping criterion evaluations together into a single Hydrologic Soil Group model. The second is to convert the model=s numeric output into a Hydrologic Soil Group. The model was applied to 1828 unique soil phases using data from Kansas, South Dakota, Missouri, Iowa, Wyoming, and Colorado and the correlation between these soils= assigned and modeled hydrologic grouping was analysed. Table shows a detailed comparison by Hydrologic Soil Group between the currently assigned HSG and the modeled HSG. The correlation between the assigned and modeled HSG A and HSG D soils is higher than the correlation between the assigned and modeled HSG B and HSG C soils.

There are several reasons for the poorer correlation between the assigned and modeled groups B and C. The first is that of the boundary condition which occurs when a soil has properties that do not fit entirely into a single hydrologic group. In this case, the soil scientist may have placed the soil into one HSG while the model placed the soil into an adjacent group. Groups B and C are the most prone to this error because they are bounded by two groups whereas HSG A and D are only bounded by one group.

Another source of correlation inconsistency is that the assigned HSG may be relatively correct, but the data in the database may not support the corresponding HSG determination by the model. Finally, correlation inconsistencies can be attributed to the fuzzy modeling of the subjective Hydrologic Soil Group criteria.

Table. Correlation Frequency Between Assigned and Fuzzy Modeled Hydrologic Soil Groups

Current HSG	Number of Soils	Fuzzy hsg Assignment Frequency A	B	C	D	A/D	B/D	C/D
A	155	0.9	0.08	0	0.01	0.01	0	0
B	821	0.25	0.54	0.17	0.02	0.01	0	0
C	405	0.04	0.25	0.34	0.31	0	0.03	0.04
D	404	0.02	0.05	0.05	0.64	0.06	0.1	0.08
A/D	1	0	0	0	0	0	0.55	0
B/D	29	0.1	0.07	0.07	0	0.1	0.31	0.1
C/D	13	0	0.08	0.08	0.39	0		0.15

CURVE NUMBERS FROM RAINFALL-RUN-OFF DATA

The watershed research programme of the USDA, Agricultural Research Service is a continuation of research initiated by the Soil Conservation Service. Much of the data collected should be directly applicable to the determination of curve numbers and to explaining the variation of curve number with the soil-cover complex. In addition, Prof. R. H. Hawkins of the University of Arizona had been developing the world=s largest event rainfall–run-off data base with software to analyse the data. Prof. Hawkins was added to the ARS/NRCS work group.

The ideal method of determining curve numbers from observed data is elusive due to the stochastic nature of the variable. Our decision to emphasize the concept that the run-off equation serves to transform a rainfall frequency distribution into a run-off frequency distribution led to use of frequency matching.

That is, curve numbers were determined by use of rainfall of a given return period with run-off of the same return period. These data may or may not come from the same storm. That is, frequency transformation leads to treating ordered pairs. In his analysis, Hawkins recognized that not all data sets are adequate to define a curve number and some watersheds do not even perform according to the Curve Number run-off equation.

He developed a graphical procedure in which the calculated curve number is plotted versus the precipitation used in calculating that curve number. In part, this plot is in recognition that, due to the random nature of the curve number, for a watershed with a given Atrue@ curve number, the actual event curve number will range above and below that Atrue@ value. For small rainfall events the event Ia will vary above and below the Atrue@ Ia. Curve numbers can only be determined if there is run-off, so if the event Ia is low, run-off will occur and a CN computed. If the Ia is high, no run-off occurs so no CN can be computed.

Thus, the process of computing CN for small events biases the CN towards high values (low Ia). The CN vs. P plot displays this bias and the storm magnitude at which the bias becomes insignificant.

The concept of the CN method being a transformation between a rainfall-depth distribution and a run-off depth distribution is applied in treating rainfall and run-off data. The rainfall depths and the run-off depths are sorted separately and then re–aligned on a rank order basis to form P:Q pairs of equal return period. The individual runoffs are not necessarily associated with the original causative rainfalls.

When CNs are calculated from real storm data as outlined above, a secondary relationship almost always emerges between CN and storm rainfall depth itself. In most of these cases, these calculated CNs approach a constant value with increasing rainfall.Three variations on this theme have been observed, however, and are described in the following:

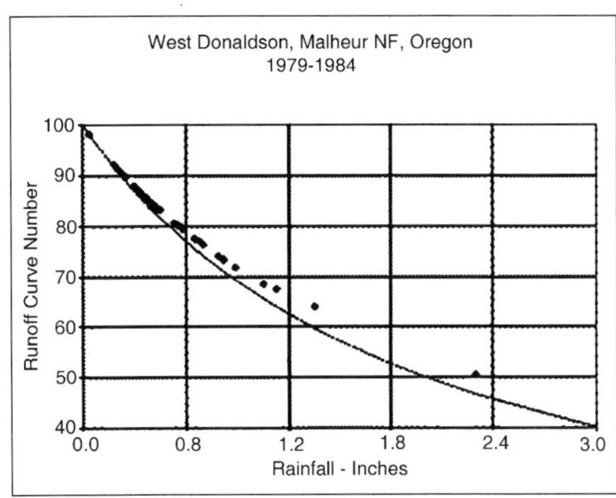

Fig. Complacent Behaviour

Complacent Behaviour

Here the observed CN declines steadily with increasing rainfall depth, and with no appreciable tendency to achieve a stable value. An example of this is given in Figure above. Curve Numbers cannot be safely determined from data which exhibit this pattern, because no constant value is clearly approached. This Curve Number behaviour has been found to indicate a partial source area situation where the source area fraction may be quite small. In these cases the run-off is more properly modeled by the linear form Q=CP rather than by the Curve Number run-off equation.

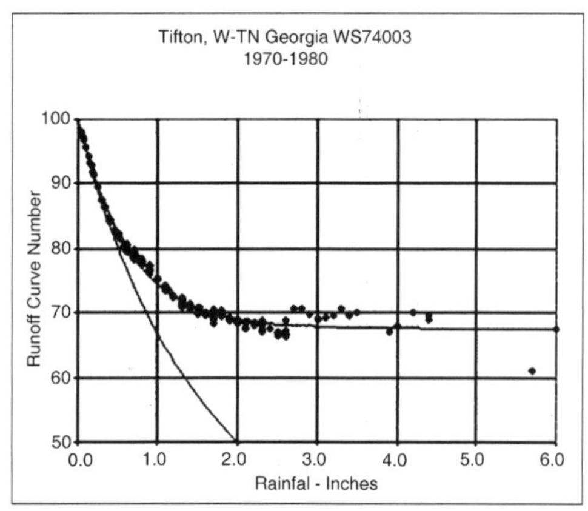

Standard Behaviour

This is the most common scenario. The observed CN declines with increasing storm size, as in the Complacent situation described. However, here the CNs approach and/or maintain a near–constant value with increasingly larger storms. The run-off itself may arise from a variety of source processes, including overland flow and rapid subsurface flow. An example of this pattern is given in Figure.

Violent Behaviour

The distinguishing feature here is that the observed CNs rise suddenly and asymptotically approach an apparent constant value. There is often accompanying Complacent behaviour at lower rainfalls. From a source process standpoint, this could be a threshold phenomenon at some critical rainfall depth value. Rietz and Hawkins used their large electronic database of rainfall-run-off data to determine data-defined CNs calculated from local rainfall-run-off data. Their study attempted to develop a better understanding of a watershed=s land use as manifested in its CN. The land use variable was isolated in a large data set of small watersheds, and land use CN=s were calculated and analysed for each of these watersheds at a local, regional, and national scale.

Data in this study contained detailed land use information on 177 watersheds covering 2,455 years of record and 32,891 events. Watershed land uses analysed in this study were: alfalfa (closec–seed legume), corn (row crop), cotton (row crop), desert shrub, fallow, forest, grassland, meadow, oats (small grain), pasture, range, sage brush, sorghum (row crop), soy bean (row crop) and wheat (small grain). Many of the cultivated watersheds had a different land use year to year due to crop rotation. When one watershed had several land uses throughout the period of record, data were segregated by date of land use and CN calculated for each land use. Curve Numbers for each land use on each watershed were determined using the Asym-ptotic data-derived procedure with ordered P:Q pairs.

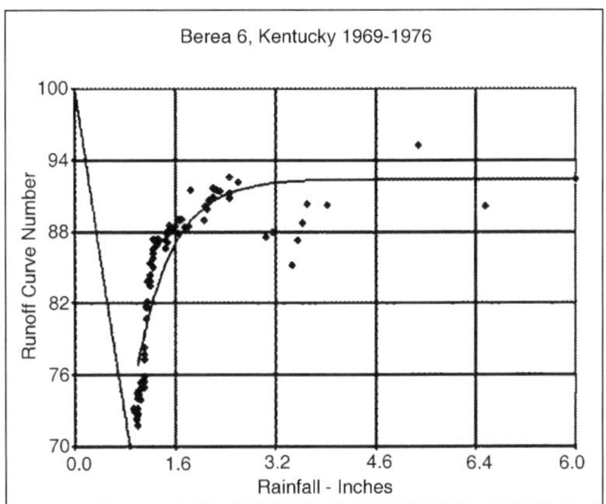

Fig. Violent Behaviour

Differences in land use CN at the local level can be attributed solely to a change in hydrological response of a watershed due to land use because all other input variables of the Curve Number model are constant.

Soil type, climate, and morphology are fixed, and watershed land conditions are constant for that land use. Of the 177 watersheds used in this study, 53 were found to have more than one land use during their period of record.

When ANOVA independent group tests were performed 96.23% of the watersheds (51 out of 53) were found to have significant differences among their land use Curve Numbers.

The results were:

- Meadow Curve Numbers were almost always the lowest CN for a watershed. Of the 19 watersheds that had a meadow in their crop rotation, 13 had meadow Curve Numbers significantly lower than any other land use CN within that same watershed. Three others had meadow Curve Numbers that ranked second lowest.
- Pasture is a grassland watershed that is grazed. This CN was generally significantly higher (6 out of 8 times) than all other land use Curve Numbers on a given watershed.
- Watersheds that experienced a land conversion had a significant difference in their data-derived CN after the conversion. Two desert watersheds in the Boco Mountains of Colorado were converted from desert brush to grass and with both, the grass Curve Number was significantly lower than desert brush. Another land use conversion study was at Riesel, Texas watershed #42036. This ARS experimental watershed was 100% rangeland that was Ainfested≅ with honey mesquite. In 1972 the watershed was treated, at which time the mesquites were killed and left standing. The Curve Number following mesquite killing was statistically higher than for live mesquites.

In order to compare land use Curve Numbers across all locations, a land use had to have been applied in more than one location, which was found to be the case with 11 single land uses. Seven of these 11 land uses (63.6%) exhibited a significant difference. The rank order of Curve Numbers was: forest and meadow were among the lowest average Curve Number, row crops or small grain were in mid-range, and desert brush exhibited the highest average Curve Number. Small grains (wheat and oats) were grouped together as were row crops (soybean, corn and sorghum). It was surprising however, that the average Curve Number for range was the third lowest average Curve Number and that row crops had a lower average CN than small grains.

The results of the work group are:

- The basic description of the Curve Number procedure is more clear, more consistent, and is in a more technically defensible state.
- The Hydrologic Soil Groups are associated with soil physical properties through fuzzy set procedures.
- Procedures for determining Curve Numbers from local data and interpretation of the results are much better established.

However, more work is needed. For example, we still need to work at verifying, adjusting, and correcting the table of CN. Regional variation in Curve Numbers should be explored. Finally, the whole issue of the application of Curve Numbers in continuous simulation models (CREAMS, GLEAMS, EPIC, SWAT) may be quite different from the design storm Curve Numbers of NEH–4. If there is a relation, that relation should be determined.

WATER PROBLEM IN INDIA

Summers are here and the cities in India are already complaining about water shortage not to mention many villages which lack safe drinking water. In the list of 122 countries rated on quality of portable water, India ranks a lowly 120.

Although India has 4% of the world's water, studies show average availability is shrinking steadily. It is estimated that by 2020, India will become a water-stressed nation. Nearly 50% of villages still don't have any source of protected drinking water. According to 2001 census 68.2% households have access to safe drinking water. The department of drinking water supply estimates that 94% of rural habitations and 91% urban households have access to drinking water. But according to experts these figures are misleading simply because coverage refers to installed capacity and not actual supply.

The ground reality is that of the 1.42 million villages in India, 1, 95,813 are affected by chemical contamination of water. The quality of ground water which accounts of more than 85% of domestic supply is a major problem in many areas as none of the rivers have water fit to drink. 37.7 million People –over 75% of whom are children are afflicted by waterborne diseases every year.

Overdependence on groundwater has brought in contaminants, fluoride being one of them. Nearly 66 million people in 20 states are at risk because of the excessive fluoride in water. While the permissible limit of fluoride in water is 1 mg per litre in states like Haryana it is as high as 48 mg in some places. Delhi water too has 32 mg. But the worst hits are Rajasthan, Gujarat and Andhra Pradesh. Nearly 6 million children below 14 suffer from dental, skeletal and non-skeletal fluorosis.

Arsenic is the other big killer lurking in ground water putting at risk nearly 10 million people. The problem is acute in Murshidabad, Nadia, North and South 24 Paraganas, Malda and Vardhaman districts of West Bengal. The deeper aquifers in the entire Gangetic plains contain arsenic.

High nitrate content in water is another serious concern. Fertilizers, septic tanks, sewage tanks etc. are the main sources of nitrate contamination. The groundwater in MP, UP, Punjab, Haryana, Delhi, Kanataka and Tamil Nadu has shown traces of nitrates.

However it is bacteriological contamination which leads to diarrhoea, cholera and hepatitis which is widespread in India. A bacteriological analysis of the water in Bangalore revealed 75% bore wells were contaminated. Iron; hardness and salinity are also a concern. Nearly 12,500 habitats have been affected by salinity.

In Gujarat it is a major problem in coastel districts. Often babies die of dehydration and there are major fights in villages for freshwater. Some villages have seen 80% migration due to high salinity.

Health is not the only issue; impure water is a major burden on the state as well. Till the 10th plan the government had spent Rs 1,105 billion on drinking water schemes. Yet it is the poor who pay a heavier price spending around Rs 6700 crore annually on treatment of waterborne diseases.

There is an urgent need to look for alternative sources of portable water in places where water quality has deteriorated sharply. Community based water quality monitoring guidelines should be encouraged. People should be encouraged to look at traditional methods of protecting water sources. Also in places where groundwater has arsenic or fluoride, surface water should be considered as an alternative.

WATER SUPPLY AND SANITATION IN INDIA

Water supply and sanitation in India continue to be inadequate, despite longstanding efforts by the various levels of government and communities at improving coverage. The level of investment in water and sanitation, albeit low by international standards, has increased during the 2000s. Access has also increased significantly.

For example, in 1980 rural sanitation coverage was estimated at 1% and reached 21% in 2008. Also, the share of Indians with access to improved sources of water has increased significantly from 72% in 1990 to 88% in 2008. At the same time, local government institutions in charge of operating and maintaining the infrastructure are seen as weak and lack the financial resources to carry out their functions. In addition, no major city in India is known to have a continuous water supply and an estimated 72% of Indians still lack access to improved sanitation facilities. A number of innovative approaches to improve water supply and sanitation have been tested in India, in particular in the early 2000s. These include demand-driven approaches in rural water supply since 1999, community-led total sanitation, a public-private partnerships to improve the continuity of urban water supply in Karnataka, and the use of micro-credit to women in order to improve access to water.

ACCESS

In 2008, 88% of the population in India had access to an improved water source, but only 31% had access to improved sanitation. In rural areas, where 72% of India's population lives, the respective shares are 84% for water and only 21% for sanitation. In urban areas, 96% had access to an improved water source and 54% to improved sanitation. Access has improved substantially since 1990 when it was estimated to stand at 72% for water and 18% for sanitation.

As of 2010, the UN estimated based on Indian statistics that 626 people practice open defecation. In June 2012 Minister of Rural Development Jairam Ramesh stated India is the worlds largest "open air toilet". He also remarked that Pakistan, Bangladesh and Afghanistan have better sanitation records.

According to Indian norms, access to improved water supply exists if at least 40 litres/capita/day of safe drinking water are provided within a distance of 1.6 km or 100 meter of elevation difference, to be relaxed as per field conditions. There should be at least one pump per 250 persons.

SERVICE QUALITY

Water and sanitation service quality in India is generally poor, although there has been some limited progress concerning continuity of supply in urban areas and access to sanitation in rural areas.

WATER SUPPLY

Challenges. None of the 35 Indian cities with a population of more than one million distribute water for more than a few hours per day, despite generally sufficient infrastructure. Owing to inadequate pressure people struggle to collect water even when it is available. According to the World Bank, none have performance indicators that compare with average international standards. A 2007 study by the Asian Development Bank showed that in 20 cities the average duration of supply was only 4.3 hours per day. No city had continuous supply. The longest duration of supply was 12 hours per day in Chandigarh, and the lowest was 0.3 hours per day in Rajkot. In Delhi residents receive water only a few hours per day because of inadequate management of the distribution system. This results in contaminated water and forces households to complement a deficient public water service at prohibitive 'coping' costs; the poor suffer most from this situation. For example, according to a 1996 survey households in Delhi spent an average of 2,182 (US$39.5) per year in time and money to cope with poor service levels. This is more than three times as much as the 2001 water bill of about US$18 per year of a Delhi household that uses 20 cubic meters per month.

Achievements. Jamshedpur, a city in Jharkhand with 573,000 inhabitants, provided 25% of its residents with continuous water supply in 2009. Navi Mumbai, a planned city with more than 1m inhabitants, has achieved continuous supply for about half its population as of January 2009. Badlapur, another city in the Mumbai Conurbation with a population of 140,000, has achieved continuous supply in 3 out of 10 operating zones, covering 30% of its population. Thiruvananthapuram, the capital of Kerala state with a population of 745,000 in 2001, is probably the largest Indian city that enjoys continuous water supply.

SANITATION

Most Indians depend on on-site sanitation facilities. Recently, access to on-site sanitation have increased in both rural and urban areas. In rural areas, total sanitation has been successful. In urban areas, a good practice is the Slum Sanitation Program in Mumbai that has provided access to sanitation for a quarter million slum dwellers. Sewerage, where available, is often in a bad state. In Delhi the sewerage network has lacked maintenance over the years and overflow of raw sewage in open drains is common, due to blockage, settlements and inadequate pumping capacities. The capacity of the 17 existing wastewater treatment plants in Delhi is adequate to cater a daily production of waste water of less than 50% of the drinking water produced. Of the 2.5 Billion people in the world that defecate openly, some 665 million live in India. This is of greater concern as 88% of deaths from diarrhoea occur because of unsafe water, inadequate sanitation and poor hygiene.

ENVIRONMENT

As of 2003, it was estimated that only 27% of India's wastewater was being treated, with the remainder flowing into rivers, canals, groundwater or the sea., For example, the sacred Ganges river is infested with diseases and in some places "the Ganges becomes black and septic. Corpses, of semi-cremated adults or enshrouded babies, drift slowly by.". News Week describes Delhi's sacred Yamuna River as "a putrid ribbon of black sludge" where fecal bacteria is 10,000 over safety limits despite a 15-year programme to address the problem. Cholera epidemics are not unknown.

HEALTH IMPACT

The lack of adequate sanitation and safe water has significant negative health impacts including diarrhoea, referred to by travellers as the "Delhi Belly", and experienced by about 10 million visitors annually. While most visitors to India recover quickly and otherwise receive proper care, the World Health Organisation estimated that around 700,000 Indians die each year from diarrhoea. The dismal working conditions of sewer workers are another concern. A survey of the working conditions of sewage workers in Delhi showed that most of them suffer from chronic diseases, respiratory problems, skin disorders, allergies, headaches and eye infections.

WATER SUPPLY AND WATER RESOURCES

Depleting ground water table and deteriorating ground water quality are threatening the sustainability of both urban and rural water supply in many parts of India. The supply of cities that depend on surface water is threatened by pollution, increasing water scarcity and conflicts among users. For example, Bangalore depends to a large extent on water pumped since 1974 from the Kaveri river, whose waters are disputed between the states of Karnataka and Tamil Nadu. As in other Indian cities, the response to water scarcity is to transfer more water over large distances at high costs. In the case of Bangalore, the 3,384 crore (US$612.5 million) Kaveri Stage IV project, Phase II, includes the supply of 500,000 cubic meter of water per day over a distance of 100 km, thus increasing the city's supply by two thirds.

RESPONSIBILITY FOR WATER SUPPLY AND SANITATION

Water supply and sanitation is a State responsibility under the Indian Constitution. States may give the responsibility to the Panchayati Raj Institutions (PRI) in rural areas or municipalities in urban areas, called Urban Local Bodies (ULB). At present, states generally plan, design and execute water supply schemes (and often operate them) through their State Departments (of Public Health Engineering or Rural Development Engineering) or State Water Boards.

Highly centralised decision-making and approvals at the state level, which are characteristic of the Indian civil service, affect the management of water supply and sanitation services. For example, according to the World Bank in the state of Punjab the process of approving designs is centralised with even minor technical approvals reaching the office of chief engineers. A majority of decisions are made in a very centralised manner at the headquarters. In 1993 the Indian constitution and relevant state legislations were amended in order to decentralise certain responsibilities, including water supply and sanitation, to municipalities. Since the assignment of responsibilities to municipalities is a state responsibility, different states have followed different approaches.

According to a Planning Commission report of 2003 there is a trend to decentralise capital investment to engineering departments at the district level and operation and maintenance to district and gram panchayat levels.

POLICY AND REGULATION

The responsibility for water supply and sanitation at the central and state level is shared by various Ministries. At the central level, The Ministry of Rural Development is responsible for rural water supply through its Department of Drinking Water Supply (DDWS) and theMinistry of Housing and Urban Poverty Alleviation is responsible for urban water supply. However, except for the National Capital Territory of Delhi and other Union Territories, the central Ministries only have an advisory capacity and a very limited role in funding. Sector policy thus is a prerogative of state governments.

SERVICE PROVISION

Urban areas. Institutional arrangements for water supply and sanitation in Indian cities vary greatly. Typically, a state-level agency is in charge of planning and investment, while the local government (Urban Local Bodies) is in charge of operation and maintenance. Some of the largest cities have created municipal water and sanitation utilities that are legally and financially separated from the local government. However, these utilities remain weak in terms of financial capacity. In spite of decentralisation, ULBs remain dependent on capital subsidies from state governments. Tariffs are also set by state governments, which often even subsidise operating costs. Furthermore, when no separate utility exists there is no separation of accounts for different activities within a municipality. Some states and cities have non-typical institutional arrangements. For example, in Rajasthan the sector is more centralised and the state government is also in charge of operation and maintenance, while in Mumbai the sector is more decentralised and local government is also in charge of planning and investment.

Private sector participation. The private sector plays a limited, albeit recently increasing role in operating and maintaining urban water systems on behalf of ULBs. For example, the Jamshedpur Utilities & Services Company (Jusco), a subsidiary of Tata Steel, has a lease contract for Jamshedpur (Jharkhand), a management contract in Haldia (West Bengal), another contract in Mysore (Karnataka) and since 2007 a contract for the reduction of non-revenue water in parts of Bhopal (Madhya Pradesh). The French water company Veolia won a management contract in three cities in Karnataka in 2005.

In 2002 a consortium including Thames Water won a pilot contract covering 40,000 households to reduce non-revenue water in parts of Bangalore, funded by the Japan Bank for International Cooperation. The contract was scaled up in 2004. The Cypriot company Hydro-Comp, together with two Indian companies, won a 10-year concession contract for the city of Latur City (Maharashtra) in 2007 and an operator-consultant contract in Madurai (Tamil Nadu). Furthermore, the private Indian infrastructure development company SPML is engaged in Build-Operate-Transfer (BOT) projects, such as a bulk water supply project for Bhiwandi (Maharashtra).

Rural areas. There are about a 100,000 rural water supply systems in India. At least in some states responsibility for service provision is in the process of being partially transferred from State Water Boards and district governments to Panchayati Raj Institutions (PRI) at the block or village level (there were about 604 districts and 256,000 villages in India in 2002, according to Subdivisions of India. Blocks are an intermediate level between districts and villages). Where this transfer has been initiated, it seems to be more advanced for single-village water schemes than for more complex multi-village water schemes. Despite their professed role Panchayati Raj Institutions, play only a limited role in provision of rural water supply and sanitation as of 2006. There has been limited success in implementing decentralisation, partly due to low priority by some state governments. Rural sanitation is typically provided by households themselves in the form of latrines.

INNOVATIVE APPROACHES

A number of innovative approaches to improve water supply and sanitation have been tested in India, in particular in the early 2000s. These include community-led total sanitation, demand-driven approaches in rural water supply, a public-private partnerships to improve the continuity of urban water supply in Karnataka, and the use of micro-credit to women in order to improve access to water.

COMMUNITY-LED TOTAL SANITATION

In 1999 a demand-driven and people-centered sanitation programme was initiated under the name Total Sanitation Campaign (TSC) or Community-led total sanitation. It evolved from the limited achievements of the first structured programme for rural sanitation in India, the Central Rural Sanitation Programme, which had minimal community participation. The main goal of Total Sanitation Campaign is to eradicate the practice of open defecation by 2017. Community-led total sanitation is not focused on building infrastructure, but on preventing open defecation through peer pressure and shame. In Maharashtra where the programme started more than 2000 Gram Panchayats have achieved "open defecation free" status. Villages that achieve this status receive monetary rewards and high publicity under a programme called Nirmal Gram Puraskar.

DEMAND-DRIVEN APPROACHES IN RURAL WATER SUPPLY

Most rural water supply schemes in India use a centralised, supply-driven approach, *i.e.* a government institution designs a project and has it built with little community consultation and no capacity building for the community, often requiring no water fees to be paid for its subsequent operation. Since 2002 the Government of India has rolled out at the national level a programme to change the way in which water and sanitation services are supported in rural areas. The programme, called *Swajaldhara*, decentralises service delivery responsibility to rural local governments and user groups. Under the new approach communities are being consulted and trained, and users agree up-front to pay a tariff that is set at a level sufficiently high to cover operation and maintenance costs. It also includes measures to promote sanitation and to improve hygiene behaviour. The national programme follows a pilot programme launched in 1999.

According to a 2008 World Bank study in 10 Indian states, *Swajaldhara* results in lower capital costs, lower administrative costs and better service quality compared to the supply-driven approach. In particular, the study found that the average full cost of supply-driven schemes is Rs 38 (US$0.7) per cubic meter, while it is only Rs 26 (US$0.5) per cubic meter for demand-driven schemes. These costs include capital, operation and maintenance costs, administrative costs and coping costs incurred by users of malfunctioning systems. Coping costs include travelling long distances to obtain water, standing in long queues, storing water and repairing failed systems. Among the surveyed systems that were built using supply-driven approach system breakdowns were common, the quantity and quality of water supply were less than foreseen in designs, and 30% of households did not get daily supply in summer. The poor functioning of one system sometimes leads to the construction of another system, so that about 30% of households surveyed were served by several systems. As of 2008 only about 10% of rural water schemes built in India used a demand-driven approach. Since water users have to pay lower or no tariffs under the supply-driven approach, this discourages them to opt for a demand-driven approach, even if the likelihood of the systems operating on a sustainable basis is higher under a demand-driven approach.

ACHIEVING CONTINUOUS WATER SUPPLY

In the cities of Hubli, Belgaum and Gulbarga in the state of Karnataka, the private operator Veolia increased water supply from once every 2–15 days for 1–2 hours, to 24 hours per day for 180,000 people (12% of the population of the 3 cities) within 2 years (2006–2008). This was achieved by carefully selecting and ring-fencing demonstration zones (one in each city), renovating the distribution network, installing meters, introducing a well-functioning commercial system, and effective grass-roots social intermediation by an NGO, all without increasing the amount of bulk water supplied. The project, known by its acronym as KUWASIP (Karnataka Urban Water Sector Improvement Project), was supported by a US$39.5 million loan from the World Bank. It constitutes a milestone for India, where no large city so far has achieved continuous water supply. The project is expected to be scaled-up to cover the entire area of the three cities.

MICRO-CREDIT FOR WATER CONNECTIONS IN TAMIL NADU

In Tiruchirapalli in Tamil Nadu, the NGO Gramalaya, established in 1987, and women self-help groups promote access to water supply and sanitation by the poor through micro-credit. Among the benefits are that women can spend more time with their children, earn additional income, and sell surplus water to neighbours. This money contributes to her repayment of the WaterCredit loan. The initiative is supported by the US-based non-profit Water Partners International.

THE JAMSHEDPUR UTILITIES AND SERVICES COMPANY

The Jamshedpur Utilities and Services Company (JUSCO) provides water and sanitation services in Jamshedpur, a major industrial centre in East India that is home to Tata Steel. Until 2004 a division of Tata Steel provided water to the city's residents. However, service quality was poor with intermittent supply, high water losses and no metering. To improve this situation and to establish good practices that could be replicated in other Indian cities, JUSCO was set up as a wholly owned subsidiary of Tata Steel in 2004.

Efficiency and service quality improved substantially over the following years. The level on non-revenue water decreased from an estimated 36% in 2005 to 10% in 2009; one quarter of residents received continuous water supply (although the average supply remained at only 7 hours per day) in 2009; the share of metered connections increased from 2% in 2007 to 26% in 2009; the number of customers increased; and the company recovered its operating costs plus a portion of capital costs. Identifying and legalising illegal connections was an important element in the reduction of non-revenue water. The utility prides itself today of the good drinking water quality provided and encourages its customers to drink from the tap. The utility also operates a wastewater treatment plant that meets discharge standards. The private utility pays salaries that are higher than civil service salaries and conducts extensive training programmes for its staff. It has also installed a modern system to track and resolve customer complaints. Furthermore, it conducts independent annual customer satisfaction surveys. JUSCO's vision is to be the preferred provider of water supply and other urban services throughout India. Together with Ranhill Malaysia it won a 25-year concession contract for providing the water supply in Haldia City, West Bengal.

EFFICIENCY

There are only limited data on the operating efficiency of utilities in India, and even fewer data on the efficiency of investments.

Concerning operating efficiency, a study of 20 cities by the Jawaharlal Nehru National Urban Renewal Mission with the support of the Asian Development Bank showed an average level of non-revenue water (NRW) of 32%. However, 5 out of the 20 cities did not provide any data. For those that provided data there probably is a large margin of error, since only 25% of connections are metered, which makes it very difficult to estimate non-revenue water. Also, three utilities show NRW levels of less than 20%, two of which have practically no metering, which indicates that the numbers are not reliable and actual values are likely to be higher. In Delhi, which was not included in the ADB study, non-revenue water stood at 53% and there were about 20 employees per 1000 connections. Furthermore, only 70% of revenue billed was actually collected.

Concerning labour productivity, the 20 utilities in the sample had on average 7.4 employees per 1,000 connections, which is much higher than the estimated level for an efficient utility. A survey of a larger sample of Indian utilities showed an average ratio of 10.9 employees per 1,000 connections.

TARIFFS, COST RECOVERY AND SUBSIDIES

Water and sewer tariffs in India are low in both urban and rural areas. In urban areas they were set at the equivalent of about US$0.10 per cubic meter in 2007 and recovered about 60% of operating and maintenance costs, with large differences between cities. Some cities such as Kolkata do not bill residential users at all. In rural areas the level of cost recovery often is even lower than in urban areas and was estimated at only 20% in rural Punjab. Subsidies were estimated at US$1.1 billion per year in the mid-1990s, accounting to 4% of all government subsidies in India. 70% of those benefiting from the subsidies are not poor.

URBAN AREAS

Metering. Water metering is the precondition for billing water users on the basis of volume consumed. According to a 1999 survey of 300 cities about 62% of urban water customers in metropolitan areas and 50% in smaller cities are metered (average 55%). However, meters often do not work so that many "metered" customers are charged flat rates. Bangalore and Pune are among the few Indian cities that meter all their customers. Many other cities have no metering at all or meter only commercial customers. Users of standposts receive water free of charge. A 2007 study of 20 cities by the Jawaharlal Nehru National Urban Renewal Mission with the support of the Asian Development Bank (ADB) showed that only 25% of customers of these utilities were metered. Most other customers paid a flat tariff independent of consumption. Some utilities, such as the one serving Kolkata, actually do not bill residential users at all. Tariff levels. According to the same ADB study the average tariff for all customers – including industrial, commercial and public customers – is Rs. 4.9

(US$0.1) per cubic meter. According to a 2007 global water tariff survey by the OECD the residential water tariff for a consumption of 15 m^3 was equivalent to US$0.15 per m^3 in Bangalore, US$0.12 per m^3 in Calcutta, US$0.11 per m3 in New Delhi and US$0.09 per m^3 in Mumbai. Only Bangalore had a sewer tariff of US$0.02 per m^3. The other three cities did not charge for sewerage, although the better-off tend to be the ones with access to sewers.

Tariff structure. The tariff for customers that are effectively metered is typically a uniform linear tariff, although some cities apply increasing-block tariffs.

Affordability. Urban water tariffs were highly affordable according to data from the year 2000. A family of five living on the poverty line which uses 20 cubic meter of water per month would spend less than 1.2% of its budget on its water bill if it had a water meter. If it did not have a water meter and was charged a flat rate, it would pay 2.0% of its budget. This percentage lies below the often used affordability threshold of 5%. However, at that time the average metered tariff was estimated at only US$0.03 per m^3, or less than three times what it was estimated to be in 2007. Apparently no more up-to-date estimates on the share of the average water bill in the budget of the poor are available.

Cost recovery. According to a 2007 study of 20 cities the average rate of cost recovery for operating and maintenance costs of utilities in these cities was 60%. Seven of the 20 utilities generated a cash surplus to partially finance investments. Chennai generated the highest relative surplus. The lowest cost recovery ratio was found in Indore in Madhya Pradesh, which recovered less than 20% of its operating and maintenance costs.

Delhi example. In Delhi revenues were just sufficient to cover about 60% of operating costs of the city's utility in 2004; maintenance has, as a result, been minimal. In the past, the Delhi utility has relied heavily on government financial support for recurrent and capital expenditures in the magnitude of Rs. 3 billion (US$54.3 million) per year and Rs. 7 billion (US$126.7 million) respectively. As financial support for both capital and recurrent expenditures has been passed on as loans by the Government of the National Capital Territory of Delhi, the utility's balance sheet is loaded with a huge debt totalling about Rs. 50 billion (US$905 million) that it is unlikely to be able to service. Accounts receivable represent more than 12 months of billing, part of it being non recoverable.

The average tariff was estimated atUS$0.074/$m^3$ in 2001, compared to production costs of US$0.085/$m^3$, the latter probably being a very conservative estimate that does not take into account capital costs. Challenges faced in attempting to increase tariffs.

Even if users are willing to pay more for better services, political interests often prevent tariffs from being increased even to a small extent. An example is the city of Jabalpur where the central government and the state government financed a Rs. 130 million (US$2.4 million) water supply project from 2000–2004 to be operated by the Jabalpur Municipal Corporation, an entity that collected only less than half of its operational costs in revenues even before this major investment.

Even so the municipal corporation initially refused to increase tariffs. Only following pressure from the state government it reluctantly agreed to increase commercial tariffs, but not residential tariffs.

RURAL AREAS

Cost recovery in rural areas is low and a majority of the rural water systems are defunct for lack of maintenance. Some state governments subsidise rural water systems, but funds are scarce and insufficient. In rural areas in Punjab, operation and maintenance cost recovery is only about 20%. On one hand, expenditures are high due to high salary levels, high power tariff and a high number of operating staff. On the other hand, revenue is paid only by the 10% of the households who have private connections. Those drawing water from public stand posts do not pay any water charges at all, although the official tariff for public stand post users is Rs. 15 (US$0.3) per month per household.

SUBSIDIES AND TARGETING OF SUBSIDIES

There are no accurate recent estimates of the level of subsidies for water and sanitation in India. It has been estimated that transfers to the water sector in India amounted to Rs. 5,470.8 crore (US$990.2 million) per year in the mid-1990s, accounting for 4% of all government subsidies in India. About 98% of this subsidy is said to come from State rather than Central budgets. This figure may only cover recurrent cost subsidies and not investment subsidies, which are even higher. There is little targeting of subsidies. According to the World Bank, 70% of those benefiting from subsidies for public water supply are not poor, while 40% of the poor are excluded because they do not have access to public water services.

INVESTMENT AND FINANCING

Investment in urban water supply and sanitation has increased during the first decade of the 21st century, not least thanks to increased central government grants made available under Jawaharlal Nehru National Urban Renewal Mission alongside with loans from the Housing and Urban Development Corporation.

INVESTMENT

The Eleventh Five-Year Plan (2007–2012) foresees investments of Rs. 127,025 crore (US$23 billion) for urban water supply and sanitation, including urban (stormwater) drainage and solid waste management.

FINANCING

55% of the investments foreseen under the 11th Plan are to be financed by the central government, 28% by state governments, 8% by "institutional financing" such as HUDCO, 8% by external agencies and 1.5% by the private sector. Local governments are not expected to contribute to the investments. The volume of investments is expected to double to reach 0.7% of GDP. Also, it implies a shift in financing from state governments to the central government. During the 9th Plan only 24% of investments were financed by the central government and 76% by state governments. Central government financing was heavily focused on water supply in rural areas.

INSTITUTIONS

State Financing Corporations (SFC) play an important role in making recommendations regarding the allocation of state tax revenues between states and municipalities, criteria for grants, and measures to improve the financial position of municipalities. According to the Planning Commission, SFCs are in some cases not sufficiently transparent and/or competent, have high transactions costs, and their recommendations are sometimes not being implemented. An important source of financing are loans from Housing and Urban Development Corporation Ltd (HUDCO), a Central government financial undertaking. HUDCO loans to municipal corporations need to be guaranteed by state governments. HUDCO also on-lends loans from foreign aid, including Japanese aid, to states. The Jawaharlal Nehru National Urban Renewal Mission initiated in 2005 also plays an increasingly important role in financing urban water supply and sanitation through central government grants. The current system of financing water supply and sanitation is fragmented through a number of different national and state programmes. This results in simultaneous implementation with different and conflicting rules in neighbouring areas. In rural areas different programmes undermine each other, adversely affecting demand driven approaches requiring cost sharing by users.

EXTERNAL COOPERATION

In absolute terms India receives almost twice as much development assistance for water, sanitation and water resources management as any other country, according to data from the Organisation for Economic Co-operation and Development. India accounts for 13 per cent of commitments in global water aid for 2006–07, receiving an annual average of about US$830 million (□620 million), more than double the amount provided to China. India's biggest water and sanitation donor is Japan, which provided US$635 million, followed by the World Bank with US$130 million. The annual average for 2004–06, however, was about half as much at US$448 million, of which Japan provided US$293 million and the World Bank US$87 million. The Asian Development Bank and

Germany are other important external partners in water supply and sanitation. In 2003 the Indian government decided it would only accept bilateral aid from five countries (the United Kingdom, the United States, Russia, Germany and Japan). A further 22 bilateral donors were asked to channel aid through nongovernmental organisations, United Nations agencies or multilateral institutions such as the European Union, the Asian Development Bank or the World Bank.

ASIAN DEVELOPMENT BANK

India has increased its loans from the Asian Development Bank (ADB) since 2005 after the introduction of new financing modalities, such as the multitranche financing facility (MFF) which features a framework agreement with the national government under which financing is provided in flexible tranches for subprojects that meet established selection criteria. In 2008 four MFFs for urban development investment programmes were under way in North Karnataka (US$862 million), Jammu and Kashmir (US$1,260 million),Rajasthan (US$450 million), and Uttarakhand (US$1,589 million). Included in these MFFs are major investments for the development of urban water supply and sanitation services.

GERMANY

Germany supports access to water and sanitation in India through financial cooperation by KfW development bank and technical cooperation by GTZ. Since the early 1990s both institutions have supported watershed management in rural Maharashtra, using a participatory approach first piloted by the Social Centre in Ahmednagar and that constituted a fundamental break with the previous top-down, technical approach to watershed management that had yielded little results. The involvement of women in decision-making is an essential part of the project. While the benefits are mostly in terms of increased agricultural production, the project also increases availability of water resources for rural water supply. In addition, GTZ actively supports the introduction of ecological sanitationconcepts in India, including community toilets and decentralised wastewater systems for schools as well as small and medium enterprises. Many of these systems produce biogas from wastewater, provide fertiliser and irrigation water.

JAPAN

As India's largest donor in the sector the Japan International Cooperation Agency (JICA) finances a multitude of projects with a focus on capital-intensive urban water supply and sanitation projects, often involving follow-up projects in the same locations. Current projects. Projects approved between 2006 and 2009 include the Guwahati Water Supply Project (Phases I and II) in Assam, the Kerala Water Supply Project (Phased II and III), the Hogenakkal Water

Supply and Fluorosis Mitigation Project (Phases I and II) in Tamil Nadu, the Goa Water Supply and Sewerage Project, the Agra Water Supply Project, the Amritsar Sewerage Project in Punjab, the Orissa Integrated Sanitation Improvement Project, and the Bangalore Water Supply and Sewerage Project (Phase II).

Evaluation of past projects. An ex-post evaluation of one large programme, the Urban Water Supply and Sanitation Improvement Program, showed that "some 60%–70% of the goals were achieved" and that "results were moderate". The programme was implemented by the Housing and Urban Development Corporation, Ltd. (HUDCO) from 1996 to 2003 in 26 cities. The evaluation says that "state government plans were not based on sufficient demand research, including the research for residents' willingness to pay for services", so that demand for connections was overestimated. Also fees (water tariffs) were rarely increased despite recommendations to increase them. The evaluation concludes that "HUDCO was not able to make significant contributions to the effectiveness, sustainability, or overall quality of individual projects. One of the reasons that not much attention was given to this problem is probably that there was little risk of default on the loans thanks to state government guarantees."

WORLD BANK

Current projects. The World Bank finances a number of projects in urban and rural areas that are fully or partly dedicated to water supply and sanitation. In urban areas the World Bank supports the Andhra Pradesh Municipal Development Project (approved in 2009, US$300 million loan), the Karnataka Municipal Reform Project (approved in 2006, US$216 million loan), the Third Tamil Nadu Urban Development Project (approved in 2005, US$300 million loan) and the Karnataka Urban Water Sector Improvement Project (approved in 2004, US$39.5 million loan). In rural areas it supports the Andhra Pradesh Rural Water Supply and Sanitation (US$150 million loan, approved in 2009), the Second Karnataka Rural Water Supply and Sanitation Project (approved in 2001,US$151.6 million loan), the Uttaranchal Rural Water Supply and Sanitation Project (approved in 2006, US$120 million loan) and the Punjab Rural Water Supply and Sanitation Project (approved in 2006, US$154 million loan).

Evaluation of past projects. A study by the World Bank's independent evaluation department evaluated the impact of the World Bank-supported interventions in the provision of urban water supply and wastewater services in Mumbai between 1973 and 1990. It concluded that water supply and sewerage planning, construction and operations in Bombay posed daunting challenges to those who planned and implemented the investment programme. At the outset, there was a huge backlog of unmet demand because of under investment. Population and economic growth accelerated in the following decades and the proportion of the poor increased as did the slums which they occupied. The intended impacts of the programme have not been realised. Shortcomings include that "water is not safe to drink; water service, especially to the poor, is difficult to access and is provided at inconvenient hours of the day; industrial water needs are not fully met; sanitary facilities are too few in number and often unusable; and urban drains, creeks and coastal waters are polluted with sanitary and industrial wastes."

WATER CRISIS LOOMS COUNTRYWIDE

Water has become the most commercial products of the century. This may sound bizarre, but true. In fact, what water is to the 21st century, oil was to the 20th century. The stress on the multiple water resources is a result of a multitude of factors. On the one hand, the rapidly rising population and changing lifestyles have increased the need for fresh water. On the other hand, intense competitions among users in agriculture, industry and domestic sector is pushing the ground water table deeper.

To get bucket of drinking water is a struggle for most women in the country. The virtually dry and dead water resources have lead to acute water scarcity, affecting the socio-economic condition of the society. The drought conditions have pushed villagers to move to cities in search of jobs, whereas women and girls have to trudge further. This time lost in fetching water can very well translate into financial gains, leading to a better life for the family. If opportunity costs were taken into account, it would be clear that in most rural areas, households are paying far more for water supply than the often-normal rates charged in urban areas. Also, if this cost of fetching water which is almost equivalent. to 150 million women days each year, is covered into a loss for the national exchequer, it translates into a whopping 10 billion rupees per year.

The government has accorded the highest priority to rural drinking water for ensuring universal access as a part of policy framework to achieve the goal of reaching the unreached. Despite the installation of more than 3.5 million hand pumps and over 116 thousand piped water supply schemes, in many parts of the country, the people face water scarcity almost every year, there by meaning that our water supply systems are failing to sustain despite huge investments.

In India, there are many villages either with scarce water supply or without any source of water. If there is no source of potable water in 2.5 kilometres, then the village becomes no source water village or problem village. In many rural areas, women still have to walk a distance of about 2.5 kms to reach the source of water. She reaches home carrying heavy pots, not to rest but to do other household chores of cooking, washing~ cleaning, caring of children and looking after livestock. Again in the evening she has to fetch water. Thus a rural woman's life is sheer drudgery.

Water is the biggest crisis facing India in terms of spread and severity, affecting one in every three persons. Even in Chennai, Bangalore, Shimla and Delhi, water is being rationed and India's food security is under threat. With the lives and livelihood of millions at risk, urban India is screaming for water. For instance, water is rationed twice a week in Bangalore, and for 30 minutes a day in Bhopal; 250 tankers make 2,250 trips to quench Chennai's thirst. Mumbai routinely lives through water cuts from January to June, when some areas get water once in three days in Hyderabad.

Harrowing midnight for a precious bucket of drinking water is a regular feature for many families of Vypuri, an Island off the mainland of Kochi. Women have to queue up in front of the public water taps, being at the lag end of the pipeline system, they get water only after the users ahead in the pipeline finish collecting water. There are nights when water pressure dips so low that some women get it after midnight. They split their day between household chores and collecting water.

Apart from the water scarcity caused by Coca-cola in Plachimada, the other districts in the state are facing a water crisis. For instance, in Kottayam district at some places, the water scarcity is so acute that people hesist to offer a glass of water to the visitor, which hitherto was a common custom. In the upper Kuttanadu area of the district during summer people collect water from a distance of 3-4 kms. Water supply from public taps is erratic and very often even after standing for an hour in the queue; people are not able to get a bucket of water. Most women and girls in Rajasthan find themselves searching water for much of the year. They trudge bare foot in the hot sun for hours over wastelands, across thorny fields, or rough terrain in search of water, often life the colour of mud and brackish, but still welcome for the parched throats back home. On an average, a rural woman walks more than 14000 km a year just to fetch water. Their urban sisters are only slightly better off- they do not walk such distances, but stand in the long winding queues for hours on end to collect water from the roadside taps on the water lorries.

In every household, in the rural areas in Rajasthan, women and girl children bear the responsibilit of collecting, transporting, storing, and managing water. In places, where there is no water for farming, men migrate to urban areas in search of work leaving women behind to fond for the old and the children. Women spend most of their time, collecting water with little time for other productive work. This impacts on the education of the girl child, if the girl is herself not collecting water, she is looking after the home and her siblings when her mother is away.

In brief:

- Water source being open dug well, the quality of water is poor; dirty, saline and has turbidity
- Women have to make at least three trips at 5 am, 11 am and 5 pm

- Sometimes, the number of trips is more
- Total distance traveled is 9-10 km, even higher
- Total Time spent is 6-9 hours
- Total number of pots/buckets is about 3 pots, 30-45 litres (one pot of 10-15 litres per trip)
- Due to long distance, they have to take rest in the middle of the way. Dust storms aggravate their problem
- At some villages water from tubewells is too saline to drink. Even animals particularly cow gets indigestion after drinking this water, so the villagers add water from the dug well. The entire life of women in rural areas like Jaisalmer is spent on water collection and cooking. Even the girls of 8-10 years cannot be spared. They cannot afford the luxury of school. For instance for Pappu a girl of hardly 10 years, water collection has become her main job. In the words of her grandmother "Water fetching is the schooling for Pappu." There are so many Pappus in the villages and dhaanis of Jaisalmer.

In Sriganganagar, the Indira Gandhi canal is the main source for drinking water. However, during the crisis period (either because of no water in the main canal/sub canal or due to the erratic power supply), the rich remain unaffected. In such crisis women from poorhouse hold draw water from the village diggis, which is totally unfit for any kind of human activity. They use this water not only for washing cloth and bathing but also for drinking. Due to the formation of algae, water becomes greenish and filthy. Women add alum to purify it.

In Orissa drinking water is being privatized. The government first insists on the formation of water associations and conveniently pass the responsibilities on to these association. When this proves inefficient, water distribution rights are given away to private contractors. For example, the Orissa government initially stressed on the formation of Paani Panchayats (water associations).

Later using police the government suppressed these panchayats justifying this by claiming that the villages were not being responsible enough. Titlagarh is the hottest town of India, but it has no water, causing great misery to the women. As the highest temperature, is recorded here 52 degrees centigrade which is also the highest temperature in India. People called "Titlagarh" as "Tatlagarh", in local language Tatla means hot. In Titlagarh water problem is acute. People are buying water throughout the year for drinking and cooking purpose. In the month of May and June the rate of water increase three times, from Rs 2 per Dabba to Rs.8 per Dabba (container). This is the picture of urban areas, but in rural areas the problem is worse, where the tubewells all are becoming dry but people have no money to buy water. Due to the water problem some villagers are migrating to other places. In Uttranchal women are suffering a lot in every village where water problem is severe. Natural sources are drying up which adds the kilometres for women everyday to quench the thirst of their family as well as animals.

Women are the major part of the workforce in Garhwal. They work from early morning to late evening to serve the family. They do all household work from cooking to cleaning and washing clothes and soiled utensils as well as look after their children and animals. Women also collect the water required for cooking, cleaning, washing, bathing and drinking both for human beings and animals.

During the survey in Jaunsar area of district Tehri Garhwal, in villages such as Nagthat, Duena, Vishoi, Gadol, Jandoh, Chi tar, Chichrad and Gangoa, it was observed that water in the region is mostly acidic in nature. The water problem in Chi tar and Gangoa villages is very severe, where men and women carry water on mules from 8-10 Km to the village. Because of the poor water quality, most of the villagers in the regions are suffering from many diseases related to skin and teeth. Natural resources of water in the area are very few and they are also disappearing very fast. During the survey, Smt. Nisha Devi of Chi tar village explained that they are not getting enough water for their animals so they take their animals to the spring about 2-3 kms away.

In Bundelkhand, women have no work but to collect drinking water on their heads from long distance. The grim situation of water may be best illustrated by one Bundelkhandi saying which roughly translated as "let the husband die but the earthen pot of water should not be broken".

The scenario is worst in Patha in Chitrakut district where women have to travel a long distance to collect water for drinking. Half of the time of women is spent to collect water, which affects their health and the well-being of their children. The paucity of time due to water crisis aggravates the domestic problem.

Instead of solving the water crisis, attempts are being made to create a disastrous situation in the region. Banda city entirely depends on the Ken river. If Ken is linked with Betwa, then it will not affect only Banda, but would also jeopardize the survival of farmers who depend on Ken. Even in Delhi the water scenario is no better, being worst in Delhi slums. For example Sanjay colony slum of New Delhi has population about 15,000-20,000 with about 4500 households in the locality.

Majority of the population is self-employed and are engaged in making daris, mats and other clothes for sale. In this area people collect water from different sources depending on the availability such as DJB tanker, MCD pipe water supply and from Sulabh International. DJB tanker comes daily but it has no fixed time for water distribution. The water that comes from MCD pipe water has fixed time for water supply but it only comes for 1-2 hr in the evening (around 4.30 p.m.). At MCD pipe line people made bore and fetch water from it. If the people don't get water from the above sources they are forced to get it from Sulabh International near Kalkaji temple for which they have pay @ Rs. 2 for 20 litre or so.

The Water crisis is same in West Bengal. In all the districts, the water commons have ceased to exist, and have become open-access resources, with hardly anyone responsible to take care of the resources. In North Bengal, some women reported they had opinions regarding the use of the water body, but their importance in management decisions is cipher. The absence of the community from the management of the water resources is indeed a tragedy, because now the resources are at the mercy of either the market or government officials.

Punjab; the name stands for abundance of water, but the present situation of water resources in the state is highly critical. The ground water availability is drastically hampered.

The village ponds are drying day by day. Women in the villages desperately need water. Near Talwandi Sabo, for some villages, the source for drinking water is about 8 km away. Near Jajjal due to contaminated water, women are suffering from a number of diseases including cancer. There have been several deaths attributed to polluted water.

For Maharashtra, water is an abiding concern. In many villages women have to walk more than 3 kilometres everyday to fetch two huge vessels of water illegally from a government reservoir. They have to make at least three trips everyday.

The state government do not send tankers to the villagers. At some places, women spend Rs 5 for two canes of water. Images of women carrying the pots of water, walking miles and miles for one single pot are common in the state of Maharashtra. Women in Maharashtra have carried the water burden both as a result of scarcity and abundance.

Drought displacement due to dams and irrigation have contributed to increasing water burden of women. Women in Nandurbar district of North Maharashtra share their woes "forget about getting safe drinking water from wells, we spend most of our time locating streams and springs that quench our thrust". Many Women came as brides, their hair have gone dry, but the search for water has not ended. Karnataka is facing the worst kind of water crisis. In Bangalore, only 35% of the city gets water on daily basis, the rest on alternative days.

In addition to the scarcity, erratic water supply is another problem. In Samadhanagar area, water generally comes in the morning at 11 A.M or in the middle of the night. Both these timings make it very difficult for women to collect water as they leave early in the morning to go to work. In Doddanagar slums in the city, women and children who are also breadwinners of the family spend 3-4 hours filling water, losing their wages. In Hosapalya locality women get severe joint pain in their shoulders, hips and knees due to carrying water pits from water sources outside their colony. In Peenya industrial area, many street fights occur among the women over water. Social conflict and tension is high due to water crisis.

In brief, at an estimate about 150 Million-Woman Days and Rs 10 Billion are lost in fetching water.

CHALLENGES OF GLOBAL WATER

Productivity is a ratio between a unit of output and a unit of input. Here, the term water productivity is used exclusively to denote the amount or value of product over volume or value of water depleted or diverted.

The value of the product might be expressed in different terms (biomass, grain, money). For example, the so-called 'crop per drop' approach focuses on the amount of product per unit of water. Another approach considers differences in the nutritional values of different crops, or that the same quantity of one crop feeds more people than the same quantity of another crop. When speaking of food security, it is important to account for such criteria.

Another concern is how to express the social benefit of agricultural water productivity. All the options that have been suggested can be summarised by the phrases 'nutrient per drop', 'capita per drop', 'jobs per drop', and 'sustainable livelihoods per drop'. There is no unique definition of productivity and the value considered for the numerator might depend on the focus as well as the availability of data. However, water productivity defined as kilogram per drop is a useful concept when comparing the productivity of water in different parts of the same system or river basin and also when comparing the productivity of water in agriculture with other possible uses of water.

Crop water production is governed only by transpiration. As it is difficult to separate transpiration from evaporation from the soil surface between the plants (which does not contribute directly to crop production), defining crop water productivity using evapotranspiration rather than transpiration makes practical sense at field and system level. In irrigated agriculture in saline areas, the leaching requirement, *i.e.* the amount of water that needs to percolate to maintain rootzone salinity at a satisfactory level, should also be included together with evapotranspiration in the amount of water that is necessarily depleted during plant growth.

Other non-productive but beneficial uses could be included. Examples are evapotranspiration by windbreaks, cover crops, and the water used in wetting seedbeds to enhance germination.

The question of considering water losses from seepage and field percolation as consumption does not receive a unique response. If this water is of no use downstream or if it generates further pollution such as that resulting from geological salt leaching (*e.g.* San Joaquin Valley, California, the United States of America), then it must be accounted for as consumption. Solutions to minimise these losses, such as canal lining or water improvement application, then have a positive effect on productivity. However, from a broader environmental point of view, it can be important to consider the impact of the outflow of an irrigation system on the overall productivity of an ecosystem.

As with the numerator, the choice of the denominator (which drops to be included) should depend on the scale, the point of view and the focus. At basin level, the choice might be between water diverted from the source and the same minus water restored, whereas at field level one might consider useful rain, irrigation water and supplemental irrigation.

WATER PRODUCTIVITY IN ECONOMIC TERMS

Data are available for agricultural water productivity in economic terms for Jordan. Water productivity ranged from US\$0.3/m^3 for potato to US\$0.03/m^3 for wheat. The average value for agricultural products was US\$0.19/m^3 and for industrial products US\$7.5/m^3.

The IWMI analysed economic water productivity data from two irrigation systems in South Asia. The values for wheat production ranged from US\$0.07 to 0.17/m^3. Average systemwide water productivity values of US\$0.10 and 0.15/m^3 were reported for two other systems in South Asia. Systemwide values for a total of 23 irrigation systems in 11 countries in Asia, Africa and Latin America ranged from US\$0.03/m^3 (for a system in India) to US\$0.91/m^3 (for one in Burkina Faso), with an overall average of US\$0.25/m^3. Comparison with the most recent cost of about US\$0.50/m^3 for desalinated seawater illustrates that this source of water is too expensive for virtually all agricultural production. However, its cost has come down to about one-tenth of what it was 20 years ago. Further improvements in the technology of seawater desalination are likely. Its cost is also likely to continue falling provided that as energy remains cheap.

SPATIAL VARIABILITY OF WATER PRODUCTIVITY

Reported data on water productivity with respect to evapotranspiration (WP_{ET}) show considerable variation, *e.g.* wheat 0.6-1.9 kg/m^3, maize 1.2-2.3 kg/m^3, rice 0.5-1.1 kg/m^3, forage sorghum 7-8 kg/m^3 and potato tubers 6.2-11.6 kg/m^3, with incidental outliers obtained under experimental conditions. Data on field-level water productivity per unit of water applied (WP_{irrig}), as reported in the literature, are lower than WP_{ET} and vary over an even wider range.

For example, grain WP_{irrig} for rice varied from 0.05 to 0.6 kg/m^3, for sorghum from 0.05 to 0.3 kg/m^3 and for maize from 0.2 to 0.8 kg/m^3. The variability occurs because data were collected in different environments and under different crop management conditions. These affected the yield and the amount of water supplied. Furthermore, it is often difficult to determine the real crop yield over a large area, *e.g.* the size of a large irrigation system. When asked for yield figures, individual farmers are likely to give a figure that depends on the situation. For a loan application, they may overstate the yield, whereas for payment of a debt or a tariff, they will probably understate the yield obtained. Vegetable yields of vegetables may change every day, and unless good records are kept, no one will know exactly how much was harvested during the total harvest period. Yields expressed in monetary terms are more doubtful as prices on the local market may fluctuate considerably over time.

Nevertheless, water productivity data across scales are useful in assessing whether water drained from upstream is reused effectively downstream. However, there are few reliable data on water productivity at different scale levels within the same system.

A study using remote sensing and GIS technologies assessed crop WP_{ET} at various irrigation system scales in the Indus Basin in Pakistan. Crop water productivity was found to vary significantly at the scale of small canal command areas.

When water productivity was aggregated for canal command areas, the highest water productivity values decreased gradually. Their variability also decreased until at a scale of about 6 million ha water productivity tended to a low value of about 0.6 kg/m^3. This arose because at the larger scale, canal commands with less fertile or saline soils and with less canal water and poorer quality groundwater were included in the average.

THE SUBSTANTIAL INCREASE OF WATER PRODUCTIVITY IN AGRICULTURE

Despite concerns about the technical inefficiency of water use in agriculture, water productivity increased by at least 100 percent between 1961 and 2001. The major factor behind this growth has been yield increase. For many crops, the yield increase has occurred without increased water consumption, and sometimes with even less water given the increase in the harvesting index.

Example of crops for which water consumption experienced little if any variation during these years are rice (mostly irrigated) and wheat (mostly rainfed), for which the recorded increases worldwide amount to 100 and 160 percent respectively. At the global level, the increase in water consumption for agriculture in the past 40 years has been 800 km^3 while world population has doubled to 6 000 million.

Considering that the arable rainfed area has not increased, one can conclude that with an additional 800 km^3 of water the world has been able to feed an additional 3 000 million people. This gives a rough estimate of 0.720 m^3/d/capita. This figure is low compared to the estimated global average for 2000 of 2.4 m^3/d/capita, which includes water for food at field level not including water losses. This is a good indicator of the significant productivity gain recorded in agriculture; a gain that has enabled the world to accommodate the doubling of the population and also increase intake.

As a whole, one can estimate that the water needs for food per capita halved between 1961 and 2001 from about 6 m^3/d to less than 3 m^3/d.

The importance of water needs for food makes any small relative gain in this sector equivalent to a significant gain for other uses. For example, given the water needs for capita in 2000, a 1-percent increase in water productivity in food production generates a potential of water use of 24 litres/d/capita. In order to produce the equivalent of the domestic water supply, a gain of 10 percent in agricultural water productivity would be required, which is a matter of years.

Therefore, it can be argued that investing in agriculture and in agricultural water is the best avenue for freeing water for other purposes.

However, future agricultural gains will need to be split into several components: (i) compensation for the reduction of agricultural production areas as a result of urban encroachment, soil degradation, and the depletion of water resource availability or access (groundwater); (ii) increased water access for the rural poor and vulnerable groups; (iii) generation of wealthier farming systems; and (iv) freezing water for other uses including the environment.

ENHANCING WATER PRODUCTIVITY AT PLANT LEVEL

Plant-level options rely mainly on germplasm improvements, *e.g.* improving seedling vigour, increasing rooting depth, increasing the harvest index (the marketable part of the plant as part of its total biomass), and enhancing photosynthetic efficiency. The most significant improvements in yield stability have usually resulted from breeding programmes to develop an appropriate growing cycle such that the duration of the vegetative and reproductive periods are well matched with the expected water supply or with the absence of crop hazards. Planting, flowering and maturation dates are important in matching the period of maximum crop growth with the time when the saturation vapour pressure deficit is low. The periods of maximum crop growth may be optimised by means of breeding technology. Improved varieties with a deeper rooting system contribute to drought avoidance and the effective use of water stored in the soil profile. Drought escape and increasing drought tolerance are also important strategies for increasing water productivity. Daylength-insensitive varieties of short to medium duration (90-120 d) enabled crops, such as wheat, rice and maize varieties developed as part of the green revolution, to increase water productivity by escaping late-season drought that adversely affects flowering and grain development. The modern rice varieties have about a threefold increase in water productivity compared with traditional varieties. Progress in extending these achievements to other crops has been considerable and will probably accelerate following the recent identification of the underlying genes. Genetic engineering, if properly integrated in breeding programmes and applied in a safe manner, can further contribute to the development of drought tolerant varieties and to increasing the water use efficiency.

KEY PRINCIPLES FOR IMPROVING WATER PRODUCTIVITY

The key principles for improving water productivity at field, farm and basin level, which apply regardless of whether the crop is grown under rainfed or irrigated conditions, are: (i) increase the marketable yield of the crop for each unit of water transpired by it; (ii) reduce all outflows (*e.g.* drainage, seepage and percolation), including evaporative outflows other than the crop stomatal transpiration; and (iii) increase the effective use of rainfall, stored water, and water of marginal quality.

The first principle relates to the need to increase crop yields or values. The second one aims to decrease all 'losses' except crop transpiration. Its phrasing does not imply that it will be impossible to increase water productivity by reducing stomatal transpiration. It is conceivable that plant breeding may find ways to overcome this constraint. The third principle aims at making use of alternative water resources. The second and third principles should be considered parts of basinwide integrated water resource management (IWRM) for water productivity improvement. IWRM recognises the essential role of institutions and policies in ensuring that upstream interventions are not made at the expense of downstream water users.

REAL IMPACTS OF VIRTUAL WATER ON WATER SAVINGS

Exchanges of virtual water through food trade first captured the attention of experts in the Near East, where water is scarce and imports represent considerable water savings. The value of virtual water of a food product is the inverse of water productivity. It is defined as the amount of water per unit of food that is or would be consumed during its production process.

Virtual water trade generates water savings for importing countries. It also generates global real water savings because of the differential in water productivity between the producing and the exporting countries.

For example, transporting 1 kg of maize from France (taken as representative of maize exporting countries for water productivity) to Egypt transforms an amount of water of about 0.6 m^3 into 1.12 m^3, which represents globally a real water saving of 0.52 m^3 per kilogram traded. In 2000, the maize imports in Egypt and the related virtual water transfer thus generated a global water saving of about 2 700 million m^3. The global real water saving is significant: a first estimate shows that water savings from virtual water transfer through food trade amounts to 385 000 million m^3.

Food storage also generates real water savings. For example, in the Syrian Arab Republic, 1988 was a good year for the cereal production with yields of

1.6 tonnes/ha, leading to a surplus. Thus, 1.9 million tonnes of cereals were stored during that year.

The following year was very dry, and the cereal yield dropped to 0.4 tonnes/ ha. About 1.2 million tonnes of cereals were then withdrawn from storage to complement internal production and imports. Based on the water productivities recorded for these years, the estimated value of virtual water was to 1 and 3.33 m^3/kg respectively.

Therefore, the use of 1.2 million tonnes of cereals from storage in 1989 is equivalent to 4 000 million m^3 of virtual water. For the two-year period of reference (1988-89), some 2 800 million m^3 of water was saved by the food storage capacity. Globally, the trade in virtual water is rising rapidly. It increased in absolute value from about 450 km^3 in 1961 to 1 340 km^3 in 2000, reaching 26 percent of the total water required for food including equivalence for sea products and sea fish. This value is shared evenly between energy, fat and protein products.

RAISING WATER PRODUCTIVITY AT FIELD LEVEL

Improved practices at field level relate to changes in crop, soil and water management. They include: selecting appropriate crops and cultivars; planting methods (*e.g.* on raised beds); minimum tillage; timely irrigation to synchronise water application with the most sensitive growing periods; nutrient management; drip irrigation; and improved drainage for water table control.

Water depletion occurs when water evaporates from moist soil, from puddles between rows and before crop establishment. All cultural and agronomic practices that reduce these losses, such as different row spacings and the application of mulches, improve water productivity. The irrigation method also affects these evaporative losses. Drip irrigation causes much less soil wetting than sprinkler irrigation. The significance of soil improvement in enhancing water productivity is often ignored. However, integrated crop and resource management practices, such as improved nutrient management, can increase water productivity by raising the yield proportionally more than it increases evapotranspiration. This principle applies to both irrigated and rainfed agriculture. Integrated weed and integrated pest management have also contributed effectively to yield increases.

One of the field-level methods for increasing water productivity is deficit irrigation, where deliberately less water is applied than that required to meet the full crop water demand. The prescribed water deficit should result in a small yield reduction that is less than the concomitant reduction in transpiration.

Therefore, it causes a gain in water productivity per unit of water transpired. In addition, it could lower production costs if one or more irrigations could be eliminated. For deficit irrigation to be successful, farmers need to know the deficit that can be allowed at each of the growth stages and the level of water stress that already exists in the rootzone. Most importantly, they need to have control over the timing and amount of irrigations. Deficit irrigation carries considerable risk for the farmers where water supplies are uncertain, as is the case with rainfall or unreliable irrigation supplies. Where water availability falls below a certain level, the value of the crop can fall to zero, either because the crop dies or because the product is of such low quality as to be unmarketable. When water is scarce, farmers could reduce the irrigation as appropriate to maximise returns to water if they have control over the timing and amount of irrigations. This degree of flexibility is usually the case with sprinkler and drip irrigation, and also with pumped groundwater if the farmer owns the pump. A totally flexible delivery system for surface irrigation in large irrigation systems is expensive because of the required overcapacity in the conveyance system. The trade-off between reduced yield and higher water productivity needs to be quantified in economic terms before recommending deficit irrigation (and other water-saving irrigations in rice production).

The often cited low water productivity per unit of water supply in rice cultivation derives from considering as losses the percolation resulting from the standing water layer on the field surface. However, this water is often recycled, and rice water productivity generally compares well with that of a dry cereal. Nevertheless, water-saving irrigation techniques such as saturated soil culture and alternate wetting and drying can reduce the unproductive water outflows drastically and increase water productivity. These techniques generally lead to some yield decline in the current lowland rice high-yielding varieties. However, some experiments are reporting substantial yield increases for local varieties using a technique called system rice intensification (SRI), a technique which originated in Madagascar. Here again there is no unique response; the fit with local resources and capacity is the most important feature to account for. Without anticipating results of current investigations in many countries, it seems that the potential of the SRI technique for the poor to increase the productivity of scarce land and water is significant provided that enough family labour is available. Other approaches are being researched as part of efforts to increase water productivity without sacrificing yield. One of these is to develop so-called aerobic rice systems that allow rice cultivation in non-flooded conditions. The development of these new rice varieties is essential if rice is to be grown like other irrigated upland crops and the deep percolation associated with paddy rice is to be avoided.

2

Fresh Water

DELTAS

Deltas are deposits of sediments (particles of sand, gravel, and silt) at the mouths of rivers that flow into the ocean. The mouth of a river is the end where the body of water flows into the sea. Deltas are shaped by interactions of the river's fresh water with the ocean water, tides, and waves. Throughout history, deltas have been important places for human settlement. They are also vital habitats for many animals and plants. In the fifth century B.C.E, Greek naturalist Herodotus coined the name delta to describe the triangular shape of the sediments deposited at the end of the Nile River. The capital Greek letter delta resembles a triangle. Most deltas are triangular in shape because rivers deposit larger amounts of sediment where they meet the sea, then fan out into the mouth of the sea to deposit the remaining sediment.

FORMATION OF DELTAS

As rivers flow through their beds (a channel occupied by a river), the water breaks up rocks and pebbles, which the river then carries with it as it flows. These pieces of rock, sediment, include sand, pebbles, and silt. When the fast-flowing waters of the river reach the ocean, they push against the ocean water. This decreases the speed of the river water, which spreads out along the coastline. As the speed of the river water slows, the sediments that it carries settle to the bottom of the ocean. Over time, the sediments accumulate and form a delta.

In most deltas, the river water is less dense (packed together) than the sea water because it contains less salt. As it flows out into the ocean, it floats on top of the ocean water. This is called hypopycnal flow. (The prefix hypo means "under" or "less" and the root word pycn means "density.") In places where hypopycnal flow occurs, the salt water that lies under the fresh water is called a salt wedge. The bigger sediments, like gravel and pebbles, are deposited at the tip of the salt wedge (nearest to shore) and the smaller sediments, like sand, are deposited farther out along the salt wedge. The smallest silt grains (fine sediment particles) are transported far offshore with the river water.

THE STRUCTURE OF A DELTA

Paths of flowing water called channels run through the sediments of deltas. These channels are called distributaries and they may be large and relatively permanent or small, transient features. The sides of the channels are made up of piles of sediments called levées. The areas between the distributaries are called interdistributary areas.

TYPES OF DELTAS

The structure of the distributaries and interdistributary areas depends on where the river empties into the ocean and the forces that affect the river water as it flows into the ocean. There are three major types of deltas: river-dominated, tide-dominated, and wave-dominated. Many deltas are formed by a combination of these forces. River-dominated deltas extend outward from the coast as the river water jets out into the ocean. The sediments deposited by the river tend to form levées that hold channels of water. The aerial view of a river-dominated delta looks like the foot of a bird with several branching channels. River-dominated deltas often have sand bars (long deposits of sand) that are perpendicular to the river. The Mississippi River Delta in Louisiana is an example of a river-dominated delta. Tide-dominated deltas are deltas where the sediments deposited by a river are redistributed by tides. These deltas have channels cut by the river water as well as channels cut by tidal currents. The result is a shoreline that looks like the fringe on the end of a carpet. Tide-dominated deltas may also have coastal features like sand bars and shoals (a sandbank seen at low tide) oriented parallel to the tidal flow. The Ganges-Brahmaputra Delta in the Bay of Bengal is an example of a tidedominated delta. Wave-dominated deltas occur in places where the sediments deposited by the river water are redistributed by waves. Because waves tend to move sediments along the shoreline, the shape of wave-dominated deltas is usually a smooth coastline. If the waves that affect the delta break parallel to the shoreline, the sediments of the delta will tend to be symmetrical on either side of the river. If the waves break at an angle to the shore, the sediments of the delta will tend to accumulate on one side of the delta. The Nile River Delta in Egypt is an example of a delta that is wave-dominated.

HUMANS AND DELTAS

Deltas play an important role in human life both historically and in present times. The land on deltas is typically very good for agriculture. On the parts of the delta close to the river, the soil is fertilized each year by nutrient-containing floodwaters when the river floods. In addition, by building aqueducts (canals or pipelines used to transport water) from the wetter lands near the river to the dryer lands farther from the water source, it is easy to expand the amount of land available for farming. This practice is called land reclamation. In particular, the fertile Nile delta has supported much of the agriculture in Egypt for thousands of years. Trade is another reason why humans have lived on deltas. Because of the many distributaries and the access to a major river and the ocean, deltas are regions where goods can be easily exported both inland and overseas. Many of the world's largest ports are in deltas. Also, communication is relatively easy in deltas. Because the land is usually flat, it is easy to build roads. The many waterways make boat travel easy as well.

LIFE ON DELTAS

The interdistributary areas of deltas can support a variety of different habitats, depending on whether they are closer to the freshwater of the river or the salt water of the ocean. If the interdistributary areas are close to the river and affected by annual floods, they are called floodplains. Other interdistributary areas near the river water may be freshwater marshes, freshwater swamps, or lakes. The interdistributary areas that are closer to the ocean are likely influenced by the tides. They may be tidal flats (flat, barren, muddy areas periodically covered by tidal waters), mangrove (a tree that grows in saltwater) swamps, salt marshes, or marine embayments (an indentation in the shoreline of the sea that forms a bay). Because deltas have such a broad range of environments, they host a diversity of species. Many different species of plants flourish on deltas, from saltwater trees called mangroves, to sea grasses, swamp sedges, and shrubs.

Deltas also serve as nursery grounds for many species of fish and invertebrates (animals without a spine) and many land animals such as snakes and birds. The marine (sea) areas are important habitats for burrowing worms and mollusks, crustaceans (sea animals with hard outer shells) that hunt for food along the seafloor, as well as a variety of different species of fish. Deltas also serve important environmental roles. They remove harmful chemicals that are deposited in them by river pollution. These chemicals are absorbed by sediments and trapped as new sediments settle on top. Over time, bacteria break down many of these harmful substances and release chemicals that are not dangerous to the health of humans or other animals. Deltas are also known as nutrient recharge zones. When animals and plants die, they are buried in sediments and bacteria digest them. This converts the chemicals in their bodies into the raw materials needed for plants to grow.

FRESHWATER LIFE

The animals and plants that live in freshwater are called aquatic life. The water that they live in is fresh, which means that it is less salty than the ocean. The terrestrial (land) environment that surrounds the freshwater environment has a large impact on the animals and plants that live there. Some factors that influence the freshwater environment include climate, soil composition, and the terrestrial animals and plants in the area. Just as on land, aquatic plants require carbon dioxide, nutrients (substances such as phosphate and nitrogen needed for growth) and light for photosynthesis, the process where plants make their food from sunlight, water, and carbon dioxide. Aquatic animals need to breathe in oxygen and consume food.

The physical conditions surrounding the body of water or wetland (lands that are covered in water often enough so that it controls the development of the soil) control the availability of these resources. For example, the concentrations of nutrients, oxygen, and carbon dioxide in the water depend on how much air gets into the water and on the chemical composition of the land nearby. The sediments (particles of sand, gravel, and silt) in the water influence how much light reaches the bottom of the lake or river. The temperature of the water affects how quickly animals and plants grow. The characteristics of the bottom of the body of water (sand, mud, rocks) and the speed of the currents (horizontal movement of water) control what kinds of plants and animals can live and reproduce in an area. In general, freshwater environments are divided into two major categories: lentic waters and lotic waters. Lentic waters are those that are moving, as in rivers and streams. Lotic waters are those that are stationary, as in lakes and ponds. Sometimes, however, rivers and streams flow into lakes and ponds and the two different habitats merge together. Some wetlands may also contain many characteristics of freshwater environments.

LIFE IN RIVERS AND STREAMS

Rivers and streams are characterized by several physical features. They are generally comprised of freshwater that flows in one direction. The flow of water is most often from an area of high altitude (like a mountain range) to an area of low altitude (like an ocean). Usually, the water flows quickly initially and slows as it moves downstream. Streams often join rivers, so there is more water at the end of a river than at the beginning. As rivers flow, they erode (wear away) rocks and pick up sediments, making rivers often murkier at the end. Because rivers and streams change so much from their beginnings to their ends, there are many different types of habitats for animals. As a result, the number of animal species that live in rivers and streams is greater than the number of species that live in lakes and ponds.

Plant life in rivers and streams

A major challenge facing plants that live in rivers and streams is staying in place, especially in swift currents. Plants have several different techniques to overcome the drag (the pull) of the water. Diatoms are a type of algae. Algae are marine organisms that range in size from microscopic phytoplankton to giant kelp and that contain chlorophyll, the same pigment used by land plants to perform photosynthesis. Diatoms avoid currents by using their small size. They grow in a single layer on the surfaces of rocks. Because of the friction between the rock surface and the water, the water flow slows nearly to a stop within about a tenth of an inch (one-quarter of a centimeter) from the rock's surface. This region is called the boundary layer, and it provides the diatoms with protection from the forces of the current that would otherwise drag them downstream.

Typical large river plants include algae, mosses, and liverworts. These plants overcome the drag of the water by using special adaptations to grip rocks. Large algae often attach themselves to rocks with root-like structures called holdfasts. In addition, plants often anchor themselves in nooks between rocks or where waters pool, to avoid the drag of the river water. River plants that live within the currents have developed techniques to withstand the forces of the water. These forces would quickly snap any plant with rigid stems or leaves. As a result, plants that live in rivers are very flexible so that they can easily bend and move with the currents.

Animal life in rivers and streams

Animals that live in rivers and streams also face the challenge of staying where they are. Many animals have hooks and suckers that they use to attach themselves to rocks. Blackfly larvae that live in streams in the northern United States and Southern Canada have suction cups that they use to stick to rocks in streams. Mayfly larvae have hooks that they use to fasten themselves to the algae growing on rocks. Other animals have streamlined shapes that minimize drag by presenting little resistance to water. Trout, which are extremely common in oxygen-rich fast-flowing waters, are shaped like torpedoes. Limpets are flattened molluscs that cling to the surfaces of rocks. Their flat shape decreases the currents' drag on them. Animals that live in streams and rivers have developed interesting ways of gathering food in the fast-flowing waters. Snails, limpets, and caddis fly larvae scrape algae from rocks using special mouthparts. Many different insect larvae, as well as freshwater clams, filter the water for small bits of food.

They have specialized mouthparts that look like brushes or combs that they use to strain the water and extract the edible plankton (animals and plants that float with currents) that float into their reach. Rivers and streams are homes to a large number of fish. Perch, smallmouth bass, largemouth bass, bullhead, carp, pike, and sunfish prefer the parts of rivers where waters slow. These fish tend to be large, visual predators (animal that hunts another animal for food) that hunt in pools for smaller fish and invertebrates (animals without a backbone). Sculpins and darters prefer the faster moving sections of the river where waters are highly oxygenated. They use the swift current to bring food to them rather than hunting for their prey. Trout are also found in these faster moving parts of the river.

LIFE IN LAKES AND PONDS

Large lakes are often divided into zones. The near-shore area is called the littoral zone. This is the part of the lake that is shallow enough for aquatic plants to grow. The limnetic zone, also called the epilimnion, is the surface water of the lake away from the shore. (The prefix epi means "on the surface" and the root word limn means "lake.") It extends down as deep as sunlight penetrates. The majority of the plant life in this zone is phytoplankton (microscopic plants that float in currents). The deep part of the lake is called the profundal zone or the hypolimnion. (The prefix hypo means "under.") No plant life exists in this zone because of the absence of light. Most of the biological activity is that of bacteria decomposing dead animals and plants.

Seasonal Changes in Lakes

Lakes and ponds are greatly influenced by the temperature changes throughout the seasons. The description below is typical for a lake in a temperate (moderate) climate, which experience seasonal temperature changes. Tropical lakes (those in hot and humid areas) will have less dramatic fluctuations in temperatures. In the summer, the Sun warms the epilimnion. Warmer water is less dense than colder water, so it floats on top of the cooler water in the hypolimnion. The region between the warm surface waters and the cold deeper waters is a transition zone where the water changes temperature very quickly with depth. This region is called the thermocline. The thermocline acts as a kind of barrier between the surface and the deep waters. In the early summer, the epilimnion is full of life. Phytoplankton can grow quickly because they have plenty of light and nutrients and the water temperature is warm. In turn, zooplankton (animals like crustaceans and small fish that float in the waters) feed on the phytoplankton. These zooplankton are food for larger fish and birds. As summer progresses, the phytoplankton use up the nutrients in the epilimnion.

They begin to die and sink to the bottom of the lake. There, decomposers, like fungi and bacteria, break up the dead phytoplankton and animals and convert them into the nutrients that phytoplankton need to grow. Because the thermocline acts as a barrier between the bottom and the top of the lake, these nutrients are unavailable to the phytoplankton in the epilimnion. Phytoplankton cannot grow in the hypolimnion, where there are nutrients, because there is no light. In the fall, the air temperature cools, which cools the surface of the lake. Eventually the temperature in the epilimnion becomes the same temperature as that of the hypolimnion. The thermocline disappears and the nutrient-rich waters from the hypolimnion mix with the waters in the surface of the lake. This is called the fall turnover. At this time, the nutrients from the bottom of the lake are mixed throughout the lake. However, because the amount of sunlight decreases in the fall and into the winter, the phytoplankton in the surface cannot grow very quickly. During the winter, the surface of the lake continues to cool. Freshwater is densest at 39°F (4°C). Ice, with a temperature of 32°F (0°C), is less dense than the deeper waters and so it forms on the surface of the lake. This provides fish and other invertebrates room to live under ice-covered lakes. The ice also acts an blanket-like insulation that helps keep the water underneath from freezing.

In the springtime, the temperatures warm so the ice melts. Eventually the whole lake becomes 39°F (4°C) and so the waters from the bottom mix with the waters from the surface. This is called the spring turnover. As summer begins, the surface waters warm and the thermocline again separates the epilimnion from the hypolimnion. Because of the fall and spring turnovers, the nutrients from the bottom of the lake are available to the phytoplankton in the surface waters. This sets the lake up for the summer's rapid growth of phytoplankton and all the animals that depend on them.

Plant Life in Lakes and Ponds

Some of the most plants in lakes and ponds are the smallest. These phytoplankton are usually single-celled plants grouped with the algae. Sometimes they connect themselves together into long strings called colonies. Common phytoplankton in lakes and ponds are diatoms, which have beautiful shells made of silica (the same material that comprises sand); dinoflagellates, which move by snapping their flagella (long whip-like cell extensions that can propel an organism; and cyanobacteria, which are bacteria that perform photosynthesis.

The larger plants in ponds and lakes include large algae and mosses, cattails, reeds, water lilies, bladderworts, willows, and button bush. These plants often grow in mud where the gases that they need to grow—such as oxygen and carbon dioxide— are scarce. Many larger plants have stems that are spongy and they pull gases from the air down into their roots. Plants on land use their roots to gather water and nutrients, however aquatic plants are surrounded by water, and nutrients are dissolved in the water. Some aquatic plants have given up their roots. For example, duckweed (or water lentil) and watermeal are small pea-sized plants that float on the surface of lakes and ponds in the spring and summer.

They absorb nutrients from the water and produce a lot of starches. By the fall, they are so heavy with nutrients that they sink to the bottom of the lake. They live out the winter in the mud at the bottom of the lake, existing on their stores of starch. By spring, they have used up so much of the starch, they are light enough to float again. They pop to the surface just in time to use the strong light of spring and summer for photosynthesis and they begin to use their starch stores once again. Other large plants, like milfoil, water soldier, and water hyacinths also float on the surface of lakes and ponds. The edges of lakes are often divided into four zones based on the physical environment and the types of plants found there. Beginning farthest from the water, the swamp plant zone contains plants that have roots in the shallow water. At times the water can recede from this zone, leaving the plants roots exposed to the air. Typical plants in the swamp plant zone are rushes and sedges (a type of plant that looks like a stiff grass). The next zone is called the floating-leaf and emergent zone. Here the water never dries up, but the lake is shallow enough that the tops of plants emerge out of the water. A typical plant that lives in this zone is the water lily, which has special gas filled chambers in its leaves that allow it to stay floating on the surface of the water. In the submerged plant zone, plants live entirely underwater. Canadian waterweed and many types of mosses live in this zone. The freefloating plant zone takes up the center of the lake. Here plants without roots, like duckweed and water soldier, float freely on the surface.

Animal life in lakes and ponds

Zooplankton float in the epilimnion of lakes and eat phytoplankton and other zooplankton. Usually, these animals are nearly transparent, in order to avoid being seen by their predators. Typical zooplankton in lakes include the water flea, Daphnia, which can reproduce without mating. Under normal conditions all of its offspring are female. However, when the animals are stressed, by lack of food for example, they will produce males. This mixes up the gene pool of the population and creates individuals that are likely to withstand environmental changes. Another typical freshwater zooplankton is the rotifer, which has bristles on top of its head that it whirls like propellers in order to move through the water and capture prey. Many insects have juvenile stages that are aquatic. Mayflies, caddis flies, mosquitoes, and dragonflies all live for some period underwater in lakes and ponds. They swim among the rocks and plants in the lake bottom for a season or several years. Then they metamorphose (change in appearance) into their adult form and fly away from the water. The bottom of the lake is also home to many different worms, mussels, and crustaceans. These animals feed on the remains of plants and animals that drop to the bottom of the lake from above. Larger animals live in lakes and ponds. In particular, fish, birds, and amphibians prey on the invertebrates that live in the lakes. Fish such as bluegills eat juvenile insects that swim in the bottom of the lake, while crappies eat zooplankton near the surface. Birds like flycatchers and warblers fly near the surface of lakes, preying on insects that are hatching from their juvenile stage. Frogs also hunt for insects that live near the pond. Still other birds and fish prey on smaller fish. Bass, salmon, osprey, loons, and heron hunt for fish by using their keen eyesight. Beavers and muskrats are mammals that depend on water for their homes. They build dams and lodges, which provide them with protection from predators.

GROUNDWATER FORMATION

Groundwater is fresh water in the rock and soil layers beneath Earth's land surface. Some of the precipitation (rain, snow, sleet, and hail) that falls on the land soaks into Earth's surface and becomes groundwater. Water-bearing rock layers called aquifers are saturated (soaked) with groundwater that moves, often very slowly, through small openings and spaces. This groundwater then returns to lakes, streams, and marshes (wet, low-lying land with grassy plants) on the land surface via springs and seeps (small springs or pools where groundwater slowly oozes to the surface). Groundwater makes up more than one-fifth (22%) of Earth's total fresh water supply, and it plays a number of critical hydrological (water-related), geological and biological roles on the continents. Soil and rock layers in groundwater recharge zones (a entry point where water enters an aquifer) reduce flooding by absorbing excess runoff after heavy rains and spring snowmelts.

Aquifers store water through dry seasons and dry weather, and groundwater flow carries water beneath arid (dry) deserts and semi-arid grasslands. Groundwater discharge replenishes streams, lakes, and wetlands on the land surface and is especially important in arid regions that receive limited rainfall. Flowing groundwater interacts with rocks and minerals in aquifers, and carries dissolved rock-building chemicals and biological nutrients. Vibrant communities of plants and animals (ecosystems) live in and around groundwater springs and seeps. Almost all of the fresh liquid water that is readily available for human use comes from underground. (The bulk of Earth's fresh water is frozen in ice in the North and South Pole regions. Water in streams, rivers, lakes, wetlands, the atmosphere, and within living organisms makes up only a tiny portion of Earth's fresh water.) For thousands of years, humans have used groundwater from springs and shallow wells to fill drinking water reservoirs, and water livestock and crops. Today, human water needs far exceed surface water supplies in many regions, and Earth's rapidly-growing human population relies heavily upon groundwater to meet its ever larger demand for clean, fresh water.

AQUIFERS: FRESH WATER UNDERGROUND

An aquifer is a body of rock or soil that yields water for human use. Most aquifers are water-saturated layers of rock or loose sediment. With the exception of a few aquifers that have water-filled caves within them, aquifers are not underground lakes or holding tanks, but rather rock "sponges" that hold groundwater in tiny cracks, cavities, and pores (tiny openings in which a liquid can pass) between mineral grains (rocks are made of minerals). The total amount of empty pore space in the rock material, called its porosity, determines the amount of groundwater the aquifer can hold. Materials like sand and gravel have high porosity, meaning that they can absorb a high amount of water. Rocks like granite, marble, and limestone have low porosity, and make poor groundwater reservoirs. Aquifers must have high permeability in addition to high porosity. Permeability is the ability of the rock or other material to allow water to pass through it. The pore space in permeable materials is interconnected throughout the rock or sediment, allowing groundwater to move freely through it. Some high-porosity materials, like mud and clay, have very low permeability.

They soak up and hold water, but don't release it easily to wells or other groundwater discharge points, so they are not good aquifer materials. Sandstone, limestone, fractured granite, glacial sediment, loose sand, and gravel are examples of materials that make good aquifers. Water enters aquifers by seeping into the land surface at entry points called recharge zones and leaves at exit points called discharge zones. (Some aquifers discharge into the ocean.) Influent or " water-losing" streams, ponds, or lakes are bodies of surface water in recharge zones that contribute groundwater from their water supply. Groundwater flows into effluent or "watergaining" streams and ponds in discharge zones. For the water level in an aquifer to remain constant, the amount of water entering at recharge zones must equal the amount leaving at discharge zones. (Imagine a bucket punched with holes under a dripping faucet. If water drips in at the same rate that it drips out, the water level stays the same.) If water discharges or is pumped from an aquifer more quickly than it recharges, the groundwater level will fall. The time an average water molecule spends within an aquifer is called its residence time. Water in some fast-flowing aquifers spends only a few days underground, while other rock layers can hold water for ten thousand years. Average aquifers have residence times of about two hundred years.

The water table and unconfined aquifers

Water enters aquifers by moving slowly down through a layer of surface rocks and soil whose pore spaces are partially filled with air (zone of infiltration). The water continues moving downwards until it reaches a level where all the pore spaces are completely filled with water (zone of saturation). The top of the zone of saturation is called the water table. In some wet, lowland regions, southern Florida for example, the water may be only a few feet (meters) below the surface. In others, like the American Southwest, water-saturated rocks may be hundreds of feet below the land surface. Groundwater reservoirs that have uniform rock or soil properties (porosity and permeability) throughout are called unconfined aquifers.

The water table forms the upper surface of an unconfined aquifer. The shape of the water table in an unconfined aquifer mirrors the shape of the land surface, but its slopes are gentler. In temperate (moderate) climates that receive moderate amounts of groundwater-replenishing rainfall, water infiltrates into unconfined aquifers in hilltop recharge zones and discharges into effluent streams and ponds in low areas where the water table intersects the land surface. Water will only rise to the level of the water table in a well, so a pump or bucket is required to extract water from an unconfined aquifer.

Confined aquifers and artesian flow

Confined aquifers are pressurized groundwater reservoirs that lie beneath layers of non-permeable rock (granite, shale) or sediment (clay). Groundwater enters a confined aquifer in recharge zones beyond the uphill edges of the confining layer and discharges beyond the downhill edges. Groundwater trapped beneath an impermeable barrier cannot rise to the height of the water table, so pressure builds up in confined aquifers. Artesian wells are wells drilled in confined aquifers where the pressure is great enough to make water flow at the surface.

LAKES

Lakes are large inland bodies of fresh or saline (salty) water. Lakes form in places where water collects in low areas or behind natural or man-made dams (barriers constructed to contain the flow of water). Some lakes are fed by streams (natural bodies of flowing freshwater), and some form where groundwater (water flowing in rock layers beneath the land surface) discharges onto the land surface. Water leaves lakes by flowing into outlet streams, infiltrating (soaking in) into groundwater reservoirs called aquifers, and by evaporating into the atmosphere (mass of air surrounding Earth). Lakes vary in size from large lakes such as the Great Lakes of North America, to small mountain lakes.

Lakes are larger than ponds, which are small bodies of fresh water that are shallow enough for rooted plants to grow. The study of ecology (relationships between living organisms and their environment) in lakes, inland seas, and wetlands is called limnology. Lakes store only a tiny percentage of Earth's fresh water. They are, however, an extremely important water resource for humans. Freshwater lakes provide water for agricultural irrigation (watering), industrial processes, municipal uses, and residential water supplies. People who live in the continental interiors use lakes for fishing and recreation, and very large lakes have important shipping and transportation routes. Humans also construct artificial lakes, called reservoirs, by building dams across rivers. In addition to providing the benefits of natural lakes, reservoirs also store water for specific communities, control floods, and generate hydroelectricity (electricity generated from water power).

HOW LAKES FORM AND DISAPPEAR

Earth scientists who study water on the continents (hydrologists and hydrogeologists) see lakes as temporary reservoirs within stream and groundwater systems. All water that falls as precipitation (rain, snow, sleet, hail) on the land surface of continents eventually makes its way to the ocean or evaporates back into the atmosphere. Water collects in lakes because it enters more rapidly than it escapes, but it is never permanently trapped there. As in a tub with a running faucet and an open drain, individual water molecules (smallest unit of water, each containing two hydrogen atoms and one oxygen atom) are constantly entering and escaping. After arriving in a lake, an average water molecule spends about one hundred years before moving to a new reservoir. (The time that an average water molecule spends in a reservoir is called it residence time. Water resides for about two weeks in rivers, forty years in glaciers (slow moving mass of ice), and between two hundred and ten thousand years in groundwater reservoirs.) To geologists (Earth scientists), lakes are temporary features. Stream-fed lakes within stream systems are destined for destruction.

Every stream seeks to create a constant slope, called a graded profile, between where the stream's waters begin and ends by eroding (wearing away) and depositing sediment (particles of sand, silt, and clay) along its course. When a natural or man-made obstruction blocks a stream, such as a river, streams deposit sediment in the lake or reservoir behind the obstruction and erode away in front of it. Eventually, the dam will collapse, and the lake will empty. Lakes that fill depressions and have no outlets fill when the regional climate becomes wetter or when warm periods melt mountain snows and glacial ice. They evaporate away during periods of dry weather and dryer climate. It may take thousands, or even tens of thousands of years, but lakes eventually drain, collapse, or dry up.

LAKE LAYERS AND OVERTURNS

Contrary to their common image as evenly mixed pools of unmoving water, lakes are complex, dynamic bodies of moving surface water. Lake water varies within the lake; its temperature, chemical content, light infiltration, and biological habitats vary from top to bottom and side to side. Furthermore, the vertical layering (stratification), horizontal variations, and circulation patterns within lakes change over time.

Waves, currents (a moving mass of water), and even tides affect circulation of water within lakes. Lakes are thermally stratified (layered according to temperature); they have layers of warm and cool water that are separated by layers where the temperature changes (thermoclines). Like the oceans, many lakes have a thin layer of warm surface water, and a thicker layer of cool deep water that is separated by a thermocline layer. Wind generates currents on lake surfaces and creates some mixing. Unlike the oceans, however, many lakes have seasonal overturns that mix their waters. water is denser than solid water (ice). Water reaches its maximum density at 39°F (4°C). Because of this odd property, the warm less-dense water rises, the cool denser water sinks, ice floats, and lakes overturn. Lakes that are ice-covered for part of the year undergo overturns that partially or completely mix their waters. Many lakes in temperate (moderate temperatures) regions like the northern United States overturn and mix completely twice a year (dimictic lakes). During the warm summer months, these lakes have a usual temperature profile with warm surface waters, a thermocline, and cool bottom water. In the fall, when the surface water cools down to 39°F (4°C), it becomes denser than the water underneath it and the surface layer sinks to the bottom. The bottom water rises to the surface, and the lake overturns. Over the winter, the bottom water is the warmest, and the frozen surface water is the coldest. (Plants and animals survive the winter on the lake floor in the chilly, but not frozen, bottom water.) In the spring, when the ice melts, and the water warms to 39°F (4°C), it sinks, and the lake overturns again. Limnologists classify lakes according to the number of mixing events they undergo each year. Lake type classifications have the root term mictic, meaning "to mix," and include:

- Oligomictic: Warm, ice-free lakes that rarely mix. They are warmest at the top, and coolest at the bottom. Tropical, oligomictic lakes have warm bottom water and very warm surface water. They rarely overturn because their water does not near 39°F (4°C).
- Meromictic: Warm, ice-free lakes that mix incompletely. These are deep lakes that are warmest at the top, and coolest at the bottom.
- Monomictic/dimictic/polymictic: Lakes with seasonal ice covers that overturn and mix completely once (monomictic), twice (dimictic), or many times per year (polymictic). Lake overturns are the norm in temperate regions, but local conditions affect the timing and number of overturns in specific lakes.
- Amictic: Lakes that never overturn because they are icecovered throughout the year. These lakes exist near the North and South Poles and atop very high mountains. They have cold bottom water that hovers near 39°F (4°C) and frozen surface water.

LAKE CHEMISTRY: SALINE LAKES

Many of Earth's largest and most important lakes contain salt water. All surface water contains some dissolved chemicals, called salts. Groundwater, streams, and freshwater lakes all contain the chemical components of rocks and minerals. Humans can drink fresh water because our bodies can use or at least tolerate the types and concentrations of dissolved chemicals it contains. Salt water, on the other hand, has a very high concentration of dissolved salts, and is undrinkable. The Dead Sea, on the border between Israel and Jordan, is Earth's saltiest body of water. It is truly a dead sea because it is too salty to support life. Saline lakes generally form in arid (dry) regions where surface water evaporates quickly. When water evaporates, the salts stay behind. Over time, the lake water becomes saltier. Some saline lakes, such as the Great Salt Lake, are all that remains of a much larger fresh water lake that has evaporated over time. Others, like the Caspian Sea in central Asia, began as saltwaterfilled ocean basins that have since closed. Saline lakes are often temporary features that fill during periods of wetter climate and then dry up when stream flow or groundwater discharge slows. Playa lakes are flat desert basins that occasionally fill with water.

Desert oases (watering holes) form and disappear with such regularity that thirsty travelers think they imagined them. The Great Salt Lake, Caspian Sea, Aral Sea, and Dead Sea are all presently evaporating. Over time, the dissolved chemicals become so concentrated in drying lakes that they bond together and form solid salt crystals. Thick layers of salt cover dry lake beds.

LAKE BIOLOGY

Lakes support rich communities of plants and animals (ecosystems) that have adapted to live within ever-changing conditions on lake beds, within the water column (water running from the surface to the lake floor, often showing differences in temperature, nutrients, etc.), and along lake shores. Lakes, like islands, are often closed systems that only rarely gain new species or individuals from other lakes. Many lakes host groups of rare species that have evolved (changed over time) together in their specific lake. These ecosystems are rich and unique, but fragile.

They have little defense against foreign predators or diseases. Human alterations and water pollution have threatened many lake species. Environmental groups and government agencies are presently attempting to protect and revive threatened lake species such as cichlids (rare doublejawed fish) that inhabit the lakes of the Great Rift Valley in east Africa. Lake organisms live in zones that are determined by the physical structure of their lakes such as the amount of available light, water depth, and distribution of nutrients. Most lake plants and animals live in shallow, well-lit surface waters called the euphotic zone. Most plants depend on the Sun's energy to produce food by the chemical process of photosynthesis, and they cannot grow in water that is too deep or too cloudy for light to penetrate. Lake animals such as fish need oxygen that plants give off during photosynthesis, so they live mostly in the euphotic zone as well. Plants with roots grow in shallow water along edges of lakes where light reaches the lake floor (littoral zone) and floating plants perform photosynthesis in the open surface waters (limnetic zone). Oxygen-consuming bacteria inhabit the deepest, darkest parts of lakes (benthic zone) where dead plant and animal materials accumulate. Limnologists also classify lakes by the balance of organisms and nutrients in their waters. Types include lakes that are described as oligotrophic, eutrophic, and mesotrophic.

- Oligotrophic: Nutrient poor lakes that support very few plants and animals. Oligotrophic lakes are typically cool, deep, and have very clear water. Very little organic (relating to or from living organisms) mud accumulates in oligotropic lakes, and they often have sand and gravel beds.
- Eutrophic: Lakes rich in plant nutrients that support abundant plant life in their surface waters. Their water is often clouded by microscopic plants, and their beds covered with thick layers of decaying plant material. Bacteria that live on the organic mud use up oxygen, and eutrophic lakes often have oxygen-poor deep water. Plants and bacteria eventually take over eutrophic lakes. They become oxygen-poor bogs and marshes where fish cannot live. Some chemicals that humans use, including fertilizers and detergents, cause a process called eutrophication when they run off into lakes, which causes the population of plants to increase to such an extent that eventually oxygen-starved fish die.
- Mesotrophic: Lakes with moderate amounts of nutrients and healthy, balanced communities of plants, animals and bacteria. Mesotrophic lakes receive adequate amounts of fresh water and nutrients, and seasonal overturns allow nutrient-poor and nutrient-rich layers to mix. Mesotrophic lakes are intermediate between crystal-clear, lifeless oligothrophic lakes and cloudy, muddy eutrophic lakes.

WHERE LAKES FORM: LAKE BASINS

Lakes form where water collects in depressions, or basins. Many lakes fill low areas created by plate tectonic movements (tectonic basins) and volcanic activity. (Plate tectonics is the movement of large, rigid pieces of Earth's outer rock shell called the lithosphere.) Retreating glaciers and ice sheets leave behind large basins and small depressions that fill with meltwater. Though flowing streams and rivers generally act to fill in and drain lake basins, other sedimentary processes can create landscape depressions and natural dams that confine water in lakes.

Lakes in tectonic basins

Rift valley lakes fill long, linear valleys within rift zones. (Rifts are areas where the continental lithosphere is stretching and beginning to break into pieces. They are the precursors of ocean basins.) A chain of large lakes including Tanganyika, Naiveté, and Malawi follows the Great Rift Valley through eastern Africa. Lake Victoria, the world's second-largest lake, lies between two branches of the rift valley. The Red Sea, Sea of Galilee, Dead Sea, and Gulf of Ababa fill the northern branches of the rift where it crosses the Arabian Peninsula in the Middle East. Russia's Lake Baikal, the world's deepest lake, fills an ancient, inactive rift valley in central Asia. Lakes also form in places where continents are moving toward each other. The Black Sea, Caspian Sea, and Mediterranean Seas fill a closing ocean basin between Africa and Europe. When continents collide, water fills depressions in the landscape over folded and broken (faulted) rock layers that were caught between the land masses. Slopes that are too steep collapse and block rivers with natural dams. Blocks of uplifted, erosion-resistant rock form bedrock that holds back mountain lakes.

Volcanic lakes

Volcanoes are mountains that form from eruptions of molten rock (lava) on the land surface. When a volcanic peak collapses into its emptied magma chamber (a pool or room of magna held under tremendous pressure within a volcano prior to a volcanic eruption), it forms a large circular basin called a caldera. (Craters, the small basins near the top of active volcanoes, sometimes also contain small lakes, but most significant volcanic lakes, including inaccurately-named Crater Lake, fill calderas.) Yellowstone Lake in Wyoming and Crater Lake in Oregon are examples of caldera lakes. Volcanic ash, mud, and lava flows also create natural dams in river valleys. A dam of volcanic rock confines Lake Tahoe in a high valley of the Sierra Mountains on the California-Nevada border.

Glacial lakes

The thick continental ice sheets that covered northern North America, Europe, and Asia during the Pleistocene ice ages (a division of geologic time that lasted from two million to ten thousand years ago) left behind thousands of lake and ponds when they retreated about twenty thousand years ago. The weight of the ice sheets pushed down on the continents, leaving broad basins that filled with melt water when they retreated. The Great Lakes of North America (Superior, Huron, Michigan, Erie, and Ontario) formed this way. Hundreds of lakes, such as the Winnipeg, Athabasca, Great Slave, and Great Bear cover the central and eastern provinces and territories of Canada that are still rebounding from their heavy ice load. Advancing glaciers also pile tall ridges of sediment, called moraines, at their toes (the end of extensions of glaciers along the ground). When glaciers retreat, moraines hold back meltwater. Small lakes and ponds also form in glacial depressions called kettles that form when blocks of ice buried in glacial sediment melt. Melting mountain glaciers feed many mountain lakes and glacial sediment traps streams and meltwater.

Groundwater discharge lakes

Water moving through pore spaces in rock and soil layers discharges on the land surface in places where the water table (level below which pore spaces are saturated with water) intersects the land surface. In regions with wet climates, the water table is near the land surface and ground water discharges in low spots. Groundwater chemically erodes limestone and other rocks and creates caves, cavities, sink holes, and collapse basins called karst features. Florida's many lakes, including Lake Okeechobee, are groundwater filled karst features.

PONDS

A pond is a depression in the ground that is filled with water that remains year round. Ponds range in size from the artificial backyard projects about the size of a bathtub to bodies of water that are about the size of a football field. Ponds support a variety of animal and plant life, and are also used as recreational sites by people. The difference between a pond and a lake involves size and water depth. A lake is big enough to have at least one beach (sand or rock that slopes down to the water) and contains enough water to generate waves from the wind that blows across the surface of the water. In contrast, a pond is usually too small for waves of any size to form. At the center of a lake, the water can reach depths of many hundreds, even thousands of feet (meters). A pond, however, is a shallow and still body of water where sunlight can usually reach down to the bottom.

HOW PONDS FORM

Natural ponds form in shallow depressions where rainwater (including runoff from nearby higher areas) collects. Water from an underground source such as an underground spring can also collect into a pond. Ponds that people enjoy in their backyard are often artificial, created by preparing the hole and adding water and plants to create a backyard oasis. These ponds can provide relaxation and a habitat for attracting insects, birds, and amphibians (such as frogs and salamanders), even in backyards located in a bustling city. Other artificial ponds are workhorses. One example is a sewage treatment pond. This type of pond keeps the sewage in a place where the growth of microorganisms can occur in the shallow and warm water. As microorganisms such as algae grow, they can use some of the materials in the sewage as food. This helps clean the water, and is an example of bioremediation, the process of using natural substances such as bacteria, to clean a contaminated natural resource, such as water.

LIFE IN AND AROUND PONDS

Ponds are havens for plants. Because the sunlight is abundant all through the water, plant can grow from every location in a pond. (Plants need sunlight to live as they convert the Sun's energy into food in a process called photosynthesis.) Often, the surface of a pond will be almost entirely covered with pond-loving plants such as the water lily and other plants that need higher levels of sunlight or that need direct exposure to air. Ponds also support various species of animal life, both in and surrounding its waters. Often, the bottom of a pond will be muddy, rather than rocky, and the mud hosts a variety of living creatures, such as crayfish.

The still pond water and muddy bottom are also favorable conditions for the eggs of insects and creatures such as frogs to develop (often attached to the stems or leaves of plants). For microscopic life such as bacteria and algae, a pond offers plenty of food and the sunlit water provides a suitable temperature for the microscopic cells to grow and divide. Animals such as deer often use natural ponds as a source of drinking water. Birds feed upon fish that live in ponds. Beavers find the still pond waters a good place to build their lodge. Ponds are often a source of relaxation and recreation. In warmer times of the year, a pond's edge can be a place where people picnic or rest outdoors. In the cold winter season of northern climates, ponds can freeze solid and host winter sports such as ice skating.

THE FATE OF PONDS

The flow of water into and out of a pond can be slow. This feature, along with its shallow depth, makes a pond vulnerable to contamination. If chemicals that upset the natural composition of the pond are introduced, then the water quality necessary to sustain life can be destroyed. Ponds that form in arid (dry) regions where rainfall is briefly heavy then sparse throughout the rest of the year continue a cycle of filling up, then slowly drying. These ponds attract animal life only when water is abundant, which can sometimes cause conflicts with humans. In some regions of Africa, crocodiles return during the rainy season to newly filled ponds that form near populated villages. Hungry after hibernating (being in an inactive state) the rest of the year, the crocodiles pose a threat to livestock that also drink from the pond, and the people who tend the livestock. As time passes, the vast majority of ponds will naturally fill in, as sediment (particles of gravel, sand, and silt) and other debris collect in the shallow water. After about one hundred years, what was once a pond often becomes a field, and the water source of the pond is diverted by the changing landscape or by changes in rainfall amounts.

RIVERS

Rivers are bodies of flowing surface water driven by gravity. Hydrologists, scientists who study the flow of water, refer to all bodies of flowing water as streams. In common language, it is accepted to refer to rivers as larger than streams. Water flowing in rivers is only a very small portion of Earth's fresh water. The oceans contain about 96% of the water on Earth, and most fresh water is bound up in glacial ice near the North and South Poles. Rivers shape the landscape and are integral to the hydrologic cycle (circulation of water on and around Earth) on the continents. Rivers shape the lands as they erode (wear away) and deposit sediment (particles of gravel, sand, and silt) along their courses. Running river water acts to level the continents. When geologic forces slowly raise (uplift) mountain ranges, rivers wear them away. The streams that form the Ganges River of India (headwater streams), for example, are presently tearing down the Himalayas almost as quickly as they are uplifted by the movements of Earth's crustal plates (plate tectonics).

When geologic forces create depressions or low areas on the continents, rivers act to fill them. River sediment replenishes floodplain (Flat land next to rivers that are subject to flooding) soils and coastal sands. Earth's major rivers, including the Nile, Amazon, Yangtze, and Mississippi, drain the waters of vast continental areas and set down (deposit) huge deposits of sediments at the ends of rivers that flow into the ocean (for example, in deltas at the end of many rivers) Rivers host vibrant communities of plants and animals, and refill groundwater reservoirs and wetlands that support biological life far beyond their banks. Rivers are a main focus of human interaction with the natural environment. Human agriculture, industry, and biology require fresh, accessible water from rivers.

Ancient human civilizations first arose in the fertile valleys of the world's great rivers: the Yangtze and Yellow Rivers in China, the Tigris and Euphrates Rivers in the Middle East, and the Nile River in Egypt. The distribution of Earth's rivers and systems of rivers has influenced human population patterns, commerce, and conquest since ancient times. Rivers flow through the great cities of the world, and the imagery of rivers is deeply embedded in our language, culture, and history.

Today, billions of people depend directly and indirectly on rivers for food and water, transportation and recreation, and spiritual and religious inspiration. Almost all major rivers are today confined by man-made dams and levees (walls along the banks) that provide people with the means to generate electricity and protection from floods.

These alterations to rivers have come at an environmental cost. When floodwaters are contained by levees or other flood-control dams, they no longer supply nutrients and sediment to floodplain soils that support agriculture. Furthermore, dams and levees that upset a river's natural path and profile (side view) cause changes to the patterns of erosion and deposition (depositing sediments) throughout the entire river system. Dams have contributed to beach erosion on many coastlines because dams trap sediment in reservoirs. Agricultural and urban development along riverbanks has threatened many species of plants and animals that live in riverside wetlands. Also, the very dams and levees that prevent frequent small floods create an increased risk of infrequent, disastrous flooding. The city of New Orleans, for example, lies at a lower elevation than the bed of the Mississippi River that runs through the center of the city in an artificial channel behind massive levees. If the levees failed, a flash flood would engulf the city and potentially threaten the lives of its residents.

MAJOR RIVERS

Earth's largest river systems define the natural and human environment within their watersheds. A watershed is the land area that drains water into a river or other body of water. A list of the world's major rivers is also a list of the major natural and cultural geographic regions on six continents. (The continent Antarctica is too cold for liquid water. Its fresh water is bound up in large masses of moving ice called glaciers.) ü Africa: The Nile is, by most measurements, the world's longest river. (River lengths are difficult to measure because rivers constantly shift their courses and change length. There is also disagreement about which branches of water (tributaries) are considered part of the main river. By some measurements, the Amazon River in South America is actually slightly longer than the Nile.) The Nile has sustained life in the inhospitable Sahara desert of eastern Africa for thousands of years. Its headwater (uphill end) streams flow from lakes in Ethiopia and Uganda and feed two branches, the White Nile and the Blue Nile, which meet in the Sudanese city of Khartoum. From there, the Nile cuts a green-bordered lifeline through the Egyptian desert.

It flows through Cairo, the bustling capital of modern-day Egypt, past the pyramids of Giza and the ancient Egyptian capital of Thebes, to its outlet in the Mediterranean Sea. The Congo River (called the Zaire River from 1971 to 1997) makes a long loop through the equatorial rainforests and war-torn nations of central western Africa. The Congo is the main trade and travel route into the African interior, and it is the setting for Joseph Conrad's famous novel Heart of Darkness. The Limpopo, Okavango, Ubangi, and Zambezi are other major African rivers. ü Asia: Huge rivers drain water from the massive Asian continent into the Pacific, Indian, and Arctic oceans.

In China, the Yangtze (Chang Jiang), Yellow (Huang He) and Pearl Rivers carry flowing waters (runoff) from the northern slope of the Himalayan Mountains and western China to the East China Sea. Hundreds of millions of Chinese people depend on these rivers for their electricity, food, and livelihoods. Water moving south from the Himalayas flows into the rivers of India and South Asia, including the Ganges-Bramaputra system and the Mekong River. The Ganges River of northern India is sacred in the Hindu religion. Hindus travel to its banks to meditate and wash away their sins. Upon death, cremated remains are placed into the Ganges in hopes of improving the deceased's fortunes in the afterlife. The Ob, Ikysh, Amur and Lena Rivers run across the northern forests and wind-swept tundra (treeless arctic plains) of Siberia (the Asian portion of Russia) into the icy Arctic Ocean. In the Middle East, rivers play an important role in the history and mythology of western civilization. The ancient civilizations of Sumeria and Mesopotamia arose in the "fertile crescent" between the Tigris and Euphrates Rivers (Shat-al-Arab) in what is today Iraq. Along with the Jordan River, they play major roles in Jewish, Christian, and Islamic history. ü Australia: The island continent of Australia has only a few major rivers, and its central desert, the outback, is extremely dry. The Murray River and its major tributary (major branch), the Darling, make up Australia's largest river system. The Murray drains water from the southeastern states of Victoria, New South Wales and southern Queensland and its floodplains are Australia's most productive farmlands. ü Europe: Rivers are intertwined in the history, culture, and geography of Europe. The capital cities of Europe are synonymous with their rivers (London and Thames, Paris and Seine, Vienna, Budapest and Danube). By their very names, the Rhone (France), Rhine (Germany), Volga (Russia), Oder and Elbe (Germany, Poland, Czech Republic), Po and Tiber (Italy), and Ebro (Spain) conjure images of great art and fine wine, desperate battles and bloody conquests, grand castles and ancient hamlets. ü North America: The Mississippi and its major tributaries, the Missouri, Ohio, and Arkansas Rivers, collect water from a huge drainage basin that spans the central plains of North America between the Rocky Mountains and the Appalachians. Canada's Mackenzie and Churchill Rivers empty into the Arctic Ocean, and the St. Lawrence River empties the Great Lakes into the Atlantic Ocean. The mighty Yukon River of northern Canada and Alaska carried prospectors to mines and mills during the Alaskan gold rush (1898–99).

Many of the great ports of the Atlantic seaboard and Gulf of Mexico lie near river mouths (the end of a river where the river empties into a larger body of water): New York (Hudson), Philadelphia and Washington, D.C. (Potomac, Susquahana), Norfolk (Delaware), New Orleans (Mississippi), and Houston (Brazos).

Rivers, including the Mississippi, Missouri, Colorado, Rio Grande, and Columbia, played central roles in European exploration and settlement of the American West. Today, the rivers that carried explorers Meriwether Lewis, William Clark, John Wesley Powell, and other legendary frontiersmen across the continent are used for agricultural irrigation, drinking water, recreation, and power generation. Their water is a valuable and heavily-sought resource. ü South America: The Amazon is the largest river in the world. It flows from the Andes Mountains of Peru, across the Brazil and empties into Atlantic Ocean on the northeast coast of Brazil.

The Amazon has more than 1,100 tributaries, 17 of which are longer than 1,000 miles (1,609 kilometers) long. The main river runs from west to east just a few degrees south of the equator, and its massive watershed lies entirely within the warm, wet tropical zone. The central Amazon contains Earth's lushest, wettest, most biologically diverse rainforest. The Orinoco (Venezuela),

Sao Francisco (Brazil), Parana (Argentina, Paraguay) and Uruguay (Uruguay, Brazil) rivers are other major waterways of South America.

STREAM SYSTEMS

Streams are any size body of moving surface fresh water driven towards sea level by gravity (force of attraction between two masses). Water scientists refer to all bodies of flowing sur- face water as streams regardless of size, yet in common language, streams are considered smaller than rivers. Stream systems are networks that collect fresh water runoff from the land and carry it to the ocean. Together, tree-shaped systems of small branch streams drain vast areas of the continents into large rivers. Stream systems of all sizes erode (wear down) sediment (particles of gravel, sand, and silt) along their courses and carve complex patterns into the landscape. They wear down slowrising mountains and fill valleys and lowlands (low and level lands) with layers of sediment.

Stream systems change character along their courses. Steep mountain streams feed shallow elevated streams that in turn flow into meandering rivers that snake across broad floodplains (flat, low-lying land near a stream that is covered with water when the stream overflows its banks). Deposits of sediment form at river mouths, the area where fresh river water enters the ocean. If a rubber duck was dropped into a mountain stream on Pike's Peak in Colorado, it might tumble down the mountainside in whitewater rapids to Cripple Creek. From there, the duck would rush over gravel beds where Colorado miners once panned for gold, and then float serenely across Kansas, Oklahoma, and Arkansas on the Arkansas River. It would pause to drift across huge man-made reservoirs, and then plunge through the spillways of dams before entering the swift, muddy waters of the Mississippi River. A few weeks or months later, you might spot the duck heading out to sea amid barges and river boats in New Orleans.

WATERSHEDS AND DRAINAGE PATTERNS

The land area that drains water into a stream is called a watershed or a drainage basin. A basin is a natural depression in the surface of the land. Watersheds can be as small as a hillside that feeds a wet-weather creek, and as large as a drainage system like the Amazon Basin that carries the runoff from most of a continent. Large watersheds are composed of many smaller drainage basins.

The boundaries between watersheds, called drainage divides, are ridge lines or high points where water flows down and away in all directions. A divide can be limited, like a ridge between two mountain gullies (deep ditches or channels cut in the earth by running water, usually after a rainstorm), or extensive, like the North American Continental Divide along the spine of the Rocky Mountains. Water that falls east of the Continental Divide eventually flows into the Atlantic

Ocean, and water that falls west of the Rockies ends up in the Pacific Ocean. Streams are arranged within watersheds in networks that feed water into larger and larger streams. Tree-shaped (dendritic) systems composed of small branch tributaries (small streams that flow into larger streams) that join and flow into large trunk streams are the most common type of stream drainage pattern. Less common drainage patterns develop where rock layers and geologic features affect the paths of streams. Drainage patterns shaped like cross-hatched garden trellises develop in hilly areas where there are ridges and valleys, and streams flow out from round volcanic mountains in radial patterns like spokes on wheels.

VALLEY AND CHANNELS

Streams cut down into the land surface and create valleys. A stream valley includes the entire area between hills on either side of a stream. The water-filled path of the stream at a specific point in time is called a channel. Over time, channels migrate back and forth and fill stream valleys with thick layers of river sediment. Some streams, particularly those in steep, mountainous terrain have narrow, V-shaped valleys and channels that fill most of the valley floor. Others, including most streams in gently- sloping basins and coastal lowlands have narrow channels that snake across wide sediment filled valleys. For example, the Mississippi River has carved a valley more than 100 miles (161 kilometers) wide and filled it with sediment hundreds of feet (meters) thick over thousands of years.

CHANNEL PATTERNS

Stream channels assume different patterns within their valleys: straight, braided and meandering. While many channels have straight segments between meanders or braids, truly straight channels are quite rare. They develop in steep, mountainous areas where geologic forces are slowing lifting up the land surface. Water flowing rapidly downhill from mountains saws straight channels down into solid rock.

Braided streams have many intertwined channels and islands of loose gravel that constantly shift across gravel-filled valley floors. They are common in streams that receive large pulses of water and course-grained sediment. The sediment-choked streams that carry water from the toes of melting glaciers are typically braided. Streams that bend and curve across gently sloping valleys and coastal plains are called meandering streams. (Individual loops and bends are called meanders.) During normal weather conditions, water flows in a narrow channel that snakes across broad plains of soft sediment. During floods, muddy water overflows the banks of the channel and deposits layers of mud and silt on the surrounding floodplains. River floodplains are typically fertile farmlands that have been replenished by floodwaters. The coarser grained sediment settles out of flood waters closer to the channel builds natural levees (walls along the banks of a stream channel) along its banks. The path of a meandering channel changes over time. Meanders grow from slight bends into nearly-circular loops. At a river bend, fast-flowing water erodes the outer channel bank and sediment accumulates on the inside of the curve in a deposit called a point bar. Eventually, the bends at the neck of the meander grow so close that the water bypasses the loop. This process strands crescent-shaped segments of the former channel and round point bar deposits called oxbows on the floodplain. Oxbow lakes are abandoned meanders that contain water. Channel patterns change down the course of a stream system between headwater streams and lowland trunk rivers. They also change over time as streams adjust to changing conditions of water flow, land incline, and amounts of sediment. Stream waters continuously erode and deposit sediment over time, and stream channels constantly shift across valley floors.

STREAM WATER FLOW

Water flows downhill due to Earth's gravity (force of attraction between two masses) pulling it. Streams, like rivers, are gravity-driven bodies of moving surface water that drain water from the continents. Water scientists, called hydrologists, refer to all bodies of running water as streams, no matter their size so, in one sense, rivers are large, well-established streams). In everyday communication, it is common to refer to streams as smaller than rivers. Streams transfer water that falls on the land as precipitation (rain, snow, sleet, and hail) to the oceans. Streams, again like rivers, constantly shift their courses and change length.

The stream is carried along a defined path, called a channel. Water flowing in stream channels is a powerful sculptor that carves landscapes and molds sediment (particles of rock, sand, and silt). It wears down mountain ranges and cuts deep canyons through solid rock. Stream waters support vibrant communities of plants and animals, and they have been the lifeblood of human civilization for thousands of years. Streams shape the land and are also integral to the hydrologic cycle (circulation of water on and around Earth).

EROSION AND DEPOSITION

Streams are the main agent of erosion (wearing away) on land. Water in fast-moving streams is usually turbulent. The flowing water is filled with swirls and small localized whirlpools of swirling water called eddies. Turbulent water picks up particles of sediment that have weathered from rock and soil and carries them downstream. (Weathering is the breaking up of rocks by physical and chemical processes, such as being exposed to the actions of water, ice, chemicals, and changing temperature.) Faster-moving water can carry more sediment in the water, and can push larger stones along the bottom of the channel. Some mountain streams move huge boulders, while sluggish lowland (low country and level) streams carry only fine grains of silt and mud. The sand grains and larger rock fragments that slide and bounce along stream beds wear away solid rock. In a straight stream, the fastest-moving water and area of greatest erosion is generally in the middle of the channel. Where a stream bends, the strongest current (a moving mass of water) is on the outside of the curve.

When water slows down, it drops its sediment load, causing sedimentary deposits to form along stream courses in areas of slowmoving water. The slower the current, the finer the sediment it deposits. In straight channels, stream water lays down sediment along the stream banks. In bending channels, sedimentary deposits called point bars form on the inside of the bends. Individual sediment grains travel downstream like hitchhikers. Sometimes the grains are picked up by a strong current or flood that moves them far downstream, but usually they don't go very far in a single trip.

The grains of sand on a beach each made a long trip with many stops before they arrived at the ocean. Whether an individual grain of sediment moves depends on the speed of water currents that vary as the amount of water moving through a stream changes. As water currents become faster they can move larger grains. Stream waters also erode rocks by dissolving its minerals, which causes them to crumble. Chemical weathering, also called dissolution, occurs when the slightly acidic water chemically alters the minerals in rocks, which causes them to break down. Clear stream water carries the chemical components (parts) of the rocks' minerals called ions (electrically charged particles). When conditions in the water change (the water slows or cools), the ions recombine into solid mineral crystals. This form of sedimentary deposition is called precipitation. Limestone, salt, and gypsum form by precipitating from water. Ocean animals like corals and shellfish take in ions and use them to build their shells. Some types of rocks, including chalk and flint (also known as chert) form from the remains of organisms.

GRADED STREAMS AND BASE LEVEL

All streams strive to reach a constant slope (incline) called a graded profile by eroding and depositing sediment. The profile (side-view) of a graded stream (a stream with a graded profile) is steep near the uphill end and gently sloping near the point at the end where a stream pours its water into a larger body of water. The position of the downstream end of the profile is determined by the water level at the outlet, called base level.

Streams cannot erode below base level. Almost all stream systems run to the sea, so sea level is the ultimate base level for most streams. Conditions change constantly in all streams, and the process of readjustment by erosion and deposition is ongoing. As conditions change along its course, a stream will readjust its profile by eroding sediment in some places and depositing it in others. If base level falls, stream waters cut down into the land surface. If it rises, they deposit more sediment. If the movements of the underlying plates of Earth's crust rise (geologic uplift) to steepen the upper part of a stream, it will erode down to regain its graded profile. Streams also attempt to level out obstructions along their path. They work to tear down dams, both natural and man-made, by erosion and filling the reservoir behind it with sediment. Lakes are, therefore, only temporary features of stream systems, and dams are interrupting the natural flow of a stream's water.

3

Tourism Products: Characteristics and Forms

INTRODUCTION

Along with this you already know by now the various perspectives of tourism. In this current session, we discuss what is a tourism product. As suggested, look at the characteristics and the forms of the tourism product. There will be a discussion on the forms like natural and man made tourism products. We go on to reading about the symbiotic, event based and site based products as well. We also see the new tourism products that have developed. In the end you can answer questions that will assess your understanding of the topic we have discussed.

DEFINITION OF TOURISM PRODUCT

A tourism product can be defined as the sum of the physical and psychological satisfaction it provides to tourists during their travelling en route to the destination. The tourist product focuses on facilities and services designed to meet the needs of the tourist. It can be seen as a composite product, as the sum total of a country's tourist attractions, transport, and accommodation and of entertainment which result in customer satisfaction. Each of the components of a tourist product is supplied by individual providers of services like hotel companies, airlines, travel agencies, etc. The tourist product can be analysed in terms of its attraction, accessibility and accommodation.

ATTRACTIONS

Of the three basic components of a tourist product, attractions are very important. Unless there is an attraction, the tourist will not be motivated to go to a particular place. Attractions are those elements in a product which determine the choice made by particular tourist to visit one particular destination rather than another. The attractions could be cultural, like sites and areas of archaeological interest, historical buildings and monuments, flora and fauna, beach resorts, mountains, national parks or events like trade fairs, exhibitions, arts and music festivals, games, etc.

Tourist demands are also very much susceptible to changes in fashion. Fashion is an important factor in the demand for various tourist attractions and amenities. The tourist who visits a particular place for its natural beauty may decide to visit some other attractions due to a change in fashion. Peter has drawn up an inventory of the various attractions which are of significance in tourism. However, the attractions of tourism are, to a very large extent, geographical in character.

Location and accessibility (whether a place has a coastal or inland position and the ease with which a given place can be reached) are important. Physical space may be thought of as a component for those who seek the wilderness and solitude. Scenery or landscape is a compound of landforms; water and the vegetation and has an aesthetic and recreative value. Climate conditions, especially in relation to the amount of sunshine, temperature and precipitation (snow as well as rain), are of special significance.

Animal life may be an important attraction, firstly in relation to, bird watching or viewing game in their natural habitat and secondly, for sports purposes, eg. fishing and hunting. Man's impact on the natural landscape in the form of his settlements, historical monuments and archaeological remains is also a major attraction. Finally, a variety of cultural features-ways of life, folklore, artistic expressions, etc. provide valuable attractions to many.

ACCESSIBILITY

It is a means by which a tourist can reach the area where attractions are located. Tourist attractions of whatever type would be of little importance if their locations are inaccessible by the normal means of transport. A Tourist in order to get to his destination needs some mode of transport. This mode may be a motor car, a coach, an aeroplane, a ship or a train which enables him to reach his predetermined destination. If tourist destinations are located at places where no transport can reach or where there are inadequate transport facilities, they become of little value.

The tourist attractions, which are located near the tourist-generating markets and are linked by a network of efficient means of transport, receive the maximum number of tourists. The distance factor also plays an important role in determining a tourist's choice of a destination. Longer distances cost much more in the way of expenses on travel as compared to short distances. An example can be that of India. About two and a half million tourist arrivals for a country of the size of India may look rather unimpressive. However if one looks at certain factors like the country's distance from the affluent tourist markets of the world such as the United States, Europe, Canada, Japan and Australia, one may conclude that the long distance is one of the factors responsible for low arrivals. It costs a visitor from these countries, quite a substantial amount, to visit India for a holiday. It has been stated earlier that Europe and North America continue to be the main generating and receiving areas for international tourism, accounting for as much as 70% and 20% respectively, of international tourist arrivals. Easy accessibility, thus is a key factor for the growth and development of tourist movements.

ACCOMMODATION

The accommodation and other facilities complement the attractions. Accommodation plays a central role and is very basic to tourist destinations. World Tourism Organization in its definition of a tourist has stated that he must spend at least one night in the destination visited, to qualify as a tourist. This presupposes availability of some kind of accommodation. The demand for accommodation away from one's home is met by a variety of facilities. The range and type of accommodation is quite varied and has undergone considerable change since the last half century. There has been a decline in the use of boarding houses and small private hotels.

Larger hotels are increasing their share of holiday trade, especially in big metropolitan areas and popular spots. In more traditional holiday and sea-side resorts in Europe and elsewhere, big hotels are keeping their share of holiday resorts. In recent years, some changes have been reflected in the type of accommodation. There has been an increasing demand for more non- traditional and informal types of accommodation. The latest trends in accommodation are holiday villages. In recent years there has been an increase in the popularity of such accommodation.

Accommodation may in itself be an important tourist attraction. In fact, a large number of tourists visit a particular destination or town simply because there is a first class luxury hotel or resort which provides excellent services and facilities. Some countries like Switzerland, Holland, France, Austria, and Belgium have gained a reputation for providing excellent accommodation with good cuisine. Many hotel establishments elsewhere in various countries, especially the resort hotels, have gained a reputation for their excellent cuisine, services and facilities. The French government for instance, paved the way for tourist development of Corsica by launching a big hotel development programme.

CHARACTERISTICS OF TOURISM PRODUCT

By now, you must have understood what a tourism product is. Now let us look at some of its characteristics:-

INTANGIBLE

Unlike a tangible product, say, a motor car or refrigerator, no transfer of ownership of goods is involved in tourism. The product here cannot be seen or inspected before its purchase. Instead, certain facilities, installations, items of equipment are made available for a specified time and for a specified use. For example, a seat in an aeroplane is provided only for a specified time.

PSYCHOLOGICAL

A large component of tourism product is the satisfaction the consumer derives from its use. A tourist acquires experiences while interacting with the new environment and his experiences help to attract and motivate potential customers.

HIGHLY PERISHABLE

A travel agent or tour operator who sells a tourism product cannot store it. Production can only take place if the customer is actually present. And once consumption begins, it cannot be stopped, interrupted or modified. If the product remains unused, the chances are lost *i.e.* if tourists do not visit a particular place, the opportunity at that time is lost. It is due to this reason that heavy discount is offered by hotels and transport generating organisations during off season.

COMPOSITE PRODUCT

The tourist product cannot be provided by a single enterprise unlike a manufactured product. The tourist product covers the complete experience of a visit to a particular place. And many providers contribute to this experience. For instance, airline supplies seats, a hotel provides rooms and restaurants, travel agents make bookings for stay and sightseeing, etc.

UNSTABLE DEMAND

Tourism demand is influenced by seasonal, economic political and others such factors. There are certain times of the year which see a greater demand than others. At these times there is a greater strain on services like hotel bookings, employment, the transport system, etc.

FIXED SUPPLY IN THE SHORT RUN

The tourism product unlike a manufactured product cannot be brought to the consumer; the consumer must go to the product. This requires an in-depth study of users' behaviour, taste preferences, likes and dislikes so that expectations and realities coincide for the maximum satisfaction of the consumer. The supply of a tourism product is fixed in the short run and can only be increased in the long run following increased demand patterns.

ABSENCE OF OWNERSHIP

When you buy a car, the ownership of the car is transferred to you, but when you hire a taxi you buy the right to be transported to a predetermined destination at a predetermined price (fare). You neither own the automobile nor the driver of the vehicle. Similarly, hotel rooms, airline tickets, etc. can be used but not owned. These services can be bought for consumption but ownership remains with the provider of the service. So, a dance can be enjoyed by viewing it, but the dancer cannot be owned.

HETEROGENEOUS

Tourism is not a homogeneous product since it tends to vary in standard and quality over time, unlike a T.V set or any other manufactured product. A package tour or even a flight on an aircraft can't be consistent at all times. The reason is that this product is a service and services are people based. Due to this, there is variability in this product. All individuals vary and even the same individual may not perform the same every time. For instance, all air hostesses cannot provide the same quality of service and even the same air hostess may not perform uniformly in the morning and evening. Thus, services cannot be standardised.

RISKY

The risk involved in the use of a tourism product is heightened since it has to be purchased before its consumption. An element of chance is always present in its consumption. Like, a show might not be as entertaining as it promises to be or a beach holiday might be disappointing due to heavy rain.

MARKETABLE

Tourism product is marketed at two levels. At the first level, national and regional organisations engage in persuading potential tourists to visit the country or a certain region. These official tourist organisations first create knowledge of its country in tourist –generating markets and persuade visitors in these markets to visit the country. At the second level, the various individual firms providing tourist services, market their own components of the total tourist product to persuade potential tourists to visit that region for which they are responsible.

FORMS OF TOURISM PRODUCT

By now you must be aware of what a tourism product is and what its peculiar features are. It is necessary to understand the components of the tourist product from the point of view of the consumer. The product for the tourist covers the complete experience from the time he leaves home to the time he returns. The tourist product today is developed to meet the needs of the consumer and techniques like direct sales, publicity and advertising are employed to bring this product to the consumer.

The tourist product is the basic raw material, be it the country's natural beauty, climate, history, culture and the people, or other facilities necessary for comfortable living such as water supply, electricity, roads, transport, communication and other essentials. The tourist product can be entirely a man-made one or nature's creation improved upon by man. A consumer can combine individual products in a large number of ways.

There would be many possible destinations, each with a number of hotels, each to be reached by more than one airline. Thus, the potential choice facing the consumer is very large. The large number of tourist destinations have placed at the disposal of a tourist a very large variety of tourist products in abundant quantity from a large number of competing destinations. This eventually, has led to the adoption of the new concept *i.e.*, the marketing concept in tourism by various countries promoting tourism. Tourism, basically, is an infrastructure based service product. The nature of the service here is highly intangible and perishable offering a limited scope for creating and maintaining the distinctive competitive edge.

The effective marketing of tourism needs constant gearing up of infrastructure to international standards and presupposes in its coordination with the tourism suppliers. In strategic terms, it calls for the action of an integrated approach to management and marketing. In operational terms, it means the implementation of a better defined, better targeted market-driven strategy for realizing the defined objectives. The important point to note here is that marketing is applied to situations where the choice can be limited to a relatively small number of brands giving the consumer a reasonable choice. The process of selection thus becomes easier. In the field of tourism this process is taking place by the increased use of 'package tours'.

A package tour is a travel plan which includes most elements of vacation, such as transportation, accommodation, sight- seeing and entertainment. The tourist product is a composite product, whether it is sold as a package or assembled by the individual himself or his travel agent. There are many tourism products that are available to the consumer today.

In modern times these products, whether traditional in nature like culture and pilgrimage, or modern like adventure, conventions and conferences, health, medical, etc. are being packaged, promoted and priced appropriately to woo as many tourists as possible. Tourism products can be classified as under for a better understanding of each of their peculiar characteristics.

NATURAL TOURISM PRODUCTS

These include natural resources such as areas, climate and its setting, landscape and natural environment. Natural resources are frequently the key elements in a destination's attraction.

Let us look at some examples:

- Countryside
- Climate- temperature, rains, snowfall, days of sunshine

- Natural Beauty- landforms, hills, rocks, gorges, terrain
- Water- lakes, ponds, rivers, waterfalls, springs
- Flora and Fauna
- Wildlife
- Beaches
- Islands
- Spas
- Scenic Attractions

The climate of a tourist destination is often an important attraction. Good weather plays an important role in making a holiday. Millions of tourists from countries with extreme climates visit beaches in search of fine weather and sunshine. The sunshine and clear sea breeze at the beaches have attracted many people for a very long time. In fact, development of spas and resorts along the sea coasts in many countries were a result of the travellers. urge to enjoy good weather and sunshine. In Europe, countries like France, Italy, Spain and Greece have developed beautiful beach resorts. North Europeans visit the Mediterranean coast searching for older resorts like Monte Carlo, Nice and Cannes on the Riviera and new resorts in Spain and Italy.

Beautiful beaches of India, Sri Lanka, and Thailand, Indonesia and Australia and some other new destinations are more examples of how good weather can attract tourists. All these areas capitalise on good weather. Destinations with attractive winter climates, winter warmth and sunshine are also important centres of tourist attraction. Many areas have become important winter holiday resorts attracting a large number of tourists. Around these winter resorts, winter sport facilities have been installed to cater to the increasing needs of tourists. People from warm climates travel especially to see snowfall and enjoy the cold climate. In countries with tropical climates, many upland cool areas have been developed as 'hill stations'. Hence climate is of great significance as a tourism product. The scenery and natural beauty of places has always attracted tourists.

Tourists enjoy nature in all its various forms. There are land forms like mountains, canyons, coral reefs, cliffs, etc. One of the great all time favourite tourist destination is the Grand Canyon, Arizona. Mountain ranges like the Himalayas, Kilimanjaro, and Swiss Alps, etc. There are water forms like rivers, lakes waterfalls, geysers, glaciers, etc. The Niagara Falls shared by Canada and the United States is an example of how scenic waterfalls attract tourists. Lake Tahoe in California and the, deserts of Egypt are other examples of great tourist products.

Other great natural wonders that attract tourists are the Giants Causeway of Northern Ireland, the Geysers of Iceland, the glaciers of the Alps, the forests of Africa etc. Vegetation like forests, grasslands, moors deserts, etc. has all been developed as tourist products. Flora and Fauna attract many a tourist.

Tourists like to know the various types of plants and trees that they see and which trees are seen in which seasons. There are many plants which are specific to certain regions and many times students and travellers visit those areas especially to see those varieties of plants.

Thick forest covers, attract tourists who enjoy trekking and hunting activities. Fauna attracts tourists who like to watch birds, wild mammals, reptiles and other exotic and rare animals. Countries in South East Asia have crocodile gardens, bird sanctuaries, and other tourist products that display the fauna of their region. Spas are gaining popularity as modern tourism products all over the world.

While most parts of the world have their own therapies and treatments that are effective in restoring the wellness and beauty of people. New kinds of health tours that are gaining popularity are spa tours. Spas offer the unique advantages of taking the best from the West and the East, combining them with the indigenous system and offering best of the two worlds. For example Swedish massages work well with the Javanese Mandy, lulur, aromatherapy, reflexology and traditional ayurvedic procedures. Now various spa products are being combined with yoga, meditation, and pranayama, giving a holistic experience to tourists. Spa treatments are now combined with other medical treatments to treat blood pressure, insomnia, depression, paralysis and some other diseases.

People are now travelling to spas and clinics for curative baths and medical treatment. In some countries like Italy, Austria and Germany, great importance is given to spa treatments. In Russia along the Black Sea coast and in the foothills of the Caucasus Mountains, there are many world famous sanatoria where millions of Russians and international tourists throng every year. Beach tourism is very popular among the tourists today. Tourists of all age groups, backgrounds, cultures and countries enjoy this tourism product. Besides attraction and saleability, beach holidaying has lead to overall development of tourism in many parts of the world.

The basic importance of beaches is that they provide aesthetic and environmental value of the beach such as beautiful natural scenery with golden sands, lush green vegetation and bright blue sky. The water should be clear, free of currents and underwater rocks. Beach tourism activities include water and land resource use. The water usage involves swimming, surfing, sailing, wind surfing, water scootering, Para- sailing, motorboat rides, etc.

The land use has multifacets like sunbathing, recreational areas for tourists (parks, playgrounds, clubs, theatre, amusement parks, casinos, cultural museums, etc.), accommodation facilities (hotels, cottages, villas, camping sites, etc.), car and bus parking areas, entertainment and shopping complexes, access roads and transportation network. Due to its multidimensional requirements the beach product needs special care. A beach resort needs to be developed as an integrated complex to function as a self-contained community. Environmental management should also ensure the availability of necessary infrastructure in the immediate hinterland to the coastal region in support of the development on the coast to maintain its ecosystem. Islands abound with natural beauty, with the rare flora and fauna and tribes. This makes islands an ideal place for adventure, nature and culture lovers to visit.

This tourist product has great scope as these islands are being developed as tourist paradises. For example, Hawaii, Maldives, Mauritius, Tahiti, Andaman and Nicobar Islands, etc. has developed with tourism activity over the past few decades. The topography is generally undulating and they offer natural scenic beauty with exotic flora and fauna. Most of these islands have places of worship like churches, temples, etc. As an added attraction some of these islands have developed as tax havens thereby encouraging commercial development of these economies.

They offer social and cultural attractions as tourists can experience the local lifestyle, local food, fairs and festivals, etc. Scenic attractions, like good weather, are very important factors in the development of tourism. Breath-taking mountain scenery and the coastal stretches exert a strong fascination on the tourist the magnificent mountain ranges provide an atmosphere of peace and tranquillity. Tourists visiting the northern slopes of the Alps in Switzerland and Austria and the southern slopes in Italy and also the Himalayan slopes of India and Nepal for the first time, cannot but be charmed by their physical magnificence.

MAN- MADE TOURISM PRODUCTS

Man- made tourism products are created by man for pleasure, leisure or business.

Man- made tourism products include:

CULTURE

- Sites and areas of archaeological interest
- Historical buildings and monuments
- Places of historical significance
- Museums and art galleries
- Political and educational institutions
- Religious institutions

Cultural tourism is based on the mosaic of places, traditions, art forms, celebrations and experiences that portray the nation and its people, reflecting the diversity and character of a country. Garrison Keillor, in an address to the 1995 White House Conference on Travel and Tourism, best described cultural tourism by saying, "We need to think about cultural tourism because really there is no other kind of tourism. It's what tourism is...People don't come to

America for our airports, people don't come to America for our hotels, or the recreation facilities....They come for our culture: high culture, low culture, middle culture, right, left, real or imagined—they come here to see America." Two significant travel trends will dominate the tourism market in the next decade.

- Mass marketing is giving way to one-to-one marketing with travel being tailored to the interests of the individual consumer.
- A growing number of visitors are becoming special interest travellers who rank the arts, heritage and/or other cultural activities as one of the top five reasons for travelling.

The combination of these two trends is being fuelled by technology, through the proliferation of online services and tools, making it easier for the traveller to choose destinations and customise their itineraries based on their interests. Today we can witness large masses of people travelling to foreign countries to become acquainted with the usages and customs, to visit the museums and to admire works of art. One way of hastening the beneficial effects resulting from tourism is to bring the cultural heritage into the economic circuit, thus justifying the investments made at the cost of the national community, for its preservation.

Taking an economic view of the cultural heritage of a nation may not altogether be justified, considering that the preservation of its culture is one of the basic responsibilities of any community.

But considering the financial obstacles especially for the developing countries, this may appear to be a rational approach. Hence mass tourism can contribute unique benefits to the exploiting of the cultural heritage of a nation and can serve indirectly to improve the individual cultural levels of both citizens and travellers. Cultural resources have another specific characteristic, which many tourists want to experience the exotic.

There will be a great urge on the part of the tourist to visit and become acquainted with the ancient civilization in their quest for novel human knowledge. Culture means the prospect of contact with other civilizations, their original and varied customs and tradition with their distinct characteristics. This entire process creates a powerful motivator towards travel. Various Museums also attract tourists like Madame Tussauds Museum in London, the Louvre Museum in Paris, Smithsonian Washington Museum, Museums of famous painters like Salvador Dali, Pablo Picasso, Natural History Museum, British Museum, Museum of Modern Art are also popular tourist products. Sites of archeological interest like remains of Mohenjodaro and Harrapan civilizations, museums for fossils and dinosaurs.

Sites for historical interest like city of Hiroshima and Nagasaki, sites of holocaust in Germany, tombs of various leaders and emperors. Historical buildings like Warwick Castle, Tower of London, Stratford-on-Avon which is Shakespeare's birthplace, the Roman Baths are all popular with tourists. Even historical cities like Varanasi in India get a lot of tourists due to its status as one of the oldest cities of the world. Stonehenge in United Kingdom, The White House, Buckingham Palace and other places of political significance, are also great tourist draws.

TRADITIONS

- Pilgrimages
- Fairs and festivals
- Arts and handicrafts
- Dance
- Music
- Folklore
- Native life and customs

A pilgrimage is a term primarily used for a journey or a search of great moral significance. Sometimes, it is a journey to a sacred place or shrine of importance to a person's beliefs and faith. Members of every religion participate in pilgrimages. A person who makes such a journey is called a pilgrim. Secular and civic pilgrimages are also practiced, without regard for religion but rather of importance to a particular society. For example, many people throughout the world travel to the City of Washington in the United States for a pilgrimage to see the Declaration of Independence and the Constitution of the United States. British people often make pilgrimages to London to witness the public appearances of the monarch of the United Kingdom.

A large number of people have been making pilgrimages to sacred religious places or holy places. This practice is widespread in many parts of the world. In the Christian world, for instance, a visit to Jerusalem or the Vatican is considered auspicious.

Among Muslims, a pilgrimage to Mecca is considered a great act of faith. In India there are many pilgrimage centres and holy places belonging to all major religions of the world. India is among the richest countries in the world as far as the field of art and craft is concerned. Tourists like to visit and see the creative and artistic treasures of various countries.

Every country has certain traditional arts like soap sculptures and batik of Thailand; gems and jewellery, tie and dye works, wood and marble carving in Indonesia; ivory, glasswork, hand block printing, sandalwood, inlay work; are some of the examples of traditional art that attract tourists. There are many forms of dance in the world like Salsa, Hip- Hop, Jazz, Flamingo, Ballet and Traditional Dances. People who travel like to watch these dance performances and sometimes even take some introductory classes.

Music can be either traditional or modern. Traditional music like folk music and classical and country music is specific to every region and country. Modern forms include Blues, Rock, Pop, Jazz, Rap, Techno and Hip- Hop. Music also adds to the attraction of a destination. Fairs and Festivals capture the fun loving side and bring out the joyous celebrations of the community. Festivals like Christmas, Easter, Thanksgiving, Eid, Ramadan, Diwali, and Holi and so on, also bring people to destinations where the celebration can be enjoyed. Some popular Fairs which cater to fun and work are Pushkar Mela in Rajasthan, Prêt fair in Paris, Magic Fair in Vegas for garments, Hong Kong Fashion Week and various job fairs where people are recruited.

ENTERTAINMENT

- Amusement and recreation parks
- Sporting events
- Zoos and oceanariums
- Cinemas and theatre
- Night life
- Cuisine

Tourist products that have entertainment as their main characteristic are many. Just to name a few there are amusement and recreational parks like Disneyworld in United States, Hong Kong, Paris, Singapore and theme parks in various countries and cities like Appu Ghar and Fun and Food Village in Delhi, Essel World in Mumbai and so on.

Tourists may come to attend sports events and it is also an opportunity to explore the country. The fundamental concept is that all tourist activities have an influence on providing economic benefits and have a powerful influence in some definite locality, like the Olympics in Athens has given immense benefit to all in tourism business in Athens in particular and Greece in general.

Many countries organise year round sports events like swimming meets, athletic meets, weight lifting events, cricket matches, baseball and football events and many more such events which encourage tourism. India will be hosting the Common-Wealth Games on 2010 and it is anticipated to give the tourism industry a big boost.

Night Life is one of the prime attractions in a holiday. Tourists like to especially visit areas in cities where the night life activity is promoted. These areas are usually lit up with street stalls like flea markets and food areas. Bars, night clubs, casinos and very often open air bands attract and add to the psychological satisfaction and experience of tourists.

Cuisine is very often an understated but highly important part of any holiday. Now-a-days there is cuisine from all areas of the world which is found at most tourist destinations. Specialty restaurants serve Indian, Continental, Chinese, Italian, Japanese, Thai, Indonesian, Fast food, Mexican, Mediterranean, and Arabic and so on. However, tourists usually like to eat the local food of the areas they visit.

BUSINESS

- Conventions
- Conferences

People who travel in relation to their work come under the category of business tourism. However such travel for business purposes is also linked with tourist activity like visiting places of tourist attraction at the destination, sight seeing and excursion trips. Business travel is also related to what is termed today as convention business, which is a rapidly growing industry in hospitality and tourism.

A business traveller is important to the tourism industry as it involves the usage of all the components of tourism. He travels because of different business reasons- attending conventions and conferences, meetings, workshops etc. Participants have a lot of leisure time at their disposal.

The conference organisers make this leisure time very rewarding for participants by organising many activities for their pleasure and relaxation. The spouses and families accompanying the participants are also well looked after by the organisers. The organisers plan sight seeing tours and shopping tours for the participants and their families. In India, cooking classes for learning Indian food cooking from the various states, visits to the craft bazaars where tourists see how artisans make clay pots and other handicrafts, they visit tie and dye units to see Indian printing eg. Batik printing etc. Women tourists enjoy henna demonstrations. Conferences are events which require meticulous planning and efficient implementation, co-coordinating various activities so that the right things happen at the right time.

There are a number of players in the convention business. On one hand are the customers or the consumers and on the other hand are the principle suppliers like hotels, transporters, convention centres, tour operators and travel agencies, tourism departments, exhibition organisers, sponsors etc.

SYMBIOTIC TOURISM PRODUCTS

Wildlife sanctuary, Marine parks, Aero products and Water sports, Flower festivals are the example of tourism products which are a blending of nature and man. Nature has provided the resource and man has converted them into a tourism product by managing them. National parks for example, are left in their natural state of beauty as far as possible, but still need to be managed, through provision of access, parking facilities, limited accommodation, litter bins etc.

Yet the core attraction is still nature in this category of product. These products are symbiosis of nature and man. In case of adventure sports tourists can be participants. The basic element of adventure is the satisfaction of having complete command over one's body, a sense of risk in the process, an awareness of beauty and the exploration of the unknown. Adventure tourism can be classified into aerial, water based and land based.

Aerial adventure sports include the following activities:

- Parachuting, which involves jumping off from an aircraft or balloon and descending by means of a parachute. The infrastructure required, includes an aircraft, parachutes and large landing zones
- Sky Diving, which involves a sky diver jumping off an aircraft or balloon at a much greater height without deploying his parachute initially and opening it after some interval at a pre determined height.
- Hang Gliding, which involves running off a mountain or being towed by a winch and essentially flying like a glider where the directional control is achieved by a shift in his own weight by the pilot.
- Para Gliding, is the latest aero-sport which has taken the world by storm. A Para Glider is a specially designed square parachute, along with a harness attached by lines.
- Para Sailing is a simple sport that involves towing a parachutist to a height of a few hundred feet in the air and then descending by means of a parachute. As a year round activity, Para sailing can be done on land and water.
- Bungee Jumping, which requires no equipment except a 'bungee cord' made of nylon fibre of enough elasticity to be able to absorb the shock at the end of the jump. The jumper makes a headlong jump into empty space and the resultant rush of adrenalin makes the experience very exhilarating.
- Ballooning, where a balloon is attached to a basket by steel wire ropes. By regulating hot and cold air, the pilot can steer the balloon along any charted course.

Water based adventure sports include the following:

- White water rafting which is one of the most important and exciting water sports, which involves riding down water rapids in an inflatable raft which is used to negotiate fast flowing rivers.
- Canoeing and Kayaking are adventure sports which begin upstream where the water is wild and white. The gradient best suited for canoeing is the stage near the river's entry into the plains where the trip can be combined with a natural holiday in a forest. Kayaking is appealing as it enables innovation on the river by one or two oarsman seated in tandem.
- Adventure sports in the waters of the sea like wind surfing, scuba diving, snorkeling, yachting, water skiing, etc. also offer thrilling activities to the tourists.

Land based adventure tourist products include the following:

- Rock climbing which originated as a means of practicing techniques for ascending high mountains. It was earlier provided as training to mountaineers but has now evolved into a highly developed sport. The climber moves up, using knowledge of rope handling, climbing, securing one to another, etc. Very sophisticated techniques and equipments are used nowadays to ascend or descend on very steep terrain.

- Mountaineering requires trained physical ability and suitable equipment. The higher peaks need better equipment which is also costly. The challenges which mountains like the Indian Himalayas pose attract mountaineers from various countries.
- Trekking the mighty Himalayas which spread across five Indian states form a sweeping arc and compress in its expanse a wide geographical variety and contrasting cultures.
- Skiing is the practice of sliding over snow on runners, called skis, attached to each foot. There are three types of ski resorts, the first are large towns, second type are alpine villages and the third resorts built for skiing.
- Heli skiing is a type of alpine skiing where the skier is dropped to the top of a mountain by a helicopter and then he slides down on his own.
- Motor Rally is a sport that tests the navigational skills of man and his endurance with the machine. Motor rallies, grand prix racing, hill climbing rallies, vintage car rallies, sports car racing, etc. are some forms of this tourism product.
- Safaris were earlier taken on camel, horse and elephants as an excursion for hunting or a journey. As a modern tourist product now safaris are taken on jeeps and in the form of caravans. Viewing and enjoying nature, meeting the local villagers, seeing their traditions, customs and lifestyle, entertainment and camp fires are some of the characteristics of modern safaris. Eg, Egypt desert safaris. Horse and elephant safaris are arranged in most of the national parks and wildlife sanctuaries.

EVENT BASED TOURISM PRODUCTS

Where an event is an attraction, it as an event based tourist product. Events attract tourists as spectators and also as participants in the events, sometimes for both. The Ocktoberfest organised in Germany, Dubai and Singapore shopping festivals, the camel polo at Jaisalmer, Kite flying in Ahmedabad attracts tourists, both as spectators and participants.

Whereas in case of the Snake Boat race of Kerala can be enjoyed witnessing it. Event attractions are temporary, and are often mounted in order to increase the number of tourists to a particular destination. Some events have a short time scale, such as the Republic Day Parade, others may last for many days, for example Khajuraho Dance Festival or even months like the Kumbh Mela.

A destination which may have little to commend it to the tourist can nevertheless succeed in drawing tourists by mounting an event such as an unusual exhibition.

SITE BASED TOURISM PRODUCTS

When an attraction is a place or site then it is called a site based tourist product. Site attractions are permanent by nature, for example Taj Mahal, The Great Wall of China, The Grand Canyon in Arizona, Eiffel Tower, Statue of Liberty, Temples of Khajuraho, etc. A site destination can extend its season by mounting an off season event or festival. A large number of tourists are attracted every year by the great drawing power of Stratford on Avon in England because of its association with Shakespeare, the city of Agra in India with its famous Taj Mahal, Pisa in Italy for its famous Leaning Tower. Some new features have been added to the same product to keep the tourist interest alive in the products. For example now visitors can see Taj by night, music shows have been organised with Taj as the backdrop so that there are repeat tourists.

OTHER TOURISM PRODUCTS

HEALTH TOURISM

Holidaying is generally considered as an investment in health, a subject that presents opportunities of cost- benefit analysis. The medical expertise of various countries has added a new product to the existing tourism products. People are travelling to various countries for treatment of various ailments and medical procedures like Cardio care, Bone Marrow Transplant, Dialysis and Kidney transplant, Neuro surgery, Joint Replacement Surgery, Urology, Osteoporosis, and numerous other diseases.

Even cosmetic surgery, alternative medicines like homeopathy, acupressure, ayurvedic medicines and naturopathy are also becoming tourism products wherein travel companies are offering Yoga and Rejuvenation packages. Tourists travel for what is illegal in one's own country, *e.g.* abortion, euthanasia; for instance, euthanasia for noncitizens is provided by Dignitas in Switzerland. Tourists travel also for advanced care that is not available in one's own country, in the case that there are long waiting lists in one's own country or for use of free or cheap health care organisations.

ECO-TOURISM

Tourism that combines local economic development, protection of the quality of the environment and promotion of the natural advantages and the history of an area. The combination of all or some of the above kinds of tourism could contribute significantly to the development of tourism in any country. The availability of tourist packages involving gastronomy, entertainment and information about the cultural wealth of a country should be regarded as a priority issue for tourist agents, as it will reduce the concentration of tourist activity in certain areas and will improve and enrich the tourist.

RURAL TOURISM

Any form of tourism that showcases the rural life, art, culture and heritage at rural locations, thereby, benefiting the local community economically and socially as well as enabling interaction between the tourists and the locals for a more enriching tourism experience an be termed as rural tourism. It is multifaceted and may entail farm/agricultural tourism, cultural tourism, nature tourism, adventure tourism, and eco- tourism.

The stresses of urban lifestyles have lead to this counter- urbanisation approach to tourism. There are various factors that have lead to this changing trend towards rural tourism like increasing levels of awareness, growing interest in heritage and culture and improved accessibility and environmental consciousness, Tourists like to visit villages to experience and live a relaxed and healthy lifestyle.

ETHNIC TOURISM

Ethnic tourism is travelling for the purpose of observing the cultural expressions of lifestyles of truly exotic people. Such tourism is exemplified by travel to Panama to study the San Blas Indians or to India to observe the isolated hill tribes of Assam. Typical destination activities would include visits to native homes, attending traditional ceremonies and dances, and possibly participating in religious rituals.

SENIOR CITIZEN TOURISM

A newly emerging trend in tourism, basically for senior citizens or old people who live in isolation, especially in the west, because of daily busy schedules of their children and more importantly the attitudes. The characteristic feature of this type of tourism is that the senior people are less demanding in the form of facilities and services, besides leaving minimum impact on the destination community and their main consideration is on personalised service.

SPIRITUAL TOURISM

Many people when living under conditions of stress turn to spirituality. The Eastern world is considered to be very spiritual with many of the new age Gurus and their hermitages. This takes the form of another tourism product, that is, spiritual tourism. Tourists visit places to attend spiritual discourses and meditation workshops. For example, The Osho Foundation, Art of Living Foundation which have centres all over the world, Buddhist Monasteries and Ashrams.

GOLF TOURISM

Golf has been enjoyed by many for a long time. Earlier it was enjoyed as a sport but in recent times it has developed into a hot tourism product. Many tourist organizations plan promotional packages to woo the golf tourist especially from Japan where the green fees are very high. These tourists take exclusive golfing holidays wherein their accommodation is also arranged near the course and they return after serious golf playing.

CONCLUSION

You must be now clear about what really is a tourism product along with its unique and distinguishing features. We have discussed in the various forms of tourism products. By now you know natural, man-made, symbiotic, event based and site based tourist products. Now when you look around you, in any newspaper, magazine or even T.V. programmes, you will see the various tourism products and will be able to identify their forms. At this stage it's important for you to understand and identify how each tourism product has a distinguishing feature and its marketing strategy must highlight this feature.

Advertising, publicity, sales promotion, brochures, pamphlets, posters, direct mailing, personal selling and advertorial are some of these strategies. The tourism product has to be packaged and priced keeping in mind the target customer. Without any doubt, tourism is the main sector that can play a significant part in achieving rapid economic growth and drastically reducing unemployment in our country. Currently, it is the largest foreign exchange earner for our country. The development of the tourism industry on a priority basis is the need of the hour. You will study about Tourism as an industry and the economic impact of tourism.

4

Types and Forms of Tourism

RELIGIOUS TOURISM

Religious tourism, also commonly referred to as faith tourism, is a form of tourism whereby people of faith travel individually or in groups for pilgrimage, missionary, or leisure purposes.The International Conference on Religious Tourism estimates the worldwide faith tourism industry at $18 billion. North American religious tourists comprise an estimated $10 billion of this industry.

TOURISM SEGMENTS

Religious tourism comprises many facets of the travel industry including:

- Christian and faith-based camps
- Crusades, conventions, and rallies
- Faith-based cruising
- Leisure vacations
- Missionary travel
- Monastery visits and guest-stays
- Pilgrimages
- Religious tourist attractions
- Retreats

STATISTICS

Although no definitive study has been completed on worldwide religious tourism, some segments of the industry have been measured,

- The Religious Conference Management Association, in 2006 more than 14.7 million people attended religious meetings, an increase of more than 10 million from 1994 with 4.4 million attendees.
- The U.S. Office of Travel and Tourism Industries, Americans traveling overseas for "religious or pilgrimage" purposes has increased from 491,000 travellers in 2002 to 633,000 travellers in 2005.
- The World Tourism Organization, an estimated 300 to 330 million pilgrim's visit the world's key religious sites every year.

- One-quarter of travellers said they were currently interested in taking a spiritual vacation. More than one in ten travellers said they were more interested now compared to five years ago in taking a spiritual vacation. The appeal of a spiritual vacation spans the ages, with approximately one-third of each age group expressing current interest in taking such a vacation.
- Religious attractions including Sight and Sound Theatre attracts 800,000 visitors a year while the Holy Land Experience and Focus on the Family Welcome Centre each receives about 250,000 guests annually. Religious tourism, also commonly referred to as faith tourism, is a form of tourism whereby people of faith travel individually or in groups for pilgrimage, missionary, or leisure purposes. The International Conference on Religious Tourism estimates the worldwide faith tourism industry at $18 billion.
- The 50,000 churches in the United States with religious travel programmes
- The Christian Camp and Conference Association states that more than eight million people are involved in CCCA member camps and conferences, including more than 120,000 churches.
- The United Methodist Church experienced an increase of 455% in mission volunteers from 1992 with almost 20,000 volunteers compared to 110,000 volunteers in 2006.

COUNTRIES, TOURIST BOARDS AND RELIGIOUS TOURISM

- *Bahamas*: One of the few countries with a Director of Religious Tourism and staff dedicated to attracting faith-based visitors
- *Cypress*: Launching new marketing efforts to increase religious tourism of its current 100,000 faith-based visitors annually
- *India*: Largest portion of visitors are religious pilgrims
- *Israel*: Tourism ministry looks to boost tourism from North America
- *Italy*: Religious tourism in Italy alone generates over $4.5 billion each year.
- *Jordan*: Promoting niche markets such as religious tourism is a large part of Jordan's overall tourism strategy
- *Scotland*: Projected to triple from religious tourism dollars of GBP 80-100 to GBP 300 million by 2014
- *Switzerland*: Seeking to highlight its religious sites and attract more visitors

PILGRIMAGE

In religion and spirituality, a pilgrimage is a long journey or search of great moral significance. Sometimes, it is a journey to a sacred place or shrine of importance to a person's beliefs and faith. Members of every major religion participate in pilgrimages. A person who makes such a journey is called a pilgrim. Buddhism offers four sites of pilgrimage: the Buddha's birthplace at Kapilavastu, the site where he attained Enlightenment Bodh Gaya, where he first preached at Benares, and where he achieved Parinirvana at Kusinagara.

Israel acts as a focal point for the pilgrimages of many religions, such as Judaism, Christianity, Islam and the Bahá'í Faith. In the kingdoms of Israel and Judah, the visitation of certain ancient cult-centres was repressed in the 7th century BC, when the worship was restricted to Jahweh at the temple in Jerusalem. In Syria, the shrine of Astarte at the headwater spring of the river Adonis survived until it was destroyed by order of Emperor Constantine in the 4th century AD. In mainland Greece, a stream of individuals made their way to Delphi or the oracle of Zeus at Dodona, and once every four years, at the period of the Olympic games, the temple of Zeus at Olympia formed the goal of swarms of pilgrims from every part of the Hellenic world.

When Alexander the Great reached Egypt, he put his whole vast enterprise on hold, while he made his way with a small band deep into the Libyan desert, to consult the oracle of Ammun.

During the imperium of his Ptolemaic heirs, the shrine of Isis at Philae received many votive inscriptions from Greeks on behalf of their kindred far away at home. Although a pilgrimage is normally viewed in the context of religion, the personality cults cultivated by communist leaders ironically gave birth to pilgrimages of their own. Prior to the demise of the USSR in 1991, a visit to Lenin's Mausoleum in Red Square, Moscow can be said to have had all the characteristics exhibiting a pilgrimage—for Communists. This type of pilgrimage to a personality cult is still evident today on people who pay visits of homage to Mao Tse Tung, Kim Il Sung, and Ho Chi Minh.

BELONGINGS ON TRADE

Pilgrims contributed an important element to long-distance trade before the modern era, and brought prosperity to successful pilgrimage sites, an economic phenomenon unequalled until the tourist trade of the 20th century. Encouraging pilgrims was a motivation for assembling relics and for writing hagiographies of local saints, filled with inspiring accounts of miracle cures. Lourdes and other modern pilgrimage sites keep this spirit alive.

NEW PILGRIMAGE

Pilgrimages are still made throughout the world: modern-day pilgrimages include the Way of St. James, the Hajj, and the pilgrimage to Mount Kailash. In modern usage, the terms pilgrim and pilgrimage can also have a somewhat devalued meaning as they are often applied in a secular context. For example, fans of Elvis Presley may choose to visit his home, Graceland, in Memphis,

Tennessee. Similarly one may refer to a cultural centre such as Venice as a "tourists' Mecca".

PILGRIMAGE CENTRES IN DIFFERENT TIMES AND CULTURES

Antiquity

Many ancient religions had holy sites, temples and groves, where pilgrimages were made.

- Baalbek Lebanon.
- Delphi, Greece. Oracle.
- Dodona, Epirus, Greece. Oracle.
- Ephesus Temple of Diana.
- Karnak, Egypt.
- Kurukshetra, India
- Thebes, Egypt.

Bahá'í Faith

A Bahá'í pilgrimage currently consists of visiting the holy places in Haifa, Akká, and Bahjí in Northwest Israel. Bahá'ís do not have access to other places designated as sites for pilgrimage. Bahá'u'lláh decreed pilgrimage in His Motherbook to two places: the House of Bahá'u'lláh in Baghdad, Iraq, and the House of the Báb in Shiraz, Iran. In two separate Tablets, known as Suriy-i-Hajj, He prescribed specific rites for each of these pilgrimages. It is obligatory to make the pilgrimage, "if one can afford it and is able to do so, and if no obstacle stands in one's way".

Bahá'ís are free to choose between the two Houses, as either has been deemed sufficient. And although women are not bound to perform pilgrimage, they are certainly not prohibited to do so.

Buddhism

Gautama Buddha spoke of the four sites most worthy of pilgrimage for his followers to visit:

- *Bodh Gaya*: Place of Enlightenment
- *Kusinara*: Where he attained mahaparinirvana.
- *Lumbini*: Birth place
- *Sarnath*: Where he delivered his first teaching

Other pilgrimage places in India and Nepal connected to the life of Gautama Buddha are: Savatthi, Pataliputta, Nalanda, Gaya, Vesali, Sankasia, Kapilavastu, Kosambi, Rajagaha, Varanasi.

Other famous places for buddhist pilgrimage in various countries include:

- *Cambodia*: Angkor Wat, Silver Pagoda.
- *China*: Yung-kang, Lung-men caves.

- *India*: Sanchi, Ellora, Ajanta.
- *Indonesia*: Borobudur.
- *Japan*: Kyoto, Nara.
- *Laos*: Luang Prabang.
- *Myanmar*: Bagan, Sagaing Hill.
- *Nepal*: Bodhnath, Swayambhunath.
- Sri Lanka: Polonnaruwa, Temple of the Tooth, Anuradhapura.
- *Thailand*: Sukhothai, Ayutthaya, Wat Phra Kaew, Wat Doi Suthep.
- *Tibet*: Lhasa, Mount Kailash, Lake Nam-tso.

Communism

- *China*: Peking, Mausoleum of Mao Tse Tung in Tiananmen Square.
- *Germany*: Trier, Birthplace of Karl Marx in Trier
- *USSR*: Moscow, Mausoleum of Lenin in Red Square.

Christianity

Pilgrimages were first made to sites connected with the birth, life, crucifixion and resurrection of Jesus. Surviving descriptions of Christian pilgrimages to the Holy Land date from the 4th century, when pilgrimage was encouraged by church fathers like Saint Jerome. Pilgrimages also began to be made to Rome and other sites associated with the Apostles, Saints and Christian martyrs, as well as to places where there have been apparitions of the Virgin Mary. The crusades to the holy land are also considered to be mass armed pilgrimages. The second largest single pilgrimage in the history of Christendom was to the Funeral of Pope John Paul II after his death on April 2, 2005. An estimated four million people travelled to Vatican City, in addition to the almost three million people already living in Rome, to see the body of Pope John Paul II lie in state. World Youth Day is a major Catholic Pilgrimage, specifically for people aged 16-35. It is held internationally every 2-3 years. In 2005, young Catholics visited Cologne, Germany. In 1995, the largest gathering of all time was to World Youth Day in Manila, Philippines, where four million people from all over the world attended.

The major Christian pilgrimages are to:

- *Constantinople*: Former capital of the Byzantine Empire and the see of one of the five ancient Patriarchates and spiritual see of the Eastern Orthodox Church. Hagia Sophia, former cathedral and burial place of many Ecumenical Patriarchs.
- *Jerusalem*: Site of the crucifixion and resurrection of Jesus.
- *Lourdes, France*: Apparition of the Virgin Mary. The second most visited Christian pilgrimage site after Rome.
- *Rome on roads such as the Via Francigena*: Site of the deaths of Saint Peter, Saint Paul and other early martyrs. Location of sacred relics

of various saints, relics of the Passion, important churches and headquarters of the Catholic Church.

- Santiago de Compostela in Spain on the Way of St James. This famous medieval pilgrimage to the shrine of Saint James is still popular today.

Other important Christian pilgrimage sites include:

- Assisi, Italy, St. Francis of Assisi and St Clare, relics
- Avila, Spain, St Theresa of Avila, relics
- Bethlehem, in Israel, Birthplace of Jesus and King David.
- Canterbury Cathedral associated with Saint Thomas Becket.
- Cap-de-la-Madeleine, Quebec, Canada in honour of Our Lady of the Cape.
- Carey, Ohio to the Basilica and National Shrine of Our Lady of Consolation. Catholic pilgrims from the Middle East journey here to mark the Feast of the Assumption.
- Cathedral of Chartres, France.
- *Cologne, Germany*: Relics of the Three Magi.
- Conques, France
- *Croagh Patrick, Ireland*: Saint Patrick.
- *Czestochowa, Poland*: Black Madonna of Czêstochowa is housed pernamently in theJasna Góra Monastery
- *Fatima, Portugal*: Apparition of the Virgin Mary.
- Glastonbury, England. St Joseph of Arimathea.
- Goa, India. St. Francis Xavier
- Guadalupe, Spain
- Hill of Crosses, Lithuania
- House of the Virgin Mary, Turkey. Pope John-Paul II declared the Shrine of Virgin Mary as a pilgrimage place for Christians.
- *Issoudun, France*: Notre-Dame du Sacré-Coeur
- Kapel in 't Zand, Limburg
- Kevelaer, Germany
- Knock, Ireland
- Lakefield, Ontario, Canada
- Licheñ Stary, Sanctuary of Our Lady of Licheñ
- *Lisieux, France*: Saint Therese of Lisieux, burial place.
- *Lourdes, France*: Apparition of the Virgin Mary. Place of healing.
- *Mariazell, Austria*: Marian Shrine to Austria and Hungary
- *Meaugorje, Bosnia-Herzegovina*: Apparitions of the Virgin Mary at the present.
- *Miercurea Ciuc, Transylvania, Romania*: Whit Sunday gathering of Catholics.
- *Montserrat, Catalonia, Spain*: The Virgin of Montserrat is housed pernamently in the monastery of Santa María de Montserrat.

- *Mount Athos, Greece*: Orthodox monastic centre.
- *Mount Nebo, Jordan*: Traditional site of the death of Moses.
- Mount Sinai, Egypt, holy mountain to the ancient Hebrews, traditional site has been commemorated since time of Constantine
- Nazareth, Israel, hometown of Jesus
- Nidaros, Trondheim, Norway. Shrine of St. Olav. 4th most visited pilgrimage site in Middle Ages.
- Padua, Italy, St Anthony, relics
- Paris
- PemaiEion Kalvarija, Samogitia, Lithuania.
- Rosslyn Chapel, Scotland
- *Sacri Monti, Italy*: The Sacred Mountains of Piedmont and Lombardy.
- San Giovanni Rotondo, Italy, St Pio from Pietrelcina
- Sea of Galilee, Israel, site of Jesus' early ministry.
- Shrine of Our Lady of Guadalupe, Mexico City. Apparition of the Virgin Mary.
- St. Andrews, Scotland, it is said that Saint Andrew was given, by God, directions to the location of St Andrews
- St. Patrick's Purgatory, Donegal, Ireland
- St. Thomas Mount, India. Place where St. Thomas was martyred.
- Taize Community, France, modern monastery that actively encourages pilgrimages to it
- *Trondheim, Norway*: Nidaros Cathedral, shrine of St. Olav.
- *Turin, Italy*: Holy Shroud.
- Vailankanni, India. 16th-century Mary apparition site.
- Vierzehnheiligen, Germany.
- *Walsingham, England*: Virgin Mary apparition site.
- *Wittenberg, Germany*: Church of Martin Luther and centre of the Protestant Reformation.

Hinduism

Hindus are required to undertake pilgrimages during their lifetime.

Most Hindus who can afford to go on such journeys travel to numerous sites including those below:

- Allahabad
- Arunachala
- Ayodhya
- Benares
- Chidambaram
- Dakshineshwar
- Dharmasthala
- Dwarka
- Gaya
- Guruvayoor
- Hampi
- Haridwar
- Kalahasti
- Kanchipuram
- Kanyakumari
- Kateel

- Kollur
- Kumbakonam
- Kukke Subramanya
- Kunrakudy
- Madurai
- Mahabalipuram
- Marudamalai
- Mathura
- Mandher Devi temple in Mandhradevi
- Mayapur
- Mount Kailash
- Nashik
- Nathdwara
- Palani
- Pazhamudircholai
- Puri
- Pushkar
- Puttaparthi
- Rameswaram
- Rishikesh
- Sabarimala
- Shirdi
- Sikkal
- Sivagiri, Kerala
- Somnath
- Sringeri
- Srirangam
- Swamimalai
- Swamithope
- Talapady
- Tanjavur
- Thiruchendur
- Thiruparamkunram
- Thiruthani
- Tirupati
- Ujjain
- Udupi
- Malai Mandir
- Vaishno Devi
- Vayalur
- Viralimalai
- Virpur
- Vrindavan
- Badrinath
- Gangotri
- Kedarnath
- Yamunotri

The last four sites in the list together comprise the Chardham, or four holy pilgrimage destinations. It is believed that travelling to these places leads to moksha, the release from samsara. Vrindavan is most important place of pilgrimage for every Vaishnava, especially for the followers of Gaudiya Vaishnavism who regard Krishna as the original Personality of Godhead. Here one can attain love of God.

Islam

The pilgrimage to Mecca–the Hajj–is one of the Five Pillars of Islam. It should be attempted at least once in the lifetime of all able-bodied Muslims who can afford to do so.

It is the most important of all Muslim Pilgrimages. Many Muslims also undergo ziyarat, which is a pilgrimage to sites associated with the prophet Muhammad, his companions, or other venerated figures in Islamic history, such as Shi'a imams or Sufi saints. Sites of pilgrimage include mosques, graves, battlefields, mountains, and caves. Local Pilgrimage traditions-those undertaken as ziarah visits to local graves, are also found throughout Muslim countries. In some countries, the grave sites of heroes have very strong ziyarah traditions as visiting the graves at auspicious times is a display of national and community identity. Some traditions within Islam have negative attitudes towards grave visiting. The third religiously sanctioned pilgrimage for Muslims is to the Al Quds mount in Jerusalem which hosts Al-Aqsa Mosque and the Dome of the Rock.

Judaism

Within Judaism, the Temple in Jerusalem was the centre of the Jewish religion, until its destruction in 70 AD, and all who were able were under obligation to visit and offer sacrifices known as the korbanot, particularly during the Jewish holidays in Jerusalem. Following the destruction of the Second Temple and the onset of the diaspora, the centrality of pilgrimage to Jerusalem in Judaism was discontinued. In its place came prayers and rituals hoping for a return to Zion and the accompanying restoration of regular pilgrimages. Until recent centuries, pilgrimage has been a fairly difficult and arduous adventure. But now, Jews from many countries make periodic pilgrimages to the holy sites of their religion. The western retaining wall of the original temple, known as the Wailing Wall, or Western Wall remains in the Old City of Jerusalem and this has been the most sacred site for religious Jews. Pilgrimage to this area was off-limits from 1948 to 1967, when East Jerusalem was controlled by Jordan. Some Reform and Conservative Jews who no longer consider themselves exiles, still enjoy visiting Israel even if it is not an official "pilgrimage."

ADVENTURE TOURISM

Adventure tourism is a type of niche tourism involving exploration or travel to remote areas, where the traveller should expect the unexpected. Adventure tourism is rapidly growing in popularity as tourists seek unusual holidays, different from the typical beach vacation.

Adventure Tourism can take many forms with the increase in numbers of people with disabilities around the World and recent veterans from Wars have opened the doors to Adventure Travel for the Disabled. Albeit this may not be in exotic areas some tourism areas that have been developing include Australia, USA and Canada.

Whistler and Vancouver British Columbia, Canada have been taking the lead with the 2010 Paralympics coming up fast. Adapting to the needs of the Disabled to attract a $ 13 billion dollar a year industry in North America alone. The global Adventure Travel Trade Association, "adventure travel" may be any tourist activity including two of the following three components: a physical activity, a cultural exchange or interaction. Mountaineering expeditions, trekking, bungee jumping, rafting and rock climbing are frequently cited as an examples of adventure tourism.

MOUNTAINEERING

Mountaineering is the sport, hobby or profession of walking, hiking, trekking and climbing up mountains. It is also sometimes known as alpinism, particularly in Europe. While it began as an all-out attempt to reach the highest point of unclimbed mountains, it has branched into specializations addressing different aspects of mountains and may now be said to consist of three aspects: rock-craft, snow-craft and skiing, depending on whether the route chosen is over rock, snow or ice. All require great athletic and technical ability, and experience is also a very important part of the matter.

Snow

While certain compacted snow conditions allow mountaineers to progress on foot, typically some form of mechanical device is required to travel efficiently over snow and ice. Crampons 10-12 point spikes which are attached to a mountaineers boots, are used on hard snow and ice to provide additional traction and allow very steep ascents and descents. There a many different varieties, ranging from lightweight aluminum models intended for walking on glaciers to aggressive steel models intended for vertical and overhanging ice and rock.

Snowshoes can be used to walk through deep snow approaching the mountain or on lesser slopes up the mountain. Skis can be used almost everywhere snowshoes can and also in steeper, more alpine landscapes although it takes more practice to develop sufficiently strong skiing skills for difficult terrain. The practice of combining the techniques of alpine skiing and mountaineering to ascend and descend a mountain is a form of the sport by itself, called Ski Mountaineering. Ascending and descending a snow slope involves many different techniques of the feet and an ice axe which have been developed over the last hundred years, originating in Europe. The progression of footwork from the lowest angle slopes to the steepest terrain is first to splay the feet to a rising traverse, to kick stepping, to front pointing the crampons.

The progression of the ice axe technique from the lowest angle slopes to the steepest terrain is to use the ice axe first as a walking stick, then a stake, then to use the front pick as a dagger below the shoulders or above, and finally to swing the pick into the slope over the head. This also involves different designs of ice axe depending on the terrain to be covered, and even whether a mountaineer uses one or two ice axes.

Glaciers

When traveling over glaciers, crevasses pose a grave danger. These giant cracks in the ice are not always visible as snow can be blown and freeze over the top to make a snowbridge. At times snowbridges can be as thin as a few inches. Climbers use a system of ropes to protect themselves from such hazards.

Basic gear for glacier travel includes crampons and ice axes. Teams of two to five climbers tie into a rope equally spaced. If a climber begins to fall the other members of the team perform a self-arrest to stop the fall. The other members of the team enact a crevasse rescue to pull the fallen climber from the crevasse.

Ice

Multiple methods are used to safely travel over ice. If the terrain is steep but not vertical, then protection in the form of pickets or ice screws can be driven into the snow or ice and attached to the rope by the lead climber. Each climber on the team must clip past the anchor, and the last climber picks up the picket. This allows for safety should the entire team be taken off their feet. This technique is known as Simul-climbing. If the terrain becomes vertical then standard ice climbing techniques are used.

Shelter

Climbers use a few different forms of shelter depending on the situation and conditions. Shelter is a very important aspect of safety for the climber as the weather in the mountains is very unpredictable. Tall mountains require many days of camping on the mountain.

Hut

The European alpine regions, in particular, have a network of mountain huts. Such huts exist at many different heights, including in the high mountains themselves–in extremely remote areas bivouac shelters may have been provided. The mountain huts are of varying size and quality but each is typically centred on a communal dining room and have dormitories equipped with mattresses, blankets or duvets, and pillows–guests are expected to bring and to use their own sleeping bag liner.

The facilities are usually rudimentary but, given their locations, huts offer vital shelter, make routes more widely accessible and offer good value. In Europe, all huts are staffed during the summer and some are staffed in the spring. Elsewhere, huts may also be open in the fall. Huts also may have a part that is always open, but unmanned, a so-called winter hut. When open and manned, the huts are generally run by full-time employees, but some are staffed on a voluntary basis by members of Alpine clubs. The manager of the hut, termed a guardian or warden in Europe, will usually also sell refreshments and meals–both to those visiting only for the day and to those staying overnight.

The offering is surprisingly wide–given that most supplies, often including fresh water, must be flown in by helicopter–and may include glucose-based snacks on which climbers and walkers wish to stock up, cakes and pastries made at the hut, a variety of hot and cold drinks, and high carbohydrate dinners in the evenings. Not all huts do offer a catered service, though, and visitors may need to provide for themselves. Some huts offer facilities for both, enabling visitors wishing to keep costs down to bring their own food and cooking equipment and to cater using the facilities provided. Booking for overnight stays at huts is deemed obligatory, and in many cases is essential as some popular huts–even with over 100 bed spaces-may well be full during good weather and at weekends. Once made, the cancellation of a reservation should be advised to the hut as a matter of courtesy–and, indeed, potentially of safety, as many huts keep a record of where climbers and walkers state they planned to walk to next. Most huts are contactable by telephone and most take credit cards as a means of payment for the service they provide.

Bivy

A bivy or bivouac is simply getting a sleeping bag and Bivouac sack and laying down to sleep. Many times small half sheltered areas like cracks in rocks or simply a trench dug in the snow are used to provide a basic means of shelter as well.

This technique is performed by most people only in cases of emergency, however in good weather this can be pleasant. Some climbers steadfastly committed to Alpine Style climbing plan on bivying in order to save the weight of a tent when snow conditions are not suitable for a snow cave.

Tent

Tents are the most common form of shelter used on the mountain. A four season tent is recommended for any camp above timberline in the mountains. Some climbers do not use tents at high altitudes unless the snow conditions do not allow for snow caving, although digging a snow cave is a time consuming and work intensive endeavor.

Sometimes walls of snow or rock can be built instead to shelter the tent from high winds and storms. One of the downsides to tenting is that high storm winds and snow loads can be unnerving and cause the tent to collapse, however modern mountaineering tents are usually tested for wind speeds up to 125 mph. Even so, constant flapping of the tent fabric can hinder sleep and raise doubts about the security of the shelter in windy conditions.

Snow Cave

Snow caves are another way for some climbers to shelter high on the mountain. Unlike tents snow caves are silent and actually warmer. A correctly made snow cave will hover around freezing, which relative to outside temperatures can be very warm.

They require carrying a snow shovel, which some may consider to be extra equipment, to build easily. They can be dug from a deep snowdrift, out of a slope, or anywhere there is at least four feet of snow. Another shelter that works well is a quinzee, which is excavated from a pile of snow that has been work hardened or sintered. Igloos are used by some climbers, but are deceptively difficult to build and require specific snow conditions.

Hazards

The craft of climbing has been developed to avoid three main types of danger: the danger of things falling on the climber, the danger of the climber falling and inclement weather. The things that may fall include rocks, ice, snow, other climbers or their gear; the mountaineer may fall from rocks, ice or snow, or into a crevasse. In all, there are eight chief dangers: falling rocks, falling ice, snow-avalanches, falls, the climber falling, falls from ice slopes, falls down snow slopes, falls into crevasses and dangers from weather. To select and follow a route using one's skills and experience to mitigate these dangers is to exercise the climber's craft.

Falling Rocks

Every rock mountain is slowly disintegrating due to erosion, the process being especially rapid above the snow-line. Rock faces are constantly swept by falling stones, which are generally possible to dodge. Falling rocks tend to form furrows in a mountain face, and these furrows have to be ascended with caution, their sides often being safe when the middle is stoneswept. Rocks fall more frequently on some days than on others, just as to the recent weather. Ice formed during the night may temporarily bind rocks to the face but warmth of the day or direct sun exposure may easily dislodge these rocks. Local experience is a valuable help on determining typical rockfall on such routes. The direction of the dip of rock strata often determines the degree of danger on a particular face; the character of the rock must also be considered. Where stones fall frequently debris will be found whilst on snow slopes falling stones cut furrows visible from a great distance. In planning an ascent of a new peak mountaineers must look for such traces. When falling stones get mixed in considerable quantity with slushy snow or water a mud avalanche is formed. It is vital to avoid camping in their possible line of fall.

Falling Ice

The places where ice may fall can always be determined beforehand. It falls in the broken parts of glaciers and from overhanging cornices formed on the crests of narrow ridges. Large icicles are often formed on steep rock faces, and these fall frequently in fine weather following cold and stormy days. They have to be avoided like falling stones. Seracs are slow in formation, and slow in arriving at a condition of unstable equilibrium.

They generally fall in or just after the hottest part of the day, and their debris seldom goes far. A skillful and experienced ice-man will usually devise a safe route through a most intricate ice-fall, but such places should be avoided in the afternoon of a hot day. Hanging glaciers often discharge themselves over steep rock-faces, the snout breaking off at intervals. Their track should be avoided.

Falls from Rocks

The skill of a rock climber is shown by one's choice of handhold and foothold, and his adhesion to those one has chosen. Much depends on a correct estimate of the firmness of the rock where weight is to be thrown upon it. Many loose rocks are quite firm enough to bear a person's weight, but experience is needed to know which can be trusted, and skill is required in transferring the weight to them without jerking. On rotten rocks the rope must be handled with special care, lest it should start loose stones on to the heads of those below. Similar care must be given to handholds and footholds, for the same reason.

When a horizontal traverse has to be made across very difficult rocks, a dangerous situation may arise unless at both ends of the traverse there be firm positions. Mutual assistance on hard rocks takes all manner of forms: two, or even three, people climbing on one another's shoulders, or using an ice axe propped up by others for a foothold.

The great principle is that of co-operation, all the members of the party climbing with reference to the others, and not as independent units; each when moving must know what the climber in front and the one behind are doing. After bad weather steep rocks are often found covered with a veneer of ice, which may even render them inaccessible. Crampons are useful on such occasions.

Avalanches

The avalanche is the most underestimated danger in the mountains. People generally think that they will be able to recognize the hazards and survive being caught. The truth is a somewhat different story. Every year, 120-150 people die in small avalanches in the Alps alone. The vast majority are reasonably experienced male skiers aged 20-35 but also include ski instructors and guides. There is always a lot of pressure to risk a snow crossing. Turning back takes a lot of extra time and effort, supreme leadership, and most importantly there seldom is an avalanche to prove the right decision was made. Making the decision to turn around is especially hard if others are crossing the slope, but any next person could become the trigger.

The Slab Avalanche

This type of avalanche occurs when a plate of snow breaks loose and starts sliding down; these are the largest and most dangerous.

- Hard slab avalanche-formed by hard-packed snow in a cohesive slab. The slab will not break up easily as it slides down the hill, resulting in large blocks tumbling down the mountain.
- Soft slab avalanche-formed again by a cohesive layer of snow bonded together, the slab tends to break up more easily.

The Loose Snow Avalanche

This type of avalanche is triggered by a small amount of moving snow that accumulates into a big slide. Also known as a "wet slide or point release" avalanche. This type of avalanche is deceptively dangerous as it can still knock a climber or skier off their feet and bury them, or sweep them over a cliff into a terrain trap. Dangerous slides are most likely to occur on the same slopes preferred by many skiers: long and wide open, few trees or large rocks, 30 to 45 degrees of angle, large load of fresh snow, soon after a big storm, on a slope 'lee to the storm'. Solar radiation can trigger slides as well. These will typically be a point release or wet slough type of avalanche. The added weight of the wet slide can trigger a slab avalanche. Ninety per cent of reported victims are caught in avalanches triggered by themselves or others in their group. When going off-piste or traveling in alpine terrain, parties have a moral responsibility to always carry:

- Avalanche beacon
- Probe
- Shovel

Paradoxically, expert skiers who have avalanche training make up a large percentage of avalanche fatalities; perhaps because they are the ones more likely to ski in areas prone to avalanches, and certainly because most people do not practice enough with their equipment to be truly fast and efficient rescuers. Even with proper rescue equipment and training, there is a one-in-five chance of dying if caught in a significant avalanche, and only a 50/50 chance of being found alive if buried more than a few minutes. The best solution is to learn how to avoid risky conditions.

Ice Slopes

For travel on slopes consisting of ice or hard snow, crampons are a standard part of a mountaineer's equipment. While step-cutting can sometimes be used on snow slopes of moderate angle, this can be a slow and tiring process, which does not provide the higher security of crampons. However, in soft snow or powder, crampons are easily hampered by balling of snow which reduce their effectiveness. In either case, an ice axe not only assists with balance but provides the climber with the possibility of self-arrest in case of a slip or fall. On a true ice slope however, an ice axe is rarely able to effect a self-arrest. As an additional safety precaution on steep ice slopes, the climbing rope is attached to ice screws buried into the ice. True ice slopes are rare in Europe, though common in mountains located in the tropics, where newly-fallen snow quickly thaws on the surface and becomes sodden below, so that the next night's frost turns the whole mass into a sheet of semi-solid ice.

Snow Slopes

Snow slopes are very common, and usually easy to ascend. At the foot of a snow or ice slope is generally a big crevasse, called a bergschrund, where the final slope of the mountain rises from a snow-field or glacier. Such bergschrunds are generally too wide to be stepped across, and must be crossed by a snow bridge, which needs careful testing and a painstaking use of the rope. A steep snow slope in bad condition may be dangerous, as the whole body of snow may start as an avalanche. Such slopes are less dangerous if ascended directly than obliquely, for an oblique or horizontal track cuts them across and facilitates movement of the mass.

New snow lying on ice is especially dangerous. Experience is needed for deciding on the advisability of advancing over snow in doubtful condition. Snow on rocks is usually rotten unless it is thick; snow on snow is likely to be sound. A day or two of fine weather will usually bring new snow into sound condition. Snow cannot lie at a very steep angle, though it often deceives the eye as to its slope. Snow slopes seldom exceed 40°. Ice slopes may be much steeper. Snow slopes in early morning are usually hard and safe, but the same in the afternoon are quite soft and possibly dangerous; hence the advantage of an early start.

Crevasses

Crevasses are the slits or deep chasms formed in the substance of a glacier as it passes over an uneven bed. They may be open or hidden. In the lower part of a glacier the crevasses are open. Above the snow-line they are frequently hidden by arched-over accumulations of winter snow. The detection of hidden crevasses requires care and experience. After a fresh fall of snow they can only be detected by sounding with the pole of the ice axe, or by looking to right and left where the open extension of a partially hidden crevasse may be obvious. The safeguard against accident is the rope, and no one should ever cross a snow-covered glacier unless roped to one, or even better to two companions. Anyone venturing onto crevasses should be trained in crevasse rescue.

Weather

The primary dangers caused by bad weather centre around the changes it causes in snow and rock conditions, making movement suddenly much more arduous and hazardous than under normal circumstances. Whiteouts make it difficult to retrace a route while rain may prevent taking the easiest line only determined as such under dry conditions. In a storm the mountaineer who uses a compass for guidance has a great advantage over a merely empirical observer. In large snow-fields it is, of course, easier to go wrong than on rocks, but intelligence and experience are the best guides in safely navigating objective hazards. Summer thunderstorms may produce intense lightning.

If a climber happens to be standing on or near the summit, they risk being struck. There are many cases where people have been struck by lightning while climbing mountains. In most mountainous regions, local storms develop by late morning and early afternoon. Many climbers will get an "alpine start"; that is before or by first light so as to be on the way down when storms are intensifying in activity and lightning and other weather hazards are a distinct threat to safety.

Altitude

Rapid ascent can lead to altitude sickness. The best treatment is to descend immediately. The climber's motto at high altitude is "climb high, sleep low", referring to the regimen of climbing higher to acclimatize but returning to lower elevation to sleep. In the South American Andes, the chewing of coca leaves has been traditionally used to treat altitude sickness symptoms.

Common symptoms of altitude sickness include severe headache, sleep problems, nausea, lack of appetite, lethargy and body ache. Mountain sickness may progress to High Altitude Cerebral Edema and High Altitude Pulmonary Edema, both of which can be fatal within 24 hours.

In high mountains, atmospheric pressure is lower and this means that less oxygen is available to breathe. This is the underlying cause of altitude sickness. Everyone needs to acclimatize, even exceptional mountaineers that have been to high altitude before. Generally speaking, mountaineers start using bottled oxygen when they climb above 7,000 m. Exceptional mountaineers have climbed 8000-metre peaks without oxygen, almost always with a carefully planned programme of acclimatization. In 2005, researcher and mountaineer John Semple established that above-average ozone concentrations on the Tibetan plateau may pose an additional risk to climbers.

Locations

Mountaineering has become a popular sport throughout the world. In Europe the sport largely originated in the Alps, and is still immensely popular there. Other notable mountain ranges frequented by climbers include the Caucasus, the Pyrenees and the Tatra mountains. In North America climbers frequent the Rockies and Sierra Nevada of California, the Cascades of Washington and the high peaks of Alaska. There has been a long tradition of climbers going on expeditions to the Greater Ranges, a term generally used for the Andes and the high peaks of Asia including the Himalaya, Pamirs and Tien Shan. In the past this was often on exploratory trips or to make first ascents. With the advent of cheaper long-haul air travel mountaineering holidays in the Greater Ranges are now undertaken much more frequently and ascents of even Everest and Vinson Massif are offered as a "package holiday". Other popular mountaineering areas of more local interest include the Southern Alps of New Zealand, the Japanese Alps the Scottish Highlands and the mountains of Scandinavia.

HISTORY

- Though it is unknown whether his intention was to reach a summit, Ötzi ascended at least 3,000 m in the Alps about 5,300 years ago. His remains were found at that altitude, preserved in a glacier.
- The first recorded mountain ascent in the Common Era is Roman Emperor Hadrian's ascent of Etna to see the sun rise in 121.
- Peter III of Aragon climbed Canigou in the Pyrenees in the last quarter of the 13th century.
- The first ascent of the Popocatépetl was reported in 1289 by members of a local tribe
- Jean Buridan climbed Mont Ventoux around 1316.
- The Italian poet Petrarch wrote that on April 26, 1336 he, together with his brother and two servants, climbed to the top of Mont Ventoux. His account of the trip was composed later as a letter to his friend Dionigi di Borgo San Sepolcro.
- The Rochemelon in the Italian Alps was climbed in 1358.
- In the late 1400s and early 1500s ascents were made of numerous high peaks in the Andes, for religious purposes by the citizens of the Inca Empire and their subjects. They constructed platforms, houses and altars on many summits and carried out sacrifices, including human sacrifices. The highest peak they are known for certain to have climbed is Llullaillaco. They may also have ascended the highest peak in the Andes, Aconcagua as a sacrifice victim has been found at over 5,000 m on this peak.
- In 1492 the ascent of Mont Aiguille was made by order of Charles VIII of France. The Humanists of the 16th century adopted a new attitude towards mountains, but the disturbed state of Europe nipped in the bud the nascent mountaineering of the Zurich school.
- Leonardo da Vinci climbed to a snow-field in the neighbourhood of the Val Sesia and made scientific observations.
- In 1642 Darby Field made the first recorded ascent of Mount Washington, then known as Agiocochook, in New Hampshire.
- Konrad Gesner and Josias Simler of Zurich visited and described mountains, and made regular ascents. The use of ice axe and rope were locally invented at this time. No mountain expeditions of note are recorded in the 17th century.

- Richard Pococke and William Windham's historic visit to Chamonix was made in 1741, and set the trend for visiting glaciers.
- In 1744 the Titus was climbed, the first true ascent of a snow-mountain.
- The first attempt to ascend Mont Blanc was made in 1775 by a party of natives. In 1786 Dr Michel Paccard and Jacques Balmat gained the summit for the first time. Horace-Bénédict de Saussure, the initiator of the first ascent followed next year.
- The Norwegian mountain climber, Jens Esmark was the first person to ascend Snøhetta in 1798, part of the Dovrefjell range in Southern Norway. The same year he lead the first expedition to Bitihorn, a small mountain in the southernmost outskirts of Jotunheimen, Norway. In 1810 he was the first person to ascend Mount Gaustatoppen in Telemark, Norway.
- The Jungfrau was climbed in 1811, the Finsteraarhorn in 1812, and the Breithorn in 1813. Thereafter, tourists showed a tendency to climb, and the body of Alpine guides began to come into existence as a consequence.
- Citlaltépetl was first climbed in 1848 by F. Maynard and G. Reynolds.
- Systematic mountaineering, as a sport, is usually dated from Sir Alfred Wills's ascent of the Wetterhorn in 1854. The first ascent of Monte Rosa was made in 1855.
- The Alpine Club was founded in London in 1857, and was soon imitated in most European countries. Edward Whymper's ascent of the Matterhorn in 1865 marked the close of the main period of Alpine conquest–the Golden age of alpinism–during which the craft of climbing was invented and 'perfected', the body of professional guides formed and their traditions fixed.
- Passing to other ranges, the exploration of the Pyrenees was concurrent with that of the Alps. The Caucasus followed, mainly owing to the initiative of D. W. Freshfield; it was first visited by exploring climbers in 1868, and most of its great peaks were climbed by 1888.
- The Edelweiss Club Salzburg was founded in Salzburg in 1881, and had 3 members make the First Ascent on 2 Eight-thousanders, Broad Peak and Dhaulagiri.
- Trained climbers turned their attention to the mountains of North America in 1888, when the Rev. W. S. Green made an expedition to the Selkirk Mountains. From that time exploration has gone on apace, and many English and American climbing parties have surveyed most of the highest peaks; Pikes Peak having been climbed by Mr. E. James and party in 1820, and Mt. Saint Elias by the Duke of the Abruzzi and party in 1897. The exploration of the highest Andes was begun

in 1879-1880, when Whymper climbed Chimborazo and explored the mountains of Ecuador. The Cordillera between Chile and Argentina was visited by Dr. Gussfeldt in 1883, who ascended Maipo and attempted Aconcagua. That peak was first climbed by the Fitzgerald expedition in 1897.

- The Andes of Bolivia were first explored by Sir William Martin Conway in 1898. Chilean and Argentine expeditions revealed the structure of the southern Cordillera in the years 1885-1898. Conway visited the mountains of Tierra del Fuego.
- New Zealand's Southern Alps were first visited in 1882 by the Rev. W. S. Green, and shortly afterwards a New Zealand Alpine Club was founded, and by their activities the exploration of the range was pushed forward. In 1895, Major Edward Arthur Fitzgerald, made an important journey in this range. Tom Fyfe and party climbed Aoraki/ Mount Cook on Christmas Day 1894, denying Fitzgerald the first ascent. Fitzgerald was en route from Britain with Swiss guide Matthias Zurbriggen to claim the peak. So piqued at being beaten to the top of Mount Cook, he refused to climb it and concentrated on other peaks in the area. Later in the trip Zubriggen soloed Mount Cook up a ridge that now bears his name.
- The first mountains of the arctic region explored were those of Spitzbergen by Sir W. M. Conway's expeditions in 1896 and 1897.
- Of the high African peaks, Kilimanjaro was climbed in 1889 by Dr. Hans Meyer, Mt. Kenya in 1899 by Halford John Mackinder, and a peak of Ruwenzori by H. J. Moore in 1900.
- The Asiatic mountains were initially surveyed on orders of the British Empire. In 1892 Sir William Martin Conway explored the Karakoram Himalaya, and climbed a peak of 23,000 ft. In 1895 Albert F. Mummery died while attempting Nanga Parbat, while in 1899 D. W. Freshfield took an expedition to the snowy regions of Sikkim. In 1899, 1903, 1906 and 1908 Mrs Fannie Bullock Workman made ascents in the Himalayas, including one of the Nun Kun peaks. A number of Gurkha sepoys were trained as expert mountaineers by Major the Hon. C. G. Bruce, and a good deal of exploration was accomplished by them.
- The Rucksack Club was founded in Manchester, England in 1902.
- The American Alpine Club was founded in 1902.
- In 1902, the Eckenstein-Crowley Expedition, lead by mountaineer Oscar Eckenstein and occultist Aleister Crowley, was the first to attempt to scale Chogo Ri. They reached 22,000 feet before turning back due to weather and other mishaps.
- In 1905, Aleister Crowley led the first expedition to Kanchenjunga, the third highest mountain in the world. Four members of that party

were killed in an avalanche. Some claims say they reached around 21,300 feet before turning back, however Crowley's autobiography claims they reached about 25,000 feet.

- The 1950s saw the first ascents of all the eight-thousanders but two, starting with Annapurna in 1950 by Maurice Herzog and Louis Lachenal. The world's highest mountain, Mount Everest was first climbed on May 29, 1953 by Sir Edmund Hillary and Tenzing Norgay from the south side in Nepal. Just a few months later, Hermann Buhl made the first ascent of Nanga Parbat, a remarkable solo climb, the only eight-thousander to be solo'd on the first ascent. K2, the second highest peak in the world was first scaled in 1954. In 1964, the final eight-thousander to be climbed was Shishapangma, the lowest of all the 8,000 metre peaks.

BACKPACKING

Backpacking combines hiking and camping in a single trip. A backpacker hikes into the backcountry to spend one or more nights there, and carries supplies and equipment to satisfy sleeping and eating needs. A backpacker packs all of his or her gear into a backpack. This gear must include food, water, and shelter, or the means to obtain them, but very little else, and often in a more compact and simpler form than one would use for stationary camping. A backpacking trip must include at least one overnight stay in the wilderness. Many backpacking trips last just a weekend but long-distance expeditions may last weeks or months, sometimes aided by planned food and supply drops. Backpacking camps are more spartan than ordinary camps. In areas that experience a regular traffic of backpackers, a hike-in camp might have a fire ring and a small wooden bulletin board with a map and some warning or information signs. Many hike-in camps are no more than level patches of ground without scrub or underbrush. In very remote areas, established camps do not exist at all, and travellers must choose appropriate camps themselves. In some places, backpackers have access to lodging that are more substantial than a tent.

In the more remote parts of Great Britain, bothies exist to provide simple accommodation for backpackers. Another example is the High Sierra Camps in Yosemite National Park. Mountain huts provide similar accommodation in other countries, so being a member of a mountain hut organization is advantageous to make use of their facilities.

On other trails there are somewhat more established shelters of a sort that offer a place for weary hikers to spend the night without needing to set up a tent. Most backpackers purposely try to avoid impacting on the land through which they travel. This includes following established trails as much as possible, not removing anything, and not leaving residue in the backcountry.

The Leave No Trace movement offers a set of guidelines for low-impact backpacking.

Professional Backpacking

For some people, backpacking is a necessary and integral part of their job. In the military a framed backpack is referred to as a "rucksack" or simply a "ruck". Soldiers who serve in the militaries of most nation-states usually receive at least some rudimentary backpacking training while infantrymen are often trained to a more advanced backpacking skill level. They share many common attributes with amateur backpackers: being self-contained, use of land-navigation skills and actively minimizing their environmental foot-print.

Although there are also a few differences such as the need to carry an assault rifle, other weapons, ammunition and communication equipment as well as at times maintaining "noise and light discipline", which means remaining silent and in darkness to avoid detection. Other professional backpackers may be scientific and academic researchers, professional guides, photographers, park-rangers and "search and rescue" personnel.

Motivation

People are drawn to backpacking primarily for recreation, to explore places that they consider beautiful and fascinating, many of which cannot be accessed in any other way. A backpacker can travel deeper into remote areas, away from people and their effects, than a day-hiker can. However, backpacking presents more advantages besides distance of travel. Many weekend trips cover routes that could be hiked in a single day, but people choose to backpack them anyway, for the experience of staying overnight. These possibilities come with disadvantages. The weight of a pack, laden with supplies and gear, forces backpackers to travel more slowly than day-hikers would, and it can become a nuisance and a distraction from enjoying the scenery. In addition, camp chores can easily consume several hours every day. Backpackers face many risks, including adverse weather, difficult terrain, treacherous river crossings, and hungry or unpredictable animals. They are subject to illnesses, which run the gamut from simple dehydration to heat exhaustion, hypothermia, altitude sickness, and physical injury. The remoteness of backpacking locations exacerbates any mishap. However, these hazards do not deter backpackers who are properly prepared. Some simply accept danger as a risk that they must endure if they want to backpack; for others, the potential dangers actually enhance the allure of the wilderness.

BUNGEE JUMPING

Bungee jumping is the sport that originated from New Zealand and was created by maverick daredevil A J Hackett, and his original jump from a bridge in Greenhithe, Auckland. The sport denotes jumping from a tall structure while connected to a large rubber cord. The tall structure is usually a fixed object, such as a building, bridge, or crane; but it is also possible to jump from a movable object, such as a hot-air-balloon or a helicopter, that has the ability to hover over one spot on the ground; fixed-wing aircraft are clearly unsuitable because they only stay aloft when moving rapidly forward.

The intense thrill comes as much from the free-falls as from the rebounds. When the person jumps, the cord stretches to absorb the energy of the fall, then the jumper flies upwards again as the cord snaps back. The jumper oscillates up and down until all the energy is used up. The word bungee first appeared around 1930 and was the name for rubber eraser. The word bungy, as used by A J Hackett, is said to be "Kiwi slang for Elastic Strap".

Cloth-covered rubber cords with hooks on the ends have been available for decades under the generic name bungee cords. In the 1950s David Attenborough and a BBC film crew had brought back footage of the "land divers" of Pentecost Island in Vanuatu, young men who jumped from tall wooden platforms with vines tied to their ankles as a test of courage. This film inspired Chris Baker of Bristol, England to use elastic rope in a kind of urban vine jumping. The first modern bungee jump was made on 1 April 1979 from the 250ft Clifton Suspension Bridge in Bristol, and was made by four members of the Dangerous Sports Club. The jumpers, led by David Kirke, were arrested shortly after, but continued with jumps in the US from the Golden Gate and Royal Gorge bridges, spreading the concept worldwide.

By 1982 they were jumping from mobile cranes and hot air balloons, and putting on commercial displays. One of the first operators of a commercial bungee jumping concern enabling the general public to experience these leaps of faith was New Zealander, A J Hackett, who made his first jump from Auckland's Greenhithe Bridge in 1986. During the following years Hackett performed a number of jumps from bridges and other structures building public interest in the sport. Hackett remains one of the largest commercial operators, with concerns in several countries.

The worlds first permanent commercial bungee site was the Kawarau Bridge Bungy at Queenstown in the South Island of New Zealand. Despite the inherent danger of jumping from a great height, several million successful jumps have taken place since 1980. This is attributable to bungee operators rigorously conforming to standards and guidelines governing jumps, such as double checking calculations and fittings for every jump. As with any sport, injuries can still occur, but there have been few fatalities. A relatively common mistake in fatality cases is to use too long a cord.

The cord should be substantially shorter than the height of the jumping platform to allow it room to stretch. When the cord reaches its natural length the jumper either starts to slow down or keep accelerating. depending upon the speed of descent. One may not even start to slow until the cord has already stretched somewhat, because the cord's resistance to distortion is zero at the natural length, and increases only gradually after, taking some time to even equal the jumper's weight.

RAFTING

Rafting or whitewater rafting is a recreational activity utilizing a raft to navigate a river or other bodies of water. This is usually done on whitewater or different degrees of rough water, in order to thrill and excite the raft passengers. The development of this activity as a leisure sport has become popular since the mid 1970s. Rafting is one of the earliest means of transportation, used as a means for shipping people, hunting, and transferring food. In 1842, Lieutenant John Fremont of the U.S. Army first journalized his rafting expedition on the Platte River.

Horace H. Day designed the equipment he used in rafting. Day's rafts were constructed from four independent rubber cloth tubes and wrap-around floor. In 1960s, rafting was then recognized and paths like Grand Canyon were routed and whitewater rafting companies were established. In 1970s, rafting marked its major development as a leisure sport when it was then included in the Munich Olympic Games.

In 1980s, as rafting continued to gain its popularity, a lot of rivers were opened for rafting activities. Rivers in South America and Africa were just a few of them. In 1990s, rafting was included in major game events like the Barcelona Games in 1992, Atlanta Games in 1996, and the whitewater events of the Summer Olympic Games hosted by Ocoee River in Tennessee Valley.

In addition, the International Federation of Rafting was instituted in 1997 and in 1999 the first Official International Championship was held. Nowadays, river rafting is still gaining popularity among extreme water sports in order to thrill and excite the raft passengers.

ROCK CLIMBING

Rock climbing, broadly speaking, is the act of ascending steep rock formations. Normally, climbers use gear and safety equipment specifically designed for the purpose. Strength, endurance, and mental control are required to cope with tough, dangerous physical challenges, and knowledge of climbing techniques and the use of essential pieces of gear and equipment are crucial.

Although the practice of rock climbing was an important component of Victorian mountaineering in the Alps, it is generally thought that the sport of rock climbing began in the last quarter of the nineteenth century in various parts of Europe. Rock climbing evolved gradually from an alpine necessity to an athletic sport in its own right. As rock climbing matured, grading systems were created in order to more accurately compare relative difficulties of climbs.

Over the years, both climbing techniques, and the equipment climbers use to advance the sport, have evolved in a steady fashion.

ADVENTURE TOURISM IN INDIA

ANGLING IN INDIA

Today, in India, the sport of angling is combined with conservation. As per the existing Indian protection laws, the fish is allowed to be caught, but must be released within a stipulated time period. The average time taken to land a Mahseer is in ratio to its weight—5 minutes to 5 lbs. With just enough time to record its weight, and preserve your moment of glory with the prize catch of film, before the fish is revived-you have to be really quick or else it could just end up as one of those fishy stories of, "the great one that got away."

CAMEL SAFARI IN INDIA

Thar Desert Camel Safaris of India are now one of Asia's fastest selling adventure holidays. These include camel treks ranging from short rides around Jaisalmer to extensive trips that remind you of Lawrence of Arabia on his epic journey across the Sahara, Marco Polo, on the historic silk route, a medieval trader leading his caravan through the hostile spice route or a royal caravan serai heading for one of the medieval kingdoms of the Thar desert- without many of the hardships of course! They are a great way to see the desert and to enjoy a novel and adventurous holiday.

The Great Indian Desert may not have great expanses of sand dunes and incredible spaces of wilderness as large as those of the Sahara and Namibia, but more than makes up for it with some glorious citadels and extremely colourful and unspoilt villages. Its sand dunes are more easily accessible from airports and railway stations than those of many African countries.

CAMEL SAFARI CIRCUIT IN INDIA

The Camel Safari Circuit in India comprises of Jaisalmer, Jodhpur, and Bikaner, all in Rajasthan. They were the princely kingdoms in the desert belt of India Rajasthan. Each was comparable in size to many modern nations of Europe. All the former capitals prospered from trade with the camel caravans that traveled from West Asia and Europe to Mongolia, and were impressively fortified to protect these riches. The result was a wealth of palaces built for royalty, havelis or courtyard mansions built for merchants and nobility and intricately carved temples for the subjects.

Materials used were normally sandstone, which was easily available and provided a better medium to the silavats who specialized in making stone resemble lace. A camel safari is a great way to see the desert-visiting the villages, seeing wildlife, and riding across the open desert sands. Typical camel safaris organized around Jaisalmer take in the architectural ruins of Lodurva which was the former capital of the Bhatti Rajput desert kingdom before the founding of Jaisalmer, the Anasagar oasis, the sand dunes of Samm and the water source of Moolsagar where village women gather with pitchers at dusk. Night halts on basic safaris are at villages on the way or temporary bivouac camps in the desert scrub where camels are hobbled and let out to browse.

CAMEL SAFARI IN INDIA -TRAVEL KIT

The climate is extreme in the desert-afternoons may seem much hotter than the actual 26-30 degree temperature may suggest. Night temperatures may drop below zero on the dunes. It is essential to stock both woolen and cotton clothing. Shorts and skirts are comfortable wear for camel safaris but remember some of the off beat routes visit villages that have not seen many tourists and locals may look askance at ladies who do not wear ankle length clothing and men in shorts. Sun hats with large rims or cotton caps that can be dipped in water when it gets too hot around midday, are essential preferably with a balaclava or scarf for covering the neck and forehead.

At Jodhpur you can buy umbrellas that are quite convenient for camel safaris. Sunscreen cream, moisturizers and lip salve area must. A water bottle can be comfortably slung on the camel saddle and it is practical also to carry tangerines as even on a deluxe safari it may not be practical to dismount each time to drink from the carted water supply. Bottled mineral water is available at Jodhpur and Jaisalmer. Find out if the baggage is being transferred by camel cart or vehicle. In case of the latter, a small handbag can carry the essentials you are likely to need on the way. If prone to sickness, carry suitable medication against the swaying gait of the camel. A torch, penknife an even cutlery will be required. Finally patience is an important piece of baggage on a camel safari as it takes time to get to grips with camel travel and to reach destinations that may be on your travel priorities.

MOUNTAINEERING IN INDIA

Mountaineering as a sport has a history as old as the history of the evolution of human race itself. Mountaineering started when the need was felt for people who could climb difficult heights and terrains to meet people across the border, to trade, or to conquer new territories. In the course of time, man developed new modes of transportation and communication and venturing out on these difficult routes were not needed. Nevertheless, what remained was his nature to take risks and getting pleasure in conquering something totally unknown and unexplored.

This inner urge to take up challenges has led man to do things that are quite daring. In India, mountaineering as a sport came with the Europeans in the 18th century. That was a time when entire Europe was experiencing a new phase. New regions were being explored, won, and native peoples were being made to become civilized. This zeal of adventurism found its ultimate fruition in the Himalayas-lofty, extremely difficult to conquer, and challenging enough to send a man back to his mother's womb. But, being men, these challenges were accepted and there began a tussle between men's ambitions and nature's reluctance.

New heights were conquered, new routes were discovered, many lives lost, but the mission was accomplished. Today, almost all the major peaks are conquered and even general people have started taking mountaineering as a serious hobby. For starters, India offers a wide spectrum of options for mountaineering as well as other related sports. Peaks and trekking routes are classified and maps are available for the interested travellers. Many institutes provide basic and advanced level courses in mountaineering and other related sports. All the equipment is locally available and other support resources can be found here.

PARAGLIDING IN INDIA

If you like Icarus ever wished to fly, as suggested, make your dream realise. The adventure of paragliding is something you just cannot miss. Soar over the hills, dip whenever you aspire to get a better view of the Earth, glide and sail, feel the freedom of the bird. The adventure of being at the altitude needs an attitude! No noise pollution, no smoke just plain fun. The thrill of have your own wings, the big wide sky with no traffic jams is a safe and easy aero adventure. Paragliding is fun for the people who constantly would love to reach new heights. Be amongst the stars during the day and count the constellations at night! Live life happily in the lap of Mother Nature. The package offers training for the novice too. Come fly, with us. The paraglider, harness, helmets, radios and ankle boots are equipments required for the adventure. Besides the monsoon season, the sky is your road for the escapade, come on touch the sky.

ELEPHANT SAFARI

How about a safari atop an elephant? Jeeps and other mechanical means of transportation may distract the fellow animals in the jungle. The Elephant is the best possible option available to admire the beauty of nature. The wildlife adventure in India is incomplete if an Elephant safari is not include in the itinerary. Come and explore the wild terrain of the Corbett National Park on the most majestic animal of all. Even horse safaris do well with the tourists in India. The strong and sturdy animal has since long been galloping across the terrific terrain in India.

ROCK CLIMBING IN INDIA

It is not quite easy to define rock climbing, but it is not difficult too. Anyone who claims to be a rock climber has his own version of the game. Rock climbing for some is to challenge their spirits and explore new heights, to give a fillip to their unbounded imaginations; for others, it is a way telling the world that he/she has finally arrived. For many of the professional rock climbers, it is not a sport. Can you call a mission to moon a sport or pastime? If not, then why should rock climbing be called a sports is the argument. For them, rock climbing is an adventure of the greatest magnitude; it is a fight against self, against the elements, and the ultimate goal is to reach the summit and return back alive.

SCUBA DIVING IN INDIA

One of the greatest adventures in life can be to explore the totally unknown and unexplored world under sea. The joy of floating inside the sea like a fish where every creature is your friend and every new sight is a discovery can be immense. In addition, the sheer thrill of watching the rich flora and fauna of the sea in their natural habitat is unparalleled. The curiosity to know the underwater world of the sea is not a new phenomenon for human civilization. We have so many stories from the epic Ramayana describing the world beneath the sea when Hanuman was crossing the sea to reach Lanka.

The origin of many mythical characters and objects are related to the sea. There is a legend about Samudra Manthan that tells us that the sea was churned around a hill known as Meru with a snake around it. The gods pulled one end of the snake while the other end was pulled by the demons. Many amazing things came out of this exploration-an elephant called Airavata that became the property of Indra, a tree called Kalpavriksa that could grant anything, a cow known as Kamdhenu that gave milk everyday, the Goddess of wealth Lakshmi, the god of Ayurveda Dhanawantari, the Visha and Amrit. Scuba diving and snorkeling as sports came with the Europeans who saw the vast expanse of the Indian coastline. Besides, many Indians who experienced this unique adventure also brought with them a new and exciting option for their fellow countrymen.

Stretching many thousand kilometers, the Indian coastline spans the mighty waters of the Arabian Sea, the Indian Ocean and the Bay of Bengal. Dotted with the finest beaches, cliff promontories, mangroves, backwater, jewel-like island groups and marine life, there are wide diving possibilities. While there are many popular easily accessible sites, many more can be explored which are not at all known. The sight of the smashing waves creating foaming breakers on the coral reef, which enclose azure lagoons whose crystal clear waters wash the fine grained white sands of the palm dotted low islands, is one of the few marvels of God's creations left untouched by the encroaching hands of industrialization and progress. The underwater city is a unique and diverse collection of colourful and weirdly patterned sea animals. Corals take pride of place in these reef cities. Rich in variety and colour, the thousands of types of corals range from tall sea fans to small hydroids, from languidly waving sea anemones to glassy jellyfish. Danger there is, but only enough to add to the sense of adventure and thrill. This fun is multiplied many times over as you don the scuba gear. This gear has been especially devised for the deep sea diver and gives an opportunity for thrill and adventure unparalleled and unimagined by ones who think of the sea as nothing but a large saltwater lake.

India is fast becoming the adventure tourism destination of the world; and scuba diving and snorkeling as well as other water sports are going to be an integral part of this. If you have not had adventure in India, you do not know what adventure is all about.

SKIING IN INDIA

The sheer joie de vivre inspired by one's first successful slide down a ski slope defies description. Once limited to a privileged few, the adrenalin-producing pastime of skiing has been brought within the range of the common man now. For the purist, there is unsullied, powdery snow. For the accomplished and ego-conscious, there are punishing runs. For wobbly beginners and confident intermediates, there are easy slopes and understanding instructors who soon inspire dreams of Olympic glory.

With a first run to buoy one under the belt, there follows a succession of blissful days. Each day brings a fresh challenge to conquer and relish when you are at any skiing resort. Mastering the twists and turns and jumps of skiing, completing a longer ski run, and achieving faster speed are all part of this process. Every winter in the Indian Himalayas the slopes are warmed by the excited cries and laughter of entrants being introduced to the joys of winter sports: the magic of the wind rushing past as you whiz down a slope of skis, or the sheer pleasure of gliding gracefully, artistically cutting figures of eight in the snow. Skiing, like any other high-altitude adventure sports in India, is a contribution of the Europeans. The summers in north India have always been unpleasant, more so for the Europeans who were mostly from the cold countries.

To save themselves from this oppressive heat, they went to the Himalayas, not too far from major centres in north India. Many hill stations were established, the prominent among them being Shimla, Manali, Mussoorie, and Nainital. These places served not only as the home away from home for them but also as the centre where they could participate in recreational activities like skiing and trekking. Some of these places still have the best skiing slopes in the country. Affluent Indians started participating in this sport even before independence.

After independence, with the efforts of adventure sport bodies, local youths were encouraged to participate in this sport. They took to it enthusiastically and later helped in training hordes of tourists coming from other parts of the county and even abroad. Today, skiing is quite popular in the hill stations of

North India and new facilities have added up to make it more popular among the masses.

TREKKING IN INDIA

Off late, trekking in India is becoming popular among the tourists all over the world. This might have been a new phenomenon for the travellers from abroad, for Indians, these mountains signify not only the natural beauty but also a source of spiritual guidance. Trekking has remained men's passion from the day he took his first step on the earth. He always ventured out of home and his natural surroundings to explore something new, a world that was unknown to him. It is astonishing to learn that the human race migrated from one continent to another when there were no means of communication, no helping hands, and most of them who left their home could never return back.

WHITE WATER RAFTING IN INDIA

If you want to get some kick, some change in life, or just to have some fun, river rafting can satisfy most of your desires. If you have the zeal, then go for the challenge and show others that you can do it. White-water rafting is not for fashionable thrill seekers, but for those who thrive on hair-soaking risks, which keep the adrenalin flowing overtime! The thrill of rushing down fast-flowing mountain streams a froth with huge waves, dashing against dangerous boulders and dizzy rapids, while you cling for dear life dependent on a fragile, inflatable rubber raft or dinghy. Be swept along a rushing river in a rubber raft, tumble over rapids, plunge over waterfalls and feel the icy spray splash on your face, as your raft races along a mountain river in India.

Experience the thrill of white water rafting in India along tumbling snow-fed Himalayan rivers in summer destinations in India. River rafting in India is an exhilarating experience that you can enjoy on your Indian Holiday. One of the best regions for river rafting in India is the stretch upto Rishikesh in Uttaranchal. White water rafting on Alaknanda, Bhagirathi and Ganga rivers is a popular adventure tourism activity in summer in India. For the more adventurous traveller, white water rafting tours in India can also be organized on the Indus River in Ladakh and Brahmaputra River in Arunachal Pradesh White water rafting in India on the Alaknanda River is the most easily accessible white water river rafting stretch from Delhi. We drive from Delhi to Rishikesh and further north to Devprayag, where the Alaknanda River and Bhagirati River combine to form the Ganges, a river considered holy by Hindus in India.

Further North is Rudraprayag, where the Alaknanda and Mandakini Rivers combine. The white water rafting Alaknanda tour, consists of an approximately 130 Km long stretch from Rudraprayag to Shivpuri near Rishikesh in Uttaranchal, India. You will be given training by experienced river rafting instructors and guides. You will travel in groups in rafts, with an instructor at all times. Life jackets and other essential safety equipment are provided. You can stay overnight in luxury tents, pitched on beaches alongside the river, as we halt each night.

You can also enjoy campfires and bonfire nights on river rafting tours in India. As you swoop and tumble over the rapids with exotic names such as 'Roller Coaster;' 'Crossfire' and 'The Wall' you will feel the excitement and heart-racing thrill of white water rafting in India, on adventure tours to India this summer, with Indian Holiday.

MEDICAL TOURISM

Medical tourism can be broadly defined as provision of 'cost effective' private medical care in collaboration with the tourism industry for patients needing surgical and other forms of specialized treatment. This process is being facilitated by the corporate sector involved in medical care as well as the tourism industry-both private and public. Medical tourism refers to traveling to other countries to obtain medical, dental, and surgical treatment. At the same time they could also tour, and fully experience the attractions of the countries they visit. Exorbitant costs of healthcare in industrialized nations, ease and affordability of international travel, favourable currency exchange rates in the global economy, rapidly improving technology and standards of care in many countries of the world, and most importantly proven safety of healthcare in select foreign nations have all led to the rise of medical tourism. Medical tourism is a term initially coined by travel agencies and the mass media to describe to the rapidly-growing practice of traveling to another country to obtain health care.

Such services typically include elective procedures as well as complex specialized surgeries such as joint replacement cardiac surgery, dental surgery, and cosmetic surgeries. The provider and customer use informal channels of communication-connection-contract, with less regulatory or legal oversight to assure quality and less formal recourse to reimbursement or redress, if needed. Leisure aspects typically associated with travel and tourism may be included on such medical travel trips. The concept of medical tourism is not a new one. The first recorded instance of medical tourism dates back thousands of years to when Greek pilgrims traveled from all over the Mediterranean to the small territory in the Saronic Gulf called Epidauria. This territory was the sanctuary of the healing god Asklepios. Epidauria became the original travel destination for medical tourism. Spa towns may be considered an early form of medical tourism.

DESCRIPTION

Factors that have led to the recent increase in popularity of medical travel include the high cost of health care or wait times for procedures in industrialized nations, the ease and affordability of international travel, and improvements in technology and standards of care in many countries of the world. Medical tourists can come from anywhere in the world, including Europe, the UK, Middle East, Japan, U.S. and Canada. This is because of their large populations, comparatively high wealth, the high expense of health care or lack of health care options locally, and increasingly high expectations of their populations with respect to health care. A large draw to medical travel is convenience and speed. Countries that operate public health-care systems are often so taxed that it can take considerable time to get non-urgent medical care.

The time spent waiting for a procedure such as a hip replacement can be a year or more in Britain and Canada; however, in Singapore, Hong Kong, Thailand, Cuba, Colombia, Philippines or India, a patient could feasibly have an operation the day after their arrival. In Canada, the number of procedures in 2005 for which people were waiting was 782,936. Additionally, patients are finding that insurance either does not cover orthopedic surgery or imposes unreasonable restrictions on the choice of the facility, surgeon, or prosthetics to be used.

Medical tourism for knee/hip replacements has emerged as one of the more widely accepted procedures because of the lower cost and minimal difficulties associated with the traveling to/from the surgery. Colombia provides a knee replacement for about $5,000 USD, including all associated fees such as FDA approved prosthetics and hospital stay over expenses. However, many clinics quote prices that are not all inclusive and include only the surgeon fees associated with the procedure.

Medical tourists may seek essential health care services such as cancer treatment and brain and transplant surgery as well as complementary or 'elective' services such as aesthetic treatments.

A research found in an object by a famous university: "the cost of surgery in Bolivia, Argentina, Cuba, India, Thailand, Colombia, Philippines or South Africa can be one-tenth of what it is in the United States or Western Europe, and sometimes even less. A heart-valve replacement that would cost US$200,000 or more in the U.S., for example, goes for $10,000 in the Philippines and India—and that includes round-trip airfare and a brief vacation package. Similarly, a metal-free dental bridge worth $5,500 in the U.S. costs $500 in India or Bolivia and only $200 in the Philippines, a knee replacement in Thailand with six days of physical therapy costs about one-fifth of what it would in the States, and Lasik eye surgery worth $3,700 in the U.S. is available in many other countries for only $730.

Cosmetic surgery savings are even greater: A full facelift that would cost $20,000 in the U.S. runs about $3,000 in Cuba, $2,700 in the Philippines or $2,500 in South Africa or $ 2,300 in Bolivia."To understand the phenomenon of medical travel, we can compare the average costs of cosmetic surgeries between the industrialized nations and Latin America countries where medical tourism and cosmetic surgery tourism are becoming popular, such as Argentina, Bolivia, Brazil, Costa Rica, Colombia, Philippines, and Mexico.

Popular medical travel worldwide destinations include: Brunei, Cuba, Colombia,Hong Kong, Hungary, India, Israel, Jordan, Lithuania, Malaysia, The Philippines, Singapore, South Africa, Thailand, and recently, UAE and New Zealand. Popular cosmetic surgery travel destinations include: Argentina, Bolivia, Brazil, Colombia, Costa Rica, Cuba, Mexico and Turkey. In Europe Belgium, Poland and Slovakia are also breaking into the business. South Africa is taking the term "medical tourism" very literally by promoting their "medical safaris": Come to see African wildlife and get a facelift in the same trip. However, perceptions of medical tourism are not always positive.

In places like the U.S., where most have insurance and access to quality health care, medical tourism is viewed as risky. In some parts of the world, wider political issues can influence where medical tourists will choose to seek out health care; for example, in late 2006, some patients from the Middle East were choosing to travel to Singapore or Hong Kong for health care rather than to the U.S. because of international tensions. While the tourism component might be a big draw for some Southeast Asia countries that focus on simple procedures, India is positioning itself the primary medical destination for the most complex medical procedures in the world.

India's commitment to this is demonstrated with a growing number of hospitals that are attaining the U.S. Joint Commission International accreditation to help to capture the US medical tourism market, while others looking beyond just the US market to potential clients from the United Kingdom, Europe and Australia may also look towards other international healthcare accreditation schemes for brand advantage. Singapore positions itself as a medical hub for health care services, medicine, biomedical research and pharmaceutical manufacturing converge. Singapore has made international news for many complex surgeries in specialties such as neurology, oncology, and organ transplants procedures.

Currently Singapore boasts the largest number of U.S. Joint Commission accredited hospitals in the region. In South America, countries such as Argentina, Bolivia, Brazil and Colombia lead on plastic surgery medical skills relying on the vast experience their surgeons have in treating the style-obsessed. It is estimated that 1 in 30 Argentineans have had plastic surgery procedures, making this population the most operated in the world after the U.S. and Mexico.

In Bolivia and Colombia, plastic surgery has become quite common. The "Sociedad Boliviana de Cirugia Plastica y Reconstructiva", more that 70% of middle and upper class women in the country have had some form of plastic surgery. Colombia also provides advanced care in cardiovascular and transplant surgery. Companies are beginning to offer global health care options that will enable North American and European patients to access world health care at a fraction of the cost of domestic care. Companies that focus on 'Medical Value Travel' typically provide experienced nurse case managers to assist patients with pre- and post-travel medical issues. They also help provide resources for follow-up care upon the patient's return. While these services will initially be of interest to the self-insured patient, several studies indicate that the rapid growth of Health Savings Accounts in the U.S. will also drive interest to health care in other countries.

INDIA

India is known in particular for heart surgery, hip resurfacing and other areas of advanced medicine. The government and private hospital groups are committed to the goal of making India a world leader in the industry. The industry's main appeal is low-cost treatment. Most estimates claim treatment costs in India start at around a tenth of the price of comparable treatment in America or Britain. Estimates of the value of medical tourism to India go as high as $2 billion a year by 2012. The Indian government is taking steps to address other infrastructure issues that can serve as a deterrant to the country's growth in medical tourism. The south Indian city of Chennai has been declared India's Health Capital, as it nets in 45% of health tourists from abroad and 30-40% of domestic health tourists.

CULTURAL TOURISM

'Cultural tourism' is the subset of tourism concerned with a country or region's culture, especially its arts. It generally focuses on traditional communities who have diverse customs, unique form of art and distinct social practices, which basically distinguishes it from other types/forms of culture. Cultural tourism includes tourism in urban areas, particularly historic or large cities and their cultural facilities such as museums and theatres. It can also include tourism in rural areas showcasing the traditions of indigenous cultural communities and their values and lifestyle. It is generally agreed that cultural tourists spend substantially more than standard tourists do. This form of tourism is also becoming generally more popular throughout Europe.

DEFINITION

By definition, the term destination refers broadly to any given area where tourism is a relatively important activity, like for instance having an economy significantly influenced by tourism revenues. However, it is complicated by the fact that a single, recognizable destination may include several cities, towns or municipalities, provinces, or other government entities-in island archipelago it may be the entire country.

LIVING CULTURAL AREAS

Due to globalization, technology and the onset of cultural tourism and ecotourism, the number of living cultural areas is continually declining. For an indigenous culture that has stayed largely separated from the surrounding majority, tourism can present both advantages and problems. On the positive side are the unique cultural practices and arts that attract the curiosity of tourists and provide opportunities for tourism and economic development. On the negative side is the issue of how to control tourism so that those same cultural amenities are not destroyed and the people do not feel violated.

Chiloé, Chile

Chiloé is Chile's largest island, located at the midway point between the capital, Santiago, and the country's extreme south at Tierra del Fuego. Chiloé is the site of the Chiloé Model Forest, member of the same network as the Calakmul and Eastern Ontario Model Forests. Having evolved for centuries isolated from mainland Chile, the "Chilotes" developed a strong, self-reliant culture, rich in folklore, mythology and tradition. This very identity is what constitutes the island's major attraction for domestic tourists in Chile and increasingly, for international tourists. As in the Calakmul case above, tourism to Chiloé is very strongly based on the island's cultural heritage, predominantly consisting of crafts markets, appreciation of cultural landscapes, museum exhibitions, seafood cuisine and architectural heritage.

However, the average tourist to the island will have little opportunity to see Chilotes involved in their living cultural activities, such as the elaborate preparation of the islands famous "curanto" meal, rich in shellfish, meat and potatoes, the management practices of their farm and forest lands, boat building and more. In order to overcome the cultural and organizational barriers that keep suppliers of living cultural heritage and tour operators apart, the Chiloé diocese of Ancud established a private foundation called "Fundación con Todos". Among other activities, the Foundation has played a key role in helping a number of Chilote households organize themselves into an "agrotourism" network.

The Foundation helped Chilote households make the preparation required to accommodate tourists and complemented this effort with a professional marketing campaign. These works were undertaken with the financial support of other agencies. Again, in cooperation with the EOMF and the Chiloé Model Forest, a cultural and natural heritage tour was organized to Argentina and Chile, including a three-day visit to Chiloé, permitting some of the Chilote households to host a group of cultural heritage tourists for the first time. The visits were very successful and should be the first of more to come, helping establish the credibility of Chiloé's agrotourism network among other tour operators.

Orrissa Tribes

Nestling on the eastern coast of India, Orissa is one of the most exquisite regions dominated by exotic sandy beaches, plenteous wild life, and holy temples famous for their architectural splendor and primitive lifestyle.

The charm of the city is still well- nigh chaste and unrevealed by the visitors, up to its full extent. The other lure of the city lies in its tribal population dotted with more than 62 tribal communities. The tribal communities of Orissa constitute about 23% of its total population. Orissa is inhabited by tribes like Saora or Sabar that had a respectable mentioning in the epic of Mahabharata. Mostly the Orissa tribes are high land habitats with opulent ethnic trait, cultures and customs dominated by varying languages. The culture conscious tribes are able to preserve their social customs and dignified values. The most primitive tribes are Bondas, Gadabas, Koyas, Kondhas and Sauras.

The culture of tribal Orissa is affluent with their own folk songs and dances, their tattoos. Tribal culture of Orissa is well depicted in its modern city in form of poems, art and craft or music. The tribes have adapted the Hindu traditions and culture from centuries, which is mixed with their own culture giving a distinct zest to the entire racial. Songs and dances are the essence of the tribal culture of Orissa.

The traditions and the ceremonies for wedding, birth and death all are represented by singing songs, rural dances along with feasts. The Tribal Folk Orissan tribes are strong, assiduous and simple hospitable tribes, normally like to be reserved and maintain distance from the people of other communities, as they are too shy. The major occupation of these tribes is agriculture and fishing and hunting.

Men usually wear loin attire and women rap long stretch of cloth around them. Women are adorned with ornaments like bangles, armlets, bracelets, necklaces, rings, hairpins etc usually made of silvers, aluminum, and brass. The practice of tattooing is prevalent among women folk. Girls above 5 years are found with tattoo mark on their faces and hands. Festival Celebration Numbers of deities are worshiped by the tribes for their happy life. Many festivals are also celebrated with much of enthusiasm and excitement. The ceremony rituals are observed through out the year in order to appease their deities and ascendant. The most significant festival of the year are the chaita parab and push parab- this day all able men of the village go on a hunting expedition. The tribes with their cultural dance, song and music all distinguish custom of their artistic life, which demarcate them from the other non tribal groups.

Orissa acquire every thing Orissa is a state, embellished with hilly terrain of the Eastern Ghats, where primitive tribes dwell and a beautiful stretch of the Indo-Aryans coast where modern life persists. A blend of 2 discrete civilization with contrast cultures, beautiful landscapes, beaches, rich wildlife, offers the best of India to its visitors. As the issue of globalization takes place to this modern time, the challenge of preserving the few remaining cultural community around the world is becoming hard. In a tribal based community, reaching economic advancement with minimal negative impacts is an essential objective to any destination planner. Since they are using the culture of the region as the main attraction, sustainable destination development of the area is vital for them to prevent the negative impacts because of tourism.

MANAGEMENT ISSUES

Certainly, the principle of "one size fits all" doesn't apply to destination planning. The needs, expectations, and anticipated benefits from tourism vary greatly from one destination to another. This is clearly exemplified as local communities living in regions with tourism potential develop a vision for what kind of tourism they want to facilitate, depending on issues and concerns they want to be settled or satisfied.

DESTINATION PLANNING RESOURCES

Culture: The Heart of Development Policy

It is important that the destination planner takes into account the diverse definition of culture as the term is subjective. Satisfying tourists' interests such as landscapes, seascapes, art, nature, traditions, ways of life and other products associated to them -which may be categorized cultural in the broadest sense of the word, is a prime consideration as it marks the initial phase of the development of a cultural destination.

The quality of service and destination, which doesn't solely depend on the cultural heritage but more importantly to the cultural environment, can further be developed by setting controls and policies which shall govern the community and its stakeholders. It is therefore safe to say that the planner should be on the ball with the varying meaning of culture itself as this fuels the formulation of development policies that shall entail efficient planning and monitored growth.

Local Community, Tourists, the Destination and Sustainable Tourism

While satisfying tourists' interests and demands may be a top priority, it is also imperative to ruminate the subsystems of the destination's. Development pressures should be anticipated and set to their minimum level so as to conserve the area's resources and prevent a saturation of the destination as to not abuse the product and the residents correspondingly. The plan should incorporate the locals to its gain by training and employing them and in the process encourage them to participate to the travel business. Keep in mind that the plan should make travellers not only aware about the destination but also concern on how to help it sustain its character while broadening their travelling experience.

SOURCES OF DATA

The core of a planner's job is to design an appropriate planning process and facilitate community decision. Ample information which is a crucial requirement is contributed through various technical researches and analyses.

Here are some of the helpful tools commonly used by planners to aid them:

- Key Informant Interviews
- Libraries, Internet, and Survey Research
- Census and Statistical Analysis
- Spatial Analysis with Geographical Information System and Global Positioning System technologies

KEY INSTITUTIONS

Participating structures are primarily led by the government's local authorities and the official tourism board or council, with the involvement of various NGOs, community and indigenous representatives, development organizations, and the academe.

Cultural and Ecotourism in the Mountainous Regions of Central Asia and in the Himalayas

Tourism is coming to the previously isolated but spectacular mountainous regions of Central Asia, the Hindu Kush and the Himalayas. Closed for so many years to visitors from abroad, it now attracts a growing number of foreign tourists by its unique culture and splendid natural beauty. However, while this influx of tourists is bringing economic opportunities and employment to local populations, helping to promote these little-known regions of the world, it has also brought challenges along with it: to ensure that it is well-managed and that its benefits are shared by all. As a response to this concern, the Norwegian Government, as well as the UNESCO, organized an interdisciplinary project called the Development of Cultural and Eco-tourism in the Mountainous Regions of Central Asia and the Himalayas project. It aims to establish links and promote cooperation between local communities, national and international NGOs, and tour agencies in order to heighten the role of the local community and involve them fully in the employment opportunities and income-generating activities that tourism can bring.

Project activities include training local tour guides, producing high-quality craft items and promoting home-stays and bed-and-breakfast type accommodation. As of now, the project is drawing on the expertise of international NGOs and tourism professionals in the seven participating countries, making a practical and positive contribution to alleviating poverty by helping local communities to draw the maximum benefit from their region's tourism potential, while protecting the environmental and cultural heritage of the region concerned.

ETHNIC TOURISM

Ethnic tourism is related to the more popularly known nature or eco-tourism. In nature tourism, people visit a region, usually in a third world country, in order to enjoy its natural beauty. Nature tourism can also imply social awareness because it "creates an understanding of cultural and natural history, while safeguarding the integrity of the ecosystem and producing economic benefits that encourage conservation".

Ethnic tourism is the addition of an indigenous or traditional group of people who live in this environment and interact and depend upon it. Visitors enjoy both the natural environment and the singular ethnic experience. Because of the ethnic groups' dependence on the environment, it is difficult to separate ethnic tourism from the landscape in which it occurs. Hence, nature and ethnic tourism are often interrelated and inseparable.

From the visitor's point of view, ethnic tourism is "travel motivated by the search for the firsthand, authentic and sometimes intimate contact with people whose ethnic and/or cultural background is different from the tourists". Ethnic tourists are also driven by the desire to see some of the "threatened" cultures which may soon disappear through assimilation into the nation's majority. The visitor's experience usually includes opportunities to see and photograph people in their traditional dress, observe their living conditions, and purchase local handicrafts.

Ethnic and nature tourism can help protect indigenous people and their environments by providing a sustainable alternative to subsistence agriculture and extractive activities such as timber harvesting. The added income and exposure can satisfy national goals of development while contributing to cultural pride and autonomy. Ethnic tourism can also have many negative consequences including commoditization of culture, social tension, and loss of cultural identity. In any case, tourism brings changes as groups gain or lose ownership, access, and use rights, and adjust to a new economic system. The varying controllers of tourism play a major role in the changes and effects wrought by tourism on the resident population.

National parks and similar protected areas are the most recognizable forms of nature and ethnic tourism. These large scale, federally controlled land management systems preserve the land which is often in danger of encroachment and extraction activities. Some national parks are designed to protect the environment and the indigenous group dependent on that environment such as Odzalla National Park in Congo, the Kalahari Reserves in Botswana, Manu Park in Peru, Gates of the Arctic Monument in Alaska, Kluane Park in the Yukon, Kakadu National Park in the Northern Territory in Australia, Varirata National Park in Papua New Guinea, and Honduras Rio Platano Biosphere Reserves. However, federal control of these lands often neglect the needs or input of the parks' residents.

For example, the nomadic Masai who migrate seasonally with their cattle through Amboseli and Serengeti National Parks in Kenya and Tanzania have increasingly come into conflict with park administrators who have placed priority on preserving large tracts of savanna woodlands and wildlife over that of the Masai's traditional sustainable lifestyle. Although most tourists come to see the wildlife, increasing numbers also want to view the Masai. This form of ethnic tourism brings few benefits for the Masai who have hardly any crafts and no control over tourism.

In other parks, like Sagarmatha National Park in Nepal, much of the resident population does benefit from tourism. The Sherpa have supplemented their herding lifestyle with jobs relating to tourism but have little control over tourist access. As the national government promotes Sagarmatha for tourism, the demand for material needs like wood for heat increases. As the environment is degraded due to deforestation, the Sherpa must compete with outsiders for their own resources. Hence, national parks sometimes hurt more than help the local populations who live in and around these protected areas. An alternative to national, people-exclusive projects is a project or approach to tourism that includes the resident population and recognizes the value of traditional techniques that can help manage the environment.

Outside assisted projects vary from obvious governmental or organizational influence and control to projects promoted as "grassroots" or "bottom-up" but which include outside influence in planning and implementation. "Local participation at all stages" is a phrase included in most project documents but not always strictly followed. Outside assistance can provide ideas and needed capital but can also produce many problems. One example is the Toraja of southern Sulawesi in Indonesia who receive federal assistance in planning, promotion, and infrastructure.

Although the Toraja have some control and earn most of the benefits, government interference has designated some areas over others as tourist destinations, so that competition and animosity between formerly cooperative communities has begun. Less obvious outside interference from the national majority has caused social problems among the Ladakhi of Northern India. Most tourism benefits go to the small percentage of hotel owners and to outside tour operators.

To help remedy this situation, the Swedish-backed Ledeg foundation has helped the Ladakhi develop souvenirs and promote native dancing which builds on their traditional background. It remains to be seen if Ledeg's involvement helps distribute benefits more uniformly or just allows another minority to profit over others. Outside involvement is not always apparent.

The Kuna of Panama have developed a rainforest reserve with the administrative and monetary help of multinational organizations including the Inter-American Foundation and the World Wildlife Fund. The Kuna benefit from selling their colourful weavings but have seen a decline in tourist visitation since the implementation of their project because it severed cooperative relations with individuals and groups who formerly helped to advertise, transport, and provide lodging for the visitors. One alternative to outside assistance is no assistance. This allows an approach to tourism to evolve from the existing social order and within the limits of the natural environment and culture. Of course, economic unfairness and social disruption can still occur. Indigenous-developed tourism has some clear advantages.

Tourism on Taquile island on Lake Titicaca is one example of indigenous-controlled tourism. In order to develop a tourist infrastructure, the Quechua-speaking residents of Taquile pooled together their money and energy. They bought a boat motor to speed tourist transport to the island and take turns lodging the guests. Without the influence or investment of outside groups or the government, the residents of Taquile have fostered tourism without many of the problems of outside-assisted tourism.

In Ecuador, the small community of Capirona near the Napo river wanted to avoid becoming a "tourist zoo" like many of the neighbouring villages. By designing and running their own tours and constructing a thatch guest hut as a community, Capirona residents have more control over tourist access and accommodation as well as the distribution of the resultant benefits. While there is cooperation with outside groups, the tourism project or approach is a community desire and not one imposed from the outside.

All of the examples, fit into three main categories of nature and ethnic tourism: national projects which generally exclude the resident population, smaller-scale projects that are implemented and/or assisted by outside groups, and approaches initiated by the indigenous people without outside assistance. Large national projects such as national parks and reserves are important to recognize as options. National parks in Mexico are nearly nonexistent; green dots connoting parks on tourist maps have more to do with politics than tangible reality.

5

Sustainable Tourism Management

TOURISM MANAGEMENT

Tourism management means to assess the impacts of existing and future tourism development and to monitor the impacts of tourism activities. Monitoring must be based on clear indicators, analysis of carrying capacity, limits of acceptable change and established mechanisms which are activated in case of unfavourable development. Tourism management is also a proactive approach to the regulation and the development of tourism in a specific region. It is based on a plan adopted by regional/local authorities and stakeholders. The main dimensions of tourism management are visions, common rules, control and active development strategies.

- Visions are decisions that are made on the general perspective of the development of tourism in the region.
- Zoning means that the given area is divided into clearly designated zones listing the types of tourism activities and infrastructure that would be acceptable and should be developed.
- Legislation and guidelines provide regulations of tourism activities and infrastructure / facilities according to the vision and the zoning established. Some of the rules may be set in form of laws and others as voluntary guidelines or recommendations, e.g. setting standards and/or criteria for tourism like the environmental quality and land-use criteria in and around tourism sites and the environmental and cultural sustainability guidelines for new and existing tourism development. Existing laws must be reviewed to resolve any inconsistencies between policy objectives and legislation.
- The approval, licensing and control of tourism activities and infrastructure serve to implement the regulations. Various measures can be established, e.g. the approval or licensing of new tourism infrastructure and tourism activities. Existing tourism facilities and activities must be monitored to control if they comply with the regulations.

- Tourism development: Within the tourism management, regulation and control are only one part. Stakeholders and authorities can also take an active part in tourism development by starting initiatives in tourism product development, marketing and improvement of services.
- Support of tourism development initiatives: Tourism management can also support private sector tourism development initiatives by creating incentives, implementing assistance programs and establishing a network for the tourism sector. The proactive, positive approach of tourism development can often support or even replace the enforcement of regulations by creating best practice examples, honey pots for the desired type and dimension of tourism development and discourage or squeeze out of unfavourable activities.
- The use of economic instruments, including tiered user fees, bonds, taxes or levies is part of the proactive approach of tourism management.

TOURISM MANAGEMENT PLAN

A tourism management plan is a written, approved document, which should describe the possible threats and opportunities of tourism development within the Biosphere Reserve. Based on detailed information about the environmental, social, cultural, political and legal aspects of the Biosphere Reserve, it produces a vision for tourism development in the BR. This vision covers a certain period of time, which should be stated in the document, and describes the work which has to be completed to make the vision a reality. It also establishes control measures to monitor tourism activities.

WHY IS PLANNING IMPORTANT

The well known maxim 'fail to prepare then prepare to fail' emphasizes the fact that preparation for developing a tourism management plan is critical and that the more time allocated to developing it the better. Tourism management planning is especially challenging because the involvement of many different stakeholders in the planning process is crucial if the plan is to be successfully adopted and implemented. These stakeholders have different, sometimes conflictive interests and may also have different attitudes towards conservation and tourism. The vision created through the tourism management plan should be recognized, understood and supported by all relevant stakeholders, preferably in a consensual process. Some of the benefits of a tourism management plan are shown in the box below. Benefits of a Tourism Management Plan:

- It is a tool which helps to achieve results more efficiently and in a more cost effective way.

- It shows work priorities and highlights the worst problems caused by tourism development and ways to solve these problems.
- It clearly identifies what needs to be done and who is responsible for carrying out the tasks identified.
- It helps to plan the tasks which should be completed by protected area managers, local authorities and tourism operators.
- It ensures continuous and consistent tourism management and informs future managers of what has been done, as well as why, when and how it was done.
- It communicates the goals of sustainable tourism management to all relevant stakeholders and to a wider public right from the beginning of the planning process. This assures their support and involvement in the process and can in turn help to identify possible conflicts at an early stage.
- It explains regulations, restrictions and control measures to people visiting the Biosphere Reserve as well as to individuals offering tourism facilities.
- It defines and supports the model role of the Biosphere Reserve in national and international sustainable development strategies.

HOW TO PLAN? —THE LOGICAL PROCESS OF MANAGEMENT PLANNING

The management planning process is a logical process divided into different, consecutive stages. The eight steps described in this document correspond to and explain these key stages. The first stage, getting started, clarifies the background of the planning process and also how "the team" should be assembled. The second stage identifies the key stakeholders who will participate in the planning process and establishes their working arrangements. In stage 3 the baseline information needed to make decisions about the prospective tourism development, has to be compiled. This information acts as a basis for the development of the BRs' tourism management vision. To make this vision reality, the main goals and objectives have to be agreed upon and a work plan should be produced stating how these goals and objectives will be achieved. To make sure that the tourism management plan will monitor and manage potential impacts carefully, impact management strategies should be elaborated. To find out whether the goals of the management plan are being fulfilled and whether the stakeholders are being involved appropriately, a feedback and review process needs to be designed. The last step concerns the plan approval. The template for a tourism management plan at the end of this guide provides a checklist for the contents of the plan. This document explains all of these stages and describes why they are needed, how they can be accomplished and what their problems and pitfalls are.

WHO WRITES THE PLAN AND WHO WILL USE IT?

The tourism management plan of a Biosphere Reserve should be the product of a participative and consultative process that involves all those interested in or affected by tourism. Its development should also be made known to a wider public. The body taking responsibility for the whole planning process must be clearly defined and well settled. The Biosphere Reserve's administration should take over the responsibility for coordinating the tourism management planning process because it is already responsible for organising the development strategies of the BR.

The members of the other protected areas within the Biosphere Reserve also play an important role in the planning process. Their knowledge about the region's ecosystems and biodiversity, as well as their skills and experiences in managing both biodiversity and tourism are very valuable to the process. During the planning process, there will be the need to call on locals and specialists because of their expertise in many areas. Their specific knowledge and skills should be used and contributed towards compiling the baseline information as well as the assessments which are needed for the plan. Those developing the plan should make full use of all available information sources, not only experts and specialists, but also individuals who are familiar with the BR, administrators, economists, land owners, local authorities and tourism providers. Once written and approved, the plan will be used by many different stakeholders. These include:

- Management bodies of the BR and the national park
- NGOs involved in conservation and tourism in the area
- Tour operators and individuals who provide tourism facilities
- Local communities, administrators and politicians
- Resource managers
- Scientists and experts in different areas

HOW LONG SHOULD THE PLAN BE

The length of the plan will depend strongly on the BRs' individual circumstances concerning tourism and conservation and on the reserves' vision. In theory a tourism management plan should be as short as possible without loosing its coherence, credibility or practical use.

This is, however, usually quite difficult. Individuals writing the plan should remember that the plan will not only be used by the BR and the protected area management but also by all those interested in and involved in tourism. Making the plan "complete" can lead to a document which is very long and detailed. A management plan should, however, be applicable and effective rather than "complete". The plan will be constantly monitored and evaluated anyway to find out what needs to be added, changed or updated. In this sense, a management plan never is complete.

WHAT TIMESCALE SHOULD THE PLAN COVER

Ecological processes are generally lengthy, so long term management planning is therefore necessary. In the tourism sector, however, changes can occur quickly and can have huge impacts on natural and social environments, making shorter periods of time for developing the tourism management plan more attractive.

The timescale of the tourism management plan is actually divided into three different stages which take both of the above mentioned points into consideration. Each of these stages needs to be discussed and determined at the beginning of the planning process.

Long-term or "strategic planning":

- broad, but realistic goals for the tourism management plan
- time-frame: five to ten years

Medium-term or "tactical planning":

- defines the medium term steps to achieve the long term goals
- time-frame: up to five years

Short-term or "operational planning":

- specific activities necessary if the medium-term objectives are to be fulfilled.
- time-frame: one year

WHAT AREA SHOULD BE INCLUDED IN THE TOURISM MANAGEMENT PLAN?

The BR's tourism management plan is written for the whole geographical scope of the BR. The areas surrounding the BR should also be taken into consideration where possible because they can have profound influences on the BR. The BR and the areas surrounding it are inextricably linked. Conservation is usually concentrated on the core zone of the BR, the national park.

When developing the tourism management plan, care should therefore be taken, to include and acknowledge the entire area of the BR not just the core zone. Zoning in a BR can identify areas needing different levels of tourism management. These can also ensure the inclusion of all parts of the BR in the plan. Besides the general zoning of the BR there may be special zones created for tourism management.

INTEGRATION OF THE TOURISM MANAGEMENT PLAN INTO OTHER EXISTING REGIONAL PLANS

When developing the tourism management plan it is necessary to take other regional, national or international management plans, guidelines, resolutions and laws, which refer to and may affect tourism development and biodiversity conservation into consideration. Examples of these may be a

National Park Biodiversity Management Plan, regional planning instruments, regional or local initiatives guided by tourism providers, NGO's or local authorities' and national plans, guidelines and laws on tourism and conservation etc. It is extremely important to recognise and avoid potential conflicts between plans and regulations which already exist and the tourism management plan, which is being developed.

It is also useful to be aware of what has already been accomplished in the BR in the area of sustainable tourism development and conservation promotion. This information will help while trying to create synergies and establish networks between the different stakeholders.

STAKEHOLDER INVOLVEMENT

PARTICIPATION OF LOCAL POPULATION IN THE PLANNING PROCESSES

The objectives of the Convention on Biological Diversity define resource management as a societal choice. This means, that the whole society should participate in the planning and decision-making process. Traditionally, planning was done by experts and state authorities. The people affected by the planned development were only consulted towards the end of the planning process, if at all, and had very limited opportunities to contribute to the process themselves. The local population therefore had hardly any influence on the planning process and usually could not contribute to the decision-making process at all. Modern approaches to planning recognize that participation of the local population in management planning processes is important for two reasons:

Democracy

Apart from the fact that members of democratic societies indirectly choose the planning authorities and decision-makers through general elections, the more direct involvement of the local population in planning processes is one of the main principles of the concept of sustainable development.

Success of planning

The members of the local society influence the implementation of the plan:

- They have to obey the rules set in the plan.
- They may have to undertake certain activities developed in the plan.
- They may allocate resources necessary to achieve the plan's goals.

The success of the plan's implementation depends therefore on how committed the people are towards achieving its goals. If people participate from the beginning of the planning process and can really influence its goals and objectives, they are much more likely to identify themselves with the plan and feel responsible for its implementation.

STAKEHOLDER INVOLVEMENT IN TOURISM MANAGEMENT PLANNING

When leading management institutions want to facilitate the participation of a local population, they do this by using the concept of stakeholder involvement. That doesn't mean that there are no planning processes in which really the whole population can take part. In most cases, however, individuals from societal groups will represent their groups and their interests. These representatives form a smaller group of stakeholders, which is generally easier to manage. Stakeholders in sustainable tourism management planning are all the individuals who are interested in and/or affected by tourism development and biodiversity conservation. They should participate in the planning process from the early stage. Sustainable tourism development emphasises in particular the importance of considering and respecting the wishes and needs of the local population of the tourism destination. Tourism development is usually not a primary subject of public administration, and therefore can only be managed effectively if all the stakeholders participate in the decision-making process. The goals of sustainable tourism development can only be achieved if the people involved in tourism in the area act according to the tourism management plan and commit themselves to the vision of sustainable tourism development. Reasons for stakeholder involvement when developing a tourism management plan:

- They live within the BR and are affected by tourism and conservation measures.
- They are engaged in the tourism industry and therefore influence tourism development.
- Their businesses usually benefit from the natural resources and services in the area.
- They may be required to carry out certain tasks to achieve the sustainable tourism development goals.
- They can also cause major degradation and depletion of natural resources.
- They may utilise it to such a degree that they threaten biodiversity.
- They constitute part of future generations for whom the natural and cultural heritage should be maintained.

The development of a tourism management plan takes place within the framework of the national and regional conservation strategies and the designation of the Biosphere Reserve.

For this reason, all stakeholders in the development area are also asked to act in accordance with these regional specifications. It will then be the task of the manager to create a common goal, which all stakeholders are committed to, and which is based on the principles of sustainable tourism development and the conservation of biological diversity. This means that stakeholders cannot seek any outcomes they please, especially not ones which may have too negative impacts on the natural environment.

Who are the stakeholders in tourism management planning?

The tourism sector includes a great variety of products and services and influences the local economy as well as the culture and living-conditions of the tourism destination. This means that there is a wide range of people involved in tourism, such as local tourism service providers, retailers, hoteliers, etc. Furthermore, the whole local population is affected by tourism development. The preparation of the tourism management plan means also, deciding on which of these different stakeholder groups are important for the process. Care should be taken not to exclude parts of the local population which are not directly involved in tourism. There are various methods which can be used to identify and group stakeholders. One of these is the division of all stakeholders into smaller more cohesive groups or "key stakeholders". Stakeholders come from governmental, nongovernmental and private sectors and from indigenous and local communities and can be grouped according to their background, e.g. whether they are primarily political, economical, social, technological, legislative or environmental. Another way would be to divide them into the professional public and the general public. The professional public

- individuals, groups and organisations that are involved in tourism and/ or the spatial development of the project region
- in addition: professionals – experts in various fields

General public:

- individuals, groups and organisations that are neither directly involved in tourism sector nor immediately affected by tourism
- Their participation in the process is extremely important. As tourism is an important economic and social tool for guaranteeing or even increasing the living standard of the people, communication with the public and their consultancy with issues of tourism development in "their" region are of great importance.

It is important that, in the preparation phase, managers of tourism management planning know something about the stakeholders in the region, before they begin to identify those who are the most important for the development of the tourism management plan. It is, however, normally the case that the management of the BR and/or the protected area is already familiar with the stakeholders and can quickly identify those who are vital to the success of the tourism management plan. The list of stakeholders will vary according to the size and characteristics of the BR and the actual situation of tourism development within the BR. The list of participating stakeholders may also change during the tourism management planning process. Stakeholders in tourism management planning:

- Neighbours and residents
- Farmers, foresters, hunters and fishermen
- Tourism providers such as hoteliers, restaurant owners, tourist guides, etc.
- Tours operators and tourism agencies
- Local business men, e.g. retailers
- Local authorities: local municipalities, local administration
- Local NGOs
- Educational institutions, research centres
- Visitors
- Media

It is important not to exclude those who are opposed to or sceptical about the tourism management plan and the BR or national park. They may be vital for the development of an effective tourism management plan, though they may present counterproductive facts that need to be faced. It is important to control the size and scale of stakeholder involvement so that the tourism management plan preparation process does not get out of hand. A difficult problem that might occur during the process of identifying key stakeholders is how to ensure that stakeholders represent their group well.

HOW TO WORK WITH STAKEHOLDERS

Stakeholder involvement requires careful preparation and thought, about:

- how to identify stakeholders
- how to encourage their participation
- who should facilitate the work with stakeholders
- what the basic objectives of tourism development and biodiversity conservation are.

Tourism management planning process managers should be prepared for the fact that the first steps of preparation for stakeholder involvement will be time consuming. Stakeholders should be involved into every step of tourism management planning. The participation of stakeholders is firstly part of the capacitybuilding process, and secondly, it creates a "common issue of concern" which then leads to a common vision.

That can help the stakeholders to understand why biodiversity and the ecosystems of their BR are valuable, why they are important and why their loss or degradation should be avoided. Stakeholders can contribute with their special knowledge and are therefore a useful source of information. This ensures the inclusion of all relevant information and it also reinforces the credibility and reliability of the information. In the steps of visioning, creation of goals and objectives as well as during the steps of impact management, monitoring and approval, stakeholders have the opportunity to develop their own ideas of and decide upon tourism development in the region. This fosters the ownership of the tourism management by stakeholders and facilitates their commitment to implement the plan.

METHODS OF PARTICIPATION

There are different methods of stakeholder involvement that will be applied at the different stages of plan development. Providing information to all stakeholders about the tourism management planning process is one precondition of stakeholder involvement. Another requirement for effective participation is to enable the stakeholders to take part in the planning process through capacity building, awareness raising and education.

Information and consultation

Firstly, comprehensive information has to be provided to the public so that the aim of, the reasons for and the intentions of tourism management planning are well communicated and understood. Information and consultation

- providing information: presenting significant documents and plans, providing reports about important activities, sharing experiences and findings, consulting proposals and conclusions, etc.
- motivating local people to get involved in the process, to increase their interest in the process, etc.
- guiding through an intricate process of tourism development, informing about achievements and things that yet need to be done, background information and implementation measures, etc.
- promoting tourism and its development, explaining its importance to local people in order to include it among other activities and tasks that exist in the region and/or are considered important

Information on the topics, methods and outcomes of the management planning process should be provided to all stakeholders as well as to the general public in a timely manner, throughout the whole planning process. This consultative process at all stages of management plan development tries to create "ongoing and effective dialogue and information sharing with stakeholders". Constantly informing the stakeholders not only enables stakeholders to participate, it is also useful for preventing conflicts, because people affected by the outcomes of the tourism management plan are informed about these and can communicate their opinion on them at an early stage of the process. Techniques of information and consultation are listed in appendix I.

Capacity building, awareness raising and education

The second precondition for making stakeholder participation effective is to ensure that local communities are equipped with the necessary decision-making abilities as well as with the skills and knowledge necessary for undertaking tourism management. First of all stakeholders and the general public need to be educated about the impacts of tourism on biological diversity, good management practices in sustainable tourism development and the necessity and benefits of tourism management planning.

This stage of awareness-raising and education can be realized through different methods such as media campaigns, public lectures and seminars, exhibitions, etc. Stakeholders should be informed about and become interested in the aims of tourism management and should be encouraged to participate in the planning process by making the potential benefits of tourism management clear to them. Capacity-building activities help to develop and strengthen the capacities of all stakeholders for participating in the management planning process.

Subjects of capacity-building:

- accessing, analysing and interpreting baseline information
- undertaking impact assessments and evaluations
- impact management, decision-making, monitoring and adaptive management
- sustainable tourism development
- mechanisms for approval of goals and objectives
- training of tourism professionals in conservation and biodiversity issues
- information exchange and collaboration regarding sustainable tourism implementation through networking and partnerships between all stakeholders

Capacity-building and education measures require sufficient time and adequate human, financial and technical resources. It is important that capacity-building is carried out by experts who have knowledge in public education and training and also experience in participative processes.

Notification

Notification is, in most countries, a legal requirement for the approval of tourism investments. Detailed information on the proposed tourism developments must be accessible to everybody who is affected by it. The information must be presented clearly, and written in way which all stakeholders understand.

Enough time should be given to the stakeholders to enable them to read and process this information and to express their opinions about the proposals. For the process of tourism management planning, this becomes especially important around the phase concerning impact assessment of and decision-making about the proposals for tourism development and activities at particular locations. In appendix II there is a detailed list of the information which has to be provided in the notification process.

Participation techniques

There is a variety of participation techniques which can be useful at various stages of the planning process. Establishing a multistakeholder group, whose members participate in the whole process of plan development is, however, the most important participation technique and should get the most attention. For individual tasks the managing body can also establish subgroups, workshops etc. Round tables and panel discussions:

- Round tables and panel discussions are opportunities to form networks between organisations, institutions and local stakeholders. Each round table or panel discussion should address a specific topic. The main advantage of this method is that a variety of different perspectives and opinions will be heard and should be taken into account.

Workshops and seminars:

- Workshops and seminars – either for participants with special invitations and/or open to the general public - are an efficient way to a) inform about the actual state of the project, and b) for those involved to decide on and to develop further steps together, incorporating all local standpoints.

Advisory committees / boards:

- The purpose of an advisory committee is to provide advice or recommendations which will help to facilitate cooperation between affected/involved groups at the local level.

The multi-stakeholder group

The multi-stakeholder group should include all relevant stakeholders interested in participating in the management planning process. Some of the stakeholders may only take part in special workshops and not in every part of the process. Those managing the planning process should make sure that as many stakeholders as possible participate in the multistakeholder group and that they represent their groups well. Stakeholders should commit themselves to different parts of planning and implementation and should also take over different tasks involved in the work program.

They should, however, agree all together on the vision, goals and objectives of the tourism management plan. The process of stakeholder involvement starts with one or several informal meetings, in which the rules for discussions should be established and work which needs to be carried out in the future should be discussed and decided. It is often more effective if a "neutral" moderator, who isn't directly involved in the managing institution of the tourism management plan leads these meetings. It is better to present tourism management planning as an attractive opportunity for stakeholders, who can use it to have their say on development in the region and who can therefore eventually benefit from it. Discussion in the first meetings should be open and used as an opportunity to share different points of view and to begin to establish some common objectives for sustainable tourism management. The first informal meetings should include opportunities for the participants to get to know each other even if the participants feel that they already know each other well. This will bring uncertainties and suspicions to the forefront and relationships and existing conflicts among participants can be seen. During these informal conversations common perceptions and visions of conservation and tourism development can be identified. To reduce fears of "territoriality" the venue for these meetings should be "neutral". After the initial meeting, a group of people should form the multistakeholder group. They should be prepared to commit themselves to a series of meetings which will involve organising and developing the next steps of the management plan.

BASELINE INFORMATION

WHY BASELINE INFORMATION IS NEEDED

The baseline information describes the environment, the institutional, social, economic, cultural, political and legal circumstances and the current situation of tourism in the region. The compilation of baseline information assesses the current situation and predicts the future working environment for tourism management. It also includes existing and potential threats to the natural environment and the BR's potentials for sustainable tourism development. It provides the basis for decisions which need to be made concerning measures to be taken against these threats and on the vision and the goals of the tourism management plan. An in-depth compilation of baseline information is of vital importance if the project is to proceed successfully.

WHAT KIND OF INFORMATION IS NEEDED?

Baseline information for tourism management planning can be divided into three essential parts:

- Ecological, economic, social and historic characteristics of the BR and surrounding region
- Tourism and tourism management within the BR
- Legal framework for conservation of biological diversity and for tourism development

SWOT – Analysis

To assess the BR's potentials for sustainable tourism development and to consider the negative impacts of tourism on the natural and cultural environment, the compilation of baseline information should include a SWOT analysis. It examines the strengths, weaknesses, opportunities and threats of tourism development and the conservation of biodiversity in the BR. The following box shows questions to be considered in the SWOT analysis. Strengths:

- What are the strengths of the Biosphere Reserve regarding the conservation of biodiversity?
- Which are the region's features that can foster tourism development?

Weaknesses:

- Where are lacks of management and good policies for conservation?
- Which are the constraints of tourism development in the region?

Opportunities:

- What are the opportunities for environmental conservation?
- What are the opportunities for sustainable tourism development?
- What are the current and possible positive impacts of tourism development and tourism activities?

Threats:

- What are the current and potential negative impacts of tourism development and tourism activities on the natural and cultural environment?
- What are the threats to conservation of biodiversity caused by tourism?

The process of gathering baseline information should make clear to all stakeholders that tourism in general and tourism activities in their region cause impacts which need to be addressed. The integration of impact assessment into the tourism management plan is discussed in Step 6 "Impact assessment and impact management". In appendix V there is a list of negative and positive impacts of tourism on the natural and cultural environment.

HOW TO COLLECT AND PRESENT THE DATA NEEDED

After the topics of information needed for the development of the tourism management plan are agreed upon, the information which already exists on the chosen topics should be reviewed. Much of the information which is needed will be found in studies, surveys and plans, such as the Biodiversity Management Plan of the National Park, case studies, etc. This data should be complemented by further data collection, e.g. by the conduction of surveys, and then be compiled in such a way that the practical use for the rest of the planning process is clearly evident to the reader. For efficient data compilation, the following questions should be answered:

- Who will collect the data?
- Who will analyse the collected data and how?
- How will the data be presented to the stakeholders and the general public?

A summary of the collected baseline information will later be included in the tourism management plan. It is important to present the collected information in a simple, clear and comprehensive way. It should be accessible to all stakeholders. It can enable them to understand and realise the significance of the BR's natural, economic and cultural features, whilst emphasising the importance of biodiversity conservation and the benefits of sustainable tourism development.

The compilation of baseline information should further include maps and other additional material, e.g. visualized by GIS.

VISION AND GOALS

VISION

A vision describes a state in the future, towards which development should be directed. A vision does not provide detailed goals, it is not a state that is truly intended to be achieved, but is more the direction that people intend to follow, a description of an ideal state that people dream of. Creating a vision means asking "Where do we want to go?". Developing a vision is a creative process which allows daring and even utopian ideas. Sometimes visions may be quiet easy to achieve, sometimes it might be impossible. This must be clear to the managers and stakeholders of the planning process. A vision should identify what people really want and how they wish their future to be.

CREATE A VISION

Visioning is used for participative approaches in long-term policy agenda setting using stakeholders' imagination as a source of ideas. It allows a wide public participation for the development of long-ranged regional plans. It is a democratic way to search for disparate opinions from all stakeholders and to look for common ground among participants in exploring and advocating strategies for the future.

Visioning is an integrated approach which helps to avoid fragmented and reactionary approaches to addressing problems and it also considers the relationships between issues. With visioning many different future tourism scenarios are developed and issues, problems, different points of view, and competing demands are brought to the forefront. The collected scenarios serve as a basis for generating the end vision. This vision is based on many peoples opinions and ideas and their diverse viewpoints and can therefore be considered a democratically- derived consensus.

It is easier for people to stay focused and see the direction of their work during the process of planning and implementation of the plan when they have the vision in mind. The vision is created in a process with the participation of stakeholders. Because of this it fosters communication and the relationships between stakeholders and leads to the adoption of common goals, programmes and finally projects.

VISIONING IMPORTANT IN TOURISM MANAGEMENT PLANNING

The vision of tourism management planning for sustainable tourism development may appear clearly defined before the planning process has started. The basis of the vision is usually that tourism should be developed in a way that maintains biodiversity, minimizes the negative impacts and obtains maximum benefits for the local population as well as environmental conservation. A vision for a tourism management plan should, however, be linked to the region where the plan is being developed and should reflect the region's economical, environmental and social needs. While conservation strategies and the principles of sustainable tourism are indeed the framework for sound tourism management, this does not mean that people have no choice or that they have to loose something to achieve it. Sustainable tourism development offers a wide range of opportunities. It does not restrict the types or dimensions of tourism, the targeted markets or the designation of areas for tourism activities in a way that there is no choice left for tourism developers. Furthermore, sustainable tourism development for a great part does not mean that a totally new type of tourism needs to be established. It means improving existing tourism products and tourism types so that they use natural and cultural resources in a sustainable way. People can decide on the measures that need to be taken to achieve these improvements, they can choose whether they want to establish strict rules or whether they would rather work with recommendations and incentives. The role of those managing the tourism management planning is to find out these different perspectives and to identify the underlying common goals. A continuous good working relationship with stakeholders supports this process. A common vision for future tourism development, adopted by all stakeholders and the whole public is the best way to guarantee the successful implementation of the tourism management plan.

HOW TO CREATE A VISION

Creating a vision with a range of stakeholders or the general public is done by surveys, meetings and also votes. There are, however, many different approaches to the process of visioning and towards the adoption of a common vision. Some of these are mentioned below:

- Create a draft vision in one or in several stakeholder meetings, then inform the public about it and lead a discussion with stakeholders and the general public which finally leads to the adoption of one vision.
- Conduct a survey of the publics' issues with concerns about and ideas for tourism development and biodiversity conservation. From the results different options for the vision should be developed and discussed. Finally the stakeholders and general public should vote for one of the options.

- Conduct a public survey of issues with concerns about and ideas for tourism development and biodiversity conservation, then discuss the results in stakeholder meeting and create a vision based on the discussions.

Surveys and discussion not only lead to the adoption of a common vision, but should also identify priorities and major concerns which should be integrated into the tourism management plan.

They can also provide ideas for goals which will derive from the vision and for their implementation. These ideas can then be used in the next steps of the planning process. It is important for the managers of tourism management planning to recognize that visioning will require time, staff and will need to be well prepared. A useful approach for creating a vision is the method of guided imagination.

GOALS, OBJECTIVES AND THE WORK PROGRAM

FROM VISION TO GOALS

Once a common vision is created, the next step is to break down this vision into different goals which, when attained, will make the vision a reality. The main questions to be asked during this process are:

- "How can we accomplish our vision?" and
- "What are the solutions to the problems identified during the impact assessment of current and future tourism development?"

If, for example, the vision is:

- "the development of a type of tourism which is based on nature activities with minimum impacts and on experiencing the regions historical and current economic activities while maintaining the natural environment in its present state and conserving biodiversity",

the goals for working towards this vision may be:

- supporting the region's tourism sector in focusing on hiking activities
- involving local farmers, foresters and craftsmen in tourism activities, and
- improving conservation measures.

These goals should be identified in a multi-stakeholder process. The proposals made to work towards the vision and to address the identified problems should consider the potentials, strengths and opportunities previously established.

They should be general enough to reflect the vision and precise enough to be achievable in a realistic period of time. It is crucial that no goals are included in the tourism management plan which are contrary to the overall aim of sustainable tourism development and to biodiversity conservation. This can be avoided by referring to the vision which is based on this aim.

FROM GOALS TO OBJECTIVES

To achieve the goals, each of them must be broken down into objectives. Each of these represents a detailed task which needs to be accomplished in a given period of time. The main question during this process is: "What needs to be done to achieve our goals?" For each of the defined goals, the following points need to be considered:

- define, classify and prioritise the activities necessary to reach the goal
- make the output expected from the objectives clear
- a definition of the places where the activities will be applied
- the identification of the requirements for political, legal, organisational, informative, economical, etc., resources, which are needed to put the activities into practice
- identification of institutions or persons responsible for the implementation of the activities
- identification of institutions or persons to be involved in the implementation of the activities

Finally, the proposed objectives can be grouped into programs and main activities. The agreed objectives will be integrated into the work plan of the tourism management plan as overall tasks. At this stage of planning, it is important that proposed programs and activities are realistic and not idealistic. It is of vital importance that priorities, the timescale and responsibilities for each of the objectives are clearly defined. For example, the goal concerning focusing the region's tourism on hiking activities could include the following objectives:

- the establishment of a zoning system which identifies areas where activities other than hiking are either not encouraged or totally prohibited
- the creation or the improvement of an attractive trail system which includes different hiking and educational trails
- setting up a marketing campaign, addressing tourism agencies and/ or tour operators, that promotes the region as a "hiking paradise"
- the development a training scheme for local tour guides on guided hiking tours
- the realisation of a workshop for providers of accommodations on improvement of services for hikers

AGREEING ON GOALS AND OBJECTIVES

To agree on goals and objectives, methods similar to those used in the visioning process, such as stakeholder meetings, workgroup discussions and methods of adoption may be applied. The further the planning process advances, the more discussions and decisions will be conducted in smaller stakeholder groups or within the multi-stakeholder group. Not every detail of the plan needs to be discussed and decided on by the general public. It is, nevertheless, important to inform all stakeholders and the public about discussions and the decision-making process should be transparent.

THE WORK PROGRAM

To implement the objectives, a detailed work program has to be created. It should describe the goals, objectives and each single task necessary to achieve them. The single tasks for the objective "creation or improvement of an attractive trail systems with different hiking and educational trails", for example, could include:

- Compilation of information about the existing trails and evaluate them
- Allocation of a contract to an expert team to develop proposals for a new trail system
- Publishing proposals and discuss them with the stakeholders
- Adoption of one proposal
- Implementation of the proposal: develop and build the trails, develop maps and signs, promote the trails
- Maintaining the trails
- Monitoring the use of the trails

Time schedule:

- Exact start and finish date of the activity, these are set by
- calculating the time which is needed to accomplish the activity,
- considering the circumstances in which the activity takes places,
- considering the capacity of those implementing the activity.
- Deadline: sometimes, the exact duration of an activity cannot be foreseen at the beginning, but only be estimated. Anyway, a deadline should be set on which the activity must be finished at least.

Costs:

- Exact expenses to accomplish the activity, including
- salaries
- costs for material resources
- travel expenditures, etc.
- Cost calculation must consider in detail all costs from each part of the activity: preparation, transaction, notification, implementation and reporting.

Resources:

- Identification of financial resources:
- the exact amount of existing internal resources: financial resources that are provided by the organisation implementing the activity
- the exact amount of external resources: financial resources that are allocated from elsewhere

- Identification of other resources
- the exact amount of the implementing organisation's in-kind contribution
- the exact amount of other resources provided from external parties
- The resource plan should state clearly which resources are already available and which still need to be obtained and how they will be obtained.

Responsibilities:

- Identification of the organisation and/or the individuals that are responsible for the implementation of the activity
- exact description of form of commitment
- Identification of supervising responsibilities
- Identification of the organisation and/or individual who is responsible for the monitoring

Reporting:

- Description of the ways of reporting on the implementation of the activity
- Forms and deadlines for terms of references and monitoring and evaluation procedures
- Approval system for reporting measures

Monitoring:

- Description of data collection
- time, date and methods of data collection
- form of data compilation / reporting
- Indicators to assess the results of the monitoring
- Description of action plans designed to react on results of monitoring

IMPACT ASSESSMENT AND IMPACT MANAGEMENT

A large part of tourism management involves the assessment, the monitoring and the management of the impacts that tourism has on the natural and cultural environment. Impact management means:

- Identifying the impacts of existing tourism activities
- Assessing these impacts, taking the viewpoint of sound tourism development and biodiversity conservation into consideration
- Predicting the impacts of the future tourism development
- Developing ways to monitor and react on impacts of existing tourism activities and of the future tourism development

The impact assessment is not only a question of professional analysis but also a subject of personal opinion.

The evaluation should, therefore, be reviewed and discussed within the multi-stakeholder group and with the general public. Tourism activities which benefit one societal group may have negative impacts on other groups and the natural environment. The evaluation of impacts should, therefore, also be considered part of the decision-making process.

ADDRESSING EXISTING POSITIVE AND NEGATIVE IMPACTS

The compilation of baseline information includes analysing the impacts of existing tourism activities and predicting the potential impacts future tourism development might have on the BR. The tourism management plan is an instrument which identifies negative impacts and creates measures against them. The plan should develop an overall strategy for monitoring and managing the impacts from existing tourism activities in the BR. The positive impacts of tourism are considered as opportunities for sound tourism development. It is one of the aims of the tourism management plan to enhance these positive impacts and to use them as starting points for further tourism development.

ADDRESSING FUTURE POSITIVE AND NEGATIVE IMPACTS

The tourism management plan should also consider the monitoring and management of the impacts of future tourism development. The analysis of threats and opportunities in the SWOT analysis includes predictions of further tourism development, based on experiences made at other locations and on overall trends in tourism. The tourism management plan should develop strategies on how to identify and address these future impacts. As the impacts of future tourism development cannot always been foreseen, the tourism management plan should prepare managing organisations for flexible reaction on future development. The description of worst case and best case scenarios facilitates the development of different measures to manage the impacts. Each activity of the tourism management plan must be analysed for possible negative and positive impacts and measures must be developed to handle these impacts.

IMPACT MANAGEMENT

Various internationally accepted planning methodologies such as the Recreation Opportunity Spectrum, the Limits of Acceptable Change, Environmental Impact Assessment and Social Impact Assessment are useful for the evaluation of tourism development. Impact management can include measures for the siting of tourism development and activities, measures to control tourist flows, the promotion of appropriate tourist behaviour and the limiting of the number of tourists. The tourism management plan describes the concrete measures either to avoid or to mitigate existing and potential negative impacts. Impact management can be divided into the following steps:

- definition of a clear set of indicators, that will be used to measure and assess the impacts
- measuring of impacts
- assessment of the monitoring data: are the impacts within the acceptable limits or not?

- description of action plans which will become effective in case of unacceptable negative impacts
- implementation of action plans

Those who are responsible for the implementation of the action plans, and the resources necessary for impact management should be identified in the tourism management plan. Information on the impact assessment and management should be made available to the stakeholders and the public.

MONITORING AND ADAPTIVE MANAGEMENT

MONITORING

Monitoring means constantly checking if the implementation of the goals, objectives and the work program of the tourism management plan is carried out properly and whether they have the intended effects. Monitoring and its results should help to form decisions about how the plan should be managed in the future. The tasks completed and the impacts it causes have to be monitored at different timescales. The short-term review evaluates whether the work program has been carried out. The medium-term review evaluates the outcomes of the plans objectives and the long-term review verifies the impacts of the work and therefore how well the goals have been achieved. The review should evaluate the impacts related to the overall goals of the plan and the conservation strategies of the BR.

FEEDBACK MECHANISMS

The monitoring process should consider the whole set of tourism activities and impacts addressed in the tourism development plan. Monitoring consists of three consecutive steps: data collection, evaluation and reporting. As evaluation and reporting are therefore depending on the data collected, the in-depth compilation of valid data forms the basis of a good monitoring system. In order to guarantee the good quality of dates, the tourism management plan should provide a standardised data collection process, including a determined set of indicators, which will also be used in the phase of evaluation. This will allow for a reporting system, that is able to consider also changes occurring gradually in the course of time. Another important factor is again the involvement of local stakeholders and communities. Due to their local knowledge and because not all monitoring can be accomplished by external experts, the local population can decisively contribute to the success of the monitoring process, e.g. by collecting data and delivering reports. As stakeholders live and work in the region, their insights are particularly valuable for the monitoring process. They need to use a standardised, comprehensive system for data collection and reporting. The tourism management plan should include time schedules, responsibilities and resources of monitoring. Monitoring should consist of a combination of internal and external audits. That means, that the data collected should be evaluated by internal experts of the managing organisation and/or other participating institutions, as well as by external experts, who are not responsible for the implementation of the plan. Internal evaluation should not be undertaken by people who are directly responsible for the implementation of the work plan. The data needed for the external audit can be collected by external experts, but in most cases ongoing internal data collection will be used for the external audit as well, to enable assessment of the changes over a longer period of time. The data can then be supplemented by an external survey.

ADAPTIVE MANAGEMENT

A tourism management plan is only as good as its implementation. Constant monitoring, which is clearly defined in the plan and follows standardised procedures, is the only way to control whether the intended outcomes of the plan are achieved and whether the tourism management is successful. Furthermore, monitoring facilitates early reactions on inappropriate and unexpected developments. These quick reactions are the basis of "adaptive management". Evaluating the results of monitoring, decisions can be made on whether the tourism management needs to be adjusted, where adverse impacts on biodiversity and of tourism development are discovered. These adjustments must be discussed and determined with all relevant stakeholders. The entire monitoring process needs to be transparent and should include all stakeholders and the general public. Adaptive management is needed for several reasons:

- The process might not achieve the planned outcomes. In this case, the reasons for failure must be identified and decisions made on how to handle the situation.
- The effects of the developments may not be as they were intended. Here the reasons must be identified and measures must be taken to react on the unwanted changes.

Note: Not achieving the desired results is not necessarily the fault of the management of the plan or lack of it. The reasons why the plan was not successful may also be outside it's influence. It could be due to:

- the complex and dynamic nature of ecosystems and the absence of complete knowledge or understanding of their functioning. This can lead to uncertainties. Ecosystem processes are often non-linear and the outcomes of such processes often have time-lags.
- the complex structure of the economy and social systems as well as the often unpredictable reactions of human beings.

The uncertainties and possible surprises in the dimensions above mean that a precise prediction of impacts will never be calculated. Tourism management must therefore be adjusted accordingly, taking new insights and developments into consideration as quickly as possible. Adaptive management to some extent means "learning by doing". It must be flexible and able to react to the unexpected. In some cases, rapid intervention may be required to avoid further damage caused by the negative tourism impacts. It might be necessary, for example, to decide immediately on a reduction of visitor numbers or on the redirection of tourists to less sensitive areas. These decisions still have to follow the vision of the plan as much as possible. Adaptive management, however flexible, should be incorporated into the tourism management plan by developing scenarios and action plans which can be used to make ad hoc decisions. Additionally, the plan should be updated at regular intervals in order to get adjusted to changing conditions. Changes to the plan require the participation and consultation of all stakeholders and others affected by those changes.

DECISION-MAKING, APPROVAL AND IMPLEMENTATION

DECISION-MAKING

While developing the tourism management plan, decisions will be made on:

- the overall vision and strategies
- proposals for tourism management and its development
- the adequacy of impact management measures, and
- the adequacy and frequency of monitoring and reporting

All these decisions should be made in a transparent multi-stakeholder process. The decisions on the proposals for the goals and objectives of the plan should be based on adequate information about the proposals and their impacts. Decisions should not be made at any stage of the plan without the consultation of all relevant stakeholders and local communities. The decisions should include a review of the baseline information, the impact assessment, and information on the proposed activity: in case it is a tourism development activity, its nature and size, the type of tourism involved and information on the human settlements and communities that may be affected.

APPROVAL OF THE PLAN

During the development of the plan various decisions on its content are already made. The final plan, however, must be approved, not only by the managing organisation and the multi-stakeholder group who developed it, but also by as many stakeholders, authorities and members of the general public as possible. The approval should follow an established approval system. Before the approval takes place, stakeholders and the general public must be informed and consulted about the final draft of the tourism management plan. They should be able to express their opinions and wishes, which might mean that parts of the plan need to be reconsidered. The new tourism management plan should be promoted by the managing organisation to obtain the approval of as many stakeholders as possible. Stakeholders should "own" the tourism management plan, showing that its implementation is supported by a large number of people. "Ownership" means that the people and organisations commit themselves to the vision and goals of the whole plan not just to parts of it. They should be convinced that the strategies and principles of the plan are a reasonable basis for tourism management. They also should understand the benefits the plan will have for them and others and should be willing to promote the goals of the plan. Specific stakeholders, especially local and regional authorities and decision-making bodies, should be asked to approve the tourism management plan by signing it officially. By doing so, they express their will to support the goals of the plan. Efforts should also be made to include stakeholders and authorities that were not actively involved in the development of the plan because of a lack in capacities or resources. Their approval to the plan and thus their commitment to it is still important for the success of the plan.

IMPLEMENTATION

Once the tourism management plan is approved, again clear and adequate information regarding its implementation should be provided to the stakeholders, in forms that are accessible and comprehensible to them. Stakeholders should be given an ongoing opportunity to express their wishes and concerns about the activities. This is especially important because there may be individuals who will recognize the existence of the tourism management plan and the approved activities only when implementation starts. For successful implementation, the responsibilities for each of the section in the work program must be stated clearly in the plan. Any revisions or changes to the activities approved in the plan, including additions and/or variations, must be approved by the designated authorities. Local communities and other stakeholders may require assistance as actors in implementation.

6

Tourism and the Environment

To understand the interaction that exists between tourism and the environment it is necessary to understand the complexity of tourism. Tourism is not just something that occurs in the environments of destinations overseas but is a function of the interaction of different factors in contemporary society. Since the 1950s there has been a rapid increase in the demand in western societies for people to travel internationally and visit a variety of different destinations.

This growing demand for tourism is a reflection of changing economic and social conditions in our home environment, as much as it is about the physical and cultural characteristics of the environments that await tourists in other countries. This chapter examines the meaning and complexity of tourism, its history, and how social changes since the Industrial Revolution have shaped contemporary mass participation in tourism.

The acceptance of 'going away' on holiday, commonly referred to as tourism, as a part of our lifestyle in contemporary western society may lead us to believe that it has always been a feature of people's lives.

Yet the word 'tourist' is a fairly new addition to the English language, the word 'tourist' (deliberately hyphenated), first appearing in the early nineteenth century. Boorstin draws a distinction between the arduous conditions undertaken by 'travellers' (a term originating from the French word *travail* meaning work, trouble, torment), such as pilgrims, and the 'tourist', for whom travel has become an organised and packaged affair.

The idea of travel for pleasure, for example to visit beautiful landscapes as opposed to travel for necessity or to demonstrate religious piousness, is therefore within the context of human activity a relatively recent phenomenon. Until the nineteenth century travel was not an easy option, nor was landscapes that we now regard as aesthetically pleasing, necessarily regarded in the same way.

Yet, today the word 'tourism' has become part of our common language, with over 650 million people travelling internationally at the beginning of the twenty-first century (World Tourism Organisation, 1998a).

Despite this impressive figure, trying to define what tourism actually is has proved to be more problematic than might be expected. This difficulty is a reflection of both the complexity of tourism, and the fact that different stakeholders or groups with an interest in tourism are likely to have different aspirations of what they hope to achieve from it, and subsequently hold different perspectives on what it means to them. The stakeholders in tourism include governments, the tourism industry, local communities and tourists.

DEFINITIONS AND TYPES OF TOURISM

For the majority of people who possess the financial means to participate in travel for recreational purposes, tourism is an activity that probably little conscious thought is given to beyond recollecting the enjoyment of the last holiday, and deciding where to go to for the next one. Yet this seemingly simple process involves the participation of national governments, tourism businesses and local communities, all of whom will have their own interests in tourism, which often leads them to be referred to as stakeholders in tourism.

Attempts to define tourism are made difficult because it is a highly complicated amalgam of various parts. These parts are a diverse range of factors, including the following: human feelings, emotions and desires; attractions built upon natural and developed resources; suppliers of transport, accommodation, and other services; and government policy and regulatory frameworks. Subsequently it is difficult to arrive at a consensual definition of what tourism actually is. Many authors of tourism texts comment upon the problem of defining tourism.

Yet trying to understand the meaning of 'tourism' is important if we are to plan the use of natural resources and manage impacts associated with its development. What all commentators would probably agree with is that tourism involves travel, although how far one has to travel and how long one has to be away from one's home location to be categorised as a tourist, is debatable.

A convenient definition that overcomes this difficulty is the one proposed by the World Tourism Organisation (1991) which was subsequently endorsed by the UN Statistical Commission in 1993: 'Tourism comprises the activities of persons travelling to and staying in places outside their usual environment for not more than one consecutive year for leisure, business or other purposes.'

The preceding definition challenges the commonly held perception that tourism is purely concerned with recreation and having fun. Whilst recreational tourism is the most usual form of tourism other types of tourism also exist. For instance Davidson (1993) besides recognising leisure or recreation (in which he includes travel for holidays, sports, cultural events, and visiting friends and relatives) as the main type of tourism, draws attention to the point that people also travel for business, study (or education), religious and health purposes. Indeed the origins of tourism lie in travel for reasons of faith, education and health. Although business tourism may initially seem to have little relevance to a text dealing with the interaction between tourism and the environment, it is a particularly important market sector for the economies of many urban environments. Tourism has purposefully been used in government policy as a catalyst to aid the regeneration of economically depressed areas of post-industrial cities, such as Baltimore in the USA and Liverpool in the United Kingdom. Business travel can be viewed as including travel for the purposes of commerce, exhibitions and trade fairs, and conferences.

From the previously cited World Tourism Organisation (1991) definition it can inferred that tourism involves some element of interaction with a different type of environment to the one found at home. The consequences of this interaction are commonly referred to as the 'impacts of tourism', and can be categorised into the three main types, economic, social and environmental.

All of these types of impacts can be either positive or negative and are discussed more fully in the course of this book. Recognition of the impacts that tourism can have on a destination environment are noted in the following definition of tourism given by Mathieson and Wall (1982:1): 'The study of tourism is the study of people away from their usual habitat, of the establishments which respond to the requirements of travellers, and of the impacts that they have on the economic, physical and social well-being of their hosts.'

The last word of this definition, 'host', implies an invitation from people who are happy to receive tourists. This term has received increasing criticism from academics, NGOs and the more socially aware quarters of the tourism industry, as levels of cultural and environmental awareness have grown since the early 1980s. It is now recognised that in some cases tourism is something that is tolerated or even forced upon communities as opposed to being welcomed.

Besides referring to the impacts of tourism, Mathieson and Wall's definition adds a further dimension to the concept of tourism by introducing a behavioural dimension, that is, the 'study of people away from their usual habitat'. Given that tourism would not exist without tourists, understanding the motivations of tourists and the effect of their behaviour on the environments of destinations, are areas of interest to social psychologists, sociologists and anthropologists.

In a later definition of tourism, Bull (1991:1) reiterates the behavioural and impact aspects of tourism, whilst also introducing a resource dimension: 'It [tourism] is a human activity which encompasses human behaviour, use of resources, and interaction with other people, economies and environments.'

From Bull's definition tourism can be interpreted as a form of development involving the use of natural resources. This adds another perspective to tourism's interaction with the environment, as a user of natural resources for wealth creation. The idea of wealth creation through the use of the natural and cultural environments for tourism has received increased international attention since the success of General Franco's policies on tourism development in Spain in the 1950s, as is discussed later in this chapter.

Today, the focus of using tourism for national wealth creation lies outside Europe, predominantly in the countries of the less developed world. However, the extent to which environmental resources should be used for tourism is both debatable and contentious, raising ethical and political questions. Similarly, ethical questions can be raised over tourism's 'interaction with other people', and the extent to which this is beneficial for local or indigenous communities. These are themes which are developed in the course of this book.

Although there is no definitive definition of tourism, this brief introduction to tourism demonstrates its complexity, and that it is about much more than 'going on holiday'. Tourism is based upon the economic and social processes that are occurring in the environments of the societies where tourists originate from. Its development in destinations involves the use of physical and natural resources and will subsequently impact upon the economies, cultures and ecology of the destinations it develops in.

Is there a 'tourism industry'?

According to the World Travel and Tourism Council (WTTC) (1999), travel and tourism contributed directly and indirectly to the global economy in 1999:

- 11 per cent of Gross Domestic Product;
- 200 million jobs;
- 8 per cent of total employment; and
- Will generate 5.5 million new jobs per annum until the year 2010.

Although these represent impressive statistics and reference is often made to tourism being one of the world's largest industries, trying to define the 'tourism industry' is actually extremely difficult. The problem of defining what is meant by the term is summarised by Lickorish and Jenkins (1997:1): 'The problem in describing tourism as an 'industry' is that it does not have the usual production function, nor does it have an output which can physically be measured, unlike agriculture (tonnes of wheat) or beverages (litres of whisky).'

They also add that the vague nature of the tourism industry has made it difficult to evaluate its impact upon the economy relative to other economic sectors. Similarly, in destinations where tourism development has taken place and environmental problems have arisen, it is not always that easy to disaggregate tourism's contribution to these problems from the contributions of other economic sectors.

Murphy (1985) suggests that a tourism industry does not exist because it does not produce a distinct product. He continues to point out certain industries such as transport, accommodation, and entertainment are not exclusively tourism industries, for they sell these services to local residents as well. Another key difference between tourism and other industries, is that it is the consumer who travels to the 'product', and not vice versa. The major inference of this last point is that the physical and cultural characteristics or qualities of destinations can be treated as a form of product, to be sold in the market-place. It is these characteristics of environments that create expectations in tourists and form a vital part of their experience. Yet within tourism practices are adopted that are familiar to those of industry.

For instance a common expression used in connection with tourism is 'mass tourism'. Mass tourism involves tour operators compiling a standardised package, at the very minimum usually comprising of transport and accommodation, which is then sold into the market-place *en masse* to millions of consumers. This 'package holiday', which relies on mass consumption and sales to keep the prices low, displays the characteristics of 'Fordist' production. This is a term used to describe the mass conveyor belt techniques pioneered by Henry Ford in the motor car industry in the early twentieth century, which paved the way for mass car ownership, by keeping production costs low.

Although the development of mass tourism has meant that millions of people have had the opportunity to travel to different countries, its development in destinations is often associated with environmental problems, such as pollution and a loss of local culture. Commenting on mass tourism Poon (1993:4) writes:

Mimicking mass production in the manufacturing sector, tourism was developed along assembly-line principles: holidays were standardised and inflexible; identical holidays were mass produced; and economy of scale was the driving force of production. Likewise, holidays were consumed *en masse* in a similar, robot-like and routine manner, with a lack of consideration for the norms, culture and environment of host countries visited.

Another comparison between tourism and other industries is somewhat polemically given by Krippendorf (1987:19): 'The timber industry processes timber. The metal industry processes metal. The tourist industry processes tourists.'

Although the existence of a tourism industry is debatable there are definite types of businesses that are specifically orientated to providing the services that meet the needs of tourists.

These are:

- Travel agents and tour operators;
- Airlines; and
- The international accommodation sector.

All these sectors are associated with facilitating travel. Some of these companies operate on a global scale such as Sheraton and Hilton International Hotels, whilst some tour operators have grown into major international businesses and are now listed on the stock exchange, for instance the Thomson Travel Group and Air Tours in the United Kingdom. Similarly, some airlines have become transnational businesses, with companies such as American Airlines and British Airways seeking strategic alliances to increase their global market share.

In summary it is apparent that the 'tourism industry' cannot be considered as being similar to other industries as it does not produce a single identifiable product and neither are many of its services used exclusively by tourists. Essentially when the term 'tourism industry' is used, it is important to recognise that it is an amalgam of different businesses and organisations, connected by the common factor of providing services in some capacity to tourists.

TOURISM AS A SYSTEM

Another approach to understanding tourism is to think of tourism as a system, incorporating not only businesses and tourists, but also societies and environments. Some authors interpret the different components of tourism as being interlinked thereby forming a 'tourism system'. For instance Gunn (1994) advocates that tourism should be interpreted as a system, adding that every part of tourism is related to every other part, and that no manager or owner involved in the tourism system has complete control over his or her own destiny.

It is therefore important that managers involved in any part of this system understand its complexity and possess a holistic *vis-à-vis* reductionist view of their business operations. The decisions and actions that are taken by businesses will have consequences for other components of the system. For instance, the decision of a tour operator to axe a particular destination from their schedule, will have economic and social consequences for the businesses and local community in that destination who rely upon their trade.

According to Page (1995), the advantage of a systems approach is that it allows the complexity of the real life situation to be accounted for in a simple model, demonstrating the inter-linkages of all the different elements. Mill and Morrison (1992) use the analogy of a spider's web to illustrate the inter-relatedness of different parts of the tourism system, in which touching one part of it induces a ripple effect throughout the web.

According to Laws (1991) the advantages of interpreting tourism as a system are that it avoids one-dimensional thinking and facilitates a multi-disciplinary perspective. Such an approach is beneficial with a topic that can be interpreted from a range of disciplinary perspectives including economics, psychology, sociology, anthropology and geography. The components of the tourism system modified from Laws (1991) to include a heightened environmental perspective are shown.

This model incorporates a range of different elements which together form the tourism system. Important inputs to the system from an environmental perspective include natural and human resources, the use of which are encouraged by both consumer demand in the market system for tourism, and government policy aimed at increasing entrepreneurial activity and inward investment in the sector.

Within the overall system, three distinct subsystems are recognisable, all of which overlap and are interrelated. Incorporated in these subsystems are the businesses that have been developed to cater primarily for tourists, such as tour operators, international hotel companies, global airlines, and locally owned tourism enterprises. Within the destination subsystem, the importance of natural and cultural attractions is emphasised, as the basis for attracting tourists.

The outputs of the system, which may alternatively be expressed as outcomes, suggest that tourism will bring environmental and cultural changes. These changes illustrate the dichotomy of tourism in the sense that they can be either positive or negative. Tourism can both conserve and pollute the physical environment, whilst it can also bring positive and negative cultural changes, such as employment opportunities for women or result in women being forced into prostitution.Similarly it can create economic opportunities for communities but also can result in an economic overdependence on tourism and encourage price inflation. Another output of the system, which is essential for ensuring the profits of enterprises based upon tourism and helping to secure the economic benefits desired by governments, is tourist satisfaction.

Finally, the tourism system is subjected to a range of influences exerted by changes in society. These may be classified, using a term borrowed from Poon (1993), as 'framing conditions'. Within the context of this model the term applies to those conditions in society which influence the working of the system. For instance, Poon (1993) refers to changing consumer tastes typified by the emergence of the 'new tourist'. These tourists display characteristics of being more environmentally aware, independent, flexible and quality conscious, than the tourists who form the bulk of the mass market.

Subsequently the tourism retailing subsystem must adjust its product to facilitate this new market segment, and local governments and municipalities must plan and develop their destination in a way to attract this market segment. Economic, technological and political changes can also influence tourism by making it accessible to a wider proportion of the population. For instance, rising levels of disposable income, longer holidays, and greater political

Why is it more appropriate to think of tourism as a 'system' rather than as an 'industry'?

freedoms will all encourage travel. Similarly, technological advancement, such as the development of the jet engine, has made international travel easier and encouraged tourism. Media and information technology developments have made more information and images available about potential tourism destinations than in any previous period in the history of society.

Increasing access to, and use of, computers, means it is also possible to book airline seats and holidays directly from home via the computer terminal, facilitating travel. At the end of the twentieth century environmental concerns began to exert an influence upon tourism, as suggested by the emergence of 'new' forms of tourism, such as 'ecotourism', and evidence of a growing environmental commitment in some quarters of the tourism industry, themes which are explored later in the book.

THE GROWTH IN DEMAND FOR TOURISM

Although tourism is a familiar aspect of contemporary life, particularly for the majority of people living in the countries of the developed world, it is only relatively recently that it has emerged as a significant aspect of society. The growth in demand for tourism is a reflection of a range of changes that have occurred in society, particularly since the onset of the Industrial Revolution.

This section of the chapter examines the history of tourism and reasons to explain its growth, and continues to examine a type of tourism which has been particularly popular in the latter half of the twentieth century, international mass tourism. The significance of the mass participation in international tourism from an environmental viewpoint, is that an increasing number and variety of physical and cultural environments are being exposed to tourism, with a range of consequences.

PRE-INDUSTRIAL TOURISM

Tourism is not something that happens by chance but is an activity that has developed as a consequence of the type of societies in which we live. Certainly the tendency for people to live in urban areas would seem to increase the propensity for tourism.

Although we tend to think of megacities as very much a phenomenon of contemporary times, large cities have existed in ancient history, for example Carthage at its fall in 146 BC had a population of 700,000 and Augustan Rome a population of 1 million. The desire of the Romans to escape the heat of Rome in summer time led them to travel to seaside and mountain villas. Even in Roman times there was evidence of the development of a hierarchy of resorts, possessing distinct types of cultural environments, and attracting different market segments. Holloway (1998:17) comments: Naples itself attracted the retired and intellectuals, Cumae became the resort of high fashion, Puteoli attracted the more staid tourist, while Baiae, which was both a spa town and a seaside resort, attracted the down-market tourist, becoming noted for its rowdiness, drunkenness and all-night singing.

Whilst travelling to resort areas, wealthy Romans would rest at their own private villas *en route* which although only used for three or four nights per annum were fully staffed by servants and elegantly furnished, whilst commoners rested in tavernas built by farmers on the highway between Rome and the coast.

Long-distance travel was also facilitated in the Roman Empire by the development of a transport infrastructure, the need to use only one currency whilst travelling the Empire's length from Syria in the east to Hadrian's Wall in Britain in the west, and the requirement to speak only Latin.

However, until the onset of the Industrial Revolution in the second half of the nineteenth century, the role of the environment in travel was not usually associated with aesthetic pleasure but with the benefits it could offer an individual in terms of health, religious worship, or education. Travel for healing and religious purposes, can be dated to pre-Roman times to Ancient Greece, with pilgrims travelling to visit the sites of healing gods. Religious pilgrimages have up until the last two hundred years, generally been undertaken in pretty arduous conditions, and the willingness to travel as a pilgrim was seen as a measure of a person's devotion to their god.

After the collapse of the Roman Empire in the west in the fifth century AD and the onset of the Middle Ages, travel became more difficult, and from the evidence of historical records was very limited. Travel was arduous, mostly undertaken out of a necessity to trade, or as previously stated to prove one's religious devotion through pilgrimage.

However, the early seventeenth century saw the appearance of the 'Grand Tour', a direct outcome of the freedom and quest for learning heralded by the Renaissance, a period marked by a rediscovery of the classical teachings of the civilisations of Rome and Greece. Holloway (1998) links the establishment of the Grand Tour to the reign of Elizabeth I, when young men seeking positions at court were encouraged to travel to the Continent to finish their education.

Essentially the Grand Tour consisted of a tour of European culture for aristocratic young men, the absence of references to women in the accounts of the Grand Tour is noticeable, and the aristocracies of Britain, France, Germany and Russia were particularly involved in it.

The influence of the Grand Tour on subsequent attitudes to travel was notable, as Towner (1996:96) comments: 'The Grand Tour, that circuit of western Europe undertaken by the wealthy in society for culture, education, health and pleasure, is one of the most celebrated episodes in the history of tourism.'

For the first time since Roman times, foreign environments were seen as being pleasurable, stimulating and educative. The Grand Tour included visiting the major cultural centres of Europe, and lasted from the beginning of the seventeenth century through to the onset of the Napoleonic Wars, in the first part of the nineteenth century.

The tour lasted an average of three years and the gentleman would be accompanied by a private tutor. According to Gill (1967) one of the most notable tutors was Adam Smith, the eminent economist and the author of the seminal

An Inquiry into the Nature and Causes of the Wealth of Nations (1776), in which he advocates trade liberalisation and free market economics. Although the Grand Tour is predominantly viewed as an aristocratic activity, Towner (1996) suggests that this impression is probably a consequence of the likelihood that the written records of the most prominent people are the most probable ones to have survived.

In Towner's view, social participation was likely to have been wider than just the aristocracy, with a possible figure of 15,000-20,000 British tourists partaking in the Grand Tour when it was at its zenith in the mid-eighteenth century.

The development of a travel culture during this period was supported and aided by the appearance of guide and travel books such as William Thomas's *The History of Italy* (1549). Health aspects also added another dimension to the Grand Tour, for instance Montpellier in France developed as a place to go to counteract the effects of consumption, and places in the French Riviera such as Nice also developed as places to go to for health cures. Nash (1979) describes how Nice became established as a destination for health tourism in the eighteenth century.

By the nineteenth century there were accounts of the town filling with visitors from England escaping the winter, although as Nash points out, by this stage healthy tourists probably outnumbered the infirm. It is interesting to reflect how the purpose of tourism affects the seasonal pattern of arrivals. Today, in contrast to the earlier winter visitors Nice experiences its high season in summer, as tourists arrive primarily for recreational purposes in contrast to the earlier health-driven winter visitors.

INDUSTRIALISATION AND TOURISM

The Industrial Revolution, the origins of which can be traced to the mechanisation of cotton and wool production in the north of England in the last quarter of the eighteenth century, brought great economic and social changes in society. A major change dating to this period was the urbanisation of societies of Western Europe and North America. Not only did this have the effect of removing people from direct contact with nature but also led to changes in established community structures. Subsequently, perceptions of what were desirable landscapes began to change, and for some sociologists the city became associated with the isolation of the individual.

The Industrial Revolution also made society much more time-conscious than it had been previously. In agricultural society the pattern of labour had been determined by the seasons, now it became highly structured around the need to keep industrial production functioning, with man, woman and child often working a 6-day and 70-hour week. Drinking whilst at work and breaking-off from work to attend to domestic affairs, which were not unfamiliar work practices, were aspects of work life that factory owners could not tolerate. Yet the interaction of people when performing tasks and enjoying leisure together, encompassed within the same spatial area which typified work and leisure practices in pre-industrial Britain, were essential for establishing agricultural communities. During the Industrial Revolution, work and leisure became highly differentiated, upon the criteria of time and spatial zones. This pattern is reflected in contemporary tourism, as we take defined periods of time off work, and travel long distances away from our home environment to other destinations.

The realisation that a healthy workforce was more likely to be a productive one, and perhaps the fear of a working-class uprising, led to the passing of the Bank Holidays Act in 1871 in Britain. This was a significant act, in the sense that, for the first time, taking time off work had been formalised by an Act of Parliament. With the evolution of the trade union movement and more socially progressive governments, the numbers of days off work for holidays increased, although it was not until 1938 that the Holiday with Pay Act was passed in the United Kingdom.

This Act gave workers the right to one week's paid leave from work (all leave from work before this date had been unpaid). Another major change associated with the Industrial Revolution was a technological advance in transport. Key technical advancements that encouraged mass participation in tourism in the nineteenth century were the development of the railways and steamships.

Until the nineteenth century travel was largely dependent upon the horse and carriage. Such journeys were arduous, for example a journey of approximately 640 kilometres between London and Edinburgh took 10 days by horse and carriage. In the latter part of the nineteenth century, the development of railroad systems and passenger steamship services made travel considerably easier.

This advanced technology also required a much higher level of investment than the stage coaches that had been the primary means of transport before then, subsequently necessitating the sale of large quantities of passages to secure a return upon one's investment. By 1904, P&O passenger services had already begun cruising, taking first class passengers to Australia and India.

In the twentieth century, widespread ownership of the motor car and the development of the jet engine in the 1950s, have facilitated travel by making it easier and quicker. The car has given people greater control over their own travel arrangements than at any time in the past, and the provision by governments of a good infrastructure of roads in many countries has meant that going on holiday in the motor car has become a popular option.

The development of jet-powered aircraft has led to travelling times between countries being dramatically reduced, facilitating the access of tourists to foreign countries and increasing the propensity for international travel. The development of the railways, steamships, motor car and jet engine were important technical changes that encouraged travel. Not only did they make travel quicker but it became safer and more comfortable.

The high financial investment in the railways, steamships and aircraft, also made it necessary for operators to encourage as many passengers as possible to use their services, encouraging mass participation in travel. In more contemporary times, the effects of pollution associated with travel for tourism is a major concern. In current society, the role of information technology is an increasingly important influence upon tourism.

There is little doubt that we are living at the time of an information technology revolution, which at the start of the twenty-first century is still only beginning.

Just as the development of photography and cinema offered images of foreign lands to a widening audience at the beginning of the twentieth century, the development of an increasingly sophisticated media, involving satellite and cable television, does so today. Computer technology also increasingly plays a role in many people's lives in developed countries. By the early 1990s, not only was it possible to find out the price, availability and location of a holiday spot, but the technology was already available for clients to take a visual tour of the hotel they would be staying in and the rainforest they would be walking in.

Besides technological advancement, the growth of tourism has also been encouraged by the emergence of tour operators.

Three of the best-known names in the tour operating and travel agency sector are 'Thomas Cook', 'Lunn Poly', and 'American Express', all of whom developed their tour-operating businesses in the nineteenth century. Thomas Cook organised his first fee-paying trip in 1841 as secretary of the Midland Temperance Association with 570 members travelling from Leicester to Loughborough. As Page (1999) remarks, it is rather ironic that the package tour now thrives on an image of sun, sea, sex and booze.

By the 1860s Cook had already developed tours to Europe and America, and in 1869 offered the first escorted tour to the Holy Land. In his first nine years of business, Thomas Cook handled more than one million customers. By the end of the nineteenth century, Sir Henry Lunn was organising trips to the European Alps for British people interested in winter sports, whilst in America the American Express Company had begun to offer Americans help in securing railroad tickets and hotel reservations.

The twentieth century saw a reduction in the real price of travel, with economies of scale becoming possible for suppliers, as more people wished to travel. The reduction in the real price of travel is illustrated by trans-Atlantic travel between the United States of America and Britain. At the beginning of the twentieth century to cross the Atlantic by passenger ship was a very rare and special event, restricted to a very few, and subsequently expensive.

For instance a first-class ticket on the illfated passenger ship the Titanic in 1912, cost US $3000 or approximately US $127,000 in today's money, whilst a third-class ticket cost US $40 or US $1,696 in today's money. By the end of the twentieth century, during which time incomes had risen manyfold compared to those at the beginning of the century, a typical discounted air fare between London and New York cost approximately US $250.

The changing economic and social conditions in society that are associated with the Industrial Revolution led to an increasing participation in tourism by members of different social classes. Two phases of mass participation in tourism are evident, with the first wave having taken place in the nineteenth century, fuelled by a quadrupling of the real national income per head and the development of the railways.

Primarily domestic tourism, it involved the movement of thousands of working-class people from the city areas to the coast, leading to the growth of seaside resorts as holiday destinations in northern Europe.

This trend of domestic tourism continued for the first part of the twentieth century, economic recession in the 1930s combined with two world wars greatly restricting the opportunities for the growth of international tourism. The second phase of mass tourism occurred after the Second World War and this time had an international perspective as opposed to a domestic one.

THE DEVELOPMENT OF MASS PARTICIPATION IN INTERNATIONAL TOURISM

The post-Second World War years saw the beginnings of the demise of the northern European seaside resorts, a period marked by the origins of what can be termed the 'second wave of mass tourism', this time international. Mass international tourism began in the 1950s, involving the movement of thousands of tourists from the United Kingdom to Spain, ultimately leading to the development of the western Mediterranean coastline for tourism.

A range of factors amalgamated to encourage the movement of tourists to Spain, including the following: an increasing level of disposable income from the late 1950s; a surplus of Second World War aircraft which could be used to provide cheap transport from the UK; the development of tour operators in the United Kingdom who promoted the image of Spain; the encouragement of tourism development by the Spanish dictator General Franco; and the availability of cheap land in Spain for hotel development. By 1955 two million people from the UK were travelling abroad.

The subsequent availability of cheap package holidays to Spain brought foreign travel within the reach of working-class people for the first time, the vast majority having previously had no opportunity for international travel, beyond the experiences of working-class men as soldiers in the Second World War. The factors leading to the growth of Spain as a tourism destination are discussed more fully in the case study.

CASE STUDY: THE DEVELOPMENT OF INTERNATIONAL TOURISM TO SPAIN

Although Spain is the country that is probably associated most closely with international mass tourism, its development as a destination for millions of tourists is recent. Spain was never an established part of the Grand Tour, its landscape and culture not regarded as being particularly attractive, and its geographical position rendered it fairly inaccessible.

It was not until towards the end of the nineteenth century, with the development of the Romantic Movement in northern Europe, that the wild landscape of Spain combined with its medieval and Moorish culture began to be considered attractive by an elite group of travellers, and Spain began to develop an image as being exotic.

Its geographical remoteness combined with a lack of infrastructure development, the civil war of the 1930s and two world wars in the first half of the twentieth century, meant Spain retained an exotic image even until the 1950s. In the 1950s, today's heavily developed tourism areas of the Costa Brava and Costa del Sol began to receive foreign visitors. So rare were foreign visitors in post-war Spain, their movements were monitored by the Civil Guard, a legacy of foreigners who fought in the Spanish Civil War on the side of the Republicans.

For example, in 1955 Torremolinos (a name now synonymous with large-scale tourism development) was a poverty stricken fishing village, where villagers grafted a hard living from the land and sea. The first foreign visitors to arrive in Torremolinos were wealthy foreigners who did not want to walk in the Swiss Alps or sojourn on the French Riviera. The style of the first hotels reflected a luxurious peasant style and by the 1960s Torremolinos had become a highly fashionable resort.

Beachfront property increased in price twentyfold in two years, and a villa worth £1,000 in 1955, was sold as a site for a hotel in 1963 for £146,000. Torremolinos's popularity meant increasing numbers of visitors arrived on shuttle buses from expanding airports, which led to increased hotel development. Ultimately the rich and the artistic types deserted Torremolinos and went to nearby enclaves at Marbella or as far afield as Bali and Morocco.

Apart from illustrating a typical cycle of resort development, with a destination area being discovered by a wealthy elite leading to rapid unplanned tourism growth determined by market forces, Torremolinos also illustrates the economic opportunities to be gained from tourism. General Franco encouraged the growth of tourism, based upon a need to gain political recognition of a regime that was viewed with international suspicion, and also as a means of attracting foreign exchange and modernising other sectors of the Spanish economy. Spain was marketed as an exotic, low-cost holiday destination, distinct from its chief catchment area of northern Europe. The growth of tourism to Spain was also fuelled by the development of the jet engine, bringing Spain closer to countries of northern Europe in terms of travelling time, and the expansion of the tour-operating industry particularly in the United Kingdom. Subsequently, Spanish tourism has undergone a major expansion, international arrivals increasing from 700,000 visitors in the early 1950s, to 4 million by 1959, 40 million by the early 1980s, to 47 million in 1998.

The success of Spain in using tourism as a catalyst for economic growth and development, has encouraged governments of other countries to develop tourism as a part of economic policy. Governments can offer a range of financial incentives to encourage tourism development, including the giving of grants and loans at beneficial interest rates for tourism development, relaxation of import duties and tax breaks. Examples of actual incentives that have been used to encourage tourism development are shown.

The combination of changing social conditions in society and the encouragement of tourism development by national governments, has led to a rapid increase in the number of people travelling internationally post-1950, a rate of increase that is projected to continue until at least the year 2020. The actual recorded number of international arrivals in 1950 was 25 million, in 1980 this had risen to 270 million, by 1998 it had reached 600 million, and by 2020 it is projected to be 1602 million (World Tourism Organisation, 1998a).

EXAMPLES OF INVESTMENT INCENTIVES USED BY GOVERNMENTS TO ENCOURAGE TOURISM DEVELOPMENT

Greece: Incentives were made available for the country's economic and regional development through Law 1262 passed in 1983. Tourism is considered a 'productive investment' and incentives are available for the construction, extension and modernisation of hotels (up to 300 beds), winter sports facilities, spas, tourist apartments, and for the renovation of traditional houses into hostels or hotels. Typical financial incentives include grants, preferential grants, interest rate subsidies, loans, fiscal incentives, and tax allowances.

Malaysia: Reliance is placed upon fiscal incentives rather than grants or loans. Companies may be given 'tax holidays' of up to five years providing the development meets certain criteria, such as the number of employees generated, and the geographical locality of the investment. Tax credit of up to 100 per cent is also given on capital expenditure incurred during the first five years of the operation of a tourism facility.

The dramatic growth in tourism is further underlined when the decade upon decade increases are calculated since 1950. This spatial spread of international tourism demonstrates a pattern of 'core and periphery' relationships. This was a term that originated from the development sociologist Gunther Frank, to explain the global pattern of economic dependency of lesser developed countries (the 'South') upon the more developed countries of Europe and USA (the 'North'), which according to Frank can be traced to historic patterns of colonial imperialism.

The same analogy of core to periphery relationships can also be used in tourism to describe the dependency of many less developed countries (LDCs) upon the markets of countries of Europe and the USA for international tourism.

As Cohen (1995:13) remarks, 'Tourism is essentially a modern western phenomenon', although he adds that modern tourist travel has spread in recent decades to contemporary Japan, Taiwan, and Korea. Regardless of nationality and culture, it would seem tourism is capable of being sold into any strata of society, which has both time and money. The term also refers to the dependency of many developing countries upon transnational corporations, such as the Sheraton Group, for foreign investment to develop their tourism sector.

Additionally, LDCs may be reliant upon loans, from foreign governments or banks, to develop tourism. This has led many critics of tourism to complain that tourism represents little more than a continuing form of post-colonialism, where all the power and control in the global tourism system remains in the 'North', and within which the environments and cultures of the 'South' are exploited.

Although the figures of expenditure on international tourism support the theory of the dominance of the traditional core areas of Europe and the USA, it is evident that new cores are emerging. In 1997, the world's top six spending countries on international tourism were the United States of America, Germany, Japan, the United Kingdom, Italy and France (World Tourism Organisation, 1999).

However, the complete list of countries, ranked by order of consumer spending on international tourism, reveals some interesting changes in the world order. Apart from Japan in third place, in tenth place is China, the Russian Federation is in eleventh place, and Taiwan and the Korean Republic are in seventeenth and eighteenth place respectively, ahead of Australia, Norway, Spain and Denmark (World Tourism Organisation, 1999).

The list lends support to the theory that economic development and political freedom will lead to an increased demand for tourism, and also goes some way to supporting the idea that if global political influence and economic power in the nineteenth century rested with Europe and in the twentieth century with the USA, then the twenty-first century is likely to belong to Asia.

Many countries of the world, which had previously experienced little tourism, developed as international destinations in the last four decades of the twentieth century. Areas of the world and countries as diverse as Greece, Turkey and other parts of the eastern Mediterranean; the Caribbean; Thailand

and other countries of south-east Asia; China; parts of Africa; South America; and the Pacific Isles have all developed large tourist industries based upon the attraction of their cultural and physical environments.

One of the most notable emerging tourism destinations is China, which received 24 million tourists in 1998, making it the fifth highest ranked country expressed in terms of incoming tourism.

At the beginning of the twenty-first century international tourism has expanded to include a variety of destinations and different environments. Describe the changes that have occurred in the environments of societies where tourists originate from which help to explain the growth in demand for international tourism.

As Poon (1993) points out, tourists are demanding the experience of new cultures, physical environments and activities. This has led to indigenous cultures and special physical environments such as rainforests, coral reefs and polar areas becoming the focus of tourism. With the technological advancement of the twentieth century it would seem that no environment is too remote or inaccessible for tourism. The peripheries of tourism continue to be stretched further afield and the next periphery of tourism is likely to be space.

Already one American company 'Zeaghram Space Voyages' has sold more than 250 places at £60,000 each to visit space, and plans are already developed for the construction of a space resort having room for approximately 100 guests by the year 2017.

FEASIBLE AND TOURISM

It is an ideological term. It can be used, and is used, by many if not most businesses, all the mainstream political parties, and those outside the mainstream, to illustrate and describe policies, the implications of which can be shown to be anything but sustainable in a number of ways. And it is widely used in a meaningless and anodyne way. Sustainability is perceived and described as an essential part of the ideology of the New World Order and all the trends and tendencies that are associated with it.

These tendencies, almost movements, include a 'new' consumerism, whose semantic ally is sustainability. The two notions have developed hand in hand to give mass consumption a more acceptable justification to the new middle classes who can afford to consider sustainability.

But as Selwyn remarks: 'supported by a chorus singing of the joys of economic plenty in a world scarred by scarcity, the tourist often appears as a shining hero of the most pervasive myth of our time: that which tells of the omnipotence and untrammelled sovereignty of the individual consumer' (1994:5).

In the field of tourism, the term 'sustainability' can be and has been hijacked by many to give moral rectitude and 'green' credentials to tourist activities.

And it is by no means just the tour operator and other profit-making companies standing to gain from the activity who have used the term for their own ends. Conservationists, government officials, politicians, local community organisations and tourists themselves all manipulate the term according to their own definition. But whereas the paradigms of political discourse have changed little as a result of the new word 'sustainability', the study of tourism has had to adapt itself to the creation of a whole new branch of the discipline, 'sustainable tourism'; this term is used in conjunction with many other descriptive labels, which are discussed later in this chapter.

The practice of tourism is also modifying itself to take account of the new forms of tourism; and opportunities to indulge in 'sustainable tourism' are springing up all over the world. This chapter examines the notion of sustainability as it is applied to tourism. It begins with a consideration of the development of the mass consumption of tourism and its lead into a new form of consumerism in the industry.

A brief survey of the terminology of the new forms of tourism is followed by an analysis of a range of definitions of these new forms.

This leads on to examinations of, first, a number of principles often applied to sustainability in tourism and, second, the tools and techniques commonly used to measure and describe sustainability. Finally, we speculate on the intertwined futures of sustainability and tourism.

THE GROWTH IN MASS TOURISM

The rise and rise of the importance to our lives of holidays taken collectively at a distance from our home is well documented in many texts - see, for example, Lavery (1971), Murphy (1985) and Krippendorf (1987). The early association of this feature of our lives with industrial capitalism is also well noted.

The stimulus given to the holiday industry by technological developments in the field of transport is clear from the histories of the railways (Great Britain in the nineteenth century), the motor car (widespread ownership in the First World after the 1950s) and the wide-bodied jet (post-1960s).

THE MODELS

Such a critique cannot be made without at least a brief examination of the explanatory models of tourism development.

We believe that these are generally deficient as they fail to account for the distribution of power; and the need to set an understanding of tourism in the context of its structures of power has already been presented.

Very broadly, explanatory models can be grouped into those which explain the tourist's motivation, those which explain the role of the tourist industry, and those which explain the development of the destination community. But such a categorisation is simplistic. Some models, for instance, such as Butler's

Product Life Cycle Model, attempt to explain the behaviour of both the industry and of the destination community.

Moreover, these categories and the models which follow them fail to explain the relationship between the different elements of the industry (tourist, service provider, and local populace at its simplest) and the wider context of development processes.

Probably one of the simplest models, which serves also as a definition of tourism, is the equation provided by Smith (1989):

$T = L + I + M$

where:

T = Tourism;

L = *Leisure time*, which has increased for the majority of workers in the industrialised, technocratic, western, capitalist nations since the Second World War;

I = *Discretionary income* (often referred to as surplus income), which is now commonly used up in the pursuit of instant happiness rather than in the savings for future security associated with the work ethic which was prevalent in industrialised nations in the first half of the twentieth century;

M = *Positive local sanctions* (or *motivation*), which are those factors that prompt the tourist to tour - these are many and varied, but often spring from an escapist motivation. (Thus the local sanctions or conditions may be positive in the sense of prompting travel, but negative in the sense that they reflect unchosen or unhappy aspects of the life of the traveller.)

The model should more correctly be expressed as a functional relationship which varies with a range of factors rather than as a mathematical equation, but it is obviously not intended as a precise representation. Despite its intention, however, its use, even as an aid to understanding, is restricted by its vagueness, and it offers no explicit recognition of the issue of power over the activity.

Krippendorf (1987) also referred to the surge in the importance of leisure time in modern western life: 'Most people in the industrialised countries have been seized by a feverish desire to move. Every opportunity is used to get away from the workday routine as often as possible' (1987: xiii).

His simplistic Model of Life in industrial society (Work-Home-Free Time-Travel) reflects the historical change in the balance of work and leisure in the lives of industrialised and urbanised populations.

Again, a historical inevitability underlies the model rather than a political perspective. As has already been argued, the latter is crucial to an understanding of the nature of tourism. And it is no less crucial to an understanding of the new forms of tourism.

Murphy (1985) cites the three crucial growth factors of motivation, ability and mobility as explanations of the evolution of tourism. His characterisations of each of these factors in each of four chronological eras of development. While these factors are clearly germane, neither the historical developments themselves nor tourism can be understood without an analysis of their relationship with the prevailing power structures. And all of these models fail to offer such analysis.

Albeit a little flippant, one model offered recently that does explicitly base itself on the prevailing structure of power and that also relates specifically to Third World countries is that offered by Chang Noi (a pseudonym) in the Thai newspaper The Nation.

The anger with which it was devised shines through and in this manner it clearly represents the local power structure on which the development is based. Chang Noi suggests that three stages of tourism development can be viewed throughout Thailand:

Stage: Start with a place of outstanding beauty ... Impose absolutely no controls. Allow get-rich-quick entrepreneurs to encroach on the beach, blow up the rocks, scatter garbage and pour concrete everywhere.

Stage: The resort is now popular but rapidly losing its natural charm. Add large quantities of sex and comfort. Build large, luxurious hotels. Import lots of girls.

Stage: By now the natural beauty is totally obliterated. The seafront is an essay in bad architecture. The hinterland is a shanty town of beer bars. Develop the remains as a male fantasy theme park. Add anything with testosterone appeal - big motorbikes, shooting ranges, boxing rings, archery. Bring in more and more girls (and boys).

This model is clearly based more on personal observation and political interpretation than on academic research, but for all that it may be as applicable in some Third World countries as many other models.

An attempt to summarise the major features of studies in tourism is offered. This simple summary emphasises two crucial points. First, there are many textbooks that describe in detail the existing approaches to tourism analysis. Second, it is striking how few concepts there actually are in the tourism debate and the hold that these ideas have retained in directing subsequent research. Many of them are endlessly repeated or contested in case study material.

THE 'ETHICS'

Models can explain tourist behaviour patterns through the contexts of ideology and/or political developments. One example of this is the work ethic.

The notion of the work ethic has been a contentious point in political discourse for many decades, but as an explanation of the work patterns and practices of industrialising and industrialised societies it has been and is commonly used and referred to, even if not accepted by all. In essence, it relates the pursuits of moral rectitude and economic survival as the principal motives for people's actions.

Table. Murphy's Growth Factors in the Evolution of Tourism.

Era	Motivation	Ability	Mobility
Pre-industrial	Exploration and business Pilgrimage/religion Education Health	Few travellers; those involved were wealthy, influential or received permission	Slow and treacherous
Industrial	Positive impact of education, print and radio	Higher incomes More leisure time Organised tours	Lower transport costs Reliable public transport
	Escape from city Colonial empires		
Consumer society	Positive impact of visual communication Consumer society Escape from work routine	Shorter work week More discretionary income Mass marketing Package tours	Growth of personal transportation Faster and more efficient transport
Future	Vacations a right and necessity Combined with business and learning	Self-catering Smaller families Two wage earners per household Demographic trends favour travel groups	Alternative fuels More efficient transport Greater use of public transport and package deals

The waning of the strength of the work ethic as a variable explaining the development of western capitalist trends in behaviour has been shadowed by the appearance on the scene of the notion of the leisure ethic. The two ethics are naturally closely related, for an important justification for the leisure ethic in many minds is that it is *not* work.

The leisure ethic grows in importance as the work ethic wanes when the pursuit of hedonism replaces the pursuits of moral rectitude and economic survival associated with the work ethic. But it is important to note that the two ethics are not mutually exclusive.

It is also important, however, to point out that the leisure ethic appears to have two distinctly different faces at present - the face of the urban salaried westerner and the face of the local people who have to cater for the leisure ethic of the former. In 1991 Butler wrote of the 'leisure ethic which is at least parallel to, and in some cases more powerful than, the work ethic'.

The work ethic still holds strong in many societies. The leisure ethic has not yet overtaken it, save in a few wealthy societies. But it is gaining ground, not so much as a result of the spread of wealth as something personally experienced by populations around the world, but rather more as a result of the spread of service to the wealthy around the world.

Since the early 1980s, the leisure ethic as an explanation of First World tourist behaviour has been joined by the notion of a conservation ethic which has begun to have a bearing on patterns of travel and tourism, especially in the Third World. The two recent ethics, leisure and conservation, are closely associated. The former reflects the economic power of the individual tourist, and the latter reflects their ability or desire to impose that power on the areas, communities and populations that they wish to visit.

STUDIES IN TOURISM

STRUCTURE OF THE TOURISM INDUSTRY

Attempts to identify the main actors and structures in the tourism industry usually take the form of a flow diagram. The most widely cited is Mathieson and Wall's (1982) conceptual framework of tourism. Other texts worth consulting are Shaw and Williams (1994) and Burns and Holden (1995).

IMPACTS OF TOURISM DEVELOPMENT

Seemingly a favourite among academics, who list as many impacts as they can under three headings: environment, economic, social-cultural. Mathieson and Wall (1982) started the trend which many others have followed. The best and most accessible work of this nature dealing with the Third World is John Lea's (1988) *Tourism and Development in the Third World*.

MODELS OF TOURISM DEVELOPMENT

Another 'method' with a vice-like grip on academics is to look at the way in which holiday destinations move from boom to bust. The most famous examples are Doxey's (1976) 'index of irritation' (with destination communities moving from 'euphoria' to 'antagonism') and Butler's (1980) *resort life cycle model* (with destinations moving from initial 'exploration' to 'stagnation'). An army of others have followed in testing these models out.

There is also an increasing number of texts devoted to providing blueprints - or models - for appropriate tourism development. These offer both methods and case studies. For example, see Whelan (1991), Gunn (1994) and Hawkins *et al.* (1995).

TOURIST TYPOLOGIES AND MOTIVATIONAL CHARACTERISTICS

Interesting attempts, usually from anthropologists and sociologists, have been made to place tourists into boxes. The leaders have been Erik Cohen (1972, 1979a) whose tourists range from 'recreational' to 'existential' and Valene Smith (1989) whose tourists range from 'charter' to 'explorer'. Many others have set off 'tourist spotting' too. In a Third World which is constantly faced with the denigration of its natural assets and resources, it is imperative for the new middle classes who travel that those assets and resources which they wish to travel to are preserved for that purpose.

Hence, the conservation ethic: introduced by environmental and conservation organisations (WWF, IUCN, Friends of the Earth International (FOEI), the International Ecotourism Society, the Audubon Society and private organisations such as the Caribbean Conservation Corporation (CCC) and the National Association for the Conservation of Nature (ANCON, in Panama), which suggest debt-for-nature swaps, and entice northern populations to donate towards or buy an acre of tropical rainforest in the belief that they will be contributing towards the conservation of the planet's biosphere.

According to Ryel and Grasse, the conservation ethic provides the framework within which all marketing and travelling should take place and includes several basic components: increasing public awareness of the environment, maximising economic benefits for local communities, fostering cultural sensitivity, and minimising the negative impacts of travel on the environment.

The models outlined earlier say little of the relationships of power between different elements of society with respect to the tourism industry, while it is these relationships of power which underlie the different 'ethics'. The structures of power in the industry are a crucial explanatory variable of the growth, development, patterns and types of tourism practised, and these are alluded to in an understanding of the ethics.

THE GROWTH

There is of course no doubt that the facility to take a holiday (that is, leisure) has spread, especially since the 1960s. The linking of the package holiday with increasing opportunities for large numbers of people to travel overseas has had profound effects on many areas of the world which now serve as receivers of tourists. The growth and nature of the package holiday business are conveniently and humorously summarised in the UK *Guardian*'s Pass Notes.

Cultural trend	**Economic trend**		**Tourism**	**Power**
Modernist	Fordist	The work ethic	Mass and package	Merchants and new service providers
		The leisure ethic	Package, exploration adventure	Transnational corporations (TNCs) + lending organisations
Postmodernist	Post-Fordist	The conservation ethic	Nature and sustainable	Socio-environmental organisations + TNCs + lending organisations

This global spread of tourism is explained by Prosser as the 'tidal wave of the pleasure periphery'. Assuming an origin of most tourists in Western Europe and eastern USA, Prosser identifies five peripheral regions of the world which have been successively commodified for the tourist industry over the last hundred years or so. Beyond the origin region, which represents the first periphery, these are successively: the western Mediterranean and Florida; the eastern Mediterranean, North Africa, California and the Caribbean; Africa, Asia, Latin America, the Pacific Basin and Australasia; and finally Antarctica and remote areas of all other continents and oceans. This is purely a descriptive model of the spread of tourism. But Prosser offers an analytical model to explain the changing consumption patterns and trends through the concept of successive class interventions: over time, a particular mode of consumption, fashion or lifestyle will spread downwards through the socio-economic class structure of a society. An admired elite inspires or propagates a fashion which is then aspired to by progressively broader sections of society, who as they become able, attempt to emulate the behaviour and style of the perceived elites ... As this process continues, the discoverer and elite groups, driven by the desire for novelty, uniqueness and exclusivity of experience, seek out fresh destinations and move on.

WTO/OMT projections for the year 2020 predict a continuation of this spread and growth for the industry into the foreseeable future. It should be stressed that these figures include all international arrivals using tourist visas. This includes a proportion, which probably differs with space and time, of people who travel for reasons other than tourism. Furthermore, we would draw your attention once again to the reservations concerning the WTO/OMT statistics expressed. Nevertheless, the figures are clearly illustrative of the trend.

The WTTC claims that travel and tourism is already the world's largest industry, generates more than 10 per cent of global GDP and more than 10 per cent of global employment and forecasts that the industry will create 130 million new jobs between 1996 and 2006 (WTTC, undated). The WTTC includes more than just the tourism industry in its figures, and it is in effect a lobby group for the industry; but even though their claims may be exaggerated, they are nevertheless in agreement with all other sources that tourism is a large-scale and fast-growing industry.

This growth in the importance of tourism has not passed by the Third World. Regionally, the 1990s saw rates of increase in tourist arrivals to Africa of 81 per cent, the Americas 35 per cent, East Asia and the Pacific 77 per cent, and South Asia 69 per cent. The world average growth rate over the same decade was 44 per cent. Mass tourism, then, has increased remarkably in recent years and, despite recessions, recent downturns, and terrorist attacks, most projections show a continuation of this trend.

Moreover, most pundits consider that the September 2001 terrorist attacks on the USA will not bring about anything more than a temporary reversal or slowing of this trend. The ability to holiday anywhere in the world has become an essential part of modern professional life in the wealthy world. Not surprisingly, the growing middle class in the middle-income economies of the world are also increasingly keen to participate in this pursuit of hedonism. The potential for more growth is, therefore, great.

But can the planet sustain this growth? Is the current practice of tourism suitable for us to pass down to future generations as a model of economic development which will guarantee them a source of income without the destruction of the environment from which they make it? The next section outlines just a few of the growing litany of social, cultural, economic and environmental problems created by the industry and its practices and conduct.

RESULTING PROBLEMS AND THE RISE OF NEW FORMS OF TOURISM

The phenomenon and growth of mass tourism has led to a range of problems, which have become increasingly evident and well publicised over recent years. They include environmental, social and cultural degradation, unequal distribution of financial benefits, the promotion of paternalistic attitudes, and even the spread of disease. These have been described in many publications (Bugnicourt (1977), Harrison (1979), Hong (1985), Krippendorf (1987), Lea (1988), *Cultural Survival Quarterly* (1982, 1990a, 1990b), *Equations* (various), *In Focus* (various), *New Internationalist* (various), the Tourism Investigation and Monitoring Team of Thailand (various)), and by a variety of other organisations.

They have also resulted in a range of campaigns run in recent years by NGOs: the Tear Fund, Voluntary Service Overseas (VSO), Action for Southern Africa, the WWF and others have all run tourism-related campaigns as well as those NGOs such as Tourism Concern whose principal motive is action on tourism.

Some of these problems have become matters of global concern, as in the cases of, for example, the state of the Mediterranean Sea, deforestation and consequent soil erosion in various regions of the Himalayas, litter along Nepalese mountain tracks, and the disturbance of wildlife by Kenyan safari tours. It may be most illustrative to outline the general problems associated with mass international tourism through the words of the Reverend Kaleo Patterson, a pastor on the island of Kauia, Hawaii:

I have counselled the prostitute, the desk clerk, the maid and the bartender. I have had to counsel and pray with the whole housekeeping section of a major resort development consisting of over a hundred Filipinos and Hawaiians. I have been involved in hundreds of re-burials of ancient Hawaiian grave sites because of a new resort development or existing resort renovations. I have witnessed the desecration of our sacred places and cried over the senseless pollution of our reefs and rivers. I have held picket signs in protest and given testimony at public hearings. I have organised workshops and forums on tourism. I have even chased an obstinate tourist into the sanctuary of a local pizza restaurant in an attempt to vent my anger in confrontation. I have seen the oppression and the exploitation of an 'out-of-control' global industry that has no understanding of limits or responsibility or concern for the host people of a land ... All is not well in paradise.

The problems illustrated by Patterson are tangible and identifiable and can be solved in practical ways. They are often and commonly associated with mass tourism, although there is mounting evidence from impact studies to suggest that new forms of tourism also suffer from similar problems.

It has often been claimed that, in part, the development of alternative forms of tourism has resulted from the need to address these problems. Other factors have also been cited as responsible. For instance, the rise of a population of tourists who are becoming increasingly sophisticated and aware in their leisure pursuits; socio-economic trends in northern countries; the replacement of the work ethic with a leisure ethic; and the post-Fordist production trends and postmodern cultural trends which were discussed. To a greater or lesser degree all these factors explain the rise of new forms of tourism.

While we do not deny the existence of these factors, we believe that the association of the growth of new forms of tourism with the problems arising from conventional mass tourism is misplaced. They may indeed have been used at times as an excuse for this growth in new tourism. But we believe that this growth has come about more as the 'natural' continuation of the historical inequalities between First and Third World countries.

As Fernandes argues, much of what are now seen as new forms of tourism have arisen because 'the mainstream tourism industry has in fact merely tried to invent a new legitimation for itself - the "sustainable" and "rational" use of the environment, including the preservation of nature as an amenity for the already advantaged' (1994:4).

Whatever the reasons for their growth, there now abound forms of tourism apparently attempting to grapple with the negative impacts of mass tourism and claiming to be alternative, different or sustainable. As Frank Barrett reports in the UK *Independent* newspaper:

When the *Independent* was launched in 1986, there was some debate in the Weekend department of the paper as to whether we should call the travel section 'Independent Traveller'. Hard to believe now, but as recently as the mid-Eighties, independent travellers were still considered in some quarters to be socks-and-sandals wearing, knapsack-toting, five star eccentrics.

At that time most people taking a a foreign holiday bought some sort of inclusive package from a tour operator ... As the Eighties continued, people no longer thought about package holidays being fun or good value; instead they became associated with lager louts and unseemly behaviour. Resorts like Torremolinos, Benidorm and Palma Nova emerged as the modern equivalent of a music hall joke ... By the start of the Nineties, independent travellers were no longer considered oddballs ... there is a demand from sophisticated travellers for information about sophisticated travel ... about slow boats to China, express trains to Ulan Bator, coaches across America and rambles through the Himalayas.

Within the industry, tourism to protected areas and pristine wilderness is one of the most rapidly growing sectors. This is what Boo describes as the ecotourism sector which 'has rapidly evolved from a pastime of a select few, to a range of activities that encompasses many people pursuing a wide variety of interests in nature' (1990:2). It also goes under several other names or descriptors which will be examined in the following section.

Published data on the increase in the importance of new forms of tourism are difficult to come by. Where they exist, they do so for specific sites, parks, or tours, and their overall significance in the tourism industry is still difficult to measure. For Costa Rica, a country renowned for its national parks and its promotion of ecotourism, the Costa Rican Institute of Tourism's annual surveys of visitors have regularly shown that around 70 per cent of its tourists (both national and international) visit its protected areas. Costa Rica may not be representative of Third World countries in this sense, although it is often held out as a model of tourism development for others to follow - but see the case study of the country given.

Evidence seems to suggest an increasing share of the tourism market for types of tourism which may (or, as we shall see, may not) be referred to as 'responsible', 'sustainable', 'alternative' or 'environmentally friendly', and an increase in holiday journeys to Third World countries. In the UK in 2001, the Tear Fund (2002) reports that one in ten holidays taken by British people were to Third World countries (that is, 4.3 million holidays), and points out that many of the favourite new tourist destinations are among the poorest countries in the world. It is noteworthy that many estimates are generally not dissimilar to the estimated 10-12 per cent of the First World population interested in the issues which concern the socio-environmental movement.

It is clear that one of the difficulties in measuring this growth is the uncertainty of what is being measured. The terminology associated with the type of tourism and the different definitions of these types varies, as does the debate about their degree of sustainability. The terminology and definitions of the new forms of tourism are discussed in the next two sections.

TERMINOLOGY

These have been culled from the vocabulary of relevant academic papers, journals, advertisements and tour operators' brochures. It would be tempting to dismiss the terminology as insignificant and of little consequence to the notion of sustainability except inasmuch as it provides us with descriptive labels. But the use of these terms represents an attempt to distance the activities associated with the new forms of tourism from what are presumed to be the unsustainable activities pursued by the mass.

Frank Barrett of the UK *Independent* newspaper calls this 'a reaction to the naffness of package holidays'. But, sustainability is a goal and/or claim of various sectors of the mass tourism industry as well as the sector of the industry which can be described as 'new'. With this burgeoning list of new terms has emerged a new range of travel agents and tour operators which offer their clients individually centred, flexible, personalised holidays. Phrases used to appeal to the tourist's desire for something different and exclusive include: 'designer' tourism from Cara Spencer Safaris; 'bespoke' itineraries from Journey Latin America. The markets associated with this are referred to as 'individuated' or 'specialised', as distinct from 'mass'.

It is also necessary for operators to differentiate themselves from 'conventional' travel operators. Magic of the Orient, therefore, claim their holiday brochure is 'like no other', for it is a 'collection of ideas', and Roama Travel (specialising in treks and climbs in India and Nepal) establish that they are not 'a travel agent but a specialist tour operator'. Travel consultancies, a middle-class transformation of the travel agent, have also begun to appear.

Marco Polo Travel Advisory Service, for example, offers a consultation service to the 'imaginative and independent traveller looking for an extra dimension' to their holiday. The small specialist operators catering for the new middle classes who form an increasingly significant market segment can translate their desire to be a twenty-first-century adventurer, explorer or 'traveller'.

Urry (1990b) argues that this represents a consumer reaction against being part of a mass; and, as we have discussed, the emergence of these specialised markets is a feature of a post-Fordist mode of consumption. In the same way that the new middle classes assume control of the 'new' activities through their exclusiveness, so the operators assume exclusivity, and therefore status, for themselves on the grounds of their specialised, individualised offerings.

The messy word de-differentiation (a key feature of postmodernism) is used to convey a straightforward idea. It involves the way new tourism practices may no longer be about tourism *per se*, but embody other activities. On the one hand this means combining a variety of 'activities' such as adventure, trekking, climbing, sketching and mountain biking. More significantly, on the other hand, it means the marriage of different, often intellectual, spheres of activity with tourism (that is, academic, anthropological, archaeological, ecological and scientific tourisms).

These latter forms of tourism are becoming increasingly important to the small-scale tour operator and travel agent. School, college or group tours combining elements of fieldwork and vacation offer a way of catching larger numbers of clients on a package which has to be especially designed, but for the group rather than an individual. In this book we use the phrase 'new forms of tourism' generically to cover the range of terms. Other terms, such as 'sustainable', 'alternative', 'ecotourism' and the like are used either because they appear in quotations or because they refer to a specific type of tourism that is appropriately described only by that word.

DEFINING THE 'NEW' TOURISM

Because the study of the forms of new tourism is still in its infancy, there is no clear agreement on their definitions and conceptual and practical boundaries. This lack of consensus is at its most conspicuous between those who study new forms of tourism and those who operate tours. But disagreements are also evident amongst others in the field, the conservationists, government officials and service providers.

The new tourisms are truly contested ideas and the tourism literature is peppered with claim and counter-claim, with mainly academics and interest groups advocating and defending particular terms and definitions. A little like tourism destinations themselves, the terminology of new tourism experiences a relatively rapid circulation as terms come in and fall out of fashion (although there is often little to distinguish one term from another).

As with any activity which involves many groups, the terms mean different things to different people, according to the role they have within the activity. Protagonists perceive and portray the activity they are involved in as 'sustainable', 'no-impact', 'responsible', 'low-impact', 'green', 'environmentally friendly' or use some other suitable term to convey the message. We do not intend to get sidetracked into a lengthy discussion of the many and varied definitions of new tourism types. Suffice it to say they share, in varying degrees, a concern for 'development' and take account of the environmental, economic and socio-cultural impacts of tourism.

They also share an expressed concern, again with varying levels of commitment, for participation and control to be assumed by 'local people' and the degree to which they engage and benefit the poor. Most of these terms and their meanings underlie or echo the notion of sustainability in its varying guises and again suggest an important link between sustainability, development and new tourism.

The extent to which these terms can be used interchangeably is itself a debatable point. But more significant is the extent to which the claim of sustainability can be justified, a point examined under the heading 'The principles of sustainability in tourism'.

One further point of relevance to the sustainability of tourism is the acknowledgement in some quarters that mass packaged tours may be just as sustainable as some of the new forms of tourism - which makes a qualitative comparison of the sustainability of a package sun-sea-and-sand holiday and a trekking tour. Acknowledgement is made by organisations such as Tourism Concern, Green Globe and by some in the industry that sustainability is not the exclusive concern of new forms of tourism. But the attempt to subsume sustainability is reflected in the language and terminology of the new forms of tourism.

This section sketches in turn the meaning of sustainability in the field of tourism to tourists, tour operators, host communities, national governments, regional and international organisations, and academics. The differing definitions are only briefly sketched here but much of the discussion reflects these varying interpretations.

TOURISM AND DEVELOPMENT

The seemingly endless list of new tourism terms apart, perhaps the most noteworthy activity has been the definitional battle between different forms of tourism, tourism advocates and protagonists, in defining the most ethical way to take a holiday. Here we briefly review the front runners that seek to define themselves in relationship to development and sustainability.

ECOTOURISM

Faring badly during the UN's International Year of Ecotourism. Considered by Third World protagonists as an elite form of western defined pleasure and by First World proponents as a means of protecting ecologically valuable Third World destination habitats.

Unashamedly focused on the environment, with largely incidental benefits for local host communities.

SUSTAINABLE TOURISM

Sustainable tourism concentrates on environmental issues - relabelled from ecotourism. Although pro-poor tourism advocates would agree with much that sustainable tourism stands for, the overall objective of sustainable tourism is not to reduce poverty, though this may happen as a result of sustainable tourism development.

COMMUNITY-BASED TOURISM

Seeks to increase people's involvement and ownership of tourism at the destination end. Initiates from and control stays with the local community. Has some resonance in the other types of tourism reviewed here.

FAIR TRADE AND ETHICAL TOURISM

Fair trade tourism policies seek to create social, cultural and economic benefits for local people at the destination end and minimise leakages. Such policies: adhere to national laws; establish strong First World/Third World consultation structures; are transparent; involve open trading operations (such as social accounting); are ecologically sustainable; and respect human rights. The key focus is on changing consumption patterns in the First World.

PRO-POOR TOURISM

Out to capture the emerging development consensus on poverty reduction by generating net benefits for the poor. Set to become the developmentalists' favourite; packed with the most up-to-date technical development-speak. Proponents argue that pro-poor tourism puts 'the poor at the centre of analysis', 'focuses on tourism destinations in the South' and is 'particularly relevant to conditions of poverty'.

The tourists themselves often define their activities in terms of practical details. Green, for instance, suggests that 'Environmentalists and nature lovers should be able to survive camp without disposable paper cups, use-only-once plastic groundsheets, and crates of Coca Cola'. These claims reflect the desire of the new middle classes for exclusivity and differentiation in their holidays and tours.

In countries renowned for their natural beauty, however, it is not uncommon to hear these same tourists display the same 'been-there-done-that' attitude to national parks and spectacular locations as the conventional package tourists of whom they are so disdainful. Countries and locations are there to be 'collected' - for the list, the kudos and the image. And not a few object to having to pay a higher entrance fee than local nationals for access to protected areas, thereby betraying an ignorance of the social, cultural and economic ramifications of their position of wealthy foreign visitor.

The tour operators describe new tourist activities in short advertising 'bites', such as 'spectacular views of active volcano', 'surrounded by exuberant evergreen forest', 'exciting thrills of white water rafting' and many more. Specialised ecotour operators may develop these along the lines of: 'it is our pleasure to give the visitors personalised, low-impact, rustic excursions to national parks, Mayan archaeological sites, and natural wonders of Guatemala'.

Not surprisingly, the destination communities stress the importance of their own involvement in all stages of planning and operating tours. In its lengthy definition of ecotourism, the Talamanca Association for Ecotourism and Conservation in Costa Rica (ATEC) includes the following:

Ecotourism means more than bird books and binoculars ... more than native art hanging on hotel walls or ethnic dishes on the restaurant menu. Ecotourism is not mass tourism behind a green mask. Ecotourism means a constant struggle to defend the earth and to protect and sustain traditional communities. Ecotourism is a cooperative relationship between the non-wealthy local community and those sincere, open-minded tourists who want to enjoy themselves in a Third World setting.

The debate is currently not one of whether local communities should be involved in the development of tourism to their areas, but how they should be involved and whether 'involvement' means 'control'. This struggle for power and control over the tourist activities and financial benefits is at its sharpest at the destination end. The degree of control is generally perceived as being a significant element of sustainability.

In most relevant texts these communities are referred to as 'hosts', but we try to avoid this term as it generally conveys the idea that the resident populations in these communities are willing partners in the activity. In some instances, this may be the case, but, as we shall see, in others it is not. Governments are more concerned with the national planning strategies required to exploit the potential of their natural environments - in some cases without destroying them.

But all too often, ministers who speak radically, convincingly and frequently about protection of the nation's environmental and cultural treasures are the same people who sign the agreements which allow transnational companies to build a hotel or tourism complex whose development pays no heed to the environmental, social and cultural impacts caused.

In their pursuit of sustainability, international conservation bodies, such as the WWF, see the new forms of tourism as a useful tool in ensuring the conservation of a region's natural areas. They plan 'buffer zones', 'corridors of conservation', 'biosphere reserves' and similar. And they attempt to exert pressure on national governments to implement policy to protect such areas.

The Paseo Pantera Project promoted by Wildlife Conservation International (WCI) and the CCC envisages the achievement of conservation goals through the promotion of ecotourism.

'*Properly-planned tourism can:*

- Provide funds for acquisition and management of protected areas,
- Enhance the economies of local communities and
- Promote environmental education for park visitors, both national and international' (CCC, 1992).

The interpretations of sustainability made by different strands of the international socio-environmental organisations are examined again.

Supranational institutions include the multilateral lending agencies such as the World Bank, the IMF, the European Development Fund (EDF), other regional development funds and organisations such as the Overseas Private Investment Corporation (OPIC). Their view of tourist developments is used to justify the creation and promotion of investment opportunities, especially those for transnational corporations. Indeed, it might be argued that the industry involved, tourism in this case, is largely irrelevant so long as it fits in with the prevailing ideological planks of privatisation, deregulation, reduction of public spending, tight money control, increasing production for export, and related policies which tend to concentrate wealth and power rather than distribute it.

Finally, academics agonise over the most appropriate term to use and often reach the conclusion that 'no consensus has yet emerged as to the precise nature of alternative tourism' and 'it is still not possible to be exact about whether the term 'ecotourism' is meant as a pure concept or as a term for wide public use'. Sustainability and sustainable tourism are rich fields of discourse and debate for the academic community. Wheeller points out that, while there are effective critics of new forms of tourism in academia, there are also many academics who embrace and promote the notion as if it is a new idea: 'Glib, general assertions are frequently incorporated into policy statements without any attention being given to defining in a practical sense such phrases as, for example, "the local community", "tourism education" or "good visitor management"' (1992:143).

With such a diverse range of standpoints, it is not surprising that there is little agreement on the definition of the term. In these circumstances, it cannot be surprising that there is such a plethora of terms.

THE PRINCIPLES OF SUSTAINABILITY IN TOURISM

Given that none of the definitions cited in the previous section is comprehensive and all-encompassing, an approach more frequently taken is to examine and assess tourist activities according to whether they satisfy a number of criteria of sustainability.

Whether, for instance, a specific tour, lodge or wildlife reserve is operating sustainably might be assessed by reference to the criteria listed. This list is not presented here in a prescriptive manner; rather, it has been culled from observed practice, especially the practice of those organisations which attempt to publicise lists of environmentally and ethically sound companies.

As such, it stands as descriptive of these practices. It is not our view that these principles represent a 'correct' or absolute version of the meaning of sustainability. Indeed, we believe there to be no absolutely true nature of sustainability and, as the last section has illustrated, it is not definable except in terms of the context, control and position of those who are defining it. And points out, the notion of sustainability has many ramifications. These are briefly examined in the following subsections and discussed further at various points.

ECOLOGICAL SUSTAINABILITY

The condition of ecological sustainability need hardly be stated as it is often the only way in which sustainability is publicly perceived.

The need to avoid or minimise the environmental impact of tourist activities is clear. Maldonado *et al.* (1992) suggest that the calculation of carrying capacities is an important method of assessing environmental impact and sustainability. In an important work on carrying capacity, they calculate the capacities for seven different tourist foci in Costa Rica, and in so doing take the notion of sustainability beyond a rather fatuous interpretation by so many users of the term. While the work of Maldonado *et al.* is undoubtedly a valuable contribution to the measurement of carrying capacity, it is important to understand that the notion of carrying capacity may be used to wrap a social or economic constraint in a cloak of scientific jargon. Where exclusivity is promoted by the operators, a low carrying capacity is likely to be publicised. And conservation organisations involved in the promotion of new forms of tourism are more likely than most to foster imaginary maximum capacities in pursuit of conservation and economic gain. Several examples of the variability of carrying capacity calculations are given.

Moreover, despite the progressive nature and importance of this work, the calculations are dependent on assumptions which are in some cases arbitrarily chosen (such as the maximum number in a group and the ideal management capacity) and in others widely variable (such as the degree of slope). Other assumptions and conditions affecting the physical and management capacity of the area (such as the availability of guides, maps, rest spots and the incidence of low cloud cover) might be thought of as relevant, but are not included. Furthermore, a change in one value allocated to one assumption or input could have a substantial effect on the final carrying capacity calculated.

SOCIAL SUSTAINABILITY

Social sustainability refers to the ability of a community, whether local or national, to absorb inputs, such as extra people, for short or long periods of time, and to continue functioning either without the creation of social disharmony as a result of these inputs or by adapting its functions and relationships so that the disharmony created can be alleviated or mitigated.

Some of the negative effects of tourism in the past have included the opening of previously non-existent social divisions or the exacerbation of already-existing divisions. These can appear in the form of increasing differences between the beneficiaries of tourism and those who are marginalised by it, or of the creation of spatial ghettos, either of the tourists themselves or of those excluded from tourism. Stonich *et al.*(1995) provide a clear example of these social divisions on the Bay Islands of Honduras.

If we accept the premise that tourism sets up an intrinsically false and fabricated social division between the server and the served in the first place, it is of course inevitable that tourist developments (resorts, enclaves, condominia) will create such divisions.

It is one of the purposes of the tools of sustainability, such as carrying capacity calculations, environmental impact assessments, and sustainability indicators, to minimise the effects of these divisions to a point at which they can be excused. To this end, Clark (1990) has suggested the possibility of calculating social carrying capacity.

CULTURAL SUSTAINABILITY

Societies may be able to continue functioning in social harmony despite the effects of changes brought about by a new input such as tourists. But the relationships within that society, the mores of interaction, the styles of life, the customs and traditions are all subject to change through the introduction of visitors with different habits, styles, customs and means of exchange. Even if the society survives, its culture may be irreversibly altered.

Culture of course is as dynamic a feature of human life as society or economy; so the processes of cultural adaptation and change are not assumed by all in all cases to be a negative effect. But cultural sustainability refers to the ability of people to retain or adapt elements of their culture which distinguish them from other people. Cultural influences from even a small influx of tourists are inevitable and may be insidious; but the control of the most harmful effects, emphasis on the responsible behaviour of the visitor, and the prevention of distortion of local culture might be assumed to be essential elements of sustainable tourism.

Pratt's notion of transculturation encapsulates the way in which marginalised or subordinated groups select and invent from materials transmitted to them by dominant 'metropolitan' cultures. Cultural adaptation occurs in this way, and may result in change towards the wishes of the dominant culture. Cultural impacts are more easily seen over the long term and are therefore more difficult to measure, although the cultural subversion of many local communities has been well documented, especially but not exclusively by anthropologists - the work of de Kadt (1979), Plog (1972) and Smith (1989), for instance, illustrates the cultural ill-effects of tourism. Organisations such as Survival International and Tourism Concern have also documented the cultural subversion of indigenous groups.

ECONOMIC SUSTAINABILITY

The condition of economic sustainability is no less important than all others in any tourist development. Sustainability in these terms refers to a level of economic gain from the activity sufficient either to cover the cost of any special measures taken to cater for the tourist and to mitigate the effects of the tourist's presence or to offer an income appropriate to the inconvenience caused to the local community visited - without violating any of the other conditions - or both.

The following calculations and conclusions were made by Calderón and Madriz Díaz of the Geography Department of the University of Costa Rica, and were reported in *Análisis de Capacidad de Carga Para Visitación en las Áreas Silvestres de Costa Rica* by Maldonado *et al.* (1992).

The Guayabo National Monument covers 217 hectares and is the most significant area of archeological interest in Costa Rica. Its structures date back to 500 AD.

The map shows its location in the centre of the country. Within its area there are three trails along which visitors are chanelled. In 1990 the monument received 12,356 visitors, 92 per cent of whom were Costa Rican nationals, and 80 per cent of whom arrived in their own vehicles. Among the problems of the area identified by the team of geographers who conducted the study on which the carrying capacity calculations were based, were inadequate government funding for protection of the area, increasing visitor numbers, tree felling in a buffer zone around the monument, indiscriminate hunting of birds, deterioration of the archaeological remains due to visitors, and the lack of a management plan.

CARRYING CAPACITY CALCULATIONS

Three types of carrying capacity were calculated for each of the three trails separately, as it wasn't possible to apply the three different concepts to the area as a whole.

The three different types are:

- Physical carrying capacity;
- Real carrying capacity;
- Effective or permissible carrying capacity.

They are defined by the variable used in their measurement.

Physical carrying capacity (PCC): calculated according to the space necessary for one person to move freely in a specified time and assumed to be 1 square metre per person. The average width of the trails is 1 metre, so each visitor uses 1 linear metre of the trail at any given moment. *For one of the trails, sendero Los Cantarillos, other relevant assumptions made are*:

- Visitors follow the trails in groups of no more than 25 (each group with a guide);
- A distance of at least 100 metres is maintained between groups;
- The trail has a length of 1,100 metres;
- An average time of 1 hour is required for a visitor to complete this trail;
- The monument and trail are open to the public for 7 hours per day and 360 days per year.

PCC = Length × visitors/metre × daily duration (hrs/day)
= 1,100 × 1 × 7
= 7,700 visits per day
= 7,700 × 360
= 2,772,000 visits per year

Real carrying capacity (RCC) is the physical carrying capacity 'corrected' to allow for the following factors: precipitation (FP = 1.39%), vulnerability to erosion (FE = 38.28%), degree of slope (FS = 38.28%). Correction factors were calculated for each of these and expressed as percentages. The calculations are based on survey data, for details of which the reader should consult the original work.

The real carrying capacity calculations are:

RCC = PCC × (100 - FP)/100 × (100 - FE)/100 × (100 - FS)/100

= 7,770 × 0.9861 × 0.6172 × 0.6172
= 2,892 visits per day
= 2,892 × 360
= 1,041,276 visits per year

Effective carrying capacity (ECC) is the real carrying capacity 'corrected' to allow for the difference between the actual management capacity and the ideal management capacity, and is represented as FM. The actual management capacity of the monument is given by the number of personnel (administrative staff, park guards, and guides) employed (in this case 10). The ideal management capacity is given by the number that would be required to fulfil all functions allocated to the staff of the monument (39).

FM = (39-10)/39 × 100 = 74.36%
ECC = RCC × FM = 2,892 × (100-74.36)/100
= 2,892 × 0.2564
= 741.5 visits per day
= 741.5 × 360
= 266,943 visits per year

As expressed thus, it may appear as if the other aspects or conditions of sustainability are being 'bought off'. In other words, regardless of how much damage may be done culturally, socially and environmentally, it is perfectly acceptable if the economic profitability of the scheme is great enough to cover over the damage, ease the discontent or suppress the protest.

Economic sustainability, we would argue, is not a condition which competes with other aspects of sustainability. Rather, it can be seen as equally important a condition in its own right. On the other hand, it is not the only condition of sustainability, as might appear to be the case from the thoughts of numerous active agents of the industry. The condition of this as an element of sustainability in no way reduces the significance or level of acceptance or tolerance of the other conditions.

Nor does it cloud the importance of the contextual issue of power over tourist activities. With this in mind, the question of who gains financially and who loses financially often sets the power and control issue in sharper and more immediate focus than all other facets of sustainability.

THE EDUCATIONAL ELEMENT

It is often stated that an important difference between the new forms of tourism and conventional tourism is found in an element of educational input into the activity. This does not mean that it is necessary to reach high academic levels in order to be a sustainable tourist; but a greater understanding of how our natural and human environment works is often a goal, if not always stated, of the activity. At times, however, it is stated as a goal without being practised. Pressure of business may render this so, but cynicism may also explain it - the flimsiest pamphlet of information for the tourist can be used as evidence of an educational input, and therefore of the 'genuine' motives of the operators and the real desire to aim for sustainability.

Again, it is important to refer this principle back to its context of power and development. Who is the beneficiary of the educational element? Does this enhance their degree of control over the activity and its distribution of benefits? This element, we would argue, has the potential to further widen the inequalities of tourism developments.

At conferences on the subject (First World Congress on Tourism and the Environment, Belize 1992; Ecotourism - A Sustainable Option, Royal Geographical Society 1992; Managing Tourism, Commonwealth Institute 1995; Sustainable Tourism, San Jose, Costa Rica 1995; to name just a few) education in this respect is generally taken to mean one of two things: first, the enlightenment of the new tourist in the cultural ways and norms of those they are visiting - an education for its own sake; and second, the training of the 'hosts' so that they are better able to cater for the wishes of the new middle classes who visit them.

There are very few acknowledgements of the need to educate the local populace of the destination communities about the tourists. One notable exception to this is Krippendorf (1987), who encourages the dissemination of information about the tourists to those they are visiting:

By supplying the host population with comprehensive information about tourists and tourism, many misunderstandings could be eliminated, feelings of aggression prevented, more sympathetic attitudes developed and a better basis for hospitality and contact with tourists created ... Such information should aim at introducing the host population ... to the tourists' background: their country, their daily life (working and housing conditions, etc.), their reasons for travelling and their behaviour patterns.

Another form of educational input into sustainable tourism is the provision of 'technical information on how to do ecotourism *right*' (our emphasis). Arrogance like that betrayed in this paternalistic attitude expresses the idea that 'we' know how to do it and 'the rest' just need to be educated in our ways.

LOCAL PARTICIPATION

The importance attached by many parties to the inclusion of the local populations is considerable. Indeed, there is more debate about the degree of inclusion or control to be exercised by destination communities than about the need for their involvement at all. Six different types of participation are identified by Pretty and Hine (1999:6), ranging from 'passive participation' ('people participate by being told what has been decided or has already happened') to 'self-mobilization' ('people ... taking initiatives independently ... [and] retain control over how resources are used').

This debate is thrown into sharp contrast by the two standpoints of 'host' communities as objects of tourism or as controllers of tourism. Again, this matter is often considered to be at the heart of the difference between conventional mass tourism and supposedly sustainable new forms of tourism. But it is argued here that the issue of control is the same whether it refers to mass tourism or any of the new forms of tourism. Indeed, there may be something in the idea that the local authorities and local service providers of a mass tourism clientele have a greater degree of control and power over their activities than do those of the new forms of tourism.

THE CONSERVATION ELEMENT

It is often argued that new forms of tourism assist or should assist in the conservation of specific aspects of the biodiversity or culture of a given area, and hence that an essential element of new forms of tourism is or should be such conservation. This criterion has the tendency to divide the conservationists into two distinct camps.

On the one hand, we have the proponents of the benefits of specific new forms of tourism who cite examples such as the Annapurna Conservation Area in Nepal, private nature reserves in Costa Rica and selected rainforest areas in Brazil in order to illustrate the relationship between tourist money and the conservation of natural or cultural phenomena by placing a value on their retention rather than their extraction.

Gerardo Budowski, for example (former Director General of the IUCN, former Head of Ecology and Conservation at the United Nations Educational, Scientific and Cultural Organisation (UNESCO) and former President of the International Ecotourism Society), believes that 'ecotourism cannot survive without conservation and a symbiotic relation must therefore be established'.

On the other hand, we have those who believe strongly that the disbenefits of tourism outweigh the benefits, who see the only valid form of conservation as that which excludes the malign influence of human visitors, and who claim that the former group focus exclusively on species preservation at the expense of local people. This view sees ecotourism as a new form of ecological imperialism in which western cultural values override local cultural values and thereby oppose the principles of sustainability which ecotourism claims to support.

The aspects of sustainability discussed above are not presented here as prescriptive. We are not suggesting that a given lodge, tour or reserve (or indeed a regional or national tourism strategy) can be assessed through these criteria for sustainability. In fact, it should be clear that no establishment would be able to meet all these criteria. If they were universally used for making judgements about whether a given practice was sustainable and if all criteria had to be satisfied, then clearly nothing would be judged as sustainable. But this raises the point that sustainability should perhaps be seen as a continuum, and should be assessed on a scale similar to that of probability, offering differing degrees of sustainability. Such an idea opens the concept up to distortion and misuse, but as we have seen and as we shall see, it is indeed misused already.

In any case, it is our contention that sustainability is contested and is not reducible to a series of absolute principles. If principles can be applied to the notion, then it can only be in a relative way, relative to each other without contradiction, relative to the varying perceptions of those who use them, and relative to the values, ideological and moral, of those who apply and interpret them. 'Good' and 'bad' are relative terms, as is sustainability. With this in mind, it is worth considering the priorities for sustainable development set out by Agenda 21.

AGENDA 21 AND SUSTAINABLE DEVELOPMENT IN TOURISM

Agenda 21 is a global action plan endorsed by the 1992 Rio Summit in Brazil. It sets out the priorities for sustainable development into the twenty-first century. Stancliffe (1995) provides the following summary of the points of relevance in Agenda 21 for the tourism industry.

Agenda 21 impinges on tourism in two ways. First, tourism is specifically mentioned as offering sustainable development potential to certain communities, particularly in fragile environments. Second, tourism will be affected by Agenda 21's programme of action because its many impacts may be altered by the legal framework, policies and management practices under which it operates. Among other priorities given in Agenda 21, *governments* are urged to:

- Improve and reorientate pricing and subsidy policies in issues related to tourism;
- Diversify mountain economies by creating and strengthening tourism;
- Provide mechanisms to preserve threatened areas that could protect wildlife, conserve biological diversity or serve as national parks;
- Promote environmentally sound leisure and tourism activities, building on ... the current programme of the world tourism organisation.

Business and industry, including transnational corporations, are urged to:

- Adopt ... codes of conduct promoting best environmental practice;
- Ensure responsible and ethical management of products and processes;
- Increase self-regulation.

In its widest sense, tourism is a form of trade, not of goods perhaps, although the commodification of tourist destinations and talk of the 'tourist product' is now firmly established and accepted. Shortly after the Rio Summit, Arden-Clarke argued that 'the whole of the Agenda 21 section dealing with trade amounted to an evasion of key trade and environment issues, rather than a basis for their solution' (1992:13).

Arden-Clarke's arguments about Agenda 21's treatment of the general area of trade are applicable to the field of tourism. Essentially, his criticism is based on two particular features of the Agenda: first, it endorses the GATT rules which encourage the externalisation of environmental costs; and second, it endorses the idea that only trade liberalisation will bring about sustainable development. The first of these endorsements stems from GATT's agreement that the degree to which a country internalises its costs is left to choice. This effectively fixes the externalisation of environmental costs as the norm and makes clear that those countries which deviate from this will lose short-term competitiveness. The second endorsement on trade liberalisation implicitly depends on: the 'trickle down' mechanism to solve environmental problems - free trade leads to increases in per capita income through the economic growth it engenders, which in turn creates wealth, some part of which can then be invested in environmental protection ... The argument essentially says that you must first dirty your own backyard to generate the wealth to clean it up ...

[This] ignores the facts that:

- There is no automatic mechanism which guarantees that 'trickle-down' wealth is invested in the environment;
- Environmental damage is cheaper to prevent than cure, and in many cases is irreversible.

The flaws in this argument are being learned painfully around the world, but most notably in developing countries. Arden-Clarke's critique highlights the ideological values which underpin the priorities of Agenda 21 and reinforces the arguments about the importance of relationships of power. The principles of sustainability are not absolute and immutable. In any tourism analysis there is a need to examine the questions of who is stating the principles, priorities and policies, who will benefit from related action and who will lose, and the arguments around Agenda 21 illustrate this point.

Sustainability, or certain elements of it, may be measurable; it may be judged according to given yardsticks. But in the same way that the principles of sustainability may be contested, so too may be its measurement. As with the principles of sustainability, it is necessary to examine the exercise of power in its measurement. Those who employ the tools used to measure sustainability may also exercise power over its definition.

THE TOOLS OF SUSTAINABILITY IN TOURISM

The last section made mention of the tools and techniques available for use in assessing or measuring various aspects of sustainability.

AREA PROTECTION

As applied to the field of tourism and for the purposes of this chapter, we use the term 'tools or techniques of sustainability' in a general sense. Even the designation of an area of land as a national park or as some other category of protected area can be seen as a tool of sustainable tourism. Those countries with high proportions of their land area under some form of legislated protection might be considered as practising more sustainable tourism than those with low proportions of their land protected. This assumption can of course be questioned.

Some governments, for instance, have designated large areas of land as national parks or wildlife reserves but have failed to provide the resources required to afford an appropriate level of protection on the ground. Guatemala and Brazil may be cited as examples here, but they are not alone. It is difficult to blame such governments - they simply do not have the capital resources to pay for land protection, which after all has become a fashionable policy to pursue only in recent years.

Indeed, the very idea of protected areas begs the questions of who is protecting the area for whom and from whom. Many such areas have been so designated as a result of the tide of environmental consciousness that has been promoted, especially by environmentalists and conservationists since the 1970s. In 1994, for instance, WWF International began a fund-raising and recruitment campaign with the patronising slogan: 'He's destroying his own rainforest. To stop him, do you send in the army or an anthropologist?' The advertisement that followed was, as Survival International observed, 'glibly "pro-nature" and implicitly anti-people'.

This consciousness portrays areas of natural beauty as wilderness areas, unspoiled by contact with humans, and reserved for visits by the 'discerning' and appreciative urban dweller in need of rest and recuperation. This view conveniently ignores both the indigenous inhabitants of such areas and the proportion of the national population in search of and in need of land for survival.

Lorenzo Cardenal, a Nicaraguan environmentalist, has characterised this approach as '*parquismo*'. He suggests that a progressive, integrated approach should replace it, referring to the integration of humanity and nature rather than their separation or compartmentalisation as typified by *parquismo*.

INDUSTRY REGULATION

Regulation of the tourism industry can come from local governments in the form of planning restrictions, national governments in the form of laws relating to business practice, professional associations in the form of articles of affiliation, and international bodies in the form of international agreements and guidelines to governments. It is axiomatic that government legislation is intrinsically political in multi-party democracies. International agreements may also be explicitly or implicitly political, especially when they stem from a body such as the World Tourism Organisation (WTO/OMT) whose 'overall goal is the promotion and development of travel and tourism as a means of stimulating business and economic development' (WTO/OMT, 1991). Other international agreements and guidelines, especially those stemming from the work of the scientific community, such as agreements to reduce carbon dioxide emissions, may suffer from a lack of commitment without statutory legislation on the part of national governments and a difficulty in enforcement.

Regulation imposed on the industry by industry associations is normally promoted as a more effective way of preventing unethical or illegal activity than is government legislation. In 1986 the American Society of Travel Agents (ASTA) produced a set of Principles of Professional Conduct and Ethics. They added weight to these with the threat of disciplinary action against those failing to live up to the responsibilities embodied in the set of Principles.

With this type of discipline, the industry tries to promote voluntary self-regulation and to fend off what it sees as restrictive government legislation. On the one hand, it seems to be an intrinsic part of the doctrine of monetarism that any form of regulation should be voluntary and conducted by the industry itself.

This accompanies other planks of the doctrine, such as the right to corporate privacy, reduction in public expenditure, transfer of national assets from public to private hands, deregulation of industry, and wholesale support for the notion of 'free trade' which is currently sweeping the globe 'as the key to planetary prosperity and environmental protection'. On the other hand:

It has to be appreciated that tourism is an industry and, as such, is much like any other industry ... There is no more reason to expect tourism, on its own accord, to be 'responsible', than there is to expect the beer industry to discourage drinking or the tobacco industry to discourage smoking - even though many agree that such steps would be socially desirable.

The tool of regulation is clearly one which allows specific groups to take control of the industry. The argument around regulation represents a power struggle between different interest groups. So should the industry be regulated, presumably by a branch of government? Or should it be left to regulate itself voluntarily?

VISITOR MANAGEMENT TECHNIQUES

A range of visitor management techniques exist for use by those who cater for and control the movements of tourists. There are several texts which outline these in depth. Worthy of particular note is the current trend towards the restriction of motorised vehicles in areas normally attractive to lovers of nature. On the premise that the motor car as currently run is inherently unsustainable, this trend would seem like a move which the scientific community, the hosts, and the planners could all agree works towards the goal of sustainability.

This particular issue is currently of topical concern in countries like the UK and USA where levels of car ownership and use are high. It is also a topical issue in many cities in Third World countries, although in national parks and protected areas in the Third World the problems have generally not yet prompted the same level of concern as those of the national parks in the developed countries.

There are exceptions to this, as for instance in the case of the highway through the Metropolitan National Park in Panama City, the largest area of tropical rainforest within the boundaries of a city. Wildlife safari vehicles in East Africa have also created problems sufficient to be widely noticed and publicised in recent years.

Another interesting visitor management technique is that of differential charging for foreign and national visitors. Such a policy is not always understood by the visiting tourists from the north, but it promotes the condition of local participation as an inherent aspect of sustainability.

ENVIRONMENTAL IMPACT ASSESSMENT (EIA)

A technique which has attained fashionability and respect relatively recently is that of environmental impact assessment (EIA). It has been described as 'among the foremost tools available to national decision makers in their efforts to prevent further environmental deterioration'. But it can be used at more than just the local scale: 'the EIA process is seen as a means not only of identifying potential impacts, but also of enabling the integration of the environment and development'.

According to Tourism Concern, 'For the tourism industry to develop and survive in a sustainable and responsible manner, an anticipatory approach is essential'. This is eminently sensible, as is Goodall's pronouncement that 'Only where the result of the EIA clearly demonstrates that the development will be environmentally responsible and sustain the destination's primary tourism resources should planning permission to proceed normally be granted'.

But EIAs are not an exact science and can be manipulated like most other techniques. Their results are responsive to those factors used as inputs and assessment can be qualitative and quantitative, and hence subject to degrees of subjectivity. The choice of input, then, is crucial, and it is vital that we recognise that 'If we are to account for environment ... then the idea of a politically neutral social science has to be dropped'. Mulberg's statement is a reference to the externalisation of unquantifiable factors by the practitioners (accountants) of capitalist economics. For 'externalisation' we could read 'ignoring', a practice which has indirectly led to many of the world's worst environmental catastrophes.

Environmental auditing of specific activities or processes has arisen out of the practice of EIAs, and in turn environmental auditing has more recently spawned the practice of eco-labelling and the certification of products and activities.

CARRYING CAPACITY CALCULATIONS

Carrying capacity calculations have already been briefly discussed in this chapter. It is worth adding, however, that Mulberg's point about political and social neutrality, which can be extended to include commercial neutrality, is as applicable to carrying capacity calculations as it is to EIAs. Calculations can be manipulated by, for instance, tour operators, protected area officials, officers of conservation organisations, or government officers, to promote either a destination's exclusivity (a low carrying capacity) or its ability and potential to absorb more visitors (a high carrying capacity).

Both these strategies might be seen as in the interests of different parties under different circumstances. And it is interesting to note how upper thresholds of visitors, arrived at as a result of carrying capacity calculations, have increased as time progresses. Again, examples are discussed later, along with the technique of limits of acceptable change which is becoming more fashionable than carrying capacity.

It should also be remarked that the notion of carrying capacity reflects the prevailing relationships of dominance between First World and Third World. Management of the carrying capacity of a particular national park or other protected area gives considerable power to those who have that control. And control of the technique itself offers academics their own degree of power in the debate.

CONSULTATION/PARTICIPATION TECHNIQUES

Stewart and Hams (1991) argue that 'Sustainable development must be built by, through and with the commitment of local communities. The requirements of sustainable development cannot merely be imposed; active participation by local communities is needed.' And, as we have already discussed, participation is regarded as central to people-focused and pro-poor approaches to 'development'.

In the field of tourism, those who speak of sustainable development almost always include participation of the destination communities as one essential element or principle of that sustainability. For this reason, techniques for promoting public participation and involvement in development projects are included as one type of tool available for the measurement of sustainability.

Furthermore, techniques for measuring public perceptions, attitudes and values (such as contingent valuation techniques and stated preference surveys) are seen here as a necessary stage in the measurement of sustainability. They too are included here, although for details of the application of these techniques, see Pearce (1993) and Pearce and Moran (1994).

Techniques which allow for consultation and participation (of those people affected) are still young in their development and subject to problems of definition and interpretation. They are vulnerable to the type of distortion and bias which is introduced in the selection of inputs. They can also be hijacked to give an appearance of consultation with local people while in reality there is only consultation with so-called 'experts'.

Additionally, consultation with local people has become fashionable, especially among conservationists, but as Survival International point out in relation to the role of indigenous people in managing protected areas, 'This looks good on paper, but they are hardly an adequate substitute for land ownership rights and self determination' (1996:2).

Attempts to value social costs and benefits include surveys of public perceptions of, expectations of, and attitudes towards a range of social problems and manifestations such as shopping opportunities, access to recreational facilities, noise levels, litter, standard of living, and vandalism. Measurements of perceptions are placed on a scale, generally extending from highly positive (strongly in favour of) to deeply negative (strongly opposed to). Perceptions, attitudes, expectations and values, however, vary from person to person and from group to group. Difficulties therefore arise with the interpretation of results, which often appear weak and ambiguous, but which are nevertheless used and excused as participation and consultation.

CODES OF CONDUCT

Recent years have seen a rising tide of codes of conduct for use in the tourist industry. Their design, promotion, contents, relevance, uptake, effectiveness and monitoring have become important features of the industry and are all worthy of attention. There are two general points that can be made about almost all codes. First, they attempt to influence attitudes and modify behaviour. Second, almost all codes are voluntary; statutory codes, backed by law, are very rare.

Many codes of conduct are very impressive in their range of issues and in their depth of discussion and information. But they can be abused by the industry as marketing ploys or as veils extending over many of its impacts.

There exist a number of problems associated with the use of codes of conduct which can be summarised under the following descriptions: the monitoring and evaluation of codes of conduct; the conflict between codes as a form of marketing and codes as genuine attempts to improve the practice of tourism; the debate between regulation or voluntary self-regulation of the industry; and the variability between codes and the need for coordination.

SUSTAINABILITY INDICATORS

The youngest of all the tools of sustainability are those now described as sustainability indicators, the development of which arose from the Rio Summit of 1992. It is now commonly accepted that conventional indicators of 'well-being' (such as GNP) give a restricted, partial and one-sided view of development. It is the search for indicators which show the linkages between economic, social and environmental issues and the power relationships behind them which has given rise to the development of so-called 'sustainability indicators'. Thus far, such indicators have been developed mainly as trials and are currently applied largely at local authority level.

One important aspect that has been built into these indicators from their inception has been the participation of local community members in their formulation. There is no doubting here the genuine and diligent attempt to promote such participation as part of the development of sustainability indicators. There is also no doubting that it is precisely this participation which has led to the use of indicators which are much less remote and much more comprehensible to people than are nationally and internationally derived measures such as GNP, Gross Domestic Investment and the like.

But their acceptance will face an uphill struggle. The measures most frequently used at the level of the national economy relate precisely to that: the economy. Other relevant factors are ignored (or, as economists call it, 'externalised'). Moreover, their use is well entrenched and perpetuated by conservative media which accept new ideas with great reluctance unless they are forced to do so by a public that has already moved ahead.

The need to include the social, cultural, environmental and aesthetic factors which our commercial world and controllers normally externalise has not led to a quick redress for such factors, despite public debate of the issue.

Furthermore, it has yet to be proved that these more locally accountable, more relevant and less remote indicators are less likely to be subject to bias and manipulation to suit the ends of those who use them.

FOOTPRINTING

The 'ecological footprint' provides a means of quantifying environmental impacts in a single easily understandable indicator. It also provides a means of identifying opportunities for cost savings. It is calculated on the assumption that the earth is a reserve of natural capital, each year producing interest in the form of renewable natural resources such as fish, soil, fresh water and many more. Ecological sustainability requires that we live off this interest rather than eat into the underlying 'capital'.

The interest is quantified in units of area. At present (2002) there are about two units of area available per person on the planet per year. The WWF-UK have developed the tool of ecological footprinting and estimate that on a global scale humanity is currently eating into the earth's underlying capital by annually consuming around a third more resource than the earth produces, which, if accurate, is clearly unsustainable.

Holiday footprinting quantifies the area used by a given holiday. A report commissioned by WWF-UK estimates that 'the typical Mediterranean holiday can have an environmental impact equivalent to spending up to 50 per cent of your entire annual income in two weeks' (WWF-UK, 2002). The same report details examples of the application of holiday footprinting as a practical business tool that can be used by tour operators as a guide not only to ways of making holidays more environmentally friendly in terms of the resources used - the 'footprint made' - but also to identify opportunities for cost savings.

For such a methodological tool to enter into common practice, it will have to become acceptable to the travelling public, for few tour operators and travel agents will begin to describe their holidays in terms of their holiday footprints unless the idea is already widely understood and accepted by the public. And even if such a situation is reached in the future, it would also be necessary to overcome the industry's resistance to change and new ideas by persuading them that the technique can genuinely work in their financial interests.

It is worth restating the point that the notion of sustainability has to be taken beyond its current bland usage and interpretation, as best illustrated by politicians and daily media pundits. If it remains a 'buzzword' which can be so widely interpreted that people of very different outlooks on a given issue can all use it to support their cause, then it will suffer the same distortions to which discourses such as 'freedom', 'democracy' and 'development' are commonly subjected. All of these terms, and others, are frequently and regularly distorted by most of our politicians - see Chomsky (1989, 2000), Postman (1985), Curran *et al.* (1986) and Beder (1997) for analyses of such distortions.

We move on, then, to the question of how sustainability should be taken beyond its current usage and how it should be given a substantial, tangible and unequivocal meaning. This further leads us onto the question of whether we should be promoting the principles and tools of sustainability, as outlined above, towards this end.

It has already been pointed out that the principles of sustainable tourism are open to manipulation in the service of operators and others in the industry. That is not to say that the principles are not worthy of attention by all those involved in the industry; but it does suggest that the motives of those who apply them should also be scrutinised.

On the assumption that the use of the techniques of measurement and description will help a move towards a clearer, workable and meaningful analysis of sustainability, awareness of the limitations and immaturity of the techniques is also necessary. This means that they are susceptible to manipulation for partisan purposes. In turn, this raises the need to politicise the tourism industry in order to promote its movement towards sustainability and away from its tendency to dominate, corrupt and transform nature, culture and society.

The politicisation of the tourism industry would require a clarification and emphasis of the associations between the prevailing power structures and the control of tourism developments, and a clear linking of the goal of reducing uneven and unequal development with the policies pursued by the tourism industry and the governments and international institutions which promote it.

Without this politicisation, sustainability will continue to be hijacked by the prevailing model of development, capitalism, and will increasingly fall into the service of the controllers of capital, the boards of directors of major transnational companies and other organisations which manage the industry. This tendency has already become apparent. And as the new forms of tourism gather ground and increase their share of the tourism market, as seems likely, the current power structure and the processes by which power is held and retained will attempt to subsume them, as has already been shown.

Concurrent with this trend in many areas of the Third World, however, is a grassroots groundswell to take control of, and exploit, tourist opportunities at the community level. Currently this tendency seems to assume automatically that 'sustainability' is their prerogative, and use of the term is as loose as it is in other tendencies. Automatic assumptions are often used to cover over awkward questions. The existence of these different tendencies highlights the debate between a tourism that is industry-controlled and one that is community-controlled.

The obstacles to change towards sustainability briefly mentioned above and the struggle for power over the definition of the concept are themes which run throughout the remainder of the book. The discussions on global changes, power relationships, dependency theory and sustainability in the first part of the book inform and fuel the analyses of the roles of different sectors of tourism that now follow. Specifically, the key themes (uneven and unequal development, globalisation, relationships of power) and key words (new tourism, sustainability and the Third World) of the book will reappear.

Bibliography

B.P. Sawant, H.W. Awari, A.M. Kamble and D.D. Tekale: *Fundamentals of Soil and Water Conservation Engineering*, Current Publications, Agra, 2010.

G.L. Bagdi: *People's Participation in Soil and Water Conservation Through Watershed Approach*, International Book Distributer, Delhi, 2005.

G.N. Chattopadhyay: *Chemical Analysis of Fish Pond Soil and Water*, Daya Publications, Delhi, 1998.

G.S. Narwani: *Community Water Management*, Rawat Publications, Delhi, 2005.

H.W. Dalzell, A.J. Biddlestone, K.R. Gray and K. Thurairajan: *Soil Management: Compost Production and Use in Tropical and Subtropical Environments*, Daya Publications, Delhi, 2007.

Helmut Kohnke and Anson R. Bertrand: *Soil Conservation*, Biotech Books, Delhi, 2009.

Hough Hammond Bennett: *Soil Conservation for Sustainable Agriculture*, Agrobios Publications, Jodhpur, 2001.

Hugh Hammond Bennett: *Elements of Soil Conservation*, Biotech Books, Delhi, 2009.

J. Cyril Kanmony: *Drinking Water Management: Problems and Prospects*, Mittal Publications, Delhi, 2010.

J.P.J. Van Veren: *Soil Fertility and Sewage*, Agrobios Publications, Jodhpur, 2002.

Kalyan Kumar Chakravarty; Gyani Lal Badam and Vijay Paranjpye: *Traditional Water Management Systems of India*, Aryan Books International, Delhi, 2006.

Klein Gomes: *Waste Water Management*, Oxford Book Company, Jaipur, 2009.

L K Tripathi: *Water and Soil Management*, ABD Publications, Delhi, 2005.

Madireddi V. Subba Rao: *Water Conservation Management And Analysis*, Readworthy Publications, Delhi, 2011.

Manikant Shah: *Traditional Water Management Practices of Uttarakhand*, Pentagon Press, Delhi, 2012.

Mukund Narayan, Satyendra Kumar and Nilesh Biwalkar: *A Reference Manual of Soil and Water: Conservation Engineering*, Biotech Books, Delhi, 2014.

N.K. Prasad: *Soil Fertility and Plant Nutrition*, IBDC Publishers, Delhi, 2013.

Norman W. Hudson: *Soil and Water Conservation in Semi-Arid Areas*, Scientific Publications, Chenai, 2004.

P.C. Bansil: *Water Management in India*, Concept Publications, Delhi, 2004.

Pietro Laureano: *Water Conservation Techniques in Traditional Human Settlements*, Copal Publishing Group, Delhi, 2013.

Rajendra Prasad and James F. Power: *Soil Fertility Management for Sustainable Agriculture*, CRC (Lewis Publishers), 2012.

Rakesh Hooja, Ganesh Pangare and K.V. Raju: *Users in Water Management: The Andhra Model and its Replicability in India*, Rawat Publications, Delhi, 2002.

Ratan Kumar Saha: *Soil and Water Quality Management for Sustainable Aquaculture*, Narendra Publications, Delhi, 2010.

Ravinder Kumar Kashyap: *Agriculture and Water Management*, Oxford Book Company, Jaipur, 2009.

S C Panda: *Soil Management and Organic Farming*, Agrobios Publications, Jodhpur, 2006.

S K Datta: *Soil Conservation and Land Management*, International Book Distributer, Delhi, 2006.

S. Asaithambi: *Economics of Ground Water Management in India*, Abhijeet Publications, Delhi, 2008.

S.C. Panda: *Soil Conservation and Fertility Management*, Agrobios Publications, jodhpur, 2008.

Index